GLOBAL FUTURES IN EAST ASIA

A Series Sponsored by the East-West Center

CONTEMPORARY ISSUES IN ASIA AND THE PACIFIC

John T. Sidel and Geoffrey M. White, Series Co-Editors

A collaborative effort by Stanford University Press and the East-West Center, this series focuses on issues of contemporary significance in the Asia Pacific region, most notably political, social, cultural, and economic change. The series seeks books that focus on topics of regional importance, on problems that cross disciplinary boundaries, and that have the capacity to reach academic and other interested audiences.

The East-West Center promotes better relations and understanding among the people and nations of the United States, Asia, and the Pacific through cooperative study, research, and dialogue. Established by the US Congress in 1960, the Center serves as a resource for information and analysis on critical issues of common concern, bringing people together to exchange views, build expertise, and develop policy options. The Center is an independent, public, nonprofit organization with funding from the US government, and additional support provided by private agencies, individuals, foundations, corporations, and governments in the region.

EDITED BY ANN ANAGNOST, ANDREA ARAI,
AND HAI REN

Global Futures in East Asia

*Youth, Nation, and the New Economy
in Uncertain Times*

Stanford University Press · *Stanford, California*

Stanford University Press
Stanford, California

Printed in the United States of America on acid-free, archival-quality paper

Library of Congress Cataloging-in-Publication Data
Global futures in East Asia : youth, nation, and the new economy in
uncertain times / edited by Ann Anagnost, Andrea Arai, and Hai Ren.
        pages cm. — (Contemporary issues in Asia and the Pacific)
    Includes bibliographical references and index.
    ISBN 978-0-8047-7617-2 (cloth : alk. paper) — ISBN 978-0-8047-7618-9
(pbk. : alk. paper)
    1. Youth—Employment—East Asia—Case studies.   2. Neoliberalism—
East Asia—Case studies.   3. Globalization—Economic aspects—East
Asia—Case studies.   4. East Asia—Economic conditions—21st century.
5. Ethnology—East Asia—Case studies.   I. Anagnost, Ann, editor of
compilation.   II. Arai, Andrea, 1956– editor of compilation.   III. Ren,
Hai, 1965– editor of compilation.   IV. Series: Contemporary issues in Asia
and the Pacific.
    HD6276.E18G56 2012
    320.51095—dc23
                                                          2012014296

Typeset by Thompson Type in 9.75/13.5 Janson

Contents

    and Projects of the Self in a Japanese Corporate Office   197
    Miyako Inoue

9. Workplace Dramas and Labor Fantasies in 1990s Japan   222
    Gabriella Lukacs

10. Governmental Entanglements: The Ambiguities
    of Progressive Politics in Neoliberal Reform in South Korea   248
    Jesook Song

    References Cited   277

    About the Contributors   301

    Index   305

Acknowledgments

The idea for this volume first began as a panel organized by Hai Ren and Andrea Arai on neoliberal governmentality in East Asia for the Annual Meetings of the American Anthropological Association in San Francisco in 2004. Due to the decision by the AAA to honor a bitterly contested hotel workers strike, the meetings were relocated to Atlanta, and many panels planned for the meetings that year ended up as miniconferences on campuses across the country.

Such was the fate of this panel. Andrea Arai took the lead in organizing, with Ann Anagnost, a small conference and public teach-in held April 22–23, 2005, on the theme "Nation, Culture, New Economy in East Asia" cosponsored by Pacific Lutheran University (Chinese Studies and Anthropology), the University of Washington Jackson School of International Studies (China Program, Center for East Asian Studies, Korea Program, Japan Program), the Simpson Center for the Humanities (Critical Asian Studies), and the Department of Anthropology. Among conference participants not represented in this volume but who contributed importantly to its intellectual formation were Tani Barlow, Brian Hammer, Lisa Hoffman, Nayna Jhaveri, Ken Kawashima, Gavin McCormack, Laura C. Nelson, and Pun Ngai. The chapters by Ching-wen Hsu, Miyako Inoue, Gabriella Lukacs, Nickola Pazderic, and Trang X. Ta were later additions.

As the volume began to take shape, so did the idea for an upper division course called Global Futures in East Asia, cotaught by Ann Anagnost and Andrea Arai and developed over a period of two years (2006–2008) with funding from the University of Washington Jackson School of International Studies (China Program, Center for East Asian Studies, Korea Program, Japan Program) and the Department of Anthropology. We express our thanks to Madeleine Dong, Miriam Kahn, Robert Pekkanen, Kristi Roundtree, and Clark Sorensen for their generous support of this endeavor. This teaching collaboration further developed the themes of intersecting histories and complex crossings in East Asian modernity projects that we consider as fundamental to understanding the themes of this volume. Our students, many of them originally from East Asia, brought to the course their experience of border crossing life-making projects, and this fueled our passion for understanding their complex subjectivities. The classroom became, in a very real sense, an ethnographic laboratory well suited to investigating the relationship between youth, labor, and human capital formation in tandem with students in search of critical frameworks through which to better comprehend their position in the global economy. We would like to dedicate this volume to them.

In addition, we thank the University of Washington Simpson Center for the Humanities for funding a research collaborative called Global Futures for two years (2006–2008). This research collaborative put us in dialogue with colleagues working in South Asia (Craig Jeffrey and Jane Dyson) and Africa (Danny Hoffman) around the topic of youth and globalization in relation to education, labor, and technology. The Simpson Center funding allowed us to bring Nancy Abelmann for a visit in the fall quarter of 2006, to help develop the Korea component for this volume. Other colleagues we would like to acknowledge for their input include Miyako Inoue, Karen Kelsky, Janet Poole, Stefan Tanaka, and Peter Wissoker. A special thanks goes to Stacy Wagner, our editor at Stanford University Press, for her enthusiastic embrace of this project and for her keen editorial vision in grooming it toward completion and also to Jessica Walsh for her steady support at every stage of the editorial process. We also wish to express thanks to the East-West Center for its support and for including this volume in their series Contemporary Issues in Asia and the Pacific.

GLOBAL FUTURES IN EAST ASIA

Introduction

Life-Making in Neoliberal Times

ANN ANAGNOST

A Bus to Nowhere

In 2005, a television documentary followed a group of young Japanese youth in work uniforms as they climbed aboard a bus to travel to their worksite for the day.[1] Each morning these young people were taken to a new location to work in unskilled assembly jobs. "We feel like robots" was how one young woman described her experience. When this film was first screened, Japan's economic downturn—begun in the 1990s—was well into its second decade. Recovery had proved elusive. Spiraling rates of underemployment, especially for youth, had produced a new reserve army of low-waged labor with greatly reduced life prospects. Later, when showing a still photo of the scene on the bus to a Japanese youth, my colleague Andrea Arai was asked whether it had been taken "in China."

This misrecognition of Japan for China is telling in terms of how people are experiencing the rapid remapping of economic relations in the region. By the mid-2000s, China was beginning to be talked about in ways that echoed how Japan had once been represented in the 1980s; while Japan, in turn, was becoming unrecognizable as the miracle modernizer it was once thought to be. The reasons for this turnabout cannot be fathomed within the limits of a study of Japan. They must be put into a wider context in which these transformations in national economies and societies are understood as complexly related to processes occurring regionally as well as globally.

This volume gathers together ethnographic explorations of life-making in East Asia that register these regional resonances in a time of economic globalization and neoliberal restructuring. *Life-making* here refers to investments in the self to ensure one's forward career progression as embodied human capital. In the Japanese recession, the project of building a life through education and training had become stalled with the sudden contraction of employment opportunities. China's rise as an economic power is the other side of the story of the postindustrial transformations of Japan, South Korea, and Taiwan. The off-shoring of industrial production from these once "miraculous" economies to China and Southeast Asia threatens the reproduction of middle-class livelihoods, raising the question: "What if economic miracles do not last forever?" In such changed circumstances, the future of youth in East Asia becomes much less certain; not only are the forms of life inhabited by their parents in terms of secure employment and benefits no longer available to them, but, more importantly, they may no longer seem desirable in the transfigured imaginings of what it means to make a life.

As we shall see in the case studies that follow, some embrace the "burden of self-development" of the enterprising subject with a gleeful optimism that they will realize their dreams more fully on a global stage. Indeed, one cannot help but wonder to what extent the new regime of capital accumulation relies on the energy of youth and its optimism and resilience in the face of life's challenges. Others, such as the Japanese youth who boarded the bus to their assembly jobs, may feel themselves to have been stripped bare of any value with no secure passage to a future of better times. The teleological narrative of development that buoyed Japan's postwar economic success has ended up in a most surprising place, but, instead of recognizing the political economic forces that have changed the game plan, the critique turns inward, to an implied failure of the youth themselves to reproduce the economic miracle. The increasing unevenness in the distribution of life chances in the global economy makes all the difference between success and failure, transcendence and loss.

The objectives of this volume are threefold. The first is an exploration of how "places are made through their connections with each other, not their isolation" (Tsing 2000: 330). What might it mean to talk about region as a series of intertwined histories in which ideas—civilization, modernity, development, globalization—have traveled from one place to another and have taken local form while looking at other places as a basis for comparison? Such a project, combining deep area knowledge with regional and global perspectives, is necessarily a collaborative one that is sensitive to the resonances across time and space within East Asia. We envision this volume as a way to encourage a dialogue among scholars working in their different locations but who wish to work collaboratively to understand these complex crossings.

The second objective is to demonstrate the power of anthropology to trace out the connections between people's lived experience with larger processes working at the global scale. Ethnography provides us with detailed descriptions of how people in different locations in East Asia experience their everyday realities in the midst of the new possibilities and constraints that the global economy is producing for their lives. Engagement with these transformations at the level of the everyday beyond our national borders also makes us attentive to the changing experiences of our students in U.S.-based academic settings as well. Embodying the realities of global flows of information and capital, they also bear the burden of neoliberalism's "freedoms" and self-responsibility. We have found that tracing out the connections in this new era and the histories on which they are based fosters in our students a sense of recognition (rather than competition) with youth located elsewhere of their shared experience of both the promise and uncertainty they confront as they enter the global economy as embodied human capital. We see cultivating this recognition as a political act that contributes to the formation of a very different kind of global project, one that transcends national identity formations to resist the segregations between high- and low-value subjects imposed by neoliberal globalization (Dyer-Witheford 2002).

A third objective is to illuminate the changing calculus of human worth in the production of subjects as both workers and consumers. A number of the chapters in this volume look at the contingent production of emergent "forms of being" in relation to national projects of "human engineering." In phrasing it this way, we hope to draw attention both to the intentional activities of agents of change (including individuals working on themselves) and the imaginaries of development that they inhabit along with the indeterminacy of outcomes. Amid the promises of globalization to equalize and "flatten" the world, anthropologists confront the way in which the utopian visions of this era, often invested with ideas of freedom and the promise of self-fulfillment, are also laden with the costs of greater vulnerability and uncertainty. In this respect, universalizing invocations of freedom may be understood very differently in different contexts, and the promises they offer may come with very different costs.

Living in Conditions of Neoliberal Globalization

Neoliberal globalization is a complex mix of technological and economic innovations alongside changing conceptions of human worth and philosophies of government.[2] The theoretical approach of this volume is to bring into dialogue political economic approaches to the study of neoliberal globalization as a "spatiotemporal fix" for the contradictions of late capitalism with biopolitical analyses of neoliberal projects of government as addressing the problem of how to govern free subjects in liberal societies.[3] However, neoliberalism as a strategy of governing at a distance is not limited to liberal democracies. Aspects of neoliberal governmentality have been adopted by illiberal regimes in the guise of market reforms. Historically, implementations of neoliberal thought in government, in particular the strain that focuses on the extension of free market principles into areas of social policy, have developed alongside and even facilitated economic globalization. However, the link between them must be understood not just at the level of political strategy but also as a pervasive ethos that deeply informs the subjective formation of ordinary individuals living in conditions of neoliberal globalization but in ways that may be very differently situated.

As an approach to government that emerged in the early postwar period, neoliberal thinking did not gain significant political traction until the end of the 1970s. The dismantling of the welfare state reworked the social contract between state and citizen. Michel Foucault has suggested that the Beveridge Plan, which popularized Keynesian policies in the United Kingdom during World War II, set up the exchange of patriotic self-sacrifice in a time of war in exchange for job security and universal health care. He phrased its appeal as follows: "Now we are asking you to get yourselves killed, but we promise you that when you have done this, you will keep your jobs until the end of your lives" (2008: 216). The postwar social contract took a different form in Japan, which had been shorn of its military powers after World War II. Instead, one could say that it took the form of an intensification of labor productivity (Dohse, Ulrich, and Nialsch 1985) to ensure Japan's economic success in exchange for life-long employment security. Andrea Arai (Chapter Seven in this volume), addresses how the economic recession has changed the terms of the social contract between state and citizen in conditions of high unemployment in which "the securing of the national future, it appears, no longer guarantees that all will participate in the ongoing prosperity of the national community."

These shifts in the strategies of government were deeply engaged with the crisis of capitalism beginning in the 1970s by opening national borders to flows of capital and labor worldwide. China's shift to market socialism in the late 1970s provided a timely entry into the global market as a place where foreign investment could go in search of cheaper labor, turning the challenge that Chinese socialism posed to capitalist hegemony into a new frontier for capital accumulation. Following the end of the Cold War in 1989, a transformed geopolitical order accelerated these shifts, and the technological innovations of information technologies and containerization facilitated the globalization of production chains. The "law of comparative advantage" (that is, organizing national economies around what they produce most efficiently) often meant not just a changing division of labor in global markets but also the rolling back of government responsibilities for social welfare provision in the name of remaining "competitive." Pressures to reduce the social wage meant that provision for health care, job security, and retirement benefits became expendable entitlements in the new "global arbitrage of labor" (Ross 2006). Neoliberal reforms to encourage citizens to assume responsibility for their fates in an increasingly precarious labor market promised to reduce the costs of government in a time of high unemployment. These reductions in social spending were certainly not met without contestation, as illustrated by a number of the chapters in this volume, in ways that illuminate the uncertain trajectory of neoliberal projects as they move from place to place.

Of course, not all citizens shared equally in the forms of social insurance and job security of the postwar welfare state. Later in Chapter Eight of this book, Miyako Inoue foregrounds this issue in her discussion of the situation of women workers in Japanese corporations during the high-growth era as anticipating a more precarious relationship to employment that later became more generalized. Inoue's examination of how women were required to take responsibility for their own self-development in the early 1990s ushers in a new way of relating to one's work that later becomes glamorized in the workplace teledramas explored by Gabriela Lukacs (see Chapter Nine). In the context of Chinese socialism, many of the guarantees of urban workers were not extended to rural people during the Maoist era, setting up conditions of inequality that became the conditions of possibility for the rural to urban migration instigated by the economic reforms. In Chapter Six, Yan Hairong shows us how the awakening of the "weaker groups" (*ruoshi qunti*) to the imperative of taking charge of their own self-development was used to capture the labor of rural women for domestic work in Beijing. Even the belated establishment of a welfare system following on South Korea's democratization in the 1990s takes a neoliberal spin, as argued by Jesook Song in Chapter Ten. The state's response to the increase in homelessness in the wake of the International Monetary Fund (IMF) crisis of 1997 demarcated a divide between the deserving and undeserving in terms of the allocation of welfare benefits.

The ethnographic essays collected here have been written with an awareness of the history of this capital movement and, along with it, the making and breaking of economies and the social orders they supported. Although the end of the Cold War seemed to promise a New World Order of unlimited economic possibility in a borderless world, this triumphal scenario was haunted almost from the very beginning with the specter of failure: first the bursting of the Japanese bubble in 1991; then the Asian Economic Crisis of 1997; and, a decade later, the global financial crisis of 2008. The economic crisis in 2008 was fueled in good part by speculative trading in futures and derivatives markets in which transactions of value increasingly took on more and more ephemeral forms that were traded globally. The Japanese recession of the early 1990s, triggered by a collapse in the real estate market, appears in retrospect as an eerie anticipation for the later economic troubles, often referenced as "the Japanese disease," in the global financial crisis of 2008.

The question is still open as to whether this most recent crisis marks an endpoint to an optimistic belief in the promises of economic globalization or whether it provides renewed impetus for further neoliberal reform in austerity measures. The economic crisis of 2008 revealed the hidden instabilities of an economy built on speculative futures while at the same time providing a crisis narrative for the survival of global capitalism by shoring up the banking institutions that created the problems in the first place, often at the expense of further cuts to social spending. As of this writing, crises of mounting debt are playing out worldwide, raising the specter of systemic collapse.[4]

These recurring crises are forceful reminders of the increasing integration of the global economy. The implications of these economic perturbations for those whose lives have been disrupted by them figure importantly in the chapters of this volume.

The Future as a Critical Category

In using *global futures* as a conceptual frame, the chapters of this volume attempt to capture both the global scope of imagining life trajectories by individuals as well as the restless movement of capital in search of the next frontiers of accumulation. Speculative futures conjure new horizons for investment in the hopeful projection of new knowledge economies as the promise of a postindustrial transition. The irony is, of course, that the miracle must be continually produced anew. This imperative demands an orientation to a future that is, in effect, unknowable. It requires a futurology, an ability to conceptualize a future that has not only not yet appeared but that, once conceptualized, must be performed into being. The vision of the "information society" was the product of just such a futurology in the 1980s as a calculated strategy to recharge Japan's flagging high-growth economy around the development of new information technologies, and now a similar formulation of the "knowledge society" has spread worldwide as the future dynamic of the global economy.[5] Therefore, envisioning the future becomes a performative process that powerfully shapes the present as well as the future. The study of such futurologies is a necessary step in understanding that neither globalization nor neoliberalism is a force that is exogenous to human imagination and agency; they are, rather, both dialectically produced in relation to disparate social forces that come together to mobilize in pursuit of or to resist this demand. The chapters of this volume cannot offer a prognostication of the future, but they do make important contributions to our understanding of the extent to which "the global" and "the future" have framed projects of life-making in East Asian places in this period of restructuring.

Anna Tsing has reminded us that the future orientation of globalization talk is undoubtedly connected with the promissory nature of finance capital. The verb that Tsing (2000) uses to convey the performative power of these representations of futurity is *to conjure*. She suggests that we think of "the global" in terms of projects rather than thinking of it as descriptive of something that already exists or that will, in time, be inevitable. Her suggestion derives its inspiration from recent critiques of the modernization projects of the postwar era. She asks that we view our present from a perspective of the future anterior tense: "how we will have" understood it in an imagined retrospective future of failed promise (now perhaps a moment that has already arrived). A project is by definition anticipatory. It casts its vision into the future, but in pursuit of this object it encounters material and social forces that mutate and transform its initial promise. In this sense, we can view the discourses and practice of various globalisms and neoliberalisms as projects of human engineering and in this sense not unlike the modernization projects of the postwar period and the modernity projects of national becoming that preceded them.

Human engineering refers here to projects to create new kinds of subjects for political and economic transformation. In Europe, the ideals of the Enlightenment promised the emancipation of individuals from the hierarchical orders of the past. Modern secular education provided the "enlightenment" of a national citizenry through science and reason. However, the rise of capitalism also spurred the development of "more instrumental notions of human transformation [through which] the rational perfection of an individual could be engineered by another, armed with a knowledge of scientific law, and employing modern techniques of social management" (Ewen 1988: 194). The dialectic of the Enlightenment lies precisely in this twining together of the liberation of the free individual from the oppressive hierarchies of the past with engineering new forms of being through technical reason. Projections of the knowledge society as the shape of labor to come are today intrinsically related to neoliberal conceptions of human capital and embodied value that profoundly shape how individuals calculate their life chances.

Complex Crossings in East Asian Modernities

Incorporating a regional and global frame of analysis requires deep area knowledge of a specific national context while also being in dialogue with scholars working elsewhere in East Asia. Moreover, it requires awareness that these complex border crossings are not just characteristic of neoliberal globalization but have a much deeper history that continues to shape the present. Modernity projects in East Asia have long been pursued with an awareness of the pressures nations exert on each other in response to the challenges of uneven development. In examining the impact of economic globalization and the spread of neoliberal ideologies—which are not just restructuring economies but sociopolitical relations and conceptions of citizenship—we need to comprehend how these ideas and forces touch down on deeply layered histories that subtly mutate and sometimes redirect logics that have come from somewhere else. When we talk about region we are referring to a set of intertwined histories through which an object known as East Asia is named and continually redefined. Moreover, these are ideologically diverse spaces in which state governments and other kinds of institutional contexts are themselves riven with difference, contestation, and debate. These logics (globalization, economic restructuring) open new spaces and create new kinds of actors who are often multiply located in competing regimes of value and whose daily practices are caught up in negotiating the ruptures between them. The chapters in this volume are experiments in ethnographic writing attuned to these regional interactions, layered histories, and complicated subjectivities.

A deeper sense of the intertwined histories of national modernity projects in East Asia entails the questioning of what we ordinarily understand by the terms *nation* and *modernity*. If globalization is an imagination of scale, modernity is no less an imagination of temporality. In this sense, *modernity* refers to a subjective awareness on the part of individuals of their positioning in a movement out of backwardness, ignorance, or tradition, on the one hand, and toward progress, enlightenment, and civilization on the other. What we mean by "the nation-form" is closely allied with a concept of modernity as a moment of rupture from the past.[6]

Therefore, nationalist imaginings on the part of modernizing elites in different contexts position themselves in relation to other nations as both mirror and measure of their own progress to something called "the modern." In the process they embark on projects of human engineering premised on new models for ideal citizenship as imperative for the nation's ability to progress. In this introduction, I note three particular moments of modern East Asian histories in which these human engineering projects take shape in relation to larger geopolitical processes: the colonial modernity projects of the late nineteenth and early twentieth centuries, the modernization projects of the period following World War II, and the neoliberal restructuring of national economies in the context of economic globalization following the end of the Cold War.

The modernity projects in East Asia of the late nineteenth and early twentieth centuries were mobilizations by modernizing elites in search of national sovereignty. The ability to cohere together as a "strong nation" had become the new imperative to stave off the colonial ambitions of other nations. This pursuit of wealth and power superseded the aspirations of the Enlightenment to become aspirations for becoming, in the case of Japan, a colonial power. These histories of national becoming are important in understanding the continuing salience of "the nation" as a category of political belonging in a time of globalization, in particular with the rise of sentiments of "hypernationalism" expressed through the desire for economic and military power.

Hence, we wish to note here at the very beginning the importance of comprehending both the terms *nation* and *modernity* as structures of comparison. Benedict Anderson argues that the nation concept constitutes an unbounded seriality, an open-to-the-world plurality, in which one nation is set alongside others as counterposable units in "a world understood as one" (1998: 32). He poses seriality, rather than mimicry, as the underlying grammar of a national order of things. Most importantly, the "remarkable planetary spread" of nationalism accompanied the dissemination of a "profoundly standardized conception of politics" (1998: 29) requiring an entirely new vocabulary that marked a departure from a prior cosmological order. Therefore, each national context is "haunted" (Cheah 1999: 10) by its relation to other similar national bodies, all of which possess leaders, nationalists, citizens, ethnicities, populations, religions, and so forth. These categories achieve the status of "quotidian universals" through media technologies such as newspapers, in which one views these things "simultaneously close up and from afar" as categories of intelligibility present in one's own nation as well as in others (Anderson 1998: 33, 2). The history of East Asian nation-building projects can be tracked as these new conceptual frameworks for constructing modern identities—ideas such as "individual," "society," "Enlightenment"—circulated, touched down, and developed in place in ways that reflected a local politics of meaning.[7]

This underlying grammar makes it possible even now to compare, for example, Chinese children with Japanese children or, for that matter, American children, in terms of their training for success (Anagnost 2008b, Arai 2005).[8] It also sets up the possibility, to return to our opening example, for misrecognizing Japan for China. Comparison therefore becomes the "mid-

wife of national consciousness" in terms of placing the nation into a teleological narrative from backwardness to modernity but always in relation to
certain others.[9] National awakening is an awareness that derives from the
"disquieting knowledge of material forces at work in the wider world . . . a
form of inhuman automatism conjured by capitalism's eternal restlessness"
(Cheah 1999: 11–12).

In the postwar period, the Enlightenment ideals of the modernity project
were once again superseded by the more technical solutions of modernization theory. Japan became the American "Island of Dr. Moreau" (Harootunian 2004: 81), a scientific experiment to demonstrate the truth of modernization theory through the achievement of "essential characteristics."[10] The
history of postwar economic development in East Asia has been envisioned
in terms of miracles and moments of "takeoff," animated in the figures of
"little tigers" or "flocks of geese" (played off, of course, against the "sleeping
dragon" of socialist China) as if all nations everywhere, given the proper incentives and know-how, might expect the same progression through the se-
quential stages of rural to urban transition, industrial development, middle-
class formation, and consumer utopia (Bernard 1996). What tends to be
forgotten in these stories of miracle economies is not only the geopolitical
processes shaping them but also how they are themselves animated by the
restless movement of capital as the conditions of uneven development shift.
What does it mean to be living in postmiracle times?

Therefore, the studies in this volume argue for the importance of understanding how these projects of life-making in different national contexts are
connected. We are by now well into what has been designated as the Asian
Century, in which the dynamism of the global economy is said to be shifting
away from Europe and North America to a region of emerging economies.
The rise of China, in particular, figures centrally in visions of a future world
order in ways that are reminiscent of Japan's rise to economic preeminence
in the 1980s. Japan's prior economic success was in no small part due to its
Cold War–era role as a model modernizer. China's post–Cold War rise is
in no small part due to its ability to offer foreign capital (including from
Japan, South Korea, and Taiwan) an apparently inexhaustible well of cheap
rural labor as the historical product of its socialist-era development. However, even this promise has begun to unravel as wages in China rise, due in
no small part to worker protests over abysmal labor conditions, leading to
capital flight deeper into the Chinese hinterland or to Southeast Asia.

This focus on region is not meant to naturalize the idea of East Asia as a region but to draw from a history of complex crossings that have linked modernity projects across national boundaries. It also explores the value of a more integrated area studies for global studies as well as the reverse, to recognize the importance of incorporating global perspectives in our understandings of regional and national contexts. All too often, the fields of study identified with specific nation states (China, Japan, Korea, Taiwan) remain insular and fail to address the ways in which constructions of place are bound up with their relationships to other places. Likewise, a newly constituted "global studies" tends to gloss over the deeply stratified histories that continue to shape the present and future. The chapters in this volume adopt an ethnographic approach that combines a historical depth of field with regional and global perspectives in the study of East Asian places.

Neoliberalism as Ethos

The opportunities and terrors of this new time, shaped by global forces in labor markets, frame the life prospects for youth. Defined by calculations of risk and calibrations of human capital, these conditions of existence have resulted in new forms of embodied value and self-enterprising subjects. This volume explores detailed case studies of how workers are produced for new conditions of labor in a global marketplace, how new forms of consumption appear to promise a future for capital accumulation, and how individuals may or may not embrace risk as a marker of their "freedom" within a cultural ethos that we identify as "neoliberal."

In referring to a neoliberal ethos, we reference the capillary spread of values that define self-enterprising subjects (Hoffman, DeHart, and Collier 2006: 9–10). The question of whether we can apply the term *neoliberal* to transformations of economy and society in East Asia should not be premised on the presence of a particular political form but on whether there is a prevailing ethos of "empowering" individuals as risk-bearing subjects and of unleashing the power of the markets to order human affairs in areas where market agency is deemed superior to governmental control and regulation. However, in each of these specific national contexts, neoliberal logics must confront locally specific histories and the problems of government that influence how these logics are adapted, contested, and shaped. Both South Korea and Taiwan experienced long struggles for democratization from a military dictatorship and an authoritarian ruling party; Japan's attainment of rapid economic growth in the postwar period as a client state of the United States was purchased at the cost of democratic debate; China's postsocialist government allowed for the liberalization of the economy while retaining a tight hold on political control. In each case, the term *neoliberalism* references a "new freedom" that negates the value of what came before. This means that what this new freedom may mean in the context of different national histories may be in fact quite variable.

All of the societies represented in this volume are in their different ways under pressure from the global economy to produce enterprising selves able to navigate successfully the booms and busts of an increasingly volatile economy by encouraging individuals to regard themselves as a portfolio of human capital assets that they can manage and develop.[11] In illiberal political formations, as is the case elsewhere, incitements to neoliberal subjectivity come not only in the form of more overt pedagogies but also through media portrayals of desired subjectivities. In places where liberal models of governing "at a distance" coexist with more authoritarian forms of power, these modes of representation carve out areas of "microfreedoms" that encourage the development of "self-governing subjects" that will not challenge the limits set by the state (Zhang and Ong 2008).

We are perhaps only beginning to understand how neoliberal values spread globally, touching down in disparate places with complexly layered histories, and how these ideas develop locally with an awareness of the competitive pressures that come from other places. Zhang Li and Aihwa Ong have suggested the concept of assemblage as a useful tool of analysis. "An assemblage is not framed by preconceived political or social terrains, but is configured through the intersection of global forms and situated politics and cultures. . . . [D]isparate global and situated elements co-produce a particular space, and this interplay crystallizes conditions of possibility and outcomes" (2008: 10). This framing works well for the regional approach we propose here. It helps us to capture the awareness of individual subjects of being situated within a global condition that enables a young man from Taiwan, for example, to envision building his hip-hop empire in China (Hsu, Chapter Two) or an elite student from South Korea to anticipate a global scope for her ambitions as an events manager (Abelmann, Park, and Kim, Chapter Four). However, the scale of such ambitions expands and contracts with the growth and decline of national labor markets. Bookshops in Japan now feature literature for parents wishing to prevent their children from becoming *freeters* (Arai, Chapter Seven), while in China they feature advice on how to get one's child into Harvard.

These examples suggest that although neoliberalism as an ethos may traverse uneven terrain, it has, nonetheless, "pervasive effects on ways of thought to the point where it has become incorporated into the common-sense way many of us interpret, live in, and understand the world" (Harvey 2005: 3). However, "the actual process by which it became hegemonic, to the point of becoming common sense, is not examined" (Read 2009: 25). The hegemonic force of this new ethos is "generated not from the state, or from a dominant class, but from the quotidian experience of buying and selling commodities from the market, which is then extended across other social spaces, 'the marketplace of ideas,' to become an image of society" (2009: 26). In other words, the neoliberal ethos is a "real abstraction." Although it exists only within the human mind, it does not originate there. "It is not people who originate these abstractions [in their minds] but their actions. 'They do this without being aware of it'" (Sohn-Rethel 1978: 20; embedded quote is from Marx 1976: 166). Or, to reprise Pheng Cheah, they arise from "the disquieting knowledge of material forces at work in the wider world . . . a form of inhuman automatism conjured by capitalism's eternal restlessness" (1999: 11–12).

In neoliberal globalization, enterprising selves are not just buying and selling commodities in a marketplace, they are also put into a more direct relationship with the commodity value of their labor power within a global market. However, this value can vanish overnight as once-reliable jobs migrate elsewhere, or, as in the case of China, the ready availability of migrant populations of rural workers becomes the means of displacing state sector workers. Workers are abundantly clear as to where their jobs have migrated. What is less clear is how to find a new pathway to the future. The worker who must continually add to the list of his or her assets through perpetual retraining to remain employed becomes the new norm as global capital ensures its profits. Indeed, neoliberal conceptions of human capital are useful for economic logics premised on the increasing precariousness of labor (Gordon 1991). But this vision of never-ending self-development would seem to capitalize on the energies and resilience of youth, while refusing to acknowledge the gradual erosion of life and spirit by the stresses of constantly having to remake oneself. Workers become terrorized by the specter of redundancy when their labor power will no longer be of any "use to society." Over the course of a lifetime, it becomes harder to maintain a forward-moving life-building project when one's embodied value is constantly being negated. The body is, therefore, not just an "accumulation strategy" (Harvey 2000) in neoliberal economies, but it is also that which absorbs the contradictions of global capitalism through a mounting debt of stress, a slow attrition of life that Lauren Berlant (2007) refers to as "slow death." But it also offers the possibility for projects of self-appreciation outside the circuit of commodity value (Feher 2009).

Making New Spaces, Making New People

All of the chapters in this volume focus on new kinds of spaces, institutional structures, pedagogies, discourses, and practices engineered to produce new kinds of people. In Chapter One, Hai Ren explores the emergence of the new middle class, which has acquired the status of being an anticipatory sign of China's emergence as a leading economic power. However, this project is haunted by the specter of social inequality, which has become weightier as the chasm between the haves and have-nots of China's new economy continues to widen. Ren explores the concrete social space of Beijing's ethnic theme park as both a technology and a theater of middle-class self-making by detailing the visitors' complex negotiations of the park as an engineered space designed to produce certain effects. He examines the complexity of these negotiations on witnessing the theft of an umbrella from a souvenir stand under the cover of middle-class respectability as an example of the risk taking that underlies many a middle-class economic success story.

Hence, Ren proposes the "risk subject" as an analytical fulcrum to open up the question of the root causes of inequality in China today that underlie the new models of success in an entrepreneurial culture. In this respect, the risk subject is one who is able to calculate the costs and benefits of breaking the rules rather than abiding them. The subject who is willing to embrace risk as opportunity can be counterposed to another kind of risk subject, the so-called weaker groups (*ruoshi qunti*) who are rendered vulnerable by these very same transformations. Their structural disadvantage—as rural, impoverished, uneducated—is transformed into a problem of subjective lack of awareness of how to take advantage of the opportunities offered them.

In Chapter Two, Ching-wen Hsu offers another example of producing new kinds of people by producing new kinds of spaces in the project to update the New Kujiang shopping area in Taiwan's southern port city of Kaohsiung. This project exemplifies the problem of postindustrial development: How does one transform a prior history as a place of production into a storied place of consumption? New Kujiang participates in the imagineering of Taiwan's passage to a postindustrial economy through developing the power of the attractions of place. In the case of Taiwan, the off-shoring of industrial jobs has necessitated a revisioning of what development can mean. Taiwan, as one of the East Asian Tigers, was a poster child of state-led developmentalism. However, development, which was once conceived of as the ultimate goal of modernizing states, turns out to be something that, once achieved, is not forever. In the global competition for capital investment, redevelopment becomes not only a reengineering of the built environment but also of the kind of person to inhabit these new spaces, that is, a highly educated, high-earning, consumer citizen. Moreover, this new kind of person is one who is self-enterprising and able to recognize the new, more flexible terms of the labor contract as opportunity rather than risk. The hip-hop artist encountered by Hsu in New Kujiang sees in dance an alternative career track similar to those devised by the youth identified as *freeter* in postrecessionary Japan who seek careers in the creative professions in reaction against the soul-deadening ethos of the salaryman. His dream of expanding his hip-hop empire into China can be put into the context of how a late starter such as Taiwan can see itself as more progressive than the mainland in terms of pop-cultural temporalities of the latest thing. The production of culture is where the future of accumulation lies for an economy hollowed out by the flight of industrial jobs to the very place where he plans to build his empire. At the same time, in Hsu's account of the efforts of New Kujiang planners to create a dreamscape that evokes other places (for example, the streets of Austria) to attract Chinese tourism as a strategy of accumulation, we see a triangulation of where precisely these subjects locate Taiwan in a global mapping of the hierarchy of places worth going to. As Hsu concludes, for these planners and consumers there is a "double distancing." Both the mainland of China and the streets of Austria are brought into the visual field of New Kujiang as a way of situating it within a global frame. The world is both near and far at the same time.

In Chapter Three, Trang X. Ta looks at urban space from the perspective of the weaker groups in Chinese society. In the heart of Beijing's own "Silicon Valley," where high rises gleam, the parents of a terminally ill child come from the countryside to engage unsuccessfully in the production of affects that will move people to donate money. However, in following the script of what makes a story moving, the family risks becoming misrecognized as merely a facsimile of tragedy rather than the real thing, enabling passersby to dismiss the disquiet that the family enacts on the street. This disquiet is the knowledge that China's economic miracle is not bought without incalculable cost in the growing chasm between the country and the city. The fact that these desperate parents have no access to adequate health care for their son is a story that is utterly banal, but it is this very banality that is the most shocking thing of all. The failure to recognize what is truly shocking in their condition is what the author wants us to recognize. If this is a form of affective labor enacted by subjects disadvantaged from the biopolitical effects of the economic reforms, it is a failure in its inability to produce the desired affects in others. However, the ethnographer wishes to reanimate the potential of the disquiet implicit in the practice of these parents to move her readers to critical reflection. This suggests the possibility of scholarship itself as a form of affective labor from below that works at cross-purposes to logics of capital accumulation.

Affective Economies

Many of the chapters in this volume focus on the production of affects in the formation of new kinds of embodied labor and citizen subjects. Whereas *emotion* refers to a mental state, *affect* expresses "a certain state of the body along with a certain mode of thinking" (Hardt and Negri 2004: 108). Hence, affective labor works to produce certain kinds of affect (that is, "service with a smile"), in which a focus on social skills becomes predominant.[12] In this respect, these chapters develop ethnographically the ways in which forms of affective production have been incorporated into the global capitalist economy as one of the "highest value-producing forms of labor" (Hardt 1999).

The concept of "affective economies" provides a frame for tracking transformations of value that take place in the realm of affective production. Most of the chapters in this section of the volume focus on education and training in the formation of new labor subjectivities: "A worker with a good attitude and social skills is another way of saying a worker adept at affective labor" (Hardt and Negri 2004: 108). The workers trained to do affective labor are themselves the product of another form of affective labor, called training, that is intended to produce an alignment between their emotional experience and the real material conditions of their labor.

In Chapter Four, Nancy Abelmann, Sojin Park, and Hyunhee Kim explore the production of affects in the context of higher education. A young college woman, whom the authors name Heejin, plots her course on a global stage through the deployment of the "brand capital" of the elite university she attends in Seoul. Her vision of the vital life, as one that is "not just comfortably enjoyed but more actively lived," is an endless striving for competitive advantage that excludes the possibility of any point of rest or pursuit of contemplative realms of value other than the market-driven ones of the global economy.[13] For her, the world appears open ended, and her university degree promises to be a global passport to the future. She views the failure of others to set such goals and actively pursue them as a mark of their personal insufficiency—a lacking of spirit, discipline, and will—rather than ascribing them to more structural constraints such as class, gender, and nationality. And yet, some of the other students interviewed by the authors suggest that Heejin's subjectivity is not universal. Others of her generation question the value of this perpetual striving, opting instead for other realms of value, leading not necessarily to economic rewards but to personal fulfillment and happiness.

Both Nickola Pazderic (Chapter Five) and Yan Hairong (Chapter Six) offer us a sense of how happiness, in the form of a smile, is made into an imperative for those wishing to be recognized as employable labor value, but at quite different levels and locations of the labor hierarchy. Pazderic's essay begins with a description of "Smile Chaoyang," a university campaign to exhort students to embody a new formation of human capital defined as a form of affective discipline. His discussion can be put into the context of transformations to the political shifts in Taiwan as it moved from state-led developmentalism to democratization and the changing role of education in relation to these shifts. Pazderic explores how Taiwan's unique positioning in the world system of nation-states as a U.S. client-state and poster child for developmental statism has both contributed to its miraculous economic rise and set its limits. He examines the impact of the global economy on the institutional context in which he teaches, a third-tier university specialized in training students for service sector jobs in a moment of uncertainty about the national economic future. Educational credentials now enter into a global circuit of value, institutions of higher learning become increasingly entrepreneurial to compete in a global market for tuition dollars, and faculty are under increasing pressure to publish their work in journals of international standing in a global standardization of academic credentialing. In other words, we see the restructuring of education in relation to the entrepreneurial state—Taiwan, Inc.—and its project to produce a "second miracle" to ensure Taiwan's transcendence in the new global order. Education has become a profitable investment sector. It has become the primary service provider in the production of the new knowledge economy. The graduates of Chaoyang are encouraged to be the very embodiment of flexible labor, conditioned to accept whatever changed life chances the global economy might bring—with a smile. The objective of training in Chaoyang's programs is to produce a labor force that is above average on the global scale of things. The smile effectively becomes a school brand. The student acquires the imprimatur of the school's affective disciplines as a professionalized service worker.

We see how the smile similarly figures into an economy of affects in Yan Hairong's study of a Beijing school for training rural women as domestic workers. If the Chinese state promotes migration to the city in search of wage labor as a form of "social university" (Yan 2008), we see in this case how this idea has become literalized in the founding of a school where migrant women learn to objectify their own labor as a commodity in a process of self-objectification and alienation. They are taught that they are service providers, not servants, and that their employers are their clients, not their masters. This is an education of affects: The worker becomes an eager seller of his or her own labor power. Moreover, the conflict that will occur in the labor process when the interests of master and servant inevitably collide will be successfully negotiated through the smile as the sign of sovereign self-possession and the stamp of professionalism as an asset in human capital formation. The object of the institute is not so much to teach the technical skills of domestic labor as it is to prepare the worker for the workplace at the level of her subjective transformation.

Yan explores the military imagery that she discovers in descriptions of the market given in class as a battleground, sorting out winners and losers. To put this in a regional perspective, the image of the battleground, along with survival games, is a common trope in Japan as well. The *manga*-turned-film *Battle Royale* discussed by Andrea Arai, in which schoolchildren are compelled to compete in a life-and-death struggle until a sole survivor remains (with a smile on her face), is a particularly vivid example of this. It adumbrates in a particularly ominous way what Teacher Yin, in Yan's account, meant by consequences—the loss of one's value as labor results in a symbolic death. In both these accounts, we see a subtle transposition of the battleground of the marketplace into a battleground within, one that lies internal to the self in the struggle for self-transformation. At the same time, these military metaphors resonate with the resurgence of hypernationalism in which the nation is seen as engaged in a Darwinian struggle for survival.

In Chapter Seven, Arai explores another affective economy in the form of a gift of *Notes to the Heart*, a set of booklets prepared as a supplementary curriculum for public school children in Japan in 2002. She reads this act of giving from the school to its students (but also implicit here is a gift from the state to its citizens) as an exemplification of how the Japanese people are asked to accept a profound reworking of Japanese identity formation to meet the challenges of a postmiracle Japan. Problems that had been denied, disavowed, or overlooked in postwar representations of Japan as a homogeneous society and model modernizer have suddenly become visible and are laid bare by the ending of the miracle and the grim new reality of a deepening recessionary economy. One of the key effects of this shift is the discourse of "strange kids," most horrifically exemplified by the beheading of a Kobe schoolboy in 1997 by a fellow student, and in the discourse of "abnormal nation," referring to the constitutional stripping of Japan's war powers. Both of these discourses reveal concerns about national and cultural reproduction that take their form in anxieties about youth and educational reform.

More particularly, Arai explores education as a site where issues of modernity that have a long history in Japan continue to be debated. "Love of nation" and "freedom" take on different meanings and uses in this specific context. This is not a love that can reproduce the national community as it once was, nor is it simply a reprise of the past. It is a newly individualized love, and it is a different nation than one might think of loving or devoting oneself to. The shift of focus to the individual's love and heart rather than the nation works as a form of governance by other means. The frontier within offers the promise to transcend the rigors of a harsh new economic reality by developing the strength to live in a system that can no longer offer any guarantees. Arai's analysis of this discourse raises important questions about the reworking of national cultural identity formations in the face of epochal economic shifts remapping capital flows across national boundaries. The success of Japan Inc. no longer rests on a reciprocal exchange of obligations between state and citizen but continues to demand sacrifices on the part of the latter in exchange for increasingly precarious conditions of living.

Governing "Free" Subjects

What is understood by the word *freedom* is often cast as a repudiation of a national past that continues, nonetheless, to condition its possibilities in the present and for the future.[14] In each instance, *freedom* has meant a liberation from structures of the past that are now perceived to constrain individual freedom. Often this entails a massive overturning of values under the pressure of the heightened competition of globalization. However, this shift in what constitutes value has come at the cost of making the future increasingly precarious. The erosion of job security and social insurance is also accomplished in the name of freedom through new models of citizenship (in which individuals take responsibility for themselves). The chapters in this section therefore explore the specificities of what *freedom* might mean and how libratory projects of social change can become folded into neoliberal projects of economic restructuring.

In Chapter Eight, Miyako Inoue explores the effects of corporate practices to address gender inequality in a workplace in Japan in which the underlying structural causes of inequality are left undisturbed. The confessional practices of training workshops focus on a failure of women workers to realize their full potential as professionals. Either they fully accept the requirements of full integration into the workplace or they are "free" to relinquish their professional lives for homemaking. In Inoue's analysis of how these technologies of subject production operate, we see a striking parallel to the training objectives of the Fuping School described by Yan Hairong. Both contexts teach women to objectify their labor as entrepreneurs of themselves and to optimize their opportunities by becoming self-governing subjects fully responsible for their own success or failure. Gender reform thereby becomes a process of working on the self and the production of laboring subjects of a particular determinate form. Rather than being a form of false consciousness, it is a question of how discursively difficult it becomes to think outside the construction of a rational self who pursues her own interests. In liberal governments, as Inoue is careful to remind us by citing Foucault, "Power is exercised only over free subjects, and only insofar as they are free" (1983: 221). In this respect, we can begin to see this activity of gender reform as yet another form of affective labor in which the "happiness, sense of fulfillment, and aspirations" of women workers become the central focus of management. Inoue carefully maps out how this process of subject formation is enacted by noting the limits of what can be spoken in addressing the question of gender inequality—hence, neoliberal speech acts—in new managerial tools such as the workplace climate survey. In her detailed analysis of such instruments, Inoue is able to elucidate the apparent paradox of how constructing what it is that women want can result in a new mode of subjection for women that is in tune with the new demands of competitiveness in a globalized economy. Gender issues become a problem of interpersonal EQ between supervisors and workers and therefore subject to new modes of human engineering rather than structural reform in gender relations.

Inoue's discussion of what freedom means in this new neoliberalized labor regime foreshadows Gabrielle Lukacs's discussion, in Chapter Nine, of televisual celebrations of the possibility of not taking work seriously, in which female protagonists figure prominently. Lukacs explores technologies of subject production in 1990s Japan through an ethnographic study of television dramas that focus on the workplace. In her analysis of one such drama, *Shomuni*, which proved to be an unexpected success, especially with young male viewers, we see dramatized many of the new management practices that Inoue encountered in her field research—indeed, one of the characters is assigned the task of addressing complaints about gender discrimination in the workplace. Lukacs suggests that this series, which was pitched as social realism, was really a fantasy about the emergence of a new labor subject who takes responsibility for his or her own success in the workplace and in making his or her work life meaningful—if only to have fun with it. The irreverent attitude of the principle female character epitomizes an approach to work that is meant to be a refreshing antidote to the labor contract of the high-growth era, which had been based on lifelong job security and benefits for male wage earners in exchange for rigid hierarchy, loyalty to the firm, an ethic of workaholism, and the subordination of women's labor. Instead, Chinatsu, the principle female character, projects the image of a woman who is contemptuous of her male bosses, takes on each new assignment as a challenge to her ingenuity and sense of fun, and emphasizes her individuality and strong sense of self.

Lukacs argues that Chinatsu, in fact, represents much more than women workers but becomes a stand-in for the *freeter*, the new labor subject, both male and female, that is demanded by the conditions of Japan's postrecessionary economy. The Japanese term *freeter* is a neologism that combines the English word *free* with the German word *arbeiter* (worker) to designate a new generation of Japanese workers who no longer desire the guarantees of life-long labor but wish to remain free to develop their life career as a project that entails no loyalty to any employer. If the neoliberal ethos rests on ideas of freedom, then freedom is differently articulated in each localized project of reform. This new laboring subject is one who desires his or her freedom from a labor regime that is, in fact, no longer a possibility for this generation of Japanese youth. The *freeter* is represented as a lifestyle choice rather than a condition that is imposed by the economic changes in the wake of Japan's economic recession. However, representations of this figure are fraught with contradiction, being both celebrated as figures of freedom and creative energy unleashed from the stultifying labor regime of the high-growth era and also reviled by elders as a generational failure to understand the importance of hard work. The *freeter* therefore exemplifies the "new spirit of capitalism" in which the subject seeks emancipation from what was oppressive in prior labor regimes as a project of self-fulfillment, but one that is entirely resonant with the post-Fordist reorganization of capitalism itself (Boltanski and Chiapello 2006). Neither of these two *freeters* (Driscoll 2007) adequately captures the desperation of many Japanese youth who have not been able to secure regular employment but are bused from one location to the other as a reserve army of labor with no way to map out a future.

In Chapter Ten, Jesook Song explores the meaning of freedom in post-democratization South Korea in the context of the Asian Debt Crisis of 1997–2001, which had upset the occupational stability South Korea had enjoyed in the preceding couple of decades. Under pressure from the IMF,

South Korea had to agree to a program of economic restructuring in which the downsizing of the large state-subsidized conglomerates (*chaebol*) to liberalize the market economy led to massive unemployment. However, as Song carefully lays out for us, these economic policies must also be placed within the context of Kim Dae Jung's specific problem of government as an anticorruption reformer. Hence we see here the articulation of external forces of global governance and internal forces of political liberalization.

As an "unemployed highly educated worker," Song describes how she herself became caught up in the paradoxes of this articulation. Hired on as a part-time researcher investigating the problems of homeless people, she became both an agent and a beneficiary of Kim's workfare policies. She describes with devastating detail her discomfort with her growing awareness of the forms of discrimination embedded in these policies in which homeless women are made invisible as subjects deserving social support. Song's chapter resonates strongly with Inoue's reflections on how discourses of welfare reform work through the medium of neoliberal speech acts to make gender inequality invisible. In the case of South Korea, these speech acts took on the guise of "family breakdown," "the deserving poor," and "empowerment," and their illocutionary effects turned liberal projects of social redistribution into neoliberal projects of self-responsibilization by making invisible the structural causes of women's homelessness.

Conclusion

The authors of these chapters bring ethnography to bear on what it does best by exploring the complex relationships between macrolevel processes working globally with the everyday practices of building a life in an economic landscape that has been dramatically altered. They demonstrate the value of grounded ethnographic work in exploring the processes of subject formation within locally specific conditions of possibility. Neoliberal subjecthood is not entirely the result of a process of top-down human engineering but is also the result of transnational cultural flows in which ideals of the enterprising self take shape in locally specific forms that define what it means to be competitive and forward moving.

But this volume was also conceived with a hope that these projects of life-making can be connected across national boundaries to become part of a

New International already in formation. Capitalism's strategy of segregating high- and low-value subjects by means of a global division of labor has re-created the struggle at a global level: "Intensifying the integration of the world market has made channels for unprecedented connections between different value subjects; it has formed a new, and militant industrial proletariat in new planetary zones" (Dyer-Witheford 2002: 30). The self-enterprising subjects produced by capitalism's efforts to externalize its costs may instead engage in life-making projects that lie outside the circuit of capital accumulation altogether. In a global regime that constantly undercuts the value of the enterprise of the self, the imperative of building new economies from the ground up outside the speculative logics of global capitalism may indeed open a path to a future.[15]

Notes

ACKNOWLEDGMENTS

This introduction emerged out of countless conversations with Andrea G. Arai whose intellectual collaboration has taken the form of teaching together as well as co-editing this volume. Our other volume coeditor Hai Ren and Stanford University Press editor Stacy Wagner also contributed invaluable input, which has helped shape it into its final form.

1. NHK. *Friita—Genryuu—Monozukuri no Genba de* (From the Worksite: A Story of the *Freeter*). Documentary, aired February 2005.

2. For a historical overview of neoliberalism, see Harvey 2005. For discussion of neoliberalism as a problem of government, see Foucault 2008 and Lemke 2001.

3. "Spatiotemporal fix" is a phrase taken from Harvey 2003. It is a spatial movement in that capitalism seeks geographical regions where there are large pools of cheap labor. It is a temporal move because it seeks these new conditions of doing business in areas that are "behind" in terms of capitalist development.

4. See Mike Davis's discussion (2011) of the collision course of the debt crisis in the United States, the European Union, and China. China's real estate bubble threatens an iteration of the Japanese disease in China.

5. See Morris-Suzuki 1988 for an account of how government agencies plotted Japan's future course as the information society. The knowledge economy has now diversified to include materials science and biogenetics as key areas for economic growth. China and India are engaged in a race to develop research parks and

"innovation incubators," while the labor costs for building the physical infrastructure of such facilities are still low. Likewise, we see transnational competition for becoming the new "education hubs" that are very much in service to this model of technological innovation as the driver of the new economy.

6. In East Asia, nation-building projects did not always relinquish the past completely. For example, Japan's modern emperor system employed forms of "creative anachronism" to form the diverse inhabitants of a dispersed island archipelago into the Japanese people through new forms of national pedagogies (Fujitani 1993)—a project that was extended to Taiwan and Korea as part of Japan's colonial expansion (Ching 2001; Schmid 2002). China's formation as a modern nation entailed a more deliberate break from the "feudal" structures of the past but no less a molding of the people, in this case "the masses" as new socialist subjects.

7. For the case of China, see for example the discussions by Lydia Liu (1995) on the translingual movement of conceptions of "individual" and by Tani Barlow (1991) on the emergence of the position of "intellectual" in relation to Enlightenment projects.

8. A 2006 story in the English edition of the Japanese newspaper *Asahi Shimbun* (September 27, 2006) exemplifies a more recent iteration of this mode of comparison. See "China's Gifted 'Superchildren' on a Fast Track to Success."

9. For example, Andre Schmid argues that in early-twentieth-century Korea "shifting understandings of China and Japan were integral to Korean self-knowledge, largely overshadowing the East-West dynamic and giving Koreans several others against which to compare their nation's particularity" (2002: 10).

10. See Koschmann (2003: 229) for an account of the 1960 Hakone conference, where Japan historian Jon Hall set out nine essential characteristics of a modern society.

11. Human capital could be considered the essence of neoliberal subjectivity. It marks a significant departure from earlier forms of labor subjectivity in the sense that the worker is understood as an entrepreneur who invests in his or her own self-development. Much of the literature inspired by Michel Foucault's (2008) late lectures on neoliberalism sees human capital as a mode of governmentality that incites individuals "to adopt conducts deemed valorizing and to follow models for self-valuation that modify their priorities and inflect their strategic choices" (Feher 2009: 28).

12. This emphasis on affective labor perhaps accounts for the spread of the concept of EQ (emotional quotient) among human resource managers in East Asia, as well as elsewhere, as a measure of interpersonal skills and leadership potential. A self-help literature has become widespread to teach individuals how to evaluate themselves and develop their emotional intelligence as an aspect of their overall human capital development.

13. Quoted phrase from Stacy Wagner, personal communication.

14. In Japan, the term *freedom* connotes a more individualized horizon for the development of human creativity that had been constrained by the deadening and highly gendered institutionalization of the salaryman tracked for upward mobility. As noted earlier, the *freeter* youth has been described as a figure of "the great refusal" of this sort of labor bondage. In South Korea, *freedom* signals the moment of democratization in 1987 following a long era of military dictatorship in close formation with the *chaebol* (Korean corporations). In China, freedom takes the form of "reform and opening" (*gaige kaifang*) in the dismantling of the redistributive structures of the socialist system in favor of market institutions beginning in 1976. In Taiwan, *freedom* also refers to democratization beginning in the late 1980s, during which the KMT (Kuomintang) lost its monolithic governing power.

15. For one such experiment, see Carl Cassegard's (2008) discussion of Kojin Karatani's New Associationist Movement.

Chapter One

The Middle-Class Norm
and Responsible Consumption
in China's Risk Society

HAI REN

China's neoliberalization, a process known in China as "reform and open-ing" (*gaige kaifang*), which began in the late 1970s, has extracted individu-als from the social institutions developed in socialism and reembedded them within a new sociopolitical system. The embrace of a neoliberal economic and political system, with all its attendant risks, has forced the development of new governmental and social policies to stabilize China's growing inequal-ity through the conceptual category of the middle class. Within this histori-cal context, life-making and life-building take the form of self-formation but only in such a way that they become measured by the new social norm of the middle class. I draw from my ethnographic fieldwork in Beijing to ex-amine how individuals transform themselves into entrepreneurial subjects through consumer practices and how private corporations play an important role in cultivating middle-class values and shaping consumer behavior. As is the case with other social engineering projects discussed in this book, such as the training of migrant women workers to fit China's neoliberal develop-ment (Yan, Chapter Six in this volume), the making of responsible middle-class subjects through consumption is part of the government's larger project of engineering a new society for the future.

Neoliberalization, Risk Society, and the Middle Class

Contemporary Chinese society has been transformed into a risk society, in which individuals and nongovernmental organizations take over responsibilities once assigned to the government. This shift has been tied to China's neoliberalization, the transformation of China from a socialist country to a neoliberal state, which refers to both the Chinese nation-state under a hybrid capitalist-socialist system and to China as a country where economic rationalism penetrates all aspects of society, including domains such as the political and the cultural that are usually incommensurable or incompatible with the economic realm (Ren 2010a). China's neoliberal transformation has occurred largely through establishing a relationship between "reform and opening" and national reunification, two seemingly parallel historical agendas of the socialist state since the late 1970s.[1] The former entails various national development projects addressing the modernization (*xiandaihua*) of the economy, culture, technology, and state–society relationship. The reunification issue revolves around the status of Taiwan, Hong Kong, and Macau.

The Chinese government's reform and opening project has allowed the development of new kinds of productive enterprises that are neither state controlled nor collectively owned. This policy change contradicts both the policies of Mao Zedong's socialist government, which had eliminated all forms of private ownership and their associated productive relations, and the constitution of the Chinese Communist Party (CCP), the ruling party of China founded on commitment to the causes and interests of the working class. To resolve these contradictions, Deng Xiaoping's government declared in 1978 that the Cultural Revolution (1966–1976) had been a complete failure and had caused chaos in the Chinese state. Deng's repudiation of Mao's legacy opened up possibilities for rejecting Maoist practices (including prohibition of private ownership). Building on this decision, Deng and his successors gradually modified the Communist Party constitution and incorporated key changes as amendments to the national constitution.

In 1998, Jiang Zemin, the secretary general of the CCP and the president of China, asked the party members to propose a theoretical structure for a new system of political representation. In February 2000, he proclaimed the "Three Represents" (*sange daibiao*) in which the CCP represents "the developmental requirement of the advanced productive forces in China," "the progressive direction of the advanced culture in China," and "the fundamental interest of the vast majority of the people."[2] In 2003, the Third

Plenum of the Sixteenth Central Committee of the Communist Party of China formally incorporated this theory into the revised party constitution. Meanwhile, the Chinese government formally changed its English translation from the Chinese Communist Party to the Communist Party of China (CPC). Therefore, when the Three Represents and property rights became formally institutionalized, the transformation of the Communist Party–led state from a state of the working classes to one of the capitalist class (including the nouveaux riches) was completed (Ren 2010b).

Meanwhile, the reincorporation of capitalist Hong Kong into socialist China has done what no other contemporary event could have done: It provided both the historical precondition for and the primary process of China's radical neoliberal transformation. Under British rule, Hong Kong was recognized not simply as a capitalist economy but as one of the freest market economies in the world.[3] The Sino-British Joint Declaration of 1984 that set out the conditions for Hong Kong's return to China called for Hong Kong to retain its capitalist system and a measure of political autonomy for a period of fifty years, a provision commonly referred to as "one country, two systems" (*yiguo liangzhi*) and viewed by the Chinese as a potentially long-term arrangement. This framework was first proposed by Deng Xiaoping during the Sino-British negotiation process. It was extended to create various types of special economic and political zones, enabling the practical coexistence between socialist and capitalist spaces. Thus, the legal framework of one country, two systems, on being translated into political and economic practices in China, shaped the transformation of the Chinese state into a neoliberal state. By casting reunification as an *uncompromisable* issue of national sovereignty, the Chinese government made this a default justification for all political, economic, social, and cultural changes. That is, reunification with Hong Kong demanded the supreme power of sovereignty to act ethically by not abiding by existing (Maoist) socialist norms and laws. Thus, anything incompatible with regaining sovereignty over Hong Kong was to be modified, changed, or rejected—including Maoist forms of mobilizing and empowering ordinary people, political representation of the working class, socialist productive relations, economic policies, and nationalism (Ren 2010a; 2010b; 2012).

The spatial production of neoliberal social space followed Deng's theory of one country, two systems. This is shown by the creation of a series of four special economic zones (beginning in 1980) in Guangdong and Fujian provinces, where nonsocialist systems—not only private markets but also private controls over the economy and the population—were developed. In 1984, the year of the signing of the Sino-British Joint Declaration, the government expanded the special economic zone concept to another fourteen coastal cities and to Hainan Island. In the 1990s, many priority development regions and export processing zones were established across the country. In 1997, Hong Kong became the first special administrative region of the People's Republic of China, and two years later Macau became the second. Each region is supposed to operate for fifty years according to its own miniconstitution.

Similar to the idea of the special economic zone is the proliferation of numerous privately controlled zones through urban real estate development projects. Some past and present Communist Party officials and their relatives (for example, Chen Xitong and Chen Lianyu, members of the politburo) could use their access to political capital and networks for accruing wealth in the new economy. For them, neoliberal policies like privatization of land use offered a horizon of freedom to pursue the good life, whether in terms of a "relatively comfortable life" (*xiaokang shenghuo*), in Deng Xiaoping's words, or a lifestyle oriented toward cosmopolitan or international norms. Zhang Yuchen's prior status as the head of Beijing's construction bureau, for example, gave him the opportunity to accumulate vast wealth (Kahn 2004). By contrast, those who lacked access to social and political capital were affected negatively by privatization and the erosion of social welfare institutions. As their life chances were diminished, they become marginalized as subjects in need, whether as landless peasants or laid-off workers.

During China's neoliberal transformation, the foundation of Chinese state sovereignty has shifted away from the collective body of the people and toward the individual body of the citizen.[4] The ways in which individuals become socialized as Chinese citizens have changed significantly. Not only are the institutional structures of socialist China disappearing, but forms of practical knowledge, common sense, and guiding norms associated with socialism are no longer legitimate or empowering tools. Increasingly, Chinese citizens are expected to rely on themselves in their life-building process. This life-building process, however, does not presume a straightforward, upward, or progressive trajectory, which is based on a will-have-been of future anteriority (Berlant 2007: 758). Its outcomes are more conditional and contingent. Thus, the neoliberal do-it-yourself biographical process includes not merely positive trajectories but also delayed, regressive, or sidetracked ones.

For example, the socialist work unit (*danwei*) was not only a workplace but also an entire welfare system (Yi Wang 2003; Bray 2005). It provided employment, housing, child care, health care, and education. However, the neoliberal reforms, especially of the state-owned enterprises that employed the majority of the workers, have systematically reduced the state's welfare function with the withering away of these work units and the social networks formed through them. Some individuals have taken advantage of new opportunities to become active participants in the market. Meanwhile, millions of laid-off workers face new challenges of making a living. Some have been retrained to take temporary and part-time employment, such as domestic help and service sector jobs, while others have become permanently unemployed or underemployed because they are unable to compete either with the growing number of young migrant laborers from rural areas (Pun 2005) or with new college graduates with greater knowledge of the norms of international business and work practices (Ross 2006: 18).

The neoliberal transformation of the Chinese state has led some Chinese scholars to consider its consequences. The Chinese economist Yu Wenlie, for example, mentioned four major problems in 2004:

1. The increasing gap between the rich and the poor presents a challenge to the socialist distribution system (*fenpei zhidu*).
2. The privatization of state-owned enterprises and "state-owned assets" (*guoyou zichan*) damages the socialist "collective ownership system" (*gongyouzhi*).
3. The government's "malfunctioning" or "misbehavior" (*shiwei*) in the market damage the socialist market economic system.
4. "The urban-rural twofold economic structure" (*cheng xiang eryuan jingji jiegou*) and the increasing economic disparities among regions damage the balanced development of the national economy. (2004: 20)

These shifts have turned Chinese society from one of the world's most equal societies to one of the most unequal. China has become a risk society in which responsibility for employment, welfare, education, health, poverty alleviation, and environment have become redistributed from government to nongovernmental organizations and from the collective to the individual.[5]

During China's neoliberal transformation, governmental and social policies have shifted from regarding peasants and workers as model citizens to "disadvantaged groups" (*ruoshi qunti*). Their lack of various kinds of capital (political, economic, and cultural), unequally redistributed during the economic reforms (Yi Wang 2003; Li 2003; Xiao 2003), has made them less able to take responsibility for livelihood, health care, and education. Forming the largest segment of China's population, they are viewed as a threat to the stability of Chinese society in case of a state emergency, such as an economic or political crisis or even a crisis of biosecurity, as in the case of an outbreak of severe acute respiratory syndrome (SARS) or avian flu. To address these problems of security, government officials, policy experts, and scholars advocate for the growth of a middle class (Chinese Academy of Social Sciences [CASS] 2002; Hu 2003; He 2003; Qin 2003) as necessary for balancing the contradictions between economic growth and social stability produced by neoliberal reforms.[6] They attribute a stabilizing power to the middle class in addressing such issues as social inequality, aspirational life ways, and civic discipline. Although the middle class is still statistically small in size, it is anticipated to grow to become the predominant social class so that the pyramidal shape of the present social structure will be transformed into the ideal olive shape (CASS 2002).

The conceptualization of the category of the middle class to address the structural problem of Chinese society has built on an extensive sociological and journalistic literature on China's new class strata since the early 1990s.[7] Many of these studies were proleptic in nature: representing something that has not yet come into view as if it already existed in fact (Anagnost 1997). This figure of prolepsis suggests the performativity and productivity of all the discourse on the middle class. It also marks the practical development of the middle class as a project involving many actors, including governmental and nongovernmental organizations, corporations, educational institutions, and individuals (government officials, businesspeople, and ordinary citizens). The development of the category of the middle class reflects a fundamental policy change in understanding cultural transformations in China's economic reforms (Ren 2007a).

The middle class as a normative category becomes intelligible through systematic uses of statistical surveys by population scientists, state planners, and government bureaucrats. Among many statistical surveys, the most influential one is carried out by some of China's leading sociologists in the Chinese Academy of Social Sciences (CASS). Between 1999 and 2001, they conducted the first systematic nationwide sociological study of China's social stratification since the end of the 1970s. The CASS project, under the full support of the central government, surveyed over twelve provinces and seventy-two cities, counties, and districts. Major "findings" were included in a 411-page report, entitled *The Report on Social Stratification Research in Contemporary China (Dangdai zhongguo shehui jieceng yanjiu baogao)* (CASS 2002) (for an in-depth analysis of this report, see Ren 2010b). A major study like this provides a national standard for developing the category of the middle class through statistical thinking, based on "numerical inscriptions" such as tables, figures, charts, and equations (Greenhalgh 2005: 357).

Beyond abstract statistics, the category of the middle class is primarily used in two ways in popular culture and everyday life. The emerging nouveaux riches (*xin furen*) have a special interest in advocating for the term *middle class*, along with associated concepts such as "public sphere" (*gonggong kongjian*) and "individualism" (*ziyou zhuyi*) (X. Wang 1999; Xue 1999; Luo 1999). They use the term *middle class* to characterize their experience and lifestyle as a "successful person" (*chenggong renshi*), prototypically portrayed by the mass media as a married middle-aged businessman. He wears designer labels; owns a house with a garden; drives a car; socializes in bars, nightclubs, and hotels; plays golf; and attends concerts (X. Wang 1999: 29). He enjoys a "practical existence" (*shizai*) of a comfortable life, the "freedom" (*ziyou*) of consumer choice, a "stylish appearance" (*qipai*), the "prestige power" (*zunyan*) of his wealth, and a "cultivated appreciation for the finer things" (*mei*).[8] Such a celebration of a person's success in achieving middle-class status embraces a cosmopolitan experience at the expense of the Maoist historical experience.[9]

Whether the nouveaux riches and successful people described in the preceding paragraph are proper middle-class subjects is subject to debate. Besides its representation as the experience of the nouveaux riches, the middle class is primarily used as a norm to regulate and discipline behaviors of Chinese citizens to make them become more responsible, not only for the ongoing stability of Chinese society but also for their own success or failure. In the following section, I analyze how individuals who aspire to become middle class develop their responsibility-bearing capacity by looking at a specific context of middle-class consuming practice: the Chinese Ethnic Culture Park in Beijing. Drawing on ethnographic research first begun in 1996, I show how a private corporation shapes the conduct of consumers and how consumers carefully calculate their responses to this regulation. Their deviations from the plan are tolerated as long as they also contribute to the development of certain capacities for bearing middle-class responsibilities and values.

Responsive and Responsible Consumer Practices

Themed built environments, such as department stores, shopping malls, theme parks, and specialty restaurants, are spaces designed to produce certain kinds of consumer subjects.[10] This shift represents an international trend toward integrating the combined practices of shopping, entertainment (through cinema, arcade games, and amusement rides), education (through stories and themes), merchandising (through copyrighted images and logos), performative labor (of the front-stage employees), and control and surveillance (of both employees and consumers) (Ren 2007b).[11] Each themed built environment targets a group of consumers presumed to be middle class.[12] The design of the Chinese Ethnic Culture Park targets its visitors as a coherent group who will be transformed by their movement through its space into responsible consuming subjects.

This park is an outdoor exhibition of the life ways of a number of China's fifty-six officially recognized national minority cultures through displays of housing, costume, and performance. In the broader context of the tourist industry, according to its general manager, the park is operated as "a means for distributing culture, linking together knowledge, entertainment, participation, and taste. Not only does it guide tourists to 'look,' but it also directs them to 'play'" (quoted in Zhang Tongze 2001). I argue that the park instantiates the process of middle-class self-formation in three ways: First, it encourages the internalization of the norms that define middle-classness, such as decision-making (consumer sovereignty) and the performance of civility (*wenming*). Second, the cultivation of an appreciation for ethnic minority culture marks a form of cosmopolitanism (a tolerance for difference) for the urban consumer, while also inciting subjects to engage in an ethical relation to an ethnicized Other through charitable endeavors. Third, these practices position middle-classness according to a neoliberal logic of calculation rather than observance of the law, a logic that defines citizenship in terms of entrepreneurial subjecthood.

These aspects of middle-class self-formation constitute a form of biopower: the power to "regularize" life, the authority to force living not just to happen but to appear *in a particular way* (Foucault 1995). At the park, a particular way of living takes the form of active participation in consuming practices. The carefully designed scheme of operations that constitute the park produces the park's visitors as middle-class consumer citizens who are supposed to possess the values of civility, cosmopolitanism, and morality. Visitors must negotiate the park's policing of space in the form of uniformed guards, walls, gates, warning signs, and other visible and invisible surveillance techniques. Through this process of active negotiation, the visitor as an individual consumer experiences the park as an act of self-making according to the norms defining middle-classness. Entry to the park, in itself, is contingent on the ability of the visitor to pay what might seem to many to be an exorbitant price for a ticket (60 yuan for an adult ticket, about US$7.50).[13] In this sense, entry to the park engineers a segmentation of the marketplace in which the price of a ticket exercises a form of exclusion. Along with other forms of spatial segregation in urban places, it effects a form of graduated citizenship.[14] Access to these places produces middle-classness first and foremost by being limited to those who can most afford it.[15]

My observation of visitors at the park illustrates these processes of middle-class self-formation. Established in the early 1990s, the park is located to the west of what has since become the National Olympic Center in Beijing. It occupies a total of forty-five hectares divided into two sites.[16] The north site, about twenty hectares, was first opened to the public in June 1994. Development of the south site was completed more recently, in 2001. The cost of construction for the first phase of development was about US$36.1 million, 85 percent of which came from Taiwan and Hong Kong investors.[17] As described in a brochure, the park "blends the architecture and cultures of Chinese minorities to provide visitors with a unique place to experience the life of the minorities in the metropolitan capital."

At the north site, the park is organized into sixteen life-sized replicas of ethnic "villages," each representing the vernacular housing and dwelling environment of one of China's national ethnic groups (*minzu*).[18] Each village displays artifacts used in daily life, furnishings, domestic architecture, cultural performances, and items for sale, such as food, tea, and souvenirs. Park employees who participate in the cultural performances were hired from their home villages or towns.[19] The principle for constructing each village, as a senior manager told me in 1996, is that of "respecting nature and representing reality." Based on this principle, material for each exhibit was imported from the ethnic area it represents, and construction was carried out by experienced ethnic craftspeople brought to Beijing for that purpose. For example, a dark purple plant that was used for architectural decoration in the Zang (Tibetan) village was brought from Tibet, and a company based in Lhasa did the construction work under the direction of a Tibetan architect.

The use of Tibetan design and materials by a Tibetan construction company "authenticates" the "original flavor" of the exhibit (Xie 1995: 424).

The exhibit of ethnic cultures (*minzu wenhua*) in the park participates in a form of temporality pervasive in Chinese representations of non-Han others that relegates them to a space of tradition outside of urbane modernity.[20] However, the temporality of the park is also marked by a series of monthly "festivals" (*jie*), such as New Year celebrations in January and the Dragon Boat Festival in June. These are composed of both official national holidays and the festivals of different ethnic groups.[21] In the park's operations, however, the celebration of a festival does not strictly line up to the annual succession of months but follows a more practical logic of providing for tourist consumption.[22] The Dai Water Splashing Festival, for example, has been featured as a form of cultural display since the park's opening in 1994. It begins in April when the festival in Yunnan takes place and runs as late as October. The park's management contracts with local governments in Yunnan Province (from either Xishuangbanna Prefecture or Dehong Prefecture where there are concentrations of Dai people) to employ ethnic Dai to perform.

These performances (in the name of a "festival") are scheduled in close coordination with the movement of visitors through the different exhibits, shops, and restaurants. For example, a forty-minute performance is scheduled at the Dai village at 9:30 in the morning, drawing visitors to linger there; another performance is scheduled at 10:30 in the Miao village, a twenty-minute walk away. After watching the second performance, visitors move on to new scenic spots. As they begin to feel hungry around lunchtime, they find themselves arriving at a restaurant in the Buyi village, as engineered by the park management. Many visitors choose to eat at the restaurant, although some either carry their own food or choose to continue their tour of the park. The structure that channels the flow of visitors through the park not only encourages them to consume but also produces a competitive advantage for the park management. Because of its strategic placement, more visitors eat in the restaurant located in the Buyi Village than in another restaurant that leased a retail space within the park. This arrangement reveals the park as a highly structured environment, which overdetermines how it will be consumed. Visitors are positioned as consumers who are directed toward the appropriate modes of economic behavior already set up for them.

From the tourist's perspective, the participatory experience becomes intertwined with negotiating the carefully structured time provided by the park. If consumption indeed "creates" time and does not simply respond to it (Appadurai 1997: 27), then how do visitors develop a *new* sense of time—a new temporal relationship between external time and their own personal time—through consuming practices? Visiting a theme park as an activity consumes time; it takes the form of time management. First, planning a trip to the park entails an allocation of time set outside of the rhythms of everyday life. A visit to the park is associated with spending time with family members or friends. Many people visit the park as a group (whether as a family or as a group of friends or colleagues).[23] Moreover, visiting also involves creating a memorable archive by documenting the experience at the park in the form of a photo album shared with others or posted on the Internet (via such sites as Live Spaces, MySpace, and YouTube).

Of course, time is not all that is spent here. For many, particularly those who were drawn to the park on the basis of a simple direction given by a tourist map, a calculation of the monetary value of their time may be necessary. This was the case for a family, I had observed, who had come to Beijing from Jiangxi Province in the summer of 2000. The group included a woman (a schoolteacher in her early thirties), her mother-in-law, her daughter, her sister's daughter, and two boys of other relatives. The total cost of admission for the group was 240 yuan for two adult tickets and three student tickets. The youngest boy did not require a paid ticket because he was still a preschooler. Although the younger woman, who led the group, felt the cost of the tickets to be higher than she had anticipated, she decided to spend the money anyway because they had taken all the trouble to get themselves there. Once inside, they took part in as many activities as possible, visiting all the villages, participating in the festival, and taking photos. The schoolteacher mentioned how pleased they were to see ethnic minority artifacts because they live far away from any ethnic minority region. At the Miao village, she spent twenty yuan to rent Miao costumes for all four children. The children laughed in excitement to see each other wearing the colorful and decorative clothing as the younger woman took photographs of them. In the end, the whole group wanted to be photographed.

A visit to the park is not, therefore, something that everyone can afford. In the case of my informants in this example, the admission was high enough to warrant a careful calculation of costs and benefits. The ability to pay for admission is a privileged one, thus pointing to the ways in which these practices of self-making are exclusionary, but also, as in this case, it can operate as a form of "self-fashioning" for those for whom it also acts as a form of aspiring consumption, one that is not easily affordable. If "self-fashioning" means "the unscripted, self-reflexive thinking and action that are continuously shaped and transformed by the diverse kinds of knowledge that circulate in the dynamic and globalized Chinese environment" (Ong 2008: 185), it is often an affirmative and positive mode of living (that is, life-building), one that tends to be available only to the privileged. For example, in a visit to Shenzhen's Window of the World, a group of rural migrant women had carefully saved the price of admission and wore their best jeans and T-shirts so that they could enjoy their trip in the same way as other visitors. Once they were inside, however, they were called out by middle-class patrons as *dagongmei* (rural women migrant laborers) who properly belonged in the factory rather than in middle-class spaces of leisured consumption (Pun 2003: 484–485). This example suggests that rural migrant laborers—who are among the least paid and those who work the longest hours in China—are not normally acknowledged as those capable of self-fashioning. For the visitors in this case, I wonder whether the schoolteacher was willing to invest in the experience, not so much for herself as for the investment in her children's middle-class mobility.[24] Learning about the ethnic minority cultures on display justified the value of their visit. The cultural value of ethnic minority culture on display is a form of leisured pastime that enriches middle-class identity as a form of educational play.[25] The sign of the ethnic becomes mobilized in capital accumulation and circulated through the reproduction of the tourist body as a consuming body. The photographs that capture these cross-dressed bodies (ethnic Chinese in Miao dress) commemorate a very uneasy decision of having to spend money to spend time in this way. Long after their visit, these photographs will enable them to wrest a value from their purchase again and again. In this particular case, sharing their experience with the absent husband and father of this family group will further extend the experience of their visit as a process of self-making, making their selves both known and knowable (Foucault 1988), in this context, as middle-class consumers.

The time spent at the park is a form of leisured pastime; it is, nonetheless, an instrumentalized time ordered by a logic of consumption. This carefully calculated time synchronizes the time of the cosmopolitan consumer with the time of ethnic minority cultures (in the forms of festivals and exhibitions). This synchrony operates according to a relatively coherent, homogenous, and teleological trajectory of consumption, aiming at shaping the visitor's consuming habits in a prearranged manner (for example, the regular scheduling of festival display). However, it is often affected by a visitor's personal time, which comes from the rhythms of everyday life outside the park's instrumental time. The visitor's personal time is incoherent, heterogeneous, and contingent. It is organized not only by objective rhythms of work and leisure but also by spontaneous moments of daydreaming and pleasure. In participatory consumption in forms such as doing something together with family, friends, or colleagues; learning something about ethnic minorities; and walking around in the park, the visitor often negotiates with the park's instrumental time through an enactment of personal time as a way to create a temporal consciousness of an exceptional visit.

In such a situation, contingency becomes unleashed as a power enabling a visitor to transgress the park's instrumental time. As an act of suspending the regular rule of instrumental time, this transgression is an exceptional act, transforming the visitor into a sovereign consumer.[26] In this way, experience at the park becomes memorable. Photo taking, for example, may be practiced as an interruptive activity. When the Zang performers were ready to dance and sing at 9:30 one morning in the summer of 2000, a park employee announced the performance to the visitors through loudspeakers distributed around the park. As a result, visitors rushed to the Zang village. However, according to my observation, quite a few of them did not give their full attention to the singing and dancing. The hot summer weather might have been a factor, but I noticed that most of the visitors were more interested in taking their own photos in front of the performers than in being attentive to the performance. They had spontaneously chosen to confuse two forms of consuming practice: the cultural performance versus the occasional photo-ops already set up for them along their itinerary through the park to commemorate their visit. They refused their role as passive members of the audience by inserting themselves into the performance via the photograph.

A memorable experience at the park also may take on the form of a more active interruption. I mention two examples here, one positive and one negative. A group of twenty visitors from northeastern China arrived one morning at the Dazhao Temple in the Zang village exhibit. One man went up to the second floor and stopped in front of the statue of a Buddha. While holding a water bottle, he bowed to the statue. Afterward, he deposited a few coins into the donation box and said, "This small amount of money conveys my respect to you!" The man's act of worship suggests that worship in the park is different from what might occur outside. In a normal temple, a worshiper would be either empty handed or holding a joss stick while bowing to a god.

Holding a water bottle and donating such a small amount of money marked his act of worship as an interruption of normal or conventional behavior.

The eventfulness of this interruption is threefold. First, the bowing is a demonstration (or performance) of belief rather than of faith.[27] Here, belief is maintained as a moral value, despite not being treated as an object of desire, as in institutionalized religious practices. Second, the tiny donation is insignificant, but it is a gesture toward giving, an affective expression of charity, an impulsive act rather than a rational philanthropic effort. Nevertheless, it is considered as a norm of becoming a responsible middle-class citizen in China (CASS 2002: 253).[28] The third dimension of the eventfulness of the interruption refers to the economic value of uselessness and idleness. Because the man has already paid for the admission, his worship and donation become a mode of participatory consumption. In this sense, the two activities reassure the built environment's function as a consuming environment; his acts are productive activities because they actively consume the exhibits. However, their consumption is based on an interaction with a nothingness, whether the "idleness" of the statue of Buddha, which is, in fact, not connected to the actual religious institution of the Dazhao Temple in Lhasa, or the "uselessness" of the donation, which will not be used, in fact, to help the poor but in fact has become a part of the exhibit. Therefore, the eventfulness of the incident is fabricated by a moral demonstration of belief, an affective enactment of middle-class charity, and the production of exchange value out of a disembedded enactment of worship.[29]

A second example focuses on delinquency as an act of self-making. After visiting the temple in the Zang Village, two men in the group decided to go back to the main gate to hire a tour guide. While waiting, the rest walked into a gift shop selling jewelry, T-shirts, toys, books, films, and so forth. The solitary sales clerk was overwhelmed and thus failed to notice that a woman from the group took a brightly colored paper umbrella without paying. Later that day, as the group followed the tour guide past the shop, the sales clerk suddenly recognized the umbrella held by the woman and asked the woman to pay for it or return it. The woman denied taking the umbrella at first, but, due to the sales clerk's insistence, she eventually returned the umbrella to the shop.

In this incident, delinquency is enacted as a form of negative agency. With the redistribution of social responsibility in China's neoliberalization, a middle-class citizen is an entrepreneur, someone who becomes successful in *both* calculating the rules (rather than abiding them) *and* becoming responsible for his or her own behavior. Because the middle-class citizen is responsible for minimizing social risk, the person is held liable for increasing or elevating risk. The woman clearly miscalculated her ability to flout the rules without damaging her claims to middle-class respectability. The sales clerk did not call the park security guards but, instead, chased the woman and forced her to return the umbrella. This sequence of actions created a spectacle of discipline addressed not just to the shoplifting woman herself but also to the whole group by circulating a norm of calculated self-responsibility as a civic value.

All three practices discussed in the preceding paragraphs—photo taking, Buddha worship, and souvenir buying—are common enough activities. Indeed, the park is set up to invite and authorize visitors to do all of these things. However, this arrangement does not specify how and when these activities take place, nor does it determine which visitor will engage in them. Each visitor normally has a certain degree of autonomy in decision making. When a visitor interrupts a normal activity, however, the visitor begins to reveal whether she or he can be a sovereign consumer. This process of disclosure is critical to the formation of a middle-class citizen, a subject who is capable of becoming responsible for the self *and* for maintaining social order for the Chinese state. The positive outcome of an interruptive activity means that the process of rule calculating (rather than rule abiding) becomes successfully managed. The experience of the visit is made memorable and economically worthwhile. By contrast, the negative outcome of an interruptive activity signals a failure in middle-class self-making, while also operating as a form of disciplinary spectacle. The distinction between the two outcomes marks an important differentiation between being recognized as a self-responsible entrepreneurial subject and individual failure in realizing such a goal.

This differentiation goes beyond the environment of the theme park to being a practice central to urban (re)development across the country. The socialist-era work unit (*danwei*) as the primary structure organizing urban space is being displaced by a new entity defined as "community" (*shequ*). Through community building (*shequ jianshe*) in the form of gated communities, urban planning and real estate development tend to separate self-responsible middle-class subjects (such as educated professionals) from those considered to be incapable of bearing responsibilities (such as workers laid off from state-owned factories) (Tomba 2004; n.d.; Zhang 2010). Therefore, theme parks, shopping malls, and residential gated communities are not simply products in urban development, but they also engage in class production (including the middle class) through the production of architectural space.

Conclusion: Chinese Middle-Class Risk Subjects

Although my ethnographic analysis focuses on situated practices in a themed built environment, it intends to highlight an important link between the spatial production of the middle class and of consumer practices. As economic, social, and political inequalities become increasingly visible in China's neoliberal development, the middle class becomes explicitly a governmental mechanism for balancing between economic development (or capital circulation and accumulation) and social stability (risk management). The production of the middle class as the dominant social strata—a demographic solution to the risks of Chinese state and society—is a social engineering project of making Chinese citizens into responsible subjects. At stake are two ideal types of such subjects: those who assist the Chinese state to manage the risks resulting from neoliberal policies and those who are capable of addressing any risks emerging in their everyday lives, which include the risks of failing to take responsibility for themselves. Under the regime of the middle-class norm, responsible subjects become celebrated and differentiated from both those who underperform and those who mismanage their responsibilities.

One of the major ways through which an ordinary Chinese individual becomes subject to the regulation of the middle-class norm is consumption. Not only does consumption constitute an important domain of everyday life that is inseparable from the economy, but it also underscores the individual's capacity of living with dignity. Issues of "choice," "style," and "taste" mark consumption not simply as a buying process but as a complicated sequence of activities, including but not limited to experiencing, learning, choosing, experimenting, creating, transgressing, accepting, and performing (de Certeau 1984; de Certeau, Giard, and Mayol 1998). Thus, the capacity of addressing these issues is closely tied to the empowerment or disempowerment of subjective agency in the practice of everyday life in an enterprise culture that pins great significance to consumer goods as badges of class position. It is important to note that consumption's self-transformative role cannot be overvalued. Neither can the agency of "freedom" always be positive. Consumer agency may take the form of sovereignty, but this does not necessarily lead to liberty and freedom.[30] In Deborah Davis's (2005) study of the narratives of Shanghai residents who came of age during the 1950s and 1960s and have become successful (that is, earning US$5,000 per year), the agency of freedom is positive and even revolutionary. In contrast, the migrant female factory laborers in southern China (Pun 2003; 2005) find their efforts to refashion themselves into consumer citizens to end in failure. A danger of overvaluing consumption's self-transformative role and its relation to the positive agency of liberty is that we may disconnect China's recent development of consumer culture, which includes reconfiguring the relationship between production and consumption, from its historical and global contexts of neoliberalization.[31] Consumption neither guarantees upward class mobility nor does it prohibit class status from falling. Under neoliberal policies of entrepreneurialism and self-responsibility, consuming practice often becomes an adventurous process of discovering insecurities and risks, especially those posed by actors such as monetary regulatory agencies, financial service organizations, credit rating agencies, bankers, accountants, brokers, and their benefactors, in their rule-calculating practices for the purpose of making profits.[32]

In responsive and responsible consumer practices, the middle-class norm becomes disseminated to the individualized process of life-making and life-building. In this practical context, it is practically impossible to speak of a set of consistent characteristics that positively constitute the ideal middle-class subject. At the Chinese Ethnic Culture Park in Beijing, participatory consumption is an individual-based process in which a visitor becomes a consumer and makes and builds her or his life by bearing certain responsibilities in capital accumulation and risk reduction. My ethnographic analysis highlights three important consumption-related issues that link middle-class self-formation to the risks in China's neoliberalization. First, consumption marks a distinction between those who can consume and those who cannot. For this reason, the status of the middle class achieved through consumption is indeed a *class* position. Social stratification marked by the middle class becomes inseparable from certain structural issues, especially unequal opportunities caused by unequal access to resources (economic, political, and cultural). It is also made possible by the involvement of a series of actors, ranging from organizations (government, nongovernmental organizations, corporations), individuals (the nouveaux riches and ordinary citizens), and different ethnic groups (the ethnically Chinese Han and China's ethnic minorities).

Next, one important expression of taking social responsibility is helping others, especially the poor or those facing devastating incidents such as earthquake, famine, and flood. As the Chinese government has shifted its responsibilities for addressing social and economic problems to nongovernmental organizations, corporations, and individuals, charity and philanthropy have become popular mechanisms in recent decades (Ma 2002). The rapid rise of charitable organizations in China, for example, shows a general shift from government-funded welfare to charitable work by individuals, corporations, and nonprofit organizations (Shue 1998; Chen 2004). In Chinese media, the richest members of society are called on to demonstrate their social responsibility by participating in philanthropy.[33] Meanwhile, ordinary Chinese citizens, especially college students and urban professionals, are encouraged to undertake the work of generosity, whether through donation or voluntary work. Under neoliberal conditions, however, charitable work operates in a lateral way: It surely raises funds for charitable purposes from as many people as possible (that is, not merely from wealthy populations), but it is unfolded as a politics of rerouting personal, corporate, and governmental responsibilities.[34]

In leisure and tourist contexts, some aspiring middle-class subjects often voluntarily take on the responsibility of monitoring other middle-class subjects. The incident of disciplining the woman who tried to take an umbrella without paying for it at the Chinese Ethnic Culture Park might be small, but it is related to nationwide efforts to make Chinese tourists behave more civilly. Both domestic and international news media in recent years, for example, have frequently published stories about successful mainland Chinese citizens traveling overseas, whether as students, shoppers, business people, or tourists. Some compare the spending habits of Chinese shoppers with Americans, Japanese, and Germans in the post–World War II period, while others discuss the impact of their behaviors in the host countries. One major issue repeatedly raised is about the uncivil behavior of Chinese tourists.[35] In September 2005, for instance, pictures and reports of mainland Chinese tourists spitting, sprawling on the ground, allowing their children to urinate in public, and smoking in prohibited areas at Hong Kong's newly opened Disneyland triggered scathing criticism in the Hong Kong, mainland, and overseas media. This event underscores the ways in which middle-classness is defined as a cultural category in terms of the new norms of civility and responsibility for the actions of one's self. Chinese middle-class commentators on this news story argued that their fellow citizens need to improve their "human quality" (*suzhi*) by changing their old habits and learning to conduct themselves in a more civil manner.[36] China's tourist industry and the Chinese government responded by launching a series of campaigns to promote courteous behavior. In September 2006, the China National Tourism Administration released two detailed lists of behaviors recommended for the civilized Chinese traveler, one addressing domestic travel and the other for overseas.

With the proliferation of new media such as the Internet and mobile media, Chinese netizens in recent years have developed a popular practice called "human flesh search" (*renrou sousuo*). Although it is mainly used as a popular way to expose corrupt officials, it may also be used to reveal any ordinary person's life history, especially his or her personal or private matters such as marriage, sex life, and leisure activities. The deployment of the spectacle as a means to communicate the norm of calculated self-responsibility becomes common. Online uses of images often are intended to embarrass offenders, whether individually or collectively. In the 2007 Green Woodpecker Project that curbed public spitting, its leader Wang Tao posed action shots on his website to humiliate offenders. The Shanghai World Exposition in 2010 is the latest international event that has generated numerous discussions about the behavior of Chinese visitors. The popular Chinese website Tianya.cn has even launched a special public forum devoted to the Shanghai Exposition. Since late April 2010, when the public was first allowed to visit the Exposition, pictures and reports of bad behavior have appeared on the website. Early reports focused on how panicked the crowd behaved. By July, reports and photos often addressed delinquent visitors such as those pretending to be disabled by using a wheelchair to bypass other visitors waiting in a long line. To manage the crowd, the organizing committee decided in September to allow some visitors to use one or two hours to serve as "little Chinese cabbages" (*xiaobaicai*), volunteers whose job is to both assist visitors and monitor their behavior.[37] Those visitors whose bad behavior is captured and circulated in public via the Internet will be held accountable for as long as their records are kept online.

Entrepreneurialism, a practice critical to middle-class self-formation, may enable one's success, but it may also lead to delinquency, marking social differentiation in relation to capital accumulation and risk reduction. As neoliberal policies promoting the individual's do-it-yourself biographical process are widely implemented, calculating (rather than abiding) rules and laws becomes an integral part of self-enterprise. Consequently, as in cases of memorable visits to the theme park, life-building through self-fashioning may become positive if the enterprising subject successfully exercises calculation. But it also may become a negative process, whether deferred, regressive, or sidetracked, when the exercise of calculation is recognized as a delinquency,[38] as in the case of the tourist stealing an umbrella at the ethnic theme park. In this situation, instead of a project of future anterior (anticipating the coming of the future), this form of life-building accumulates risks and liabilities to social prosperity of one sort or another. In governmental and social policies, the middle class as a responsible figure is an abstract idea. It is only in the practice of everyday life that a citizen may discover whether he or she can claim middle-class status and thus not be subject to the kind of social scrutiny that applies to the "disadvantaged groups."[39] Ironically, this discovery is, nonetheless, made at the expense of the rules and laws that regulate the social order. Therefore, the normative bifurcation of the life-building process into positive and negative directions through acts of transgression underpins neoliberal social differentiation.

Notes

ACKNOWLEDGMENTS

My fieldwork for this project was supported by the Wenner-Gren Foundation for Anthropological Research, a faculty development grant from Bowling Green State University, a visiting scholar fellowship from the Institute for Collaborative Research and Public Humanities at Ohio State University, and an international travel grant from the University of Arizona. A small section first appeared in "The Neoliberal State and the Risk Society: The Chinese State and the Middle Class" (*Telos*, Issue 151, Summer 2010, 105–128).

1. Many economists of China who have studied the process of China's economic transformation during the Deng Xiaoping era (1978–1997) argue that the transition to market-oriented system is characterized as gradualism, a developmental process based on a series of experiments (for example, Bramall 2009: chapter 10). Missing in their studies is the understanding of the way in which national reunification in general, and Hong Kong's return to China in particular, becomes inseparable from economic transformation.

2. See "Jiang Zemin zai Guangdong kaocha gongzuo qiangdiao, jinmi jiehe xin de lishi tiaojian jiaqiang dang de jianshe, shizhong dailing quanguo renmin cujin shengchanli de fazhan."

3. Hong Kong's economy has generally been ranked very high by the four major international economic indexes of free market practices and competitiveness, the *Economic Freedom Index* (jointly published by the Heritage Foundation and the *Wall Street Journal*), the *World Competitiveness Yearbook* (published by the Interna-

tional Institute for Management Development of Lausanne), the *Global Country Forecast* (published by the Economist Intelligence Unit of *The Economist*), and the *Global Competitiveness Report* (by the World Economic Forum, based in Geneva). From 1996 to 2007 the *Economic Freedom Index* consistently ranked Hong Kong as the world's freest economy. Milton Friedman (1998), the world's leading neoliberal economist, argues that since the end of World War II Hong Kong has been the only world economy close to his ideal of a private free market system.

4. Elsewhere I discuss the relationship between sovereignty, the state, and the people (Ren 2010a: xi–xv).

5. Here, risk is both real and imagined in relation to the future of the state (see Beck 1992; 1994; Beck and Beck-Gernsheim 2002; Lash 2003).

6. In this sense, the middle-class norm is inseparable from the governmental discourse of human capital on *suzhi*, as examined in detail by Yan (2003) and Anagnost (2004).

7. For a systematic examination of these studies, see Anagnost (2008a).

8. Wang Xiaoming vividly describes this lifestyle:

Among tens of thousands of matters in the world, money is the most important. Lots of money in his packet defines "practical existence"; once having money, he can do whatever he wants to do and buy whatever he wants to buy. This is the meaning of "freedom"; spending generously, treating money like dust, attracting beautiful young women, this is the meaning of style or "respect"; wearing expensive and luxurious clothing, following fashion trends, this defines beauty or "aesthetic quality." (1999: 34)

9. A number of important studies have affirmed this. Jing Wang's critical study of "Bobo" (bourgeois bohemians) argues that marketing professionals construct the middle class through their cosmopolitan taste and lifestyle rather than through their structural class position (2005: 532–548). Deborah Davis's study of housing consumption among Shanghai residents reports an explicit connection between their embrace of economic success and their rejection of historical memories associated with the Cultural Revolution (2005: 692–709).

10. In recent years, for example, more than 400 large malls have been built in China. Currently, five of the ten largest malls in the world are in China, many of which are created by real estate developers. In the context of the global economy, these malls show that the Chinese are more like consumers than producers. Thus, a *New York Times* reporter proclaims: "Retailing and real estate are radically altering the face of China, and opening the door to the possibility that soon China may not simply be the world's factory, it may own the world's shopping space" (Barboza 2005).

11. For an excellent analysis of the phenomenon, see Bryman (2004). See also Ching-wen Hsu (Chapter Two in this volume) on the production of a shopping street in Taiwan for a comparable development elsewhere in East Asia.

12. The strategy of market segmentation is used to divide mass markets into smaller market segments "defined by distinctive orientations and tastes, each to be sold different products or even the same product packaged and marketed in totally different ways" (Cohen 2006: 56). In the United States, the spread of this practice in the late 1950s paralleled the development of themed built environments (especially shopping malls and theme parks). Both played an important part in the historical development of the middle class in the United States (Cohen 2006).

13. This is based on the currency exchange rate in 1996. Until recent years, the monthly salary of an ordinary Chinese urban citizen has been below 500 yuan.

14. The term *graduated sovereignty* comes from Aihwa Ong's discussion of how populations are differentially governed in Southeast and East Asia (1999; 2006).

15. In June 2006, when I surveyed more than eighty Chinese publications on theme parks in the past decade through Wanfang's digital database, the high price of admission was often mentioned as a major problem by industry analysts and experts.

16. I learned during my fieldwork in 1996 that this tract of land was acquired in the early 1990s when Chen Xitong, a standing member of the politburo of the Chinese Communist Party, was the mayor of Beijing. Chen was charged with corruption in 1995 and given a sixteen-year jail sentence.

17. The rest of the funding came from various organizations, including government organizations in charge of administrating land use, environment regulation, and sanitation. The park's general manager Wang manages the park's operations. Her husband Bai (the son of a former mayor of the city) is the chairman of the board, and he is in charge of planning and development. In addition to managing the park, Wang also works with scholars, especially folklorists, ethnologists, and urban planning experts. She was elected as a vice director of the Ethnological Society of China. In 2002, she worked with private business people in the tourist industry to establish a nationwide nongovernmental organization titled "Chamber of Tourism All China Federation of Industry and Commerce" (see their website at www.tcc.org.cn/). A few years ago, the park launched a website (www.emuseum .org.cn/) to provide updated tourist information in both Chinese and English. In 2008, she became a member of the Eleventh National Committee of the Chinese People's Political Consultative Conference (CPPCC).

18. The sixteen national ethnic groups included in the park are the Zang ("Tibetan"), Qiang, Jingpo, Hani, Wa, Miao, Yi, Buyi, Dong, Hezhe, Dauer, Ewenke, Elunchuan, and the Korean, Taiwanese Aboriginal, and Dai cultures. There are fifty-six national minority cultures in China altogether. The cultures that are included in the park represent the ecologically diverse areas of China's borderlands.

19. As I found out in my fieldwork, the company hires these performers through three channels. First, it contracts local (that is, county or prefecture) commissions for ethnic affairs to select ethnic performers. Second, the park managers, with the help of local government, go to a village to hire people on site. Finally, the company may contract a local performance troupe to perform at the park.

20. The representation of ethnic minorities reflects how the Han (ethnically Chinese) construct a relation of the self to the other. Scholars such as Gladney (1991), Harrell (1995), Oakes (1998), and Schein (2000) have discussed issues on nationalism and internal colonialism in representations of national minority cultures. My concern here is to examine multiculturalism more generally as a mode of middle-class consumption.

21. This structure makes up an annual cycle of festivals: New Year celebrations (January), religious activities representing Zang (Tibetan) Buddhism (February), Chinese Woman's Day (March), the Dai Water Splashing Festival (April), the Qiang Hill Worshipping Festival (May), the Miao Dragon Boat Festival (June), the Hani Kuzhazha Festival (July), the Yi Torch Festival (August), the Jinpo Song Festival (September), the Wa New Rice Festival (October), the New Year celebrations of the Buyi and the Dong (November), and a sports exhibition representing the peoples of the north (December).

22. To make a monthly festival flexible, the company considers two major factors. First, the availability of ethnic minority performers is a factor determining a festival theme. During my 1996 fieldwork, for example, there were festivals representing the Miao, Dai, Qiang, Dong, and Yi. In July 2000, Zang, Jingpo, and Dai festivals were featured. Another important factor is sponsorship for special events, such as national celebrations, visits of Chinese or foreign officials, and national and international meetings and sports events. When a special event takes place, the regularly scheduled programs are modified mainly because the event usually brings in more revenue. On July 11, 2000, for example, the Preparatory Committee of the Twenty-First International University Sports Games to be held in Beijing from August 21 to September 1, 2000, came to the park to inspect whether the park might be a suitable site for the closing ceremony. During the event, managerial staff and performers curtailed their regularly scheduled programs to receive the officials of the committee.

23. This ethnographic observation of mine was confirmed by park staff members.

24. For a discussion of how aspiring middle-class professionals invest in their children's middle-class mobility, see Anagnost 2004.

25. For a detailed discussion of how leisure becomes an important domain of citizenship, see Jing Wang 2001a.

26. According to Carl Schmitt, "Sovereign is he who decides on the exceptional case" (2005: 5). Sovereignty emerges as a decisive issue only in a state of exception. A sovereign must decide what is a state of exception *and* must make the decisions appropriate to that exception. Decision in a state of exception must be based on the quality of the deciding person not on any existing rules and laws.

27. "Faith," according to Alain Badiou, belongs to the territory of truth; it refers to the fidelity to truth (the indiscernible) that always leads to the creation of a hole within a claim about truth. Thus, it is faith rather than belief that constitutes a truthful subject (2003 [1997]: 74).

28. This practice of charity cannot be considered as a gift of grace, which refers to the granting of a gift, charisma (*kharisma*), to the ethical subject who is faithful to truth. That is, becoming a subject faithful to truth does not follow any laws and thus cannot take the form of a reward or wage (Badiou 2003 [1997]: 77).

29. Here, I use the word *nothing* to mean the emptied and the disembedded. What is emptied and disembedded is the symbolic meaning or aura of the exhibit. However, the operation of the park as a commercial environment creates exchange value out of the emptied and the disembedded. The acquisition of information or knowledge about "ethnic culture" at the park becomes the accumulation of emptied and disembedded artifacts.

30. See Berlant (2007) for a clear elaboration of the negative agency of sovereignty in neoliberalism.

31. One example is that overemphasizing consumption's association with freedom would lead to a reading of China's consumer culture merely as an example of the transition from socialism to market society (in which consumption substitutes for production), a process that mirrors what has taken place in the West. A consequence of this understanding is that it disconnects what happens in China from the present process of neoliberal globalization, of which China has been an important player (Harvey 2005; Ren 2010a). For a good example of this reading, see Zukin and Maguire (2004: 189–191).

32. Consumption merely extends the process of exploitation that begins in the productive process. This situation applies both to cosmopolitan and disenfranchised subjects (Ren 2012).

33. For example, the Shanghai-based *Hurun Report* Group ranks the philanthropic activities of individuals and corporations every year. See the organization's website at www.hurun.net/.

34. For an excellent case study of charity that involves the participation of the masses, see King (2006).

35. For a summary of these problems, see an article originally published by the *Beijing Morning News* (*Beijing Chenbao* 2006).

36. These arguments were posted in a public forum on the hainan.net. Many original news articles and photos were reposted at the site. See http://1home.hainan.net/New/PublicForum/Content.asp?idWriter=0&Key=0&strItem=funinfo&idArticle=89696&flag=1, retrieved in March 2007.

37. *Xinmin wanbao*, October 2, 2010, pp. A1, A7.

38. Gary Becker, a major figure in formulating economic neoliberalism, agues that delinquency can be calculated as a neoliberal value in self-formation (1992). In fact, as Ren has shown, delinquency in popular culture is historically tied to neoliberalism (2005).

39. See, for example, Gary Sigley's (2006: 492) discussion of the divide in neoliberal governmentality between those who embody the new model of citizenship and those who must be taught.

Chapter Two

Miraculous Rebirth
Making Global Places in Taiwan

CHING-WEN HSU

It was a hot summer afternoon in 2002. The shops in downtown Kaohsiung had just opened, and people were beginning to filter into the New Kujiang shopping district, but it would take another few hours for activity to pick up on the street.[1] Standing on the side of the road, Mr. Liao, a member of the Committee for Development in New Kujiang, took refuge from the heat in the cold air escaping from an air-conditioned shop.[2] Looking through a veil of smog, he voiced his concern about the trees: "They're ugly. They look like those trees outside of the municipal cultural centers." The man had wanted to see a different style of landscaping lining the streets to create a promenade that, he had hoped, would be "like the streets in Austria." Instead, all he could see were short trees with upright branches, small leaves, and no flowers. To him, they were entirely too predictable and uninspiring—everything the shopping district in the largest urban center in southern Taiwan was not supposed to be. He had envisioned a New Kujiang that would be trendy and alive. In less than fifteen years after its emergence, New Kujiang had indeed become a popular shopping destination for young people in southern Taiwan. Nonetheless it had not quite developed the elegance that Mr. Liao had envisioned. Now he hoped that, if only New Kujiang could get the right kind of trees (and a little more help from the authorities), everything would work out as planned. As Mr. Liao imagined a shopping district simulating the streets of faraway countries, retailers from shops all around him burned spirit money to lure in real money and hoped that their prayers and offerings would reach the deities and ghosts they were intended for.[3] The old ritual may have looked out of place in the fashionable shopping district. However, on the streets where the smoke and smog were inseparable and the heat from the fires fused with the heat from the sun, ghosts and deities are in the service of the living, and the retailers' wishes were as worldly and profit oriented as Mr. Liao's plan for New Kujiang. Here, new visions and long-standing practices intersect, and imaginations and prayers frequently reach the world beyond to make earthly enterprises more profitable.

First begun as a shopping center aimed at affluent consumers during the island's burgeoning economy in the 1980s, New Kujiang was revitalized as a shopping district by a state-initiated "place-making" project in the late 1990s. Its emergence and metamorphosis reflect the economic transformation of the city of Kaohsiung as well as that of Taiwan over the years. As part of the national project to refashion the appearance of the island's towns and cities, New Kujiang exemplifies the desire for Taiwan's modern development and prosperity through urban planning and spatial reform. As an internationalized shopping district built in the image of Euro-American and Japanese shopping streets, it offers the possibility for its shoppers and merchants to imagine themselves as being a part of the larger world of upscale "quality" (*pinzhi*) places. However, subsumed under a narrative of national modernization and market success on a global scale, New Kujiang also provides the ground on which these visions are contested and where questions about Taiwan's "internationalized" future are raised. Just as the ideas of Mr. Liao and the shopowners diverge about what it would take to make the shopping district a better place for business, different visions and practices converge, compete, and clash in New Kujiang. While the developers and planners constantly allude to the city's history of colonial dependency and international trade to build for a future in the global consumer market, those who work and shop in the streets of New Kujiang may also make use of these same idioms to justify existing practices at odds with the official vision of modernization and prosperity. This chapter examines how the space and narrative of New Kujiang as an "internationalized" place has been produced and how this space provides the background against which official narratives and imaginaries of the global become reworked to tell different stories.

Blueprint on the Streets

In descriptions of New Kujiang appearing in promotional material and in the popular media, *global connectivity* and *youthfulness* are key words. The shopping street is a "young people's paradise" where one can find "the latest fashion . . . from different countries" (Chung 2004: 75–77). It has become a "synonym for fashion in Southern Taiwan" where there is "zero time difference (*ling shicha*) with Hong Kong, Tokyo, and [South] Korea" (Liu and Ho 2004: 39). But its transnational claims go beyond contemporary commodities and fashion trends. The shopping district's name came from an earlier marketplace first established by the Japanese colonizers in the 1930s that later became known for trade in imported goods during the Cold War period. In tracing New Kujiang's history to a colonial marketplace and celebrating its present status as an internationalized space for consumption, this narrative articulates the city's colonial legacy with the island's global future. It is a reminder of Taiwan's position as a "link and crossroads" where different geopolitical forces overlap (Manthorpe 2005, 23), and it provides an assurance that, despite the danger of getting swept over by these forces, Kaohsiung can build on this global connectivity to aspire to become a world-class city.

In 1864, the Tientsin Treaty designated the fishing port of Dagou in Southwest Taiwan as one of China's "treaty ports" opened to foreign trade and residence.[4] While these treaty ports brought the island into more intense contact with foreign markets, it was not until Taiwan was ceded to Japan following the Sino-Japanese War in 1895 that the island was thoroughly made over for commercial purpose. A transportation network was constructed to link towns and cities and to allow access from trading ports to the hinterland (Knapp 2007). This provided the foundation for further economic development and integration into international markets. Taiwan became a provider of raw materials for Japan's economy, a market for Japanese products, and a wartime industrial base for the empire (Lamley 2007). In the hands of the Japanese colonizer, Dagou began its transformation into the modern city of Kaohsiung. Its deepwater port made it a prime location to transport resources in and out of the island. Planning for the construction of a new downtown was sketched out in the 1920s, and subsequent projects to expand the city made it a model of Japanese urban planning and transportation development in Taiwan.[5] The outbreak of World War II further pressed the Japanese government to turn the city into a base for its advance to the south. As it became a gateway to the world in the Japanese empire's economic and political geography, the foundation of today's Kaohsiung was laid out. Wide roads set out on flat terrain in a geometric pattern character-ized the city and granted it the kind of rational appearance and accessibility that define modern urban planning (Scott 1999). After its defeat in World War II, the Japanese left Taiwan and the Chinese Nationalist (Kuomintang, or KMT) government took control of the island. Losing the civil war against the Chinese Communist Party forced the KMT and its followers to relo-cate to Taiwan. With the financial and, later, military aid from the United States, it began to reconstruct the local economy and consolidate its rule as the Republic of China.[6] Tight state planning coupled with land reforms and an educated labor force allowed Taiwan to develop rapidly into a strong eco-nomic presence in East Asia. Taiwan's strong economic growth beginning in the mid-1960s and up through the 1980s was lauded as a "miracle" and a model success story for other developing countries. In the new regime's export-oriented economic design, Kaohsiung continued to be a transporta-tion base, and it grew into an industrial center. With a population of 1.7 mil-lion, Kaohsiung is now the second largest city in Taiwan, second only to the capital city of Taipei, and its harbor is one of the largest container ports in the world.[7]

Cold War politics brought more than American military presence to Kaohsiung. During the Korean War (1950–1953), the United States sent mil-itary advisors to assist in the training of Taiwanese armed forces and estab-lished bases and residences in all major military bases in Taiwan. The island also served as a vacationing spot and a midway station for American troops during the Vietnam War (1959–1975). In Kaohsiung's waterfront Yancheng District, a marketplace by the name of Kujiang (pronounced *horie* in Japa-nese), originally established during the Japanese colonial period, began to flourish in the 1950s. Located near an American military base, it became a place where soldiers, sailors, and local merchants traded goods.[8] Part black market and part legitimate business, Kujiang became known for the itiner-ate traders who "ran a solo gang" (*pao danbang*) by shuttling between Taiwan and elsewhere to bring in shipped goods (*shuihuo*, literally "water cargo").[9] Associations with Japanese colonial history, adventurous traders, American soldiers, and the abundance of foreign goods all gave Kujiang a cosmopolitan character and an indomitable spirit associated with entrepreneurial initiative. This good fortune, however, was short lived. A number of events soon brought about Kujiang's decline. The abolition of restrictions on international travel in 1979 allowing Taiwanese to travel abroad in search of more cosmopolitan shopping places, the severance of the diplomatic relationship between Taiwan and the United States in the same year, and the construction of the Datong Department Store were all contributing factors.

In 1975, the Datong Department Store located at the northeast corner of Chung-shan Road and Wu-fu Road opened for business. Emulating the model of Japanese department stores, which combined shopping and entertainment, Datong quickly became a famous local attraction and made the surrounding area the new shopping destination in Kaohsiung. The Oscar Movie Theater, showing primarily foreign films, and the fast-food outlets that came into the area in the late 1980s further augmented the cosmopolitan atmosphere of the newer commercial district. In 1988, a group of real estate developers bought a piece of land on Wen-heng 167 Alley near the department store and converted a few apartment buildings into a shopping center named New Kujiang Shopping Mall (NKSM hereafter).[10] In adopting the name "Kujiang," the developers connected this shopping center to the older marketplace by drawing on its cosmopolitan image, which was still vivid in local memory. Bringing together the exotic image of old Kujiang with the novel modernity of the Datong Department Store, they created a shopping mall that would be recognized by increasing numbers of upscale consumers as cosmopolitan, daring, modern, and unique, combined with a tinge of nostalgia for the energetic free spirit of the old Kujiang.

From the very beginning, NKSM was carefully planned and centrally managed. Its spatial organization is meant to invoke an outside market area. Its corridors are called "streets" (*jie*) and are marked by signs, and the self-enclosed store units flanking them all have street numbers posted on the doors. Through screening applications for retail space, the management ensured that these shops sold only imported goods and were designed to complement one another. Cleanliness and visual consistency ordered the foreign novelties into easily accessible displays and constructed a distinctive space distinguished from the streets outside. All the shops have to adhere to strict codes dictating store hours and decor. With oversized glass windows facing the "streets," these shops give consumers a full view of store interiors decorated with objects from, or associated with, foreign places. Small boutiques like the ones in NKSM were becoming more common in Taiwan in the late 1980s. They attested to a growing desire in Taiwan to construct "taste" and "identity" through consumer choice. In addition to emphasizing their sophistication, boutiques also were invested with "character" or "personality" (*gexing*) built on the personal taste of store owners who handpicked their merchandise. Tian, a store manager now in her early forties, recalled that when NKSM was first established, most of the retailers were first-time business owners who saw the shops as a means to become their own bosses in a growing market and achieve financial independence. Their enthusiasm reflected the optimism of 1980s Taiwan when the island was beginning to open up economically and politically. It was also at around the same time that teenagers started to become a consumer demographic in Taiwan. Regulations on high school dress codes were loosened, and the economic miracle produced a generation of young people who had more money at their disposal. This change occurred concurrently with the democratization process on the island and the global proliferation of youth popular culture as a marketable commodity. As a result, there emerged a youth culture largely generated and influenced by commodities, advertising, and transnational cultural flows. New Kujiang's rapid fashion changes, led by *danbang* merchants; the playful juxtaposition of images and goods from all over; and the mixture of languages on business signs composed an imaginative world where consumers could imagine, touch, and consume the global. For both consumers and merchants, these enclosed spaces with windows all facing inward were experienced as an opening that connected them to a wider world beyond the city.

Less than ten years after the establishment of NKSM, the nearby residential area of Jen-chi Street, Wen-hua Road, and Wen-heng 167 Alley had developed into a shopping area that then came to be known to most Kaohsiung residents more generally as "New Kujiang." Other shopping gallerias with spatial layout and managerial style similar to NKSM were built. The Oscar Movie Theater, numerous fast-food outlets, less pricey shopping centers, and cheap knockoffs sold on the streets all drew in a younger crowd, giving New Kujiang a reputation that was becoming more hip than the sophisticated chic that NKSM had aimed for. Merchants used the arcades (*qilou*), an outside space protected from the weather by overhanging structures, either for storage or as additional display space. Street vendors set up stalls and carts in the arcades for protection from the weather or on the sidewalks right outside, blocking access to the arcades and the shops. Pedestrians were often forced to spill out onto the streets, exacerbating the already congested traffic and contributing to constant turf battles among merchants, vendors, pedestrians, and motorists. In NKSM, as a result of later expansions that incorporated previously existing buildings, the floors were not of the same height, and the corridors took strange turns and crosscut each other at unexpected intervals. The joy of discovery (or the frustration of getting lost) made shopping in New Kujiang an adventure in itself.

The expansion of New Kujiang hit a roadblock when the Datong Department Store was destroyed by fire in October 1995. Without this anchor to draw shoppers, business in New Kujiang began to dwindle. Further complicating its plight was the construction of other department stores along the axis of Wu-fu and Chung-shan Roads already begun by the time Datong burned. The economic miracle of the 1980s had brought about New Kujiang's prosperity, but it also encouraged the establishment of more and more places for shopping and entertainment competing for business. As New Kujiang began to lose its allure as a chic shopping destination in the mid-1990s, the city of Kaohsiung also began to lose its industrial base. While department stores were being built one after another, Taiwan's increasing integration into the global market and rising wages were forcing industries to move offshore in search of cheaper labor. In response to the global restructuring of capitalist production, in which capital became increasingly mobile across spatial divides and production became increasingly dispersed (Harvey 1990), the effort to transform local places to attract investment and consumers intensified.

In this context of postmiracle economy, New Kujiang found its rebirth in Taiwan's place-making project.[11] The national government's initiative to transform Taiwan's landscape in the name of modernization started as an effort to remap Taiwan's national space, consolidate a localized Taiwanese identity, and "indigenize" the KMT so as to legitimatize its rule of Taiwan (Lu 2002). Promoted mainly as a politicocultural project at first, these programs later shifted their focus to economic development.[12] Embedded in this new landscape were articulations with a global market in which Taiwan had to compete by serving up marketable images as well as easy-to-navigate marketplaces for cosmopolitan consumers. This transformation resonates with the global trend of reconstructing local places physically as well as discursively to make them attractive to investors, visitors, and residents alike (Harvey 1989; Judd and Fainstein 1999; Philo and Kearns 1993; Zukin 1995). In addition, there was an agenda of implementing social change through spatial reorganization (Chuang 2005).[13] As stated by the Council for Economic Planning and Development (CEPD), the nationwide Township Renaissance Program would incorporate previous street-making (*zaojie*) and town-making (*zaozhen*) programs in a new effort to create a "healthy, clean, and beautiful" island. With an emphasis on "prosperity, modernization, and culture," this effort would "elevate the nation's competitiveness and improve its international image, enhance the quality of life for its citizens, achieve sustainable development for cities and towns, and strengthen the investment environment to further economic development" (CEPD n.d.). Modernization, economic development, and national competitiveness were all intertwined in these projects. A vision of progress marked by tidiness, legibility, and easily recognized local identities would be perpetuated through the funded projects.

Led by NKSM's management, business owners in New Kujiang worked with local government to transform the area. In 1998, it became one of the Department of Commerce's "Exemplary Business Streets" (*shifan shangdianjie*). The area proposed for development included Wen-hua Road, Wenheng 167 Alley, and Jen-chi Street between Wu-Fu and Hsin-Tian Roads.[14] Teamed up with consultants from the Corporate Synergy Development Center (CSDC), a private firm commissioned by the Department of Commerce, the Committee for Development in New Kujiang presented a detailed plan for the New Kujiang Business Street to the Kaohsiung Municipal Government and the Department of Commerce as the blueprint of New Kujiang's development. New Kujiang's future was envisioned as an open-air pedestrian mall resembling, in the words of Mr. Liao and CSDC consultant Chen, "the streets of Austria," "the shopping malls of America," and or even "the Harajuku area of Tokyo."[15] To achieve this end, the project focused on addressing the "disorderly (*zaluan*) streetscape" and using spatial reorganization to regulate the flow of consumer traffic through the area (CSDC 1998). It sought to reduce visually chaotic elements by banning oversized business signs and street vendors to create a more consistent look. With all of these distractions removed, the plan was to set the area apart from other city streets by paving the streets with decorative bricks, planting ornamental trees, and converting the streets into a pedestrian zone. A picture of pedestrians leisurely strolling down brick walkways shaded by colorful awnings and flanked by flowering trees, outdoor cafes, and refined street furniture recalled the pedestrian malls of other urban centers striving to bring commerce and consumers together in a controlled environment closed to automobile traffic. These pedestrian zones were consciously intended to simulate "organic" urban streets nostalgic of an idealized urbanity (Boddy 1992; Crawford 1992; McMorrough 2001; Shepherd 2008). In New Kujiang, however, the purpose was not to recreate a supposedly organic urban space but to make New Kujiang more competitive with the modernity represented by the newer shopping malls and "malled" downtowns. It was to make New Kujjang stand out from the rest of Taiwan by making it look like one of those cosmopolitan shopping streets in "advanced countries" (*xianjin guojia*) that are indistinguishable from one another.

In the planning and construction of this new space, the layered narrative of New Kujiang's success story was being reworked. Starting with Kaohsiung's past history as a colonial port and then the Cold War trade of shipped goods from abroad in the old Kujiang, the spatial reorganization of New Kujiang would bring it and the city closer to other world-class cities. Built around the key words of *internationalization*, *modernization*, and *competitiveness*, the revitalization project would connect New Kujiang's previous commercial success to future success and its past association with exotic commodities to participation in an international consumer market. The active role local business people took in refashioning the streets was celebrated as a triumph of entrepreneurialism and communal self-promotion that would ensure New Kujiang's competitiveness in the global market of places. Colonial legacy, Cold War dependence, and postindustrial decline were all reoriented toward global connectivity and future prosperity. Past and future converged in the perpetual youthfulness and newness of New Kujiang through the *imagineering* (Rutheiser 1996) of a "modern" as well as "internationalized" space for consumption.

A Place for Shopping

A decade after the Development Plan was first introduced, New Kujiang has morphed into an eclectic hybrid between a Taiwanese night market and a trendy pedestrian mall. Pricey boutiques, trees (the kind that Mr. Liao dislikes), restaurants serving exotic food, and colorful banners line the brick-paved streets. But, on these same streets, in front of the boutiques and restaurants, are street vendors selling cheap accessories, low-priced clothing, iced drinks, and snacks. Although conventional shops usually open before noon, street vendors do not show up until hours later. At nightfall, shoppers begin to come in numbers. The streets come into life, and activities continue until midnight. The smell of food, the sounds, and the crowds conjure up an ambiance not unlike a "hot and noisy" (*renao*) night market. The revitalization project did not manage to rid the vendors who made New Kujiang a "chaotic" place. Instead, because they have been pedestrianized, the streets have become an even more ideal space to set up vending stalls. While "failing" to live up to the official vision of a tidy, legible, and user-friendly quality shopping district (Hsu and Yang 2001), New Kujiang was able to regain the lively and unruly energy that had made it famous and popular among youthful consumers. It continues to serve up an "internationalized" image. But this is a different image than the one that the planners had in mind. Instead, New Kujiang provides shoppers, merchants, and vendors with an internationalized space and narratives of market success through which different visions can be articulated.

The development plan looked to European, American, and Japanese downtowns and shopping streets for inspiration. But, to many Taiwanese, a night market is the kind of pedestrian shopping area they know best, and this became New Kujiang's reference point. Fang, a store clerk, explains that, while she does not think that New Kujiang is a night market, "Its position (*diwei*) in Kaohsiung's tourism is similar to Liuhe Night Market and Ruifeng Night Market." Like these popular night markets, New Kujiang is "a place you go for shopping." She asserts that there is a difference, but exactly how New Kujiang differs she is not certain. Tian makes an easier distinction. The façade at the entrance of New Kujiang and the fact that the area has been "planned" are what make New Kujiang different. Mei-li, a female shopper, on the other hand, cites that New Kujiang sells "new things" and "expensive stuff." These upscale commodities and entertainment features make it stand out. New Kujiang not only offers food and clothing as most night markets do, but it also has a movie theater, chain record stores, specialty shops, local as well as international designer brands, and dance studios. All these, however, only make New Kujiang a "bigger and newer night market" in the eyes of Tian's younger sister: "The only reason that New Kujiang is not a night market is because it's not called a night market."

Although the general consensus among shoppers and merchants is that New Kujiang is not a night market, however, the facts that these are all

"places you go for shopping" and that comparisons are constantly made between New Kujiang and night markets point to the possibility that New Kujiang could always degenerate into a night market if a careful distinction is
not maintained. To differentiate New Kujiang from these other places for
shopping, its newness, youthfulness, and trendiness are often emphasized.
Official promotional materials constantly refer back to New Kujiang's cosmopolitan past and fashionable present to set it apart from more traditional
night markets that are known to be loud, crowded, disorderly, and, most important, provincial. Comparisons to Taipei's youth-oriented Hsimenting are
often brought up to promote New Kujiang to outsiders as a shopping area
for young people. To further differentiate New Kujiang from night markets,
street vending is condemned or held in a negative light by the committee and
planning agencies. Street vendors are accused of offering unfair competition, posing a hygiene problem, and disrupting the clear order of the development plan.[16] Although the final plan did try to incorporate street vendors
as a way of soliciting their cooperation, in its execution vendors were left
out. This neglect is partly a result of the planning agencies' negative view
toward street vending and partly a result of the government's refusal to grant
funding to designs that include street vendors and their illegitimate business
operations.[17] Street vending is also overlooked in official promotional materials. Thus, while street vending is very visible on the ground, it oftentimes
becomes invisible on paper.

Even with the constant effort to promote a carefully composed image of
New Kujiang, other stories exist to justify customary practices that do not
conform to the official vision of an "internationalized" pedestrian mall. Mr.
Hong, a food vendor in his sixties, insisted that New Kujiang's development
as a shopping area began well before the establishment of NKSM. According to him, street vendors began to show up in front of the movie theater in
the early 1980s. It was a time when people who had come to the city for jobs
found that street vending might give them more economic opportunity. "We
were people of poor fortune (*pháinn-miā-lāng* in Hoklo)," he explained. "We
didn't have enough education to get good jobs. Street vending was our way
of moving up." Landlords in the area took pity on them and allowed them to
vend at street corners and in the arcades outside their buildings. It was only
after vendors had drawn shoppers to the area that developers started moving
in to build the shopping centers. Lian, another food vendor, had a slightly

different story. After his factory folded in the early 1990s due to competition from cheap products produced in Southeast Asia, Lian decided to take up street vending. New Kujiang was already a well-known shopping area by then, and he felt that it was an ideal location to start a business. Although he does not care about who initiated New Kujiang's development, he, too, thinks that street vending is the last resort for many who lack opportunity in formal employment and that the vendors should be protected by the government and respected by the development project. To him, as well as to Mr. Hong, street vending is what gives New Kujiang a distinct flavor and makes it a fun place to be. A "place you go for shopping" is constituted of elements more than (or other than) the trees, bricks, and boutiques. It has to be "hot and noisy" (*renao*) to attract people.

Both Mr. Hong and Lian frame their stories within the framework of another popular narrative in Taiwan that argues that vending helps to absorb the impact of economic transformation by offering opportunity to unemployed workers in the absence of a welfare system (Tai 1994; Yu 1999).[18] Mr. Hong's lack of formal education made it difficult for him to find a job that paid enough to support his family. Lian, once the owner of a small-sized enterprise, was driven out of the market by rising production costs and foreign imports. Taking up street vending was a conscious decision by both to improve their economic standing.[19] Through narrating their experiences, they reiterate the same story of self-initiative and market success against the background of Kaohsiung's development but with a different twist. Unlike the story celebrated in New Kujiang's promotional materials and the official narrative of the city, in Mr. Hong and Lian's stories, the city's development has marginalized them. Yet, like New Kujiang's success story, their accounts stress entrepreneurial initiative and the ability to react quickly to a changing economic context. They cast themselves as entrepreneurs and justify street vending as a legitimate route to upward mobility. Vending, along with conventional business, should be allowed or even encouraged. Moreover, by arguing that vending has always been there in New Kujiang, they insist on the vendors' right to stay where they are and reject the notion that street vending is a source of disorder threatening New Kujiang's success.

The coexistence of conventional shops and street vending is not unique to New Kujiang. In many shopping streets in Taiwan, property owners rent out the arcades and adjoining sidewalks to vendors. A vender who has paid rent feels that he or she is entitled to set up there. Therefore, vendors in New Kujiang feel that they are unfairly harassed by the police who give out citations. Shops and property owners also do not want to lose the right to rent out space in front of their shops for extra income. While some merchants feel that vendors bring unfair competition, others welcome the crowds that they attract. Conventional shops persist in renting out the space to vendors because their presence is considered beneficial to the market as a whole. Moreover, shops located in the upper levels of the shopping centers may send their salesclerks downstairs to display merchandise on the streets, and shops on the ground level may also display their merchandise on the arcades and sidewalks, blurring the line between street vending and conventional shops.

The marketing of places on the global stage requires the production of differences. The development plan attempted to engineer New Kujiang into a different place through adopting elements of pedestrian malls in "advanced" countries. Street vendors in New Kujiang, however, propose that, to stand out in the global market of places, New Kujiang needs to stress its local features. Well educated and politically savvy, Mr. Hong's daughter Yuki has emerged as a proponent for vendors' right in New Kujiang. Working with local politicians, cultural workers, and local scholars, she hopes to organize vendors to bargain for business licenses and legal status. In her view, international tourism provides the best opportunity for New Kujiang, and the only way to attract foreign tourists is through emphasizing New Kujiang's local Taiwanese character. She envisions New Kujiang as a place that offers up homey food and exotic items to tourists: "We can't compete unless we find our own distinctive feature (*tese*)." She argues, "What can be more Taiwanese than street vending?" Although Yuki considers street vending as distinctively Taiwanese, her argument in fact resonates with the global trend of using street vending in the transformation of urban space into pleasure zones for consumption (Donovan 2008; Shepherd 2008). Street vending is promoted as a way to enliven dull streets and give cities a nostalgic as well as a generic aura of urbanism. Because New Kujiang is an important location in the city's tourism promotion and street vendors contribute to the "hot and noisy" ambience of a place for shopping, their existence is quietly accepted but never encouraged by the government authorities. As street vending has come to epitomize an authentic Taiwanese culture that can distinguish it in the global tourism market (S-D. Yu 2004), Yuki and the vendors have also learned to adopt this narrative, willing to subsume themselves under more regulations but also insisting on continuing customary practices incommensurable with official visions of modernization. Competition in the global market of places is a reason offered both by the planning agencies to eliminate street vending and by the vendors to argue for their continuing presence. In stressing competitiveness and profit seeking, the official narrative inadvertently provides a ready vocabulary for local venders to persist in evading, bending, breaking, or neglecting regulations.

The islandwide place-making projects have reconfigured local marketplaces and urban streets for capital in the form of investment and consumption. In these increasingly standardized places striving to present both modern qualities and local distinctiveness, the signs of "Taiwanese-ness" are being repackaged into a desired commodity (Wu and Kuo 2001). It is within this same framework that New Kujiang's streets have been reordered to signify national progress and global connectivity and that Yuki has strategically manipulated the idioms of competitiveness and global market to advance her agenda. Images of urban space constructed by designers and political elites are "rarely consistent with the daily spatial experience of urban residents and workers" (Low and Lawrence-Zuniga 2006: 20). "Through people's social exchanges, memories, images, and daily use of the material settings," space is transformed into "scenes and actions that convey symbolic meaning" (Low 1996: 862). Designed to be a space that resembles the cosmopolitan shopping streets in "advanced" countries, New Kujiang has been inscribed with new meanings through reinterpretations of official narratives and transformed through the actions of those who work and shop there. Contradicting views of what a "place you go for shopping" should be like remain contested on a daily basis.

Flows and Connections

In Taiwan's official place-making projects, internationalization is represented by a modern streetscape characterized by tidiness and legibility. To the planning agencies, internationalization means the (re)writing of a cosmopolitan history and the engineering of a space modeled after other places in "advanced" countries. To Yuki, internationalization means constructing local difference to compete in the global market. For many merchants and shoppers, New Kujiang is internationalized not in the sense that it physically resembles Euro-American shopping streets but in the sense that these distant locales are evoked through imagination as well as material objects to build a different kind of place. Lian displays a multilingual menu on his pushcart and is proud of having a few Canadian expatriates as his regular customers. Shops put up English or Japanese business signs, and there are shops named "Tokyo" (*Dongjing*), "L.A.," "Queen's Boulevard" (*Huanghou Dadao* of Hong Kong), and "London" (*Lundun*). A poster outside of a curio shop in NKSM showed a portrait of John Wayne with the word *Texas* printed on it. Next to the poster were small postcards with signs from Route 66. A few corridors away, a shop specialized in merchandise associated with Japanese popular music displayed pictures of Japanese boy bands on its windows and hung posters from its ceilings. Posted on the door were ads for the latest paraphernalia from concert tours around Japan. In this cacophony and juxtaposition of "other" places, New Kujiang emerges as a place where imaginaries of local Taiwan and the global market are constructed and where different actors envision Taiwan's place in the global map of fashionable places and commodities.

Shop owner Sam was one of the earliest occupants of NKSM. He was in his late twenties when he began his business selling posters and photographs. Originally, he carried photo books of Japanese pop stars because they were popular among the general public. But Sam quickly realized that there was an emerging market for Japanese pop culture and turned his poster shop into an "idol shop," offering a wider range of items.[20] As an "unauthorized intermediary" (Nakano 2002) who mediated the flow of Japanese pop cultural products before transnational record companies and television stations began to formally explore the market, Sam was able to establish his business before there was much competition. Twenty years later, he owns three shops in Kaohsiung, two of them located in New Kujiang. Sam takes frequent trips to Tokyo and Osaka to obtain posters, pictures, concert merchandise, and products endorsed by Japanese pop stars. He sees his shops as places for the exchange of information and welcomes young customers to linger in the shops, watch DVDs, and chat with salesclerks. As they learn about new releases and the latest gossip, Sam also learns about new trends in what his youthful customers are looking for.

While not a big fan of Japanese pop music, Sam nonetheless admires the "business brain" (*shengyi naodai*) of the Japanese. Japanese products, he argues, are of much better quality than Taiwanese ones. Taiwan is an imitator of Japanese fashion, and there is always a slight time lag between the two. This ordering of Taiwan and Japan at different temporalities reflects not only the colonial legacy in Taiwan that identifies Japan as the symbol of modernity and technological superiority (Cheng 2002; Iwabuchi 2002, 2004) but also the rise of Japan's "soft power" in the global popular cultural market (Allison 2006, 2009; Befu and Guichard-Anguis 2001; Chua 2004). This temporal difference plays to Sam's advantage. For as long as Japan is still ahead in fashion and popular culture, its products will be desired by Taiwanese consumers. As long as Sam can stay a step ahead of the others, keeping tabs on emerging stars, and obtaining products as soon as they are available, he will have business. For those who do not understand Japanese and cannot order merchandise directly from Japan, Sam's shops and the regular shipments of magazines are the most convenient way to obtain merchandise and concert tickets unavailable in major record stores. However, no matter how frequently Sam travels to Tokyo, the arrival of new goods never seems fast enough now that the Internet has made it easy for fans to track the newest releases and the appearances of their idols in magazines and television shows. Surrounded by posters and concert merchandise (often priced higher than young fans can afford), his customers often find Sam's shop insufficient to bridge the distance between them and the place where these items come from. Sam laments that he is at best an intermediary between Taiwan and Japan: "Surely we try to satisfy the customers and sell the timeliest items. But we have no control over what the Japanese [record companies] are going to release. What am I to do if their idol just won't release a new single or go on a tour?" Constantly chasing after Japanese pop stars and products, Sam feels that his only chance in the market is to react to Japanese trends quickly. Yet, if the time lag were to be entirely eliminated, these foreign goods would cease to be different, and Sam's shop would lose its allure for consumers.

Eddie was in high school when he discovered hip-hop dance through music videos sold in New Kujiang. After he finished college and military service in the late 1990s, Eddie started moonlighting as a dance instructor in New Kujiang. The studio where he teaches is a space of "America" composed of graffiti and images. One side of the studio is covered by a large mural depicting street scenes. Large signs of Coca-Cola and Sprite are painted on the wooden façade of faux storefront that takes up another side of the studio. In front is a boardwalk reminiscent of buildings from Western movies. When asked why they chose to paint Coca-Cola signs and build the boardwalk, a member of the dance group who founded the studio answered that it was because they are "American," and America is where hip-hop started. Here, hip-hop dance is promoted as a healthy sport. Eddie explains that, while its "central idea (*zhongxin sixiang*)" originated from the streets of New York, "the whole world is influenced by hip-hop." Therefore, this global popular culture form could be dislocated from New York and become a neutral medium through which Eddie expresses his life philosophy and imagines his position in the wide world of hip-hop.

"Hip-hop is about living happily." Eddie explains. "But you need an economic basis to live happily." Regrettably, making it as a hip-hop dancer is not easy in Taiwan and even less so in Kaohsiung. Eddie has to travel to Taipei to take part in dance competitions. Adding to his difficulties, record companies prefer foreign dancers to local ones. In this global hip-hop landscape that Eddie has constructed, Taiwan remains at the margin even though it does not have to be so. Working as individuals, Taiwanese dancers cannot compete with foreigners. However, "if we can bring everybody together, we can change the situation." The solution, according to him, is that someone rich and powerful, "like the government," has to get involved. Eddie feels that an ordinary citizen (*xiao laobaixing*) like himself has limited resources and power to change things and hopes that, through government intervention such as funding programs for dancers, this distance between Taiwan and the world stage can be crossed. But if the government does not do anything, Eddie would take things into his own hands. He believes that there is a financial future in the land across the strait for Taiwanese dancers. In his view, although Taiwan lags behind America, Japan, Hong Kong, and South Korea in hip-hop dance, it is still one step ahead of China. This temporal difference and Taiwan's strong presence in Chinese-language music industry would give Eddie the required cultural and symbolic capital to operate in China. With entrepreneurial initiative, he is determined to find his way into the world—with or without the government's help.

When Eddie began to teach dancing in New Kujiang, Ming was in his final year of high school and was more enthusiastic about making money than studying. Having sold products from snacks to accessories in night markets since he was seventeen, Ming was already an experienced vendor when he decided to try his fortune in New Kujiang in 2007. Wage labor never attracted Ming. He feels that factory jobs have no future and does not like the pay of office jobs. As for sales, he says, "You might as well be your own boss if you are going to sell things." The lack of opportunities in Kaohsiung has led many of Ming's friends to leave for Taipei, the high-tech industrial zones in Hsinchu and Tainan, and China. Ming does not want to leave his hometown, so he created a job for himself. Unlike older vendors such as Mr. Hong and Lian, he never saw street vending as the last resort. Instead, it was his choice from the very beginning and a basis on which he hopes to build his own enterprise one day.

While Eddie sees his future in China, Ming feels that the only route out of Taiwan into the world is through local culture. Having spent years selling other people's products, Ming has decided to develop his own T-shirt brand. Mixing Hoklo, Mandarin, Japanese, and English, Ming proclaims his love for Kaohsiung, criticizes the government, and makes fun of Taiwanese society through his designs. He also throws in what he considers to be "Aboriginal" symbols such as ocean waves, mountain lilies, and tropical flowers, which look suspiciously like the hibiscus patterns on Hawaiian shirts. The collage of cultural elements, Ming contends, tells the "peculiar history of Taiwan," in which the island is constantly under foreign influences through colonial occupation, transnational consumption, and waves of migration from China and elsewhere. On his T-shirts is a multicultural Taiwan that is always already internationalized and ready to step into the world stage dressed as a colorful and trendy cosmopolitan person. Instead of seeking participation in the global market through brokering Japanese fashion or imitating Euro-American modernity, Ming and many of his peers now look to put Taiwan on the map through embracing a Taiwanese identity. This proliferation of a Taiwan consciousness and civic identity, as opposed to the old Chinese cultural identity, can be traced back to the nation-building project that produced the reconfigured space of New Kujiang and a Taiwanese identity through the production of locality. Moreover, this identity, as Scott Simon argues, is also a "result of globalization and transnationalism, as international Taiwanese individuals seek the same kind of social recognition enjoyed by citizens of other nation-states" (2003: 155).

Once considered the stuff of night markets, "Made in Taiwan" is becoming a sign that is more and more sought after in New Kujiang, especially as China-made products have flooded Taiwanese marketplaces. Much like Eddie's temporal ordering of Taiwan and China, the popular perception in New Kujiang is that Taiwanese products are more advanced than Chinese ones. They might not be as fashionable as Japanese or American products, but they are nonetheless a guarantee of a better quality than Chinese products. This distrust of Chinese products is built not only on the perceived temporal difference between Taiwan and China's degrees of modernization but also on the political tension between the two. The Beijing government sees Taiwan as a renegade province of China and never ceases to block Taiwan from participating in international organizations. As the two sides become more and more closely linked economically, the desire to claim a non-Chinese Taiwan becomes intensified. In postindustrial Kaohsiung, Taiwan's integration into the global market and its growing economic connection to China are experienced through a rising unemployment rate. Even though vending is still active on the streets in New Kujiang and transnational labels are opening shops in the area, small businesses are feeling the pressure from the real and imagined economic plight of Taiwan as its industries move offshore. China remains both a threat and an opportunity. Some in New Kujiang pin their hopes on the Chinese tourists who might or might not buy from them. Some, like Eddie, see China as a potential market and look for chances to explore it. Some, like Sam, prefer to align Taiwan with Japan and other advanced countries and purposefully refuse to acknowledge any possible connection with China. And some, like Ming, turn inward to look for a cosmopolitan Taiwanese identity through which to reach outward to the world. Routed through their different experiences with the transnational flows of commodities, images, and ideas in New Kujiang, the international future in Taiwan's national project becomes refracted and reworked to envision different futures that somehow remain enmeshed in the key words of global connectivity and market success.

Conclusion

A decade after the Datong Department Store fire, the surrounding commercial area has reinvented itself as a stage for youthful fashion display. Here, former residential streets have been transformed into showcases of goods and images. Across the road from the recently reopened Datong, a park long associated with the Formosa Incident has been renamed Central Park and renovated with wide walkways and outdoor cafes.[21] A subway system began operating in 2009, and the grand subway station in Central Park has become a new tourist attraction. With its sunny weather, glittering lights, wide roads, geometric street patterns, and revitalized shopping streets, Kaohsiung now attracts Taiwanese filmmakers as a generic modern city where urban characters play out their stories. New Kujiang's eclectic hybrid of a night market and a pedestrian mall allows it to double both as a traditional site and a cosmopolitan backdrop under the camera.

In this international place engineered for consumption, it is possible to dream of being a part of a world beyond Taiwan—the quality shopping districts of advanced countries; the fashion centers of Japan, America, and Europe; and the transnational hip-hop community. Moreover, the constant search to connect with the world stems from the endeavor to refashion Taiwan into a desired site for consumption and investment in the global network of capitalism. The obsession with everything international in Taiwan underscores the difficulty of a nonnation that seeks its place in the global community of nation-states. Economic participation becomes the strategy to pursue international legitimacy and way of bypassing the impossible bind between China and Taiwan. As Taiwan remains floating in political uncertainty and as neoliberalism induces nations, places, and local actors to become entrepreneurs of themselves in search of marketable values, New Kujiang and the island's past, present, and future are constantly remade and renegotiated in the hope of finding a place in the world.

Notes

ACKNOWLEDGMENTS

Parts of this chapter appeared in *City and Society* 22(2): 286–308, under the title "'Making Streets': Planned Space and Unplanned Business in New Kujiang, Taiwan." They are reproduced by permission of the American Anthropological Association from *City & Society*, Volume 22, Issue 2, excerpts from pp. 286–308, December, 2010. Not for sale or further reproduction. The research and writing of this paper were partially funded by the Taiwan National Science Council and National Tsing Hua University. The author would like to thank the anonymous reviewers for Stanford Press for their comments.

1. There are many forms of romanization of New Kujiang in official publications, including "Shin Kuchan," "New Horie," "Hsin Chueh Chiang," and "New

Jyueijiang." Although its correct pronunciation in Mandarin (the official language) is *kujiang*, locals often pronounce it as *juejiang*. I have opted to use New (*xin*) Kujiang for clarity. Throughout the article, I use modified Wade-Giles system for place names, as this is the convention in Taiwan. Some idiosyncratic romanizations such as Keelung have become conventional. In these cases, I adopt the commonly known names. Pinyin is provided as needed for clarity.

2. All personal names are pseudonyms. Because it is not uncommon for individuals in Taiwan to adopt foreign names, I follow the informants' preferences and use English and Japanese names when applicable.

3. The worship (*baibai*), called *zehqe* in the local dialect Hoklo, on the second and sixteenth day of each month on the lunar calendar is for the gods of household foundations (*degizo* in Hoklo) and the wandering ghosts (*mngkaokong* in Hoklo) who happen to pass by the door. Some have also added *caishen*, the Money God, to the list. The relationship between Taiwanese and the ancestors, ghosts, and spirits they worship is often described in terms of debt (Ahern 1973). Thus, spirit money is offered in worship. For discussion on Taiwanese religious practices, see Feuchtwang (1974); Wang (1974); and Weller (1987). While individual shops take care of *zehqe*, the Committee for Development in New Kujiang organized *baibai* on *pudu*, the communal worship for wandering ghosts, on the fifteenth day of the seventh month of the lunar calendar.

4. There were four such treaty ports in Taiwan. In addition to Dagou, Tamsui was opened in 1862, Keelung in 1863, and Anping in 1864. Written in Chinese characters that mean "beating a dog," *Dagou* is actually a transliteration of an Aboriginal phrase whose meaning is still unclear. Because *Dagou* reads too crudely, the Japanese replaced it with two Kanji characters that are pronounced similarly as "Takao" in Japanese. The name Kaohsiung (Gaoxiong) is the Mandarin pronunciation of these two characters.

5. See Wu-dar Huang et al. (1992). As Japan's first overseas colony, Taiwan served as a lab for urban planning that aimed to solve urban problems in Japan, experimenting with methods of efficient control and maximizing economic benefit (Su 2010; Ye 1993).

6. This aid was part of Cold War politics in which the United States helped to protect Taiwan from the People's Republic of China by allying itself with Taiwan, South Korea, and Japan to contain the spread of communism.

7. On December 25, 2010, Kaohsiung City was merged with Kaohsiung County to form a special municipality. The combined population of the municipality is 2.7 million.

8. The area was called Horie (canal) Machi (district) because it was built on a land next to the canal.

9. The term *danbang* originally meant itinerate traders who bring goods from one location to sell in another. *Bang* (literally "group" or "gang") can also be used

to refer to trade organizations in traditional China. Itinerate traders often operate (*pao*) alone (*dan*). Therefore, their activities are described as *pao danbang*. Here, *pao* connotes the double meaning of "run" and "operate." In Taiwan, itinerate traders frequently traveling across borders are now called *danbangke*, while the term *danbang* has come to refer to the trade instead of the trader. *Shuihuo* (water cargo) refers to foreign goods that are brought into the country through unauthorized and/or unofficial channels.

10. Xinkujiang Jingpin Shangchang. The official English translation is New Kuchan Shopping Mall.

11. *Place-making* refers to the combined effort of physical and discursive construction of "locality."

12. In the early 1990s, the Council for Cultural Affairs began to implement programs to "develop comprehensive communities" through writing local histories. While these projects were designed and promoted as cultural projects, many communities took part for economic reasons. Following the council's initiative, the Department of Commerce also implemented the Image Business Clusters Construction Program in 1995 and the Business Street Development and Advancement Program in 1996 to revitalize small towns or business areas. In 2000, the two initiatives were combined to form a single Business Streets and Districts Development Program to eliminate the official division between urban business streets and the rural business clusters.

13. Facilitating social change and transformation of consciousness through spatial reform has been an objective of modern urban planning (Scott 1999; Su 2010). Neoliberal logic, however, demands more than planning for social change. It seeks to make cities "better" through producing new kind of spaces that are more suitable for the flow of capital and new kinds of citizens who are more competitive in the market (Thrift 1999).

14. Nearly 500 shops of various sizes were located within the area, over 200 of them inside NKSM. In addition to NKSM, there were four other small-sized malls (*shangchang*).

15. New Kujiang is not the only project that was inspired by Euro-American and Japanese shopping areas. In the handbooks published by CSDC, examples are drawn from Japan's business streets and American towns (CSDC 2000; 2001). The area around the Harajuku station in Tokyo is a hangout for youth famous for its street fashion.

16. This negative view toward vending is not limited to the planners of New Kujiang. Shuenn-Der Yu observes that, in Taiwan's modernization process, vending has increasingly been "condemned as an activity sabotaging Taiwan's economic and social well-being" (2004: 133). Chuang's study (2005) in Taipei's Yongkang community shows their attempt to confine vendors in a designated area and improve the appearances of vending stalls. Tai (1994) provides detailed account

on changing policies on vending in Taiwan. Donovan (2008) and Shepherd (2008) also trace the perception of vending as a threat to public order, a cause of traffic congestion, a potential health problem, and a source of unfair competition in different countries.

17. Street vending is officially considered as illegitimate business, and the Taiwanese government stopped issuing business licenses to street vendors in the 1970s. However, when street vendors are fined, they are cited not for violation of business laws but for blocking traffic.

18. See Donovan (2008) for an overview of theories that consider street vending and informal economies as a social safety net.

19. See Tai (1994) for an account on why street vendors in Taiwan made the decision to enter this field.

20. This increasingly visible presence of Japanese popular culture in Taiwan as well as other East Asian locations has become a much-discussed topic in both popular and academic discourses. See, for example, Befu and Guichard-Anguis 2001; Chiou 2003; Chua 2004; Iwabuchi 2002, 2004; and Lee 2002. The "South Korea Wave" (*hanliu*) has also hit Taiwan since the early 2000s.

21. The incident is sometimes referred to as the Kaohsiung Incident. In 1979, an International Human Rights Day rally in the park turned into violent confrontations between the police and the demonstrators who called for reforms. Many of the participants arrested were associated with *Meilidao* (Formosa) magazine, an oppositional publication supporting Taiwan independence, thus the name "Formosa Incident."

Chapter Three

On the Streets of Beijing
Medical Melodrama in the Everyday

TRANG X. TA

Beijing Streets

Rural migrants come to the cities to find work, but sometimes they come in search of medical care.[1] As the nation's capital, Beijing is in some ways the final destination for those seeking care from urban hospitals.[2] The costs of travel to the city are part of the burden of medical expenses for rural families. Their illness narratives performed on the streets for donations from passersby have become an everyday feature of the urban landscape. One family's struggle to seek treatment for their child's leukemia, which I encountered one day on the streets of Beijing, reveals the parameters of an economy of hope and despair in postreform-era China. In "publishing" their story of medical hardship on the street, they become a reminder of rural despair haunting the urban landscape in a society where the gap between country and city marks a biopolitical divide in people's life chances. I use the metaphor of publishing to refer to the way these stories stake a claim on a public sphere that refuses to recognize their desperate need as worthy of notice.

Economic liberalization policies in the last three decades have radically transformed Chinese cities, and the presence of migrant workers is a continual reminder of the source of the labor required for urban development. At the time I encountered this family, projects to prepare Beijing for the international visitors attending the 2008 One World, One Dream Summer Olympics had begun, heightened by government efforts to sanitize the streets.[3] The sanitization campaigns not only transformed the physical landscape of the city but also included the forced relocation of the city's homeless, transients, and petitioners—all those who did not belong in spaces newly created for international visitors and middle-class Chinese citizens. Under production was the creation of a world-class city that would meet global standards of cosmopolitanism. Thus, this family's appearance in this newly designed space was an unwelcome eruption of the rural.

At the same time, however, the pathos of their performance unwittingly reproduces a banality of the everyday that fails to disrupt the uneven social order that characterizes "socialism with Chinese characteristics."[4] In this chapter, I use this street story to raise the question of why some stories are taken up as worthy of compassion and others are not. In the "postsacred" era of industrial capitalism, the state has the monopoly on spectacle. This family's story is too easily dismissed as another example of the pervasive tragedy that constitutes the everyday. They are thus caught in a paradox: They must move passersby to donate, but their very deployment of melodrama is what leaves them open to the suspicion that they are manipulating public sentiment. By way of contrast, the story of Chengcheng, a girl from a poor, rural family, also struggling with leukemia, readily received the media attention that the family on the street had longed for. However, Chengcheng's illness narrative is recast as a story of exemplary individual sacrifice, deflecting attention from the lack of rural health care to the project of infrastructural development as a priority for economic growth. Chengcheng did not stay in the city to seek medical treatment, but neither did she die anonymously in the countryside. One story demonstrates the growing disparities of the socioeconomic order, and the other serves instead to reinscribe the developmentalist logic of the state focused on economic growth. Both stories suggest the limited conditions of possibility whereby individuals, families, and communities are now "free" to develop their economic futures as they adapt to the market rationality of neoliberalism.

A Family of Three

Families are a common sight on the busy streets of Beijing, especially in an area with a high density of shopping venues and public plazas, but the family of three that I encountered on a day in October stood out in an unsettling manner.[5] A young boy was lying on a stretcher wearing a fabric facemask while his parents attended to him as if the side of the street were a hospital room. They occupied a space near the entrance to an upscale shopping complex with brand-name boutiques and a large chain grocery store. Camped out amid the cosmopolitan backdrop of gleaming high-rises they appeared out of place; nonetheless the lack of alarm from passersby signaled to me that this tableau was an unexceptional scene.

Neatly arranged in front of the family were booklets from several hospitals that in China are used to keep records for patient visits. Each hospital sells its own booklet to record a patient's medical history, usually with the name of the hospital on the cover. Patients are required to present their booklet for the doctor to record the details of each visit.[6] Added to this display was a fraying clipping from a local newspaper, identification cards, a sign relating a brief account of their son's illness, and a plastic bucket for donations. Most passersby tended to walk by, glancing in the direction of the family as they entered or exited the shopping complex; none stopped to speak with them. As I lingered over the documentation of their medical case, the father walked over and picked up a booklet to show me his son's diagnosis of leukemia. They had gone to several hospitals, and the recommended treatment was always the same: a bone marrow transplant they could not afford. As the father turned the pages of the booklet to show me the medical history of his son, the mother started crying and began speaking in more detail about their child's condition. Passersby would stop for a few minutes to listen before hurrying off. The mother continued telling the story as the father retreated into the background to give their son his herbal medicine.

They had come from Anhui, one of China's poorer provinces.[7] The boy, now ten, had been diagnosed with leukemia at age seven. He had been enrolled under the health insurance policy at his elementary school, but there was a ninety-day interim period before the coverage was to have taken effect.[8] His illness was discovered after only sixty days from the date of enrollment, so the insurance company refused to cover his medical expenses. The doctors told the family there are three likely causes of the disease: genetic predisposition, exposure to toxic chemicals, or overuse of medications at an early age. Their son had been frequently sick as a young child, and the mother believed that the overuse of the antibiotics used to treat him must have been the primary cause. She blamed the doctors in the countryside for not understanding the consequences of excessive medication (*yaowu guo-liang*) in young children.

They used the money they received from donations to cover food, medication, and hospital visits for blood transfusions every twenty days. Without the transfusions, their son would be unable to move or eat. They had been living on the street ever since he was first diagnosed, even though they were well aware that they were unlikely to collect the 300,000 yuan (approximately US$47,000) for the operation from street donations. The mother stated, "If you do not have money, do not go to the hospital, because if you are short even one penny it is not acceptable. All hospitals are like this." They had been giving their son an imported medication that cost over 100 yuan (approximately US$16) a day, which they were no longer able to afford to do. Altogether they had spent 200,000 yuan (approximately US$31,000) over the past three years on medications and hospital visits. By this point, they were reduced to giving him a less expensive Chinese herbal medication as a "psychological consolation" (*xinli anwei*), even though they felt that the medicine was not as effective. He had no remaining immune defenses, and their living conditions on the street made it difficult to maintain a sterile environment. Once, when the family had eaten at a restaurant, the son suffered from diarrhea. After that, they set up a little portable cookstove to boil his herbal medication and to cook for him. If they had been at home, she would have been able to disinfect everything properly, but this proved to be difficult on the street. People had advised them to abandon their son at a hospital, but they could not bear to do so because he might contract something that would hasten his death. As long as they were with him, they could at least care for him.

When the couple had first decided to bring their son to Beijing, they had abandoned their farmland and sold what few possessions they had. They borrowed heavily from their extended kin network knowing that they would never be able to repay such large sums of money. The provincial government had given them 1,100 yuan (approximately US$170) and the Women's Federation (Fulian) gave them 500 yuan (approximately US$78), but there were no further sources of assistance they could appeal to locally. After arriving in Beijing, the family had tried sitting in front of the Beijing Television station offices in hopes of catching the eye of a journalist or television producer. Being featured on television might have led to viewer donations, but they failed to attract media notice. The mother explained that her husband had thought of jumping off a bridge to get attention for their plight, but she said there still would not have been any guarantee of success, and she would have been left to care for their son by herself. She speculated that if her son's illness had been a case of AIDS or SARS they would have received immediate attention from the health authorities because communicable diseases were a threat to public health.

Having exhausted all other options, the mother explained that their only remaining hope was to mobilize public sympathy or attract media attention so that a hospital might volunteer to help them without payment. She knew of a case of twins with leukemia who had received free treatment after they had been featured on a television program. The mother admitted to me that she knew there were people who lied about medical conditions to swindle money from the public, but she again pointed to their display of documentation as evidence. Returning to Anhui would mean certain death for their son. As long as they remained in Beijing they would have at least a slim chance to save his life. Here they were closer to the city hospitals, and they could still solicit donations on the street to cover some of their costs. Then, in a surprising turn, she mentioned a desire to show their son something of the world before he passed away.

The Spectacle of Dying

Everything that was directly lived has moved away into a representation.

— GUY DEBORD, *SOCIETY OF THE SPECTACLE*

This family's story, filled with details of fighting against the odds, has all the elements of melodrama. Melodrama can have a powerful affective charge, but at the same time it can be easily dismissed as overwrought sentimentalism. Peter Brooks captures the term in all its connotations: "[Melodrama is] the indulgence of strong emotionalism; moral polarization and schematization; extreme states of being, situations, actions; overt villainy, persecution of the good, and final reward of virtue; inflated and extravagant expression; dark plottings, suspense, breathtaking peripety" (1976: 11–12). I extend the scope of melodrama from a literary genre to the representation of life on the street as it is performed by those playing a role already scripted for them in media portrayals of suffering among the weaker segments (*ruoshi qunti*) of society. This form of representation transforms the trials of the everyday in a manner that is not threatening to the established order. The melodramatic elements serve to limit the power of social critique if the story is too intensely personal; yet, it is also the appeal to a shared sentiment on a personal level that makes melodrama highly effective and potentially revolutionary. The side of the street becomes a mise-en-scène. The child's body on the stretcher and the parents' distraught appearance accompanied by their medical documents make the reason for their presence very clear. Melodrama exposes the ethical dilemma in an unmistakable manner. It is its own form of silent cinema where "the melodramatic body is a body seized by meaning. Since melodrama's simple, unadulterated messages must be made absolutely clear, visually present, to the audience, bodies of victims and villains must unambiguously signify their status" (Brooks 1994: 18). However, the parents' attempt to fix the meaning of their son's body is blunted by cautionary tales of scams, bogus claims, and fraudulent stories that thrive in a society where market relations are rapidly supplanting socialist redistributive logics.[9] In this case, there is no obvious villain figure because the systemic violence is obscured from view. So who is responsible for this family's suffering? Neoliberal rationalities of government shift the responsibility for costs and risks onto the individual as the state withdraws from providing social welfare. Thus, the family must bear the responsibility for their own suffering and work to represent themselves as worthy subjects of public compassion.

In Brooks's recounting, melodrama came into being out of the collapse of a clearly ordered social hierarchy caused by the French Revolution. From this historical context he writes that "the traditional imperatives of truth and ethics have been violently thrown into question, yet . . . the promulgation of truth and ethics, their instauration as a way of life, is of immediate, daily, political concern" (Brooks 1976: 15). China's turbulent history and continuous revolutions throughout the twentieth century have led to the upheaval of the social order with lingering historical traumas that the state continues to suppress and manage. The Chinese Communist Party erected a new idealized moral order with the birth of the People's Republic of China, and that project is evolving with the incorporation of economic liberalization policies. Melodrama then is deployed to represent the idealized moral order and the accommodation with that order through easily recognizable characterizations. In China, melodrama and "socialist realism" have been widely used in past revolutionary campaigns by the Chinese Communist Party. Examples of the Soviet-inspired genre can be seen in paintings, woodblock prints, and propaganda posters of the time. Plays performed in this period employed melodramatic elements to clearly communicate the exploitative practices of feudal landlords and the heroic potential of the people in overthrowing feudalism to establish a new social order (Anderson 1990; Andrews 1994).

This melodramatic imagination was also found in Meiji-era literary fiction at a time when Japan was involved in the project of modern nation building. Ken Ito argues that Meiji melodramatic fiction depicted ideological contestations of an old order unraveling as Japanese society modernized. The traditional Japanese family that served as the moral grounding for the nation was under attack:

> If modernity had brought the social dislocations attendant upon industrialization and urbanization, as well as the ideological challenges posed by such new concepts as popular rights, individualism, socialism, then the "traditional" family could be used as a force for order, an institution for the proper location and training of citizens within the national hierarchy. (Ito 2008: 21–22)

Thus, melodrama was used to save the "traditional" family instead of revolutionizing it for a modern society. Portrayals of moral battles between the forces of good and evil in Meiji melodrama were an attempt to validate the "traditional" values believed to be under assault by modern sensibilities. In the case of contemporary Chinese society, the Communist Party revolutionized the gendered and generational hierarchies of the family to pursue a socialist vision. Reform-era biopolitical projects further transformed the family through the one-child family policy.[10] The family of three on the street exposes the vulnerability and costs of having only one child, especially when that child falls ill, but this is not a sufficient moral claim in a society operating on the principles of market reform. Their subject-position (as "beggars") makes their claims open to suspicion.

Melodrama can just as easily serve to uphold the ideological status quo when the goal is to come to some accommodation with everyday trials and tribulations. In this case, the desire for a hospital to donate a bone marrow transplant keeps the social order intact because the resolution does not exceed the ideological parameters of what is permitted. Even the mother in her distraught state did not condemn the government for its failure but extended her sympathy for its overstretched capacities and only wanted the government to provide health care for children. Sacrifice is expected, and they were willing to forgo their home and even their lives to save their child. Would you call this a defeated or willing acceptance of their situation? Or is it the outcome of the material constraints they face and the language they must employ to receive public attention and medical assistance? The political order in contemporary China deploys the techniques of melodrama to transform the readily visible signs of everyday tragedy into moral cues for the people. However, in the fine line between melodrama (potential to act to change the outcome) and tragedy (the outcome has already been determined, and action is after the fact), the failure of the parents to move passersby invites public condemnation for not doing the right thing to save their child. The parents were not in the city to find work; they chose to beg. This gave them more time to care for their son, but their refusal to sell their labor can be viewed as another condition of failure. Their refusal to participate in the market marks them as improper subjects of development in the eyes of the state.[11]

The family on the street must work against being seen as failed subjects of economic development. At the same time, they must fight against what Georg Simmel calls the blasé outlook that is characteristic of mental life in the metropolis:

> The essence of the blasé attitude is indifference toward the distinctions between things. Not in the sense that they are not perceived, as is the case of mental dullness, but rather that the meaning and the value of the distinctions between things, and therewith of the things themselves, are experienced as meaningless. . . . This psychic mood is the correct subjective reflection of a complete money economy to the extent that money takes the place of all the manifoldness of things and expresses all qualitative distinctions between them in the distinction of how much. To the extent that money, with its colourlessness and its indifferent quality, can become a common denominator of all values, it becomes the frightful leveller—it hollows out the core of things, their peculiarities, their specific values and their uniqueness and incomparability in a way which is beyond repair. (Simmel 1950: 14)

This blasé attitude is also combined with suspicion. According to Simmel, a mode of thinking develops in an environment where the density of people and the multitude of external stimulation are overwhelming. The blasé attitude then is a means of self-preservation as well as the outcome of the domination of the money economy. The market reforms have produced "a changing calculus of the value of human life" (Anagnost n.d.). The urban dweller is guarded against any attempt to manipulate his or her emotions. Beggars on the streets are dismissed as calculating actors. The issue at hand is not the authenticity of the family's need but the manner through which suffering and pain are communicated. The social reality that families increasingly cannot afford medical care is a very real phenomenon in China. This is a circumstance that more and more families are experiencing every day. It is also dramatized on television. And yet I heard over and over again from Chinese friends that the people begging on the street are all scam artists, and even the mother acknowledged the existence of frauds as she tried to differentiate her family from them. The mother's mention of the television feature on the twins with leukemia showed that she too is watching television and is informed by social scripts of how the family in need should appear in public in a manner that is convincing. The observed are also doing the observing, responding to the expectations of the audience to give a more convincing performance. The stakes in this performance have very material consequences measured by the money dropped into the plastic bin.

"Life's Little Warrior"

Chengcheng was another ten-year-old child dying of leukemia. After her parents were told by medical specialists that she had only two weeks to live, they decided to return home so that she could continue with school. Chengcheng wrote a poem, "Experiencing the Language of the Heart" (*tihui xinhua*), which she sent to the local newspaper. The wife of the lead singer of the Chengdu pop music group Mix Play convinced the group to set the poem to music. She was impressed that a young girl could have such a deep comprehension of life, and in the news story she was quoted as saying, "The pain of illness led this ten-year-old child to understand a lot prematurely; she has the maturity that her age-mates do not have!" (CCTV 2007). The group arrived at the hospital to teach the song to Chengcheng, and the entire process was recorded and uploaded to Chengcheng's blog.[12] Local university students volunteered to document her struggle through photographs, videos, and entries from her diary. They also designed individual blogs for fifty other child leukemia cases to set up a blog network entitled "Life's Little

Warriors." Her story was eventually nominated as one of the "most moving stories of 2007" by Chinese Central Television (CCTV).[13] The poem was described as capturing "the laughter and tears of her ten-year-old life and to transmit her understanding of life after enduring the torture of illness."

A touching family scene depicted in the story is Chengcheng at home surrounded by her family as she takes her fourth-grade final exam. In the days leading up to the exam date, torrential rains had washed out the dirt paths. In any case, Chengcheng was too ill to attend classes. On the day of the exam, beyond the expectations of her parents, Chengcheng woke up at 5 a.m. to help her little brother prepare for school and help her mother make breakfast before she "stood quietly in the doorway as she watched her brother carry his school bag down the familiar dirt path." Nevertheless, the village teacher walked "10 *li* [five kilometers] on a dirt path against the scorching sun" to deliver the examination paper. The young girl saw her teacher arriving covered in sweat, bowed deeply in appreciation, and went to turn on the electric fan in the corner of the room before she sat down at the family table to write her exam. The newspaper story describes the scene as follows:

> In order to encourage Chengcheng, Teacher Wei sits beside the little young-
> ster, carefully explaining each question. Chengcheng's 80-year-old grandfather
> continues to stand behind her holding a fan in his hand to swat mosquitoes
> away. The father and little brother have also joined in with the grandfather,
> helping Chengcheng by pouring water, looking through the school books.
> The small room of this ordinary rural family is filled with people, but it is
> very quiet, there is only the sound of the teacher's soft voice. At this moment,
> Chengcheng's mother comes out from the kitchen and watches the scene from
> a distance, the corners of her eyes are moist and she says softly, "Happiness is
> having the family together!" (CCTV 2007)

This scene of intense care for a dying girl indicates the value of each child for rural families who are allowed to have a second child only if the first born is a girl, as was the case here. The exam asked for an essay about her favorite animal, but Chengcheng decided to turn the assignment into a letter to the leukemia sufferers she had befriended in the hospital. The article continued with excerpts from her diary detailing the course of her chemotherapy. In one entry she promised not to cry anymore and to correct her "bad behavior" during the transfusions. In another journal entry about the surprise party to celebrate her return to school, she wrote about the "strenuous effort" (*chi li*) entailed to walk to school during the rains and the walk home from school in the afternoon and how her schoolmates would fall into the muddy puddles along the dirt road. The journalists writing her story also made an appearance as she wrote of how they trekked through the dirt path to attend her surprise party at the schoolhouse and then returned to her home to share a family dinner. The story ended with the grandfather carrying Chengcheng on his back to a waiting ambulance on the outskirts of the village because the road was inaccessible to vehicles after days of heavy rain. Finally, we learn that the publicity surrounding Chengcheng's story has led to the local authorities allocating funds to pave the five-kilometer stretch of dirt road.[14]

What is arresting about this story is how the story of Chengcheng's struggle with leukemia was transformed into a public campaign for a paved road. Her story may have been nominated as one of the most moving stories in 2007, but it is certainly not about saving her life. According to a posting on her blog site, she passed away on July 23, 2007. Her death was a given, but the surprise ending that the road will finally be paved meant that their campaign was a success—of a sort. It is difficult not to read this story with some degree of cynicism as an example of how local authorities were using Chengcheng's case to receive economic aid for road construction. This suspicion is analogous to the cynicism of passersby who encounter the family on the street. However, in this case, it is the reader who suspects that this narrative has been deftly framed by local authorities by appropriating her voice, her actions, her intentionality, and her story.

Throughout the story, the mention of the dirt path can be seen to serve many roles in the narrative as well as to highlight the family's poverty and the daily difficulties she faced. The desire for a paved road was again mentioned and even included in her letter to her friends at the hospital. At the end of the letter wishing her friends to be brave in the face of their illness, she closed with, "I feel very happy today, I am at home taking my final exam. Teacher Wei is tutoring me. Finally, many journalists have come to my home; they are all here on behalf of the dirt path in our village; they have worked hard. I really wish that this dirt path would be transformed into an asphalt road. How great would that be!" (CCTV 2007). Nothing can be done for a dying girl because this is, after all, an example of everyday tragedy, but the village can be saved through the building of a road. Public attention is directed not at the inadequacies of the health care system but on how the government construction of roads is the solution to the rural and urban divide. So who is the beneficiary of the media and government attention? Is there any other way to interpret this story as other than a justification for the priorities of the government? Melodrama with its potential for critiquing the social order is appropriated to fall in line with the imperatives of the state. Chengcheng was celebrated as embodying the quality held in high esteem by the Chinese Communist Party: self-sacrifice and service to the nation.

The Spectacle of the Commodity

Nothing happens; this is the everyday.

— MAURICE BLANCHOT, *EVERYDAY SPEECH*

I went back to where I had encountered the family of three in hopes of finding them again, but with no success. To borrow a term from Avery Gordon (1997), everyday life is full of "ghostly matters" haunting social life. There are many possibilities for why they may not have appeared again. It might be that they are no longer allowed to set up at that location by the local authorities. The mother told me that sometimes the security guards would take pity on them and allow them to set up in front of the mall entrance where they can collect more money. Or the son may have died and the parents returned home. Or, perhaps, new security guards chased them away.

My attempt to track them was to find a trace of their existence, their "realness" in an urban landscape that did not recognize their legitimacy to be there. China's economic rise has been marked with the building of showcase cities such as Shanghai, Guangzhou, and Beijing, especially in anticipation for the 2008 Olympics and the 2010 World Expo. What the city has become today is a political stage set with much more sophisticated mobilization campaigns to advance a "socialism with Chinese characteristics" through the promotion of privatization, marketization, and "responsibilization" of the citizen-subject.[15] The family's appearance in this showcase space serves as an unsettling remainder of what has been excluded. With their bodies marked as rural through their clothing, speech, and mode of address, the family is caught within the effacing *signification* of the everyday that indexes

the future of urban life rather than its links to an agrarian past. The parents'
desperate desire to gain attention from the mass media affirms the promise
of this medium to escape the nullifying experience of the everyday, "a visible
negation of life" in the modern world (Debord 1994).

The problem is that there are too many of these stories out there. Their
appearance on the street is a form of protest against the conditions that have
been forced on them. They are refusing to allow their son to die unheralded
in the remote countryside. Yet the parents recounted a narrative of family
tragedy well rehearsed and likely familiar to passersby who have seen similar stories on Chinese television. The labor of publicizing their need must
be entirely taken on by themselves, and, by its very nature, this is a labor
of repetitive iteration, a story that must be told again and again. However,
there is an entire genre of television shows dedicated to telling tales of hardship and moral conflict such as "Ethical Review" (*daode guancha*) or repentant
testimonies by criminals such as "Repentant Record" (*chanhui lu*). In these
stories, if there is a failing, it is on the part of the individual, the family,
or the community, rather than being an institutional or structural failure.
These stories are compelling because they are both exceptional and familiar,
and their tragedy provides a moral lesson to the public that stops short of any
political critique of the system.

Stories of poverty and hardship exist alongside tales of entrepreneurial
success in the expanding market economy. One program on the CCTV agricultural station, called "On the Road to Good Fortune" (*zhi fu lu*), was a
favorite program for a number of my urbanite friends. Each episode documented an industrious peasant who had discovered a new market for produce
or had created useful goods from agricultural products. The freedom to
construct a lifestyle of one's choosing is the new promise of the marketplace
filled with the spectacle of commodities. Jing Wang's discussion of the government promotion of leisure culture in the mid-1990s provides an example
of how the state reinvents itself as the protector of the right to "free" access
to the market as the primary constitutive right of modern citizenship in a
postsocialist state (Wang 2001a; 2001b). However, the sensibility honed by
living in a "consumer revolution" (Davis 2000) is also increasingly perme-
ated by suspicion of self-serving neighbors, the dehumanizing marketplace,
and corrupt officials. A recognizable socialist system is receding from view,
and what is left is literally smoke from polluting factories and the mirrored
surfaces of shopping high-rises reflecting a shimmering vision of the modern

world. The social security represented in the "iron rice bowl" of the state-owned enterprise is usurped by the commodity form. As the experience of daily life becomes increasingly dominated by commodities, the banal embodied in the everyday takes on monumental importance and needs to be examined in the context of a greater spectacle of state-sponsored development.

As Guy Debord argues, the spectacle serves to justify the dominant mode of capitalist production by obscuring the social relations of production: "The spectacle is the acme of ideology, for in its full flower it exposes and manifests the essence of all ideological systems: the impoverishment, enslavement and negation of real life. Materially, the spectacle is 'the expression of estrangement, of alienation between man and man'" (Debord 1994: 151). Spectacle and distraction depoliticize the social sphere and direct public attention to the realm of the private car, the private home, and a private life. However, it is exactly private life that has become the terrain of politics. The increasing sequestration of politics in the domain of the personal is at the core of neoliberal governmentality. The Beijing Life Channel is a prime example of how the governance of personal life has expanded into a daily lineup of shows such as: "Facing Life," "Healthy Life," "Life Is Beautiful," "Happy Life," "Seven Days," "Can I Help You?", "I Love My Car," "Fashion Circles," "Charm Front," "Clever Secrets," "Big City/Little Stories," and "Fill the World with Love."[16] Programs of this nature represent consumer liberation as a democratic revolution. Consumer choice and rights are the new rallying agenda for the public and the government.

Televisual reenactments of daily concerns expose moral stakes in everyday actions. Therefore, the shows that dole out tips on cooking, home décor, and fashion on the Beijing Life Channel are broadcasting the virtues of providing for family, working hard to afford a comfortable home, and consuming appropriately to express one's standing in life. Social standing is increasingly expressed through consumption practices that validate one's place in the world (Bourdieu 1984; Ren, Chapter One in this volume). However, the family on the street lacks the means to become the valorized consumers of the new economy, and they are trying to resuscitate a subject position from which they can legitimately speak about their suffering. The new registers of public recognition dismiss the specters of failed subjects as part of the everyday marginalia undeserving of attention. The family is seeking transcendence from banality to consequentiality bestowed through the media.

The identification cards displayed by the parents not only substantiate their claims to authenticity but also express a desire to be anonymous no longer.

In a media environment already saturated with the spectacle of commodities and state propaganda, the misfortune of a dying son is not spectacular enough to attract any particular notice from an audience already numbed by "compassion fatigue." According to Susan Moeller, "compassion fatigue" comes from the way the media covers crises so that the viewer feels "overstimulated and bored all at once" (1999: 9). For example, in the coverage of famines in Africa over the past two decades, Moeller states, "The problem with famines . . . is that they just are not considered newsworthy until the dying begins" (1999: 13). The stories begin to sound alike with their redundant images and well-trodden scripts so that "once the parameters of a news story have been established, the coverage lapses into formula. . . . Formulaic coverage of similar types of crises makes us feel that we really *have* seen this story before. We've seen the same pictures, heard about the same victims, heroes and villains, read the same morality play" (1999: 13). This leads to even more sensational reporting to elicit sympathy from viewers. If the story is not gruesome enough, then it is not worth reporting, even though the stories that do get reported follow a familiar formula so that it is "déjà vu all over again." And that is truly the tragic dimension of the family on the street: They are the background noise of the radio or television program that saturates daily life but does not penetrate the consciousness of the listener or viewer. As Maurice Blanchot suggests, "The everyday loses any power to reach us; it is no longer what is lived, but what can be seen or what shows itself, spectacle and description, without any active relation whatsoever" (1987: 14). The distracted consumption of news media and the casual glance of the observer on the street are both manifestations of everyday indifference.

Morality Tales

The appearance of families and individuals seeking charity on urban sidewalks is illustrative of structural inequalities, but these people are ultimately *not disruptive* of the social order. In fact, both stories of dying children traffic in a "society of spectacle" (Debord 1994). Both narrate the resilience of the family in the face of tragic odds. The difference between them is that Chengcheng's story becomes tied to a vision of economic growth through media exposure, whereas the story of the family in Beijing is part of the everyday ephemera that quickly pass out of sight, a "ghostly matter." Both of them register in different ways the changing relationship between the city and the country. The economic policies of the state have led to what Yan Hairong calls the "spectralization of the countryside" in which the countryside has been negated as a place to build a viable life.[17]

Instead of class-based mass mobilization campaigns reminiscent of the Mao era, we see campaigns that are exemplary of liberal techniques of governance, such as the exhortations to build "a harmonious society."[18] The personal narrative lies at the heart of what Nikolas Rose (1996) has called enterprise culture. These narratives are fundamentally different from the "speaking bitterness" (*suku*) narratives used to raise class awareness of exploitation during the Maoist era. The development of the self lies at the heart of opportunities made possible by the economic liberalization policies. The structure of personal narrative tells of the individual's responsibility to overcome poverty, and this narrative allows each individual to insert his or her own glorious ending or moral failing (see Yan, Chapter Six in this volume). The narrative structure is a political technology at the level of the personal. These stories structure the boundaries of the public imaginary and motivate individuals to serve the nation while simultaneously achieving personal wealth (Kohrman 2003).

We can easily identify the spaces for celebration of the economic miracle, but how does the current social order make a space for the expression of pain, suffering, and dying? Is there a way to speak about suffering that is divorced from the state script of moral failing? Modernity has meant the adoption of a logic that embraces technology and a rationality of enterprise that makes life a continuous project (Farquhar and Zhang 2005). The extension of this logic is evident in macrolevel development policies and is also experienced individually in the atomistic realm of the everyday. While reminiscent of speaking bitterness in their evocation of pathos, the social scripts today follow a different trajectory for the Chinese nation but still employ the spectacularization of the suffering body. The encouragement to speak of past bitterness was a means to remember a past that was prior to the establishment of the People's Republic of China, and these testimonials were used to legitimate the power of the ruling party state (see Anagnost 1997). Speaking bitterness narratives in the postreform era invokes another (socialist) past to embrace how good life is *now* under market reform.

However, the market reforms have also produced new kinds of inequality. With the privatization of health care, medical attention requires money. The parents on the street were willing to use any means possible to raise money for their son's treatment. What was not being communicated in the performance of their story was their acceptance of their son's imminent death. To communicate that would be futile because the ending to their story is already obvious to passersby. Anyone living in China today is aware of the uneven conditions of the health care system and the stark reality of illness and poverty. Although the parents may well understand fully the futility of their situation, their stubborn determination to show their son something of the world before he passes away suggests a yearning on their part to give him a meaningful life. The Chinese herbal medicine they gave him was not merely to alleviate his suffering but also to alleviate the emotional pain caused by their inability to provide him with the care he needed. It was an anodyne for their failure. The underlying pathos to this story is that hope and aspiration are believed to be located only in the city, while the countryside has been drained of all that makes a life worth living in China. This sentiment was echoed in Chengcheng's appeal to bring the village a road that will serve as a link to the city and thus to prosperity.

Chengcheng's melodrama moves audiences with emotional appeals to participate in a charitable campaign that they know in the end to be an exceptional response to a specific case rather than a systematic resolution to a structural inequality. Melodrama may well be "the principal mode for uncovering, demonstrating, and making operative the essential moral universe in a post-sacred era" (Brooks 1976: 15), but the use of melodrama in this case focuses so intently on the individual, private, and banal that we begin to lose sight of "the political" and "the moral." This orientation does several things to the experience of the everyday. It evacuates it of any sense of history and thus diminishes the importance of the everyday as a site for political signification. The lack of historicity to this everyday story enables it to be portrayed as a tragedy on a singular scale rather than a public illustration of slow death for rural families. This type of individualized medical emergency requires a systemic response that is qualitatively different than the exceptional moments of humanitarian crisis or catastrophe when medical aid and rescue arrive into an underserved region, as happened with the devastating earthquakes in Sichuan in May 2008 and again in the primarily Tibetan area of Qinghai in April 2010. The Chinese government in times of natural disasters can exercise its sovereignty in a grand spectacle by prohibiting international aid agencies from entering the afflicted region.[19] However, emergency aid is not a substitute for systemic change. The ability of the Chinese government to mobilize resources in instances of highly visible "emergency" thus highlights a failure of political will in meeting the everyday medical needs of those who do not have the means of purchasing access.

Encountering Anthropology

The case of the family on the street offers an occasion to contemplate what anthropologist Kathleen Stewart calls "ordinary affects"—that is, "public feelings that begin and end in broad circulation, but they're also the stuff that seemingly intimate lives are made of" (2007: 2). In other words, these are the intensities and banalities of fleeting encounters, fragmented moments, little pleasures, partial exchanges, glimpsed events, sad episodes, and funny or unnerving scenes that constitute everyday experience. For Stewart, "ordinary affects" are dense with possibility, potential, and insights into social existence. I saw this family only once, yet their situation serves to illuminate serious questions about the direction of development in China and the human costs of a neoliberal vision of society. Why is this story not considered newsworthy enough?

Václav Havel recounts a story about his friend with asthma who was having difficulty breathing because he was imprisoned with smokers: "Newspapers need a story. Asthma is not a story. Death could make it one . . . we are unworthy of attention because we have no stories, and no death. We have only asthma. And why should anyone be interested in listening to our cough?"[20] For Havel, the story and its open-ended potential have been obliterated under totalitarianism because history is overcome by ideology. Humans experience life through stories, but under totalitarianism there is no longer potential for stories because history has already been determined by one source of truth and power. In Havel's story, the asthmatic friend is a metonym for Czechoslovakia. The attention and interest the Czech nation fails to receive from the world community is due to the fact that it is not a place of warfare and senseless murder—the stuff that is newsworthy. The killing here happens more systematically and slowly through a daily dulling of the senses and the human will. I cannot help but see resonances to the father's idea to commit a spectacular suicide to attract attention to his son slowly dying on the street.

Of course, China is not the Czechoslovakia described by Havel prior to the end of the Cold War. Beyond the obvious dissimilarities, the Chinese state has ushered in economic plurality with the introduction of markets. For Havel, the suppression of economic activity under a totalitarian system led to an environment in which citizens "can no longer participate with relative autonomy in economic life, man loses some of his social and human individuality, and part of his hope of creating his own human story" (1992: 342). On the contrary, in China stories abound of entrepreneurial citizens getting wealthy and creating their "own human story." This family, too, is free to come to the city to seek assistance and collect money. Nonetheless, these stories retain a similar moral structure precisely because what is acknowledged is not a "plurality of truths, of logics, of agents of decisions, and of manners of behavior" (Havel 1992: 332) inherent in the story but a central logic of behavior that is continually prescribed and reenacted in each variation of the same story. Is life in China now any more open ended than it was in Czechoslovakia, or are subjects bound in fact by the very promise of freedom to take responsibility for themselves? Freedom in itself may in fact be no less a mode of subjection inherent to a neoliberal ethos (Read 2009).

If this story is not worthy of media attention, it is worthy of anthropological attention in its potential to capture social phenomena in all their complexity. Kathleen Stewart argues that everyday ephemera illuminate the potential for an alternative politics. The family on the street is making a life in a complex social and symbolic field. In that sense, this story is relevant and representative of the various tactics people employ to get by each day. But even more important, it offers the possibility of seeing how more abstract processes become registered in the experience of everyday life. The fact that I came on this family and not another is inconsequential. The ephemerality of the encounter is exactly what gives stories such as this their open-ended potential. This is my attempt to write a ghost story and "strive to understand the conditions under which a memory was produced in the first place, toward a countermemory, for the future" (Gordon 1997: 22).

In the shift from the Maoist to the post-Maoist era, health care facilities have advanced and expanded primarily in the cities, but access and affordability remains problematic for impoverished families. In response to the growing rural and urban divide, this family is being resourceful in their strategies to seek medical assistance. Their performance on the street is a negotiation of the market sensibilities that now permeate everyday life. In their calculation, their chances on the streets of Beijing are better than they would be if they remained in the countryside where the odds are even more dismal. The promise of basic universal coverage sometime in the future is a hopeful sign, but the reforms may still not fully serve to rectify the growing social disparities. By appealing to public compassion, these families and individuals on the street are acknowledging the shift from government responsibility for social welfare to citizen responsibility and responding to that transformation with their own enterprising practices.

Notes

ACKNOWLEDGMENTS

The Blakemore Freeman Foundation Fellowship provided advanced language training from 2004 to 2005, and a Fulbright-Hays Doctoral Dissertation Research Abroad Fellowship and University of Washington Jackson School Chester Fritz China Studies Fellowship provided dissertation research support from 2005 through 2007. A Simpson Center Society of Scholars Fellowship at the University of Washington provided writing support. Chris Brown, Jennifer Leehey, and Leila Sievanen read earlier versions of this chapter and offered valuable comments. Ann Anagnost, Steve Harrell, Lorna Rhodes, and Janelle Taylor also provided constructive feedback. I thank the anonymous reviewers for Stanford University Press for their suggestions on revisions and Ann Anagnost for her editorial encouragement.

    1. Li Zhang (2001, 2002) has written about rural migrants and the politics of space in urban China. Elsewhere, I examine another group of migrants to Beijing, petitioners at the Ministry of Health, seeking adjudication for medical malpractice cases (Ta 2011).

    2. With the dismantling of the Rural Cooperative Medical System in the 1980s, the cost of medical care shifted to individual families. In late 2002, the central government introduced the New Rural Cooperative Medical Scheme, but participation was voluntary, and each enrolled rural resident was asked to pay 10 to 20 yuan (approximately US$1.50 to US$3.00) annually with matching funds coming from central and local government. The high deductibles, miniscule matching

funds from the government, and voluntary basis of the programs failed to provide adequate coverage. Commercial health insurance became the only available coverage with the collapse of the cooperatives. The government neglect of health care created increasing anxiety as risks to health were growing due to environmental degradation, the deteriorating relationships between patients and doctors, skyrocketing medical costs, and the commercialization of the health care industry, resulting in disparities in rural and urban medical infrastructure. In April 2009, the Chinese government unveiled plans to overhaul the health care system. Details of the plan to offer universal coverage and restructure the medical system can be found at http://english.people.com.cn/90001/90782/90880/6634394.html ("New Healthcare Reform Plan" 2009). The first phase (2009 through 2011) allocates funds to expand medical insurance coverage to 90 percent of the population; build more village-, township-, and county-level health stations, clinics, and hospitals; lower the cost of commonly used medicines; increase the number of trained health practitioners; and implement a pilot program to reform public hospitals. The reform of the health care system aims to provide basic universal health care coverage for all citizens by 2020. Additional reforms include the regulation of pharmaceutical companies, increased monitoring of medical institutions, the implementation of an essential drug-pricing scheme, and the expansion of public health services to improve preventive care.

3. Prior to the Olympics, national and local television stations aired human interest stories showing Chinese citizens learning English, redecorating their homes with Olympic memorabilia, and making their neighborhoods more welcoming for international visitors. I was living in Beijing during the period of intense construction to widen roads and build the now iconic structures in the National Olympic Park. The ideograph *chai* ("tear down" or "demolish") was painted on structures lining the streets surrounding the Park. Government efforts ranged from the temporary shutdown of polluting factories to seeding the sky to ensure rainfall to cleanse the air pollution, building new public transportation routes, and even editing Chinese menus translated into English. The reengineering of Beijing included the construction of elaborate shopping malls to attract upwardly mobile Chinese middle-class consumers. Michael Dutton argues, "In this new economy of the eye, the first task is destruction. Shopping centres are transformed from factory-style distribution points into enchanting, seductive feasts for the eye and the wallet. In the process, everything is made 'for sale'" (1998: 223). For Dutton, the changing landscape is a reflection of the changing social mentalities of the market economy. The market sensibilities that he traces on Chinese streets illustrate how neoliberal governance technologies work in a Chinese state of surveillance to patrol the movement and livelihood of citizens.

4. In a speech on June 30, 1984, entitled, "Building a Socialism with a Specifically Chinese Character," Deng Xiaoping defined it as "a socialism that is tailored to Chinese conditions and has a specifically Chinese character." Deng was

sketching out an economic system that adhered to Marxism and would focus on developing what he called the "productive forces" in China. It would be a socialism that was adapted to the specific historical conditions and strategic needs of the Chinese people. Government policies would expand the economy through the incorporation of some market principles to offer a unique strain of "socialism with Chinese characteristics." An English translation of the speech can be found at http://english.peopledaily.com.cn/dengxp/vol3/text/c1220.html (Deng 1984). A definition of the concept is also available from the Seventeenth National Congress of the Communist Party held in 2007 under "Socialism with Chinese Characteristics" on the *People's Daily Online* site at http://english.peopledaily.com.cn/90002/92169/92211/6275043.html.

5. The streets of Beijing are indeed a continuous spectacle, and this is most apparent in this high-tech district, otherwise known as "China's Silicon Valley." The area has recently filled with metal and glass high-rises that house international software companies, high-tech businesses, and one of the most famous English language training centers in China. There are several multilevel plazas selling electronics and high-tech gadgets. The streets are lined with advertisements, and a new underground and pedestrian mall opened in the beginning of 2007. Down the wide avenue are two of China's most prestigious academic institutions, Beijing University and Tsinghua University. This is a bustling district with a constant traffic of cars and pedestrians.

6. Some of the booklets sold by bigger hospitals actually contain advertisements for pharmaceuticals on the front and back cover and inside the booklet itself.

7. Anhui is one of the poorer rural provinces, where the sale of blood to unsanitary collectors led to the spread of the HIV virus. The government distribution of HIV medication has been haphazard due to the poor medical and bureaucratic infrastructures. Rural clinics provide only basic primary care and mostly serve as a dispensary for medicines. The boy's mother told me that she distrusted the medical practitioners at the rural clinics after her son was diagnosed with leukemia. Rural families with financial resources travel to the closest urban hospital that can provide diagnosis and treatment for more serious diseases. See Adams, Erwin, and Le 2009; Anagnost 2006; Erwin 2006; Gao 2005; Li Dun 2004; Shao 2006; and Zhongguo xinwen zhoukan 2005 for discussions of the vulnerability of the medical system and compromised safety of the blood supply in hospitals.

8. I am uncertain if the mother was referring to enrollment in a pilot community-based health insurance program, which would have been introduced around the time he was diagnosed, or a commercial insurance plan available through the school. The parents did not share these details with me. Currently, the medical insurance system remains a patchwork system where citizens can purchase private insurance to supplement a range of government coverage depending on household registration status.

9. Media reports highlight the criminal activities of indigents and warn citizens to not encourage their solicitations on the streets. Warned to be wary, urban citizens are suspicious of any sort of appeals.

10. See Susan Greenhalgh and Edwin A. Winckler 2005, for a history of family planning policies, including the one-child policy.

11. See Hoffman 2006. Under the early socialist system, university graduates were assigned jobs on graduation. Students must now enter the labor market, and this entails the acquisition of a new skill set of "professionalism" that follows a neoliberal prescription for self-development.

12. Chengcheng's blog can be found at http://blog.sina.com.cn/dongpengchengxzs.

13. See the story at http://finance.cctv.com/special/C19961/20071127/107110 .shtml; retrieved on December 26, 2007.

14. The story did not specify as to the specific level of government office making this promise. It was likely to be local government, but whether they received funding from higher levels for this purpose is not mentioned.

15. *Responsibilization* is a neologism that refers to a repertoire of programs and logics that espouses self-management, self-discipline, and increasing levels of individual responsibility in all matters of life as the government rolls back social welfare provisions. It is part of a neoliberal guiding principle to actively encourage individuals to be more involved in self-government through "the generalization of an 'enterprise form' to *all* forms of conduct" serving to redefine the role of government as one of securing the grounds for the rational, free individual to conduct the business of life (Burchell 1996). For further discussion of neoliberal notions of individual autonomy as a technique of government in advanced industrial Western societies, see Foucault 1988; Gordon 1991; and Miller and Rose 1990.

16. The programming contains cooking tips, household cleaning advice, fashion advice, and purchasing advice for a myriad of commodities. The mission statement of the channel is:

> 2007 BTV Life Channel pays close attention to the people's clothing, food, shelter, and travels, wholeheartedly serving as the people's life consultant. Guiding on fashionable trends, elevating consumption tastes; life everywhere is wonderful, there is no place without entertainment; spreading the concept of public good, shouting out compassionate contribution, adhering to carry forward a compassionate spirit, promoting compassionate causes. We understand life, we happily serve, life channel, making life more beautiful. 2007, love life, love life channel.

See www.btv.com.cn/btvweb/07btv7/node_2750.htm.

17. See Yan 2003. She borrows this phrase from Spivak 1988.

18. The term *harmonious society* (*hexie shehui*) refers to policy guidelines endorsed by President Hu Jintao in 2006 for the establishment of a harmonious so-

cialist society by 2020. Issues such as rural infrastructure, health care, housing, education, employment, the environment, the urban–rural wealth gap, corruption, and legal reform are included in an agenda to address the growing social disparities, unfair land seizures for property development, and environmental degradation. This focus on socially sustainable growth comes after decades of intense economic development since the late 1970s. An English translation of the full text of the Communiqué of the Sixth Plenum of the Sixteenth Central Committee of the Communist Party of China (2006) can be found at www.chinese-embassy.org.uk/eng//zyxw/t279526.htm.

19. The refusal of international aid as an assertion of sovereignty may be clarified by Peter Redfield's analysis of the political dilemmas of such work. Humanitarian aid organizations like Médecins san frontières operate in a state of "rupture" precipitated by natural and political disasters. "Their ethical position centers around an 'ethic of refusal' that resists the cleansing of moral failure on any part" (Redfield 2005: 336). According to Redfield, this tense stance reflects the group's attempt to reach some accommodation between their humanitarian mission and their practice of political witnessing and action.

20. I first encountered this analogy to asthma in Leehey 2010, where she uses Václav Havel's mention of his friend with asthma to speak about the oppressive condition of censorship under the military dictatorship in Burma (Myanmar).

Chapter Four

On Their Own
Becoming Cosmopolitan Subjects
beyond College in South Korea

NANCY ABELMANN, SO JIN PARK,
AND HYUNHEE KIM

We met Heejin, a student at Koryŏ University, one of South Korea's top-tier private schools, in the summer of 2003 and again in summer 2004. Every time we met she sported a baseball cap and sweats. We were struck by her boyish voice, androgynous look, unselfconscious mannerisms, spontaneous laughter, and high energy. Heejin compared her carefree style with that of her best friend in high school who ended up at a women's college and had transformed herself into a stylish and feminine woman who spent lots of money on shopping and body care. Heejin sketched a contrast between her friend's narrow college life focused on consumption and her own more gregarious, masculine, and vital mode of being. Strolling with her across campus revealed her popularity and her social ease. Conversations shed light on her cosmopolitan interests in being comfortable in the world at large.

As a graduate of a special-purpose high school (with a focus on foreign languages), Heejin was upset that South Korean President Roh Moo-hyun had threatened—in the name of equality of opportunity—to repeal the policy of assigning extra points on the entrance exam to graduates of these competitive schools.[1] Heejin called it "a policy to undermine students with high standards" and spoke of her entitlement: "I worked twice as hard as others to enter that school and twice as hard to stay there." For Heejin, successful entrance to Koryŏ University had particular meaning because her squarely middle-class parents had insisted that if she could not enter a top-tier coeducational college then she should attend a top-rated women's school.[2] She had, thus, succeeded in avoiding a feminized space.

In 2003, we walked away from our meeting with Heejin with one phrase still ringing: "self-management" (*chagi kwalli*). We had been surprised to hear the phrase used so directly and to hear so many other students offering similar narratives of what it takes to succeed in a transformed South Korea. In this chapter we argue that college students inhabit new discourses of human development in the context of South Korea's neoliberal turn and globalization. In addition to Heejin, we introduce three others from mid-tier colleges. While all four of these students aspire to and accept the burden of managing their personal formation for a changing world, we argue that the burden of self-development is borne variously, according to differences in the "brand capital" of the students' universities, gender, and family background.

Contemporary college students in South Korea are envisioning human development, particularly their own maturation, in ways that are dramatically transformed in a time of globalization. These newly emerging subjectivities highlight personal ability, style, and responsibility and work to obscure escalating structural inequality in South Korea, reflecting neoliberal trends in South Korea and in the larger world. Although inequalities have long been framed in South Korea by discourses of personal effort and triumph over personal circumstances, what is new are ideas of self-styling beyond formal schooling and notions of personal character formation that extend beyond long-standing South Korean measures of effort and hard work. More specifically, the emergence of this shift must be understood in the temporal context of South Korea's postauthoritarian liberalization (that is, the call for personal freedoms) and its IMF-era neoliberalization. These emergent subjectivities and structural inequality must be viewed through the lens of South Korea's highly stratified higher education system in which college ranking is significantly correlated with real returns on educational capital (Seth 2002). Although education stratification is long-standing in South Korea, the rapid embrace of neoliberal restructuring and globalization by the education sector has accentuated differences in the brand capital of universities.[3] Central to that brand capital is globalization itself, namely universities' differential ability to go global (for example, through opportunities to study abroad or English-language courses). Although students attending South Korea's upper-tier colleges benefit from the prestige of their universities, those at lower-tier schools feel the burden of taking on the project of developing their human capital value on their own. However, this burden is borne in ways that are notably inflected by gender. Our research demonstrates that the feminine is imagined to be domestic (in both senses of that word): limited and limiting in direct contrast with masculine images of free circulation on a global stage.[4]

We use neoliberal subjectivity to index personal characteristics and proclivities that embrace the pursuit of active, vital, and cosmopolitan lives. This constellation of attributes as neoliberal agrees with many scholars who argue that changed economic and political formations across the globe have led to powerful changes in ideas about desirable or required ways of being. More specifically, this literature examines the articulation of personal formation with, for example, the flexibilization of labor, the demise of job security, and the retrenchment of both state and corporate support for social welfare. For South Korea, these personal features distinguish this generation from earlier generations of college students. Today's college students are committed to becoming vital—people who lead active and enjoyable lives, people who live hard and play hard and who aim to experience the world to its fullest. Students are aware, however, that these are more than just matters of style and pleasure. They realize that this new mode of being is a requirement for leading a productive life in a rapidly transforming and globalizing world. A feature of this discourse on human development is its explicit understanding of what it takes to succeed in the contemporary economy. That the *work* of embracing these new ideals can be onerous is, therefore, not unrecognized by students. At the time of our research, we noted a shared optimism among our interlocutors in their willingness to embrace this developmental narrative. In hindsight, some of this optimism may be waning as employment prospects grow ever bleaker and South Korea enters into an era of global fatigue, in which the call for the global has perhaps become so saturated as to lose all meaning.

Nonetheless, this new generation distinguishes itself from the hardworking model students of an earlier generation who were driven by familial pressures to achieve in the highly regimented discipline of formal schooling through the well-recognized education management of their families (especially their mothers). Today's successful student must necessarily be more than simply a hard-working social conformist: He or she must be a self-starter. The new generation also sees itself as different from student movement activists who, although not model students, conformed to another sort of collectivistic pressure. Both of these earlier groups, then, are imagined as collectivist subjects driven by the external demands of families or their cohort group. In differentiating themselves from the past, contemporary students articulate a discourse of individuality, style, and self-fashioning. Additionally, the scope of this new persona extends beyond South Korea in an age of radical liberalization and the globalization of all forms of capital. Competition does not end at the boundaries of the state. Thus, the present college generation is deeply committed to a cosmopolitan ideal in which people are able to circulate in a wider and increasingly global arena. At the heart of this personal development project is English mastery, and many students described English as a necessary base (*beisŭ*) (Park and Abelmann 2004; see also Crystal 2003).

In some senses, the lives of the students today are not so radically different from student cohorts in the past. Personal development of the educated in South Korea has long demanded considerable individual energy and vitality. Family and other collectivities continue to assert considerable pressure on students; indeed, it can be argued that neoliberalization in South Korea—particularly in the form of the repeal of employee benefits and state social support—has even led to new formations of familism, namely the ideology of family as the locus of support and social welfare. However, people narrate and take responsibility for their circumstances and predicaments in ways that are quite new. Thus this generation's self-understanding and modes of narration must be situated at the juncture of neoliberal social, economic, and educational reforms in South Korea today.

Although we cannot claim that the four students we discuss in the following pages perfectly represent a generation at large, we were struck by the consistency of their narratives about self-development.[5] We do not argue that college rank, class, and gender would articulate with the new forms of subjectivity in the same manner for every young person; however, we do think that they articulate in ways that are revealing. It is in this spirit that we linger on these four narratives to examine the variable modes of articulation in more detail and to preserve the dialogic quality of their expression.

The IMF Crisis and South Korea's Neoliberal Turn

This generation of students spent their childhood in an increasingly prosperous and democratic South Korea. In their early or late adolescence, however, they experienced the IMF crisis (1997 through 2001). This crisis marked a period of economic uncertainty leading to a broad array of social and policy reforms that were neoliberal in character. South Korea's neoliberal turn involved a critique of crony capitalism and led to the call for venture capitalism in a deregulated market. Creative, global, high-tech youth were critical to this reform project (Song 2003).

Intensified privatization, individuation, and globalization are the large context for the transformations of subjectivity we write of here.[6] Increasingly, neoliberal subjecthood demands that individuals become self-managers who "produce [themselves] as having the skills and qualities necessary to succeed" (Walkerdine 2003: 240). Yan Hairong (2003) coins the term *neohumanism* to describe, after Marx, how human exchange value in China today has extended to subjectivity. Specifically, she analyses the Chinese construct of *suzhi* (quality) as follows: "*Suzhi* is the concept of human capital given a neoliberal spin to exceed its original meaning of stored value of education and education-based qualifications to mean the capitalization of subjectivity itself" (2003: 511).[7] Of course, post-IMF South Korea and market-reform-era China represent entirely distinct historical configurations, but the neoliberal spin Yan describes is one that perhaps unites youth worldwide (see Comaroff and Comaroff 2000: 307).

Similar to other structural transformations imposed by external governing bodies, the IMF crisis forced the South Korean state and the corporate sector to become leaner and meaner. Unemployment skyrocketed in the immediate aftermath of the crisis. With radical corporate and banking restructuring as well as escalating transnational investment in the South Korean corporate sector, labor had to become increasingly flexible (Shin 2000). Today's youth face a transformed South Korean economy in which full-time, secure employment is harder to procure, state and local protections and services are curtailed, the reproduction of the middle class is fraught with uncertainty, and the vagaries of transnational capital figure profoundly. These students face a reality that is ever more vulnerable and precarious, just as new models of personhood proclaim personal responsibility and authorship for one's economic and general wellbeing. Ironically, however, their deep-seated embrace of these new narratives of personhood appear blind to the structural transformations that have fashioned these new subjectivities.

Furthermore, in a South Korea that is becoming increasingly class strati-fied or, as many have argued, polarized, we are particularly interested in how students do or do not take stock of their structural positions, which are registered here through college ranking.[8] For South Korea and other recently democratized states, the trappings of neoliberal personhood are particularly appealing because they stand for liberal democratic reform in which people can enjoy self-authorship, personal freedom, and self-styled consumption (see Song 2003; 2006). Thus the ironic meeting of neoliberal and postauthoritarian/collective liberal "individuals" is such that young South Koreans can unabashedly celebrate what might otherwise appear to be so nakedly pernicious (Song 2003 and Chapter Ten in this volume). As neoliberal transformations are easily celebrated in the name of liberal values, so too are particular features of the authoritarian developmental-ist education system, especially its egalitarian ideology and standardization, which are now dismissed as backward historical burdens (Park 2006).[9]

South Korean higher education, along with South Korean mainstream K–12 education, has long been driven by social demand. In earlier decades, this was for equal access, and more recently, for neoliberal reforms, namely deregulation, privatization, diversification, and globalization. Although some charge that the state continues to lag behind consumer demand (*Hankook Ilbo* 2004; D. Lee 2004), South Korea today offers a case of state-managed deregulation of higher education in accordance with neoliberal values of ef-ficient self-management, productivity and excellence, diversification, and global competition (Mok and Welch 2003; Mok, Yoon, and Welch 2003; Or-ganisation for Economic Co-operation and Development [OECD] 2000).[10] In other words, although neoliberal reforms have been accelerated by social demand and global pressures in the aftermath of the IMF Crisis, as Mok and his coauthors (2003) argue, they have also been highly orchestrated by the South Korean state.

The new model student is an autonomous student-consumer who is re-sponsible for managing his or her own lifelong creative capital development.[11] South Korea's elite university students have benefited most from the govern-ment distribution of national resources through the selective state support of higher education. Their coeducational campuses most deeply enact the new global human capital development that these students are well able to articulate.

This is the historical context in which contemporary college students are able to narrate their human capital development while obscuring the structural workings of college rank and family capital. The self-focused narration of this new generation works against a more broadly social imagination because it celebrates individuals who do not conform to collectivist demands. We are intrigued to find young champions of flexibility when it is flexible labor structures that jeopardize the secure futures of young people and, in particular, young women. This meeting of liberal and neoliberal values—precisely to the extent that flexible labor appears to speak to personal freedom—thus champions endless reinvention and frequent career changes. Indeed, a number of students we interviewed, particularly women, looked forward to flexible work lives in which they will be able to exercise their creativity, grow, and accrue experience. We were struck by the absence of talk about the gendered constraints in this new labor market and the burden flexibility imposes on women.

This "more radically individuated sense of personhood" (Comaroff and Comaroff 2000: 305) thus obscures class and other structural differences. In the words of our interlocutors, the "machinelike" (*kigye kat'ǔn*) students—the previous generation of model students who lived "as they were directed to live" (*sik'inǔn taero*)—were, ironically, better poised to recognize the structures that constrained their futures. The burden today of "living as one wants" (*hago sip'ǔn taero*) renders invisible the forces that impinge on one's choices in life.

We now introduce four students in greater detail: Heejin from Koryŏ University, a top-tier private school, and the others from lower-tier schools: one from Myŏngji University in Seoul and two from Inch'ŏn City University outside of Seoul. The designation of university level is complicated. For example, it is hard to put any university in Seoul on a par with those outside of the city and even more so with those in the provinces (*chibang*). Inch'ŏn City University, which is located in a city not far from Seoul, is somewhat betwixt and between because it is neither a Seoul school nor a provincial one. Although Heejin busily distinguishes herself even from her own top-tier university peers, she is nonetheless deeply invested in her university's reputation for vitality and excellence and the status it confers on her—her campus capital. The students from Myŏngji and Inch'ŏn, on the other hand, articulate their projects of self-development against the grain of their campuses. Precisely because their campuses are not easily identified with these neoliberal modes of being, they understand that they must shoulder the burden of their own human development. They thus articulate a vision of how to make the most of their college studies.

An Elite College Student

It is the feeling of *energy*, the motivation to continuously do something.

We return to the Koryŏ University student with whom we opened this chapter and her thoughts on "self-management." Heejin dwelled on self-management as a way of distinguishing herself from her close associates during her *chaesu* year, the year after high school when some students study to retake the college entrance exams to ensure college admission or upgrade their eligibility for more elite schools:

> I probably shouldn't say this, but those of us here are at this level [and she motioned as if to include the campus around us]. Our society is led by people at this higher level. . . . Frankly speaking, among my friends from my *chaesu* year [that is, those who attended the same college preparation institute], I am the only one who got in here. Don't get me wrong. I'm not saying they are bad. They all go to provincial colleges or . . . We all used to hang out together, but when we parted at 1 a.m. I would go home and study until 3 a.m. before I went to bed. They just went to bed because they were tired. *So it was all about self-management.* . . . It isn't that I look down on them. If I were to talk to them like this, they would think I was a different person. But I talk to them only about fun stuff. . . . I have friends whom I hang out with, friends I study with, and friends I consult with about the future. [emphasis added]

When we met Heejin a year later in her sophomore year, her position on self-management had hardened. Koryŏ University, she said unabashedly, was an elite school that should stand, metonymically, for students like herself: self-managers invested in the kinds of new human development sketched in the preceding pages.

She described a university that was a far cry from the one that her high school teachers had described: "Hang in there, hang in there, once you get to college you can do whatever you want." Instead, to her delight, Heejin found people who studied really hard. She told us that she had been "moved" by the long line of students waiting to enter the library at 5 a.m. For Heejin, competing, self-managing, and working hard made her feel alive and vital. She described the energy that comes from activity and achievement:

> [If you have to study in college] you can feel that you have *achieved* something. . . . When I was selected to be an exchange student [she hadn't gone yet], the feeling was amazing—the sense of *accomplishment*. When I got into college, into the department I wanted, and . . . It is the feeling of *energy*, the motivation continuously to be doing something. [emphasis added]

Heejin was unfazed by the thought that this intensity of effort should be unending and that the point was not to arrive at one place or another. On hearing Heejin's litany of activities and credentials, her friend asked, "But does this leave *you* any room for *self*-development?" Heejin's retort was quick and easy: "But this is a part of self-development, too." We understand her retort as refusing to make a distinction between a private or personal self and a market-oriented or instrumental one. Minutes later, the friend pushed her again, "You enjoy competition so that you can realize your dreams, right? It isn't that you want to compete forever, right? Do you want to agonize yourself with endless competition?" While Heejin's friend was keenly aware of the external pressures that demand neoliberal selfhood, for Heejin this selfhood resonates with her sense of her own essence, a selfhood well suited to the demands of the day and therefore deserving of reward.

We spent quite a bit of time talking about the university's recently established English requirements for graduation, namely an 800 or above on the TOEIC (Test of English for International Communication).[12] The student government was busily campaigning against this change in graduation requirements and other features of Koryŏ University's aggressive globalization efforts. Heejin was quite matter-of-fact about the requirement, which she argued should be even steeper. She posited that the social circles of future Koryŏ University graduates were ones that would demand English mastery. In passing, she remarked, "Last semester I saw more English than Korean [in course readings]." Heejin was unabashed that the university should confer these *and many more* credentials on its graduates. She described that she supports "anything that asserts that I have achieved to *this* level" [motioning with her hand]. She added later that Koryŏ University is her brand (*mak'ŭ*), and hence she wanted the bar to be set high.

Heejin is a great defender of Koryŏ University's efforts to remake itself from "national Koryŏ University" into "global Koryŏ University." She described the university's newspaper campaign, "Now we have turned our back on our homeland and are marching toward the world." She praised the university's efforts to be included in the list of the world's top 100 universities,[13] in which currently there are no South Korean universities. She was also well aware of the dean's motto, "Let's make good on our [university] pride!" For Heejin the march to the world, high levels of English acquisition, endless credentials, and ever-rising standards are the registers of self-development, not an "end" as her friend prodded her, but a way of life. Heejin's career goals encompassed this sense of self-development. She detailed her ever-escalating desire for foreign languages: "My major is English [literature]. But it is unsatisfying to work only on English. After all, everybody does English. . . . Now I am learning Japanese, and I am continuing with Spanish too. And I also want to learn Chinese." She described crafting a career through which she can use her English to "contact foreigners." Heejin thus imagined herself in broad circulation, moving freely in the world, facilitated by her mastery of many tongues, and acting as an agent who can help bring South Korea to the world. Heejin wanted to become an "events director"; more specifically she hoped to orchestrate public events that would "circulate foreign culture." Heejin's description of her ideal career synthesized her aesthetics of vital self-development, as well as her sense of the global:

> I like to make plans and to act on them, to bring them to life. . . . I'm the type who initiates getting together with my friends. I want to develop this side of me. I also like to deal with people. At one point I thought about becoming a producer, but I sensed that I would be constrained and that bothered me. . . . A producer is confined to this country. Instead, I want to have a hand in circulating foreign culture.

Throughout Heejin's narrative, she was queried both by her friend as well as ourselves about those who might be left outside of her notion of vital personhood. Heejin insisted that, in today's world of nations, South Korea cannot afford to be concerned about socioeconomic inequality: "It's too early, we are still at the point where we have to make students study more and more; all we do now is play." Lest the reader imagine that this affirmation of individual striving for success might preclude national identification, comments championing "competition" in such nationalistic terms were not uncommon. Heejin was not alone in asserting that South Korea could ill afford more egalitarian policies in the face of its race for global standing. As many have argued, nationalism and cosmopolitanism often go hand in hand (Park and Abelmann 2004; Schein 1998; Cho 2008).

As for people who can't afford the private after-school education indispensable to upper-tier college entrance, Heejin merely offered, "They should work hard and make themselves rich, too." This remark perhaps betrays Heejin's squarely middle-class background, which had allowed her to receive private after-school education. In the highly personalized project of self-realization, the individual must fashion her own mobility. Heejin identified state policies for "equalization of educational opportunity" with "dumbing down" the country in a way that it can ill afford in the global race.[14] Toward the end of our meeting, her friend interjected a comment that Heejin found simply beyond comprehension. In the torrent of talk about English, her friend confessed to preferring the study of Korean literature, to which Heejin simply replied, "I don't get it." In her view, a preference for Korean literature would limit oneself to a smaller universe, a domestic scene with lower standards and a limited global circulation. Heejin's focus on market value made it clear that she felt that citizens bear a responsibility to be competitive in the global contest. Her friend's commitment to Korean literature was too localized and would be a drag on the nation's movement toward the global.

Heejin thus positioned herself as a neoliberal paragon, and all the more so as the graduate of a special-purpose high school, one that ran against the policy current of school equalization. As an elite college student, she enunciated the neoliberal turn, relishing in the project of her own creative capital formation.

A "Third-Tier" College Student

I can't get anything from this school.

We met Sori for the first time in 2004, shortly before she was to resume her senior year at Myŏngji University after a year's leave. Myŏngji University had been a disappointment to Sori in every way. Having been a hard-working high school student in a peer group headed for greener pastures, Sori had a hard time coming to terms with herself at what she dubbed a "third-tier college."[15] What is so fascinating, if semitragic, about Sori's case is that she articulated a narrative of personal development not unlike Heejin's, even as her personal circumstances had shut her out of the elite college brand capital that confers ideal human development. The profound personal costs and even trauma of Sori's college story aside, she was nonetheless willing to take on the entire burden of her own human or capital development, holding herself "responsible for [her] own regulation" (Walkerdine 2003: 239). Although she intermittently generated systematic structural and gendered critiques, she then quickly returned to the theme of personal responsibility.

It is impossible to wrest Sori's own college story from her father's college story; indeed, college is always an intergenerational conversation of one kind or another. When Sori ended up at Myŏngji University, her father, an import-export small entrepreneur and a self-made man, let her know that she had "yielded no return" on his expenditures and that there was no point to his "investing" in her any further! Sori had made her way to Myŏngji University after a year of *chaesu*. Her scores had been so low on the first round of testing that she did not even apply to college because she had no interest in those schools that her scores would have enabled her to attend. Unlike most students from middle-class families, she did not attend a private institute in her *chaesu* year but instead burrowed in a public library because her father had pronounced her, his only child, a "hopeless case."

At this turn, Sori's family's education investment became clearly gendered. She described the hapless library crew of other students, adrift in their private pursuits, many of them already years into the project of college entrance or study for one or another state exam. The irony of Sori's settling for Myŏngji University was that her father, the first in his poor family to have attended college, had himself gone to Myŏngji University; it was thus unthinkable that the daughter, who had been raised with so many more advantages, had not managed to do any better. A year later it turned out that Sori's college entrance exam scores actually went down; she explained that it seems that hers is a personal code (*k'odŭ*) or personality ill-suited to the entrance exams. Further, she admitted to the arbitrariness of it all: Her best scores, for example, were on the third go-around when she had not even studied for it. But even when we pushed, and even with her admission that she is not an "exam person," Sori refused any critique of this engine of selection in a highly competitive South Korea; instead, echoing Heejin, she accepted that exams and competitive credentialization were necessary for South Korea's competitiveness.

When Sori explained that the score that it took to enter her major at Myŏngji University's Department of Business Management was no different from that required by less desirable departments at higher-ranked schools, it seemed that she was about to criticize the stratification of higher education in South Korea with its brand capital. Instead, however, Sori was very critical of the college. She detailed the various ways in which it did not live up to her image of what a college should be, an image made all the more palpable because the vast majority of her high school and after-school institute friends ended up attending higher-ranking schools. Indeed, on the day we met, she was accompanied by a friend who was about to begin graduate school at prestigious Yŏnse University located just minutes from the Myŏngji campus. Sori mentioned the empty Myŏngji library, completely vacant except during exam season; here we can recall how moved Heejin was by the students who lined up to enter the Koryŏ University library at dawn. Also lacking for Sori were meaningful social relationships: She described that, although students at Yŏnse or Koryŏ Universities build relations with their seniors (*sŏnbae*) and join clubs or study groups, "there is nothing that I can learn from them" [other Myŏngji students].[16] She went on to enlarge her claim, "I can't get anything from this school." When we asked her why she cannot even "have a conversation" with classmates at Myŏngji, she continued:

> To give an example: I am interested in English, but if I try to talk to them about learning English, they are clueless. They know nothing about what teacher is good at what institute or how to prepare for the TOEFL [Test of English as a Foreign Language], and so forth. If they have studied English even a little, they would know that much, and I would at least be able to talk to them about how hard the TOEFL is. But all they can say is, "I don't know anything about the TOEFL," or, "I have never taken the TOEIC."

With these comments, Sori felt she was describing students with no future or little ambition. She was also remarking on the lack of network or social capital at a place like Myŏngji University; there were neither strategic ties nor helpful information to be garnered there. These same students, who knew so little about the English exam for which Koryŏ University was requiring a score of 800 for graduation (the very score that earned Sori a sizable merit fellowship at Myŏngji University), nonetheless went for study abroad, but, Sori stressed, "with no mind of their own": "They just head for China or the United States because their parents send them. I don't understand them. They say, 'Isn't it a good thing to study abroad? Doesn't it expand one's horizons?' But they have absolutely no plan to make good on their study abroad experience." For her part, she could never imagine using her parents' money without "strong determination" to really study hard. Here Sori distinguished the spirit from the letter; her classmates, she asserted, lacked the spirit—the subjecthood—that would assure meaningful returns.

Aspiring to follow in her father's footsteps, Sori had taken on the burden of self-development on her own. Sori admired her father, a well-traveled successful businessman, "a self-made man who speaks English well, considering his age." She went on to note that his English is, in fact, better than hers. In spite of admitting to being "hurt" by him and to the trials of "never being able to live up to his expectations," Sori was busily crafting her own parallel track. Foremost, she knew that she would need to identify her own import/ export "item" (transliterated into Korean as *ait'em*) if she were to succeed. Over the course of our conversation, we began to listen to this phonetic loan-word for "item" more metaphorically, to stand for the stress that many students put on discovering their own talent or nurturing their own passion. We were struck that Sori's "item"—something that she would market or bring from abroad—paralleled Heejin's "events"; both styled themselves as decidedly cosmopolitan by extending their ambition beyond South Korea and by working to acquire English capabilities that could enable such mobility. Sori did not want to be merely "a part of the machine" but aspired instead to becoming a "figure in her own right."

Like her *chaesu* year, Sori's item was a particularly gendered burden. As she described: "My dad says that his trade item is too good to let it die with his generation and that if he had had a son he could have had him take it over." To wit, her entrepreneurship was indeed a self-entrepreneurship; the matter of fashioning herself as a woman was tied up in the project of somehow identifying that perfect trade item. Denied her patrimony on the basis of her gender, Sori's dream to circulate on a larger stage became harder to realize. Interestingly, Sori related that as a young girl she had been indulged by her father, who at that time still had big dreams for her. Like Heejin, she thus never even entertained the possibility of attending a woman's college that would somehow hem in her horizons. It was as if, in the face of her failure, Sori's father relegated her to the feminine, as if to say, "Pull yourself up, if you can, with your own bootstraps."

Sori's gendered perceptions of her parents' domains are revealing. While her father moved on the world stage, she characterized her mother as the kinder and more empathetic parent, who was confined to the domestic sphere. It is telling, if ironic, that the "masculine" attributes of the healthy subjectivity that Sori admired are coldness or even cruelty, while she portrayed "feminine" kindness as hemmed in or domestic in both senses of that word. Sori's gendered worlds and evaluations collided as she mapped her own future. She described a dilemma. On the one hand, she wanted to marry and have children: "I want to have three kids and a harmonious home filled with the sounds of children. I want my kids to have siblings, and I want to hear the sounds of people making noise when I come home." On the other hand, however, Sori was aware that to become the "savvy entrepreneurial woman" who could please her father, she needed to postpone her vision of a happy home to the distant future: "Honestly, I don't think I can get married before my thirties. . . . I need to work in a company and start my own business too, but if I get married and take care of my home and my husband, I won't be able to do anything." She dismissed out of hand the possibility of help from her mother who has already, she offered, "sacrificed too much to patriarchal demands."

Sori's struggles, however, must be appreciated in the context of what she described as the "two things that matter to my father: patriarchy and money." Sori was determined to "both marry well and become a classy woman by virtue of making lots of money" so that her father will approve of her—"give her an OK"—in spite of her having attended a lesser college, as he had. The family context of Sori's situation illuminates how her burden of self-development was intricately stitched into the fabric of conservative family norms and patriarchy. In this case, middle-class advantage was withheld along gendered lines. This case is perhaps not broadly representative of trends today: With South Korea's rapidly declining birth rate, there are many families with only girls, and many such girls are afforded the same privileges that would have been accorded a boy. But gender ideologies and their transformations work their way unevenly in all populations.

Although the task of unearthing Sori's item was still a project for her future, she had been taking a year off so as to study further for the TOEIC as well as to travel and take up photography. Sori was frustrated by what struck her as an irony: Although nonelite, the university's tendency to give constant small exams throughout the semester thwarted her desires for human development. She calculated that she was better off leaving the campus to realize her project. English, travel, and photography comprise an easy trio, for they are all highly valued human development assets, assets that are all the more important for students from Myŏngji University because this is where, according to Sori, the large firms don't even interview.

In sum, Sori realized that her human development was in her own hands. Lacking both the college brand and the gendered inheritance of her father's import/export item, Sori was indeed on her own in the project of developing herself for a transformed world. At times she called attention to matters beyond the boundary of the self (for example, personal exam proclivity, college reputations at the departmental level, and gendered inequalities in family support for exam preparation), but she nonetheless considered herself responsible for ending up at Myŏngji University and having to take on the development of her own human capital. Hardly unfettered by the burden, Sori nonetheless embraced it.

Bordering the Megalopolis

Each of us has to know exactly where we are headed and then make choices accordingly.

We turn now to two male seniors at Inch'ŏn City University, Min and Kŭn, both the children of small entrepreneurs. Min was also the son of a single mother. Although we foreground university stratification here, Min and Kŭn are also clearly from a lower-class background than that of the students already discussed. However, they, too, took on the burden of human development beyond the walls of their university. Min argued for the self-management of college in which each student decides where college fits in his or her own self-development strategy. Kŭn, having recently decided to take the civil service exam, was resigned to a rather conventional occupational future while holding onto the possibility of personal development beyond the job. Inch'ŏn City University is a nonelite university attended by students from Seoul unable to gain admission to colleges in Seoul proper and also by Inch'ŏn locals and students from the provinces. Inch'ŏn, a sprawling city neighboring Seoul, presents an interesting case. Although an independent city with its own history distinct from the Seoul megalopolis, it is close enough to Seoul so as not to be easily classified as "provincial"; it is nonetheless clearly not a part of the greater Seoul metropolitan area. Inch'ŏn City University, which began as a private university, was transformed into a public university in 1994 and is currently in the process of becoming a national university. We met Min and Kŭn in a larger group of students from the Communications Department in 2003 and in a smaller group again in 2004. In 2004, Min was off campus because of an internship that had turned into full-time employment, although he still needed to finish up some coursework. He made considerable effort to come and meet us because he had an urgent story to share. In 2003, Min who was stylishly dressed in offbeat clothes, spoke of his "fate to follow a different life course" and of his distinctive childhood without a father and with a "crazily" strong mother. He introduced himself as an "eclectic philosopher," and it was clear that his classmates had heard much of this before. Min was a frequent performer of his own difference. In 2003, he spoke at great length about South Korea's impoverished culture of conversation or debate. Speaking of English as "more comfortable," Min seemed to be saying that his use of the English language was unfettered by South Korean schooling and perhaps the dictates of Korean social life. With his comments on English, Min referred both to his international travel, namely several low-budget trips in Asia, and his cosmopolitan affinities:

> When I speak English, it doesn't seem so hard. It is easy and systematic. . . . We have a real problem with our education system. We begin our schooling learning such strange things [textbook English]—and in high school and middle school, too. I don't know why we learn those kinds of things. We could just go and talk when the situation arises, but instead we study English this way. Who knows why we can't get out of our books?

Moments later, Min championed "survival English," an English born in real-life interactions and through a more natural process of acquisition:

> When I spoke English abroad, I didn't think about it consciously—I just memorized the words and sentences that people used and said them that way. . . .

It's really easy to learn how to just change the ending of sentences and put that into action, but instead [people in South Korea] just sit in the library five hours a day studying. That's meaningless. We really need to change [the education system] soon.

If the English that Min spoke and learned in his trek in India was somehow more "natural," South Korean English was a disaster, held hostage in South Korean textbooks and classrooms. On hearing Min speak about English study, Kŭn did not negate what he said but offered his own take on Min's position: "Our [that is, South Korean] criterion for English study is the TOEIC exam. He hasn't studied for the TOEIC exam, but he went to India and tried out his English a lot there. In a word, he is talking about practical English (*siljŏn yŏng'ŏ*)." Kŭn had traveled only domestically and thus had made different choices than Min, although their class backgrounds are not so different.

In keeping with his deep-seated criticisms of South Korean English education, Min was also an avid critic of South Korea's chronic competition and of the connections (through school, region, and kin) that it takes to make it. In this litany, he included South Korea's "Seoul National University sickness," referring to the pathological obsession with this one school. Interestingly, in his excursus on English, Min also asserted that his English mastery exceeded that of Seoul National University students. Like Sori, Min also made structural critiques; however, he appeared to be more deeply empowered by them in the sense that he had not internalized his failure in having to settle on being an Inch'ŏn City University student. While it is hard to generalize from this case, we think that both class and gender are relevant here.

Min was not burdened by Sori's sense of failure and lack of empowerment. Whereas Sori was burdened with the desire to please her patriarchal father, Min prided himself on his unique family background, on being unfettered by "Korean" familial convention. Min's assertion of freedom from patriarchy can be considered ironically as a gendered privilege itself; a fatherless daughter would have been very differently positioned and would by no means have been free from patriarchal constraints. In describing the many ways in which he had styled his path, from a trek in India to side jobs in college, Min detailed an entrepreneurship of the self that had begun early in his life by virtue of his cultural marginality. His position was outside of the logic of patriarchy that had so burdened Sori. In imagining his future, Min described his inspiration from Buddhism ("following one's heart").

By 2004, via an internship, Min had landed a highly desirable job in Seoul as a TV producer in a broadcasting company. In explaining how he landed the job, he made clear his understanding that each person must take responsibility for the management of his or her own future, a management that is inherently risky and driven by many choices:

> When I was taking classes, I got many calls asking, "Min, are you up for some part-time work?" And I would turn to my friends, "Hey, let's do it together," but most of the time they said, "No, I can't, I have class." But in my case, I cut class and did those jobs. Because I skipped many classes, my GPA [grade point average] was between a B and a C. . . . but I learned many skills in the field. And so I have been able to enter the work world so quickly. Those students who stuck to their classes can't enter society and begin working as easily. It was a matter of my personal judgment; I did what I did because I chose to do it. Grades are also important, and I did fret about my grades. . . . *Each of us has to know exactly where we are headed and then make choices accordingly.* I chose my course a long time ago, and I have stayed on that path without wavering. [emphasis added]

Min's thoughts here about learning "in the field" echoed his earlier pronouncements about language learning and signified his embrace of new modes of human development. However, Min had made considerable effort to meet us that evening, not to offer these reflections but to tell us a love story.

It was a very long story, spoken with almost no interruptions, other than sympathy pangs from the assembled listeners; for Kŭn and another student present, it was clear that the story was already very familiar. In brief, Min had fallen in love with an Indian woman he had come to know because she was featured in a TV program that he had spearheaded as part of the internship that had led to his present job. It was a fairy-tale story of true love and tragic parting:[17] The woman was not at liberty to marry a non-Indian. Although it was a serious and at moments melodramatic telling, there were humorous asides, mostly about the ways in which Min skimped on his work to follow his heart. We listened to the story intently. Min was skilled at keeping his auditors tuned in. As we listened, we were struck that Min seemed to be mobilizing the tale in almost the same way he had described making choices in college as an instance of living and experiencing intensely. Although at first glance the story was a very far cry from that of the credential-happy Heejin with her "events" or from "item"-seeking Sori, the intensity, the personal flair, and the interest in experience are consistent.

Min also told us a lovely story about an encounter with a Japanese traveler in India. The meeting had been serendipitous and fleeting but somehow very meaningful. It captured beautifully the allure of travel, the magic that it promises the adventuresome. The talk of travel, yet another instance of "experience," had also featured largely in the meeting the year before, especially for Kǔn. Born and raised in Inch'ŏn, Kǔn had transferred from physics to communications, finding it better suited to his interests. After stating this, he said, "And I especially like to travel." We asked about the relation between his love of travel and his new major in communications, which made everyone chuckle. Kǔn's answer was telling: "Well, there's no exact relationship between them, but . . . I think of travel as something that gives you time to contemplate. The way I think of travel is that, while passing through new environments, it allows us to think alone and to plunge into our own thoughts." For Kǔn, both his major and his love of travel were tailored to personal proclivity and to self-fashioning of the sort we have been describing. Kǔn described his lofty goals at the start of each journey, "setting out for the answers to 'how I should live,' 'what life is,' and so on." But, he continued wistfully, "After all, it's the same. Whether I travel or not, life is hard." Kǔn would have liked to travel abroad, but limited resources precluded it. The "weight of reality," which Kǔn had described in 2003, had been getting in the way of his travels.

Kǔn's comments on his future one year later must be heard in the context of his listening to Min's account. Kǔn, conservatively and neatly dressed, smiled quietly throughout the telling. It was after this tale of adventuresome travel in India, television, and international romance that Kǔn shared his decision to take the civil service exam, a decision that would foreclose the possibility of employment better suited to his studies and passions. His future course appeared all the duller against the landscape of Min's accounts. Kǔn spoke of the naked realities of contemporary circumstances for all college students but even more so for those in universities outside of Seoul: "People say that our economy is getting worse, and youth employment is becoming a serious issue. These days there are no college students who are relaxed. We hang out together, but the moment we are alone again we are overwhelmed with worry, worries about the future." Kǔn thus described an anxiety that we observed across many of our college student interviews and particularly those with students at the lower-tier universities. Kŭn, however, went so far as to note that these days even Seoul National University students struggle.

Traveler Kŭn, however, made peace with his decision to take the civil service exam this way:

> If I become a public servant, I will have enough spare time. I can't imagine working more than ten hours a day, like Min. [As a public servant] I will go to work at 9 and finish by 5:30. The rest of the time is my own. And, in the near future, public servants will have every other Saturday off. And, somewhere down the line, all Saturdays will be off.[18] With that time, I can do something for self-development.

In this way, Kŭn registered or at least performed his peace with his decision of the need to become a public servant. The peace, as he described it, came from the self-development that he charted for after hours. It is interesting how Kŭn even spoke of his shorter work day, contrasting with Min's, as liberating in its own way. Kŭn's sketch accorded with widespread images of a changed salary man who does not forsake his personal life for the company. The typical salary man of the era of the South Korean developmentalist state was the one who gave his soul to the company for the economic development of the nation; family life, in turn, was relegated entirely to women; and leisure life was merely an extension of company life (see Janelli 1993; Kim 1998). Kŭn thus described self-development as a leisure-time project. Interesting here is Kŭn's meditation on freedom, his charge that perhaps labor that one is passionate about and demands full devotion—such as Min's—is not liberating at all!

In the previous year, Kŭn had described his own convictions, not unlike Min's, to live differently. Dismissing conventional marriage and family, he had said, "*Why* should I live like that?" Now, however, as Kŭn spoke about the unparalleled benefits (for example, retirement pension) of civil service jobs, he seemed to be sketching a much more "conventional" life course. But, if a civil service career smacked of something conventional, Kŭn nonetheless reserved his after hours and the promise of Saturdays into the future of a transformed South Korean work life. It stood in for that refuge that he had once sought—if only half realized—through travel in his earlier college days. Even as he discovered how, indeed, "life is hard," Kŭn was holding firmly to his ideals of self-expression and self-development.

Conclusions

The university students discussed in this chapter all aspire to human development, and they all accept the "burden" of managing their personal formation. These "new" students mark a break from the past with their aspirations to realize values of democracy, individualism, and cosmopolitanism. We have described how a small number of students across three campuses inhabit new discourses of human development and how in turn they manage their education and chart the course of their future lives. We have paid particular attention to differences according to university prestige as well as family background to argue both that the "burden" of human development was borne variously across these campuses and that it is powerfully gendered. Heejin occupied a privileged position in which her campus conferred a brand of subjectivity itself. In her vision of becoming a cosmopolitan events maker, she narrated her self-formation as a vital person to be a matter of personal responsibility and choice, largely unfettered by structure or circumstance. Similarly, in her case, we saw how English, as a powerful sign of the global, is a project for personal endeavor and transcendence.

Although Sori equally embraced the project of vitality as a student in a nonelite institution, she assigned herself the task of managing it on her own, independent of her university whose brand capital she found to be lacking. Her cosmopolitan vision of the future, in which she secured her "item," was a gendered burden that she needed to shoulder alone, unlike a son who would have been able to take over his father's item. Against the backdrop of Heejin's triumphant projects of personal development, we register Sori's as more fraught, raw, and even pained.

Finally, Min and Kŭn, like Sori, pursued their project of human development beyond the bounds of college. These two young men, however, emerge as distinctive cases: Min, not unlike Heejin, offered an empowered narrative of choice, cosmopolitan belonging, and gendered freedom (all of this achieved, he stressed, in spite of his campus). Kŭn, on the other hand, spoke of a vital future and the riches of domestic travel but at many points returned to the limits of his own particular circumstances, as the son of a humble family and a student at a nonelite college outside Seoul.

Across these conversations there *were* mentions of circumstance, indeed by all of the students featured here except for Heejin. But, as we have noted at many points, the discourse of human development in the neoliberal era seems to obscure structural differences by foisting the burden on the self, a burden that people necessarily come to carry differently.

We are well aware of the irony that, through the embrace of the discourse of self-development, these college students appear to be blind to their structural differences and positions. This is all the more ironic in an era when young people face a record low rate of employment and high rates of underemployment. With these cases, we document with others how young people's embrace of a new and very individuated discourse of subjecthood works as a "political rationality" (Foucault 1991; Gordon 1991; Lemke 2002; Seo 2008). As many scholars argue, in the Foucauldian sense, the shifting techniques and technologies of regulation in neoliberalism focus on the technologies of the self and the self-management of citizens (Gordon 1991; Lemke 2002; Rose 1999; Walkerdine 2003). By rendering individual subjects responsible for themselves, neoliberal governing technology passes the responsibility for social risks or problems, such as poverty and unemployment, onto the shoulders of individuals. We also note that the individualistic character of neoliberal subjectivity precludes collective alliance both in South Korea, and as importantly, across Asia where so many youth face similar circumstances and technologies.[19] This individualistic character of neoliberal subjectivity tends to prevent these students from seeking out any form of collective alliance. In the logic of neoliberal political rationality, the political subject is less a collective or social citizen than an individual citizen who obsessively pursues personal fulfillment (Seo 2008: 3).

Under these new forms of regulation, neoliberal subjects are elected to understand their positions in personal terms, even as they are located in a complex web of structural positions, as articulated for example by class and gender. This is why Valerie Walkerdine (2003: 243) calls for the necessity of exploring the ways in which social inequality "is differently lived" in the era of neoliberal transformation. The ethnographic interlocutors we have introduced here have allowed us to consider the ways in which vectors of social inequality such as college rank, class, and gender are now differently lived in South Korea's neoliberal transformation. In her discussion of British class politics in the neoliberal era, Walkerdine (2003: 239) notes that, in the new mode of self-management technologies, "class differences are taken to have melted away" because diverse people, including low-paid manual and service workers, are constantly "enjoined to improve and remake themselves as the freed consumer, as the 'entrepreneur of themselves.'" Indeed, despite intensified social inequality in the context of neoliberalism, she argues that people's sense of the possibility of upward mobility seems to have flourished as they celebrate individual freedom to self-regulate and improve themselves. In a similar way, the robust discourse of self-development of the South Korean college students we introduce here can work as if their education and future are the outcomes of individual choices free from any structural constraints.

Furthermore, for South Korea and other recently democratized states, including many Asian countries, the discourse of self-development is all the more easily celebrated because of the ironic historical conjuncture between neoliberal and postauthoritarian/collective liberal transformations. This conjuncture helps to explain how and why the college students introduced here all aspire so eagerly to an individualized project of human development.

Notes

ACKNOWLEDGMENTS

We are grateful for the helpful feedback from the editors of this volume, as well as Amy Borovoy, Ed Bruner, Bong Gun Chung, Noriko Muraki, Myung-gyu Pak, Cathy Prendergast, Jesook Song, and anonymous reviewers for both Stanford University Press and *Inter-Asia Cultural Studies*, where an earlier version appeared as "College Rank and Neoliberal Subjectivity in South Korea: The Burden of Self-Development" in *Inter-Asia Cultural Studies* (2009) 10(2): 229–247. Portions of the original article are here reprinted by permission of Taylor & Francis Ltd.; available at www.tandfonline.com. Comments by Fred Carriere, Greg Brazinsky, and Kirk W. Larsen at George Washington University were very helpful. We are also indebted for feedback from seminars at Columbia, Harvard, and Stanford Universities, and at the University of Wisconsin at Madison. We thank Jinheon Jung, who assisted with research during the summer of 2004. We are also grateful to Byung-ho Chung, Hye-young Jo, Jin-Heon Jung, Donghu Lee, Deok-hee Seo, and Keehyeung Lee for facilitating introductions to interlocutors.

1. Special-purpose high schools, which originally started in the late 1970s only for art and athletics, expanded during the mid-1990s in accordance with educational reforms that emphasized the "diversification, specialization, and autonomy" of schools. These schools have special purposes to nurture talents for the new

economy, including technical, science, and foreign-language skills. These high schools run against the grain of decades of high school equalization measures, a history that is reviewed later in this chapter (Kim Young-Chol 2003; Lee 1998).

2. In South Korea, top-rated women's schools are easier to enter because of the decreasing popularity of women's schools generally.

3. Critically important is that the state has effected recent higher education transformations in a centralized manner, concentrating on the country's top-tier universities and thus intensifying the already enormous stratification of South Korean education with neoliberal reforms (J. H. Lee 2004). Although our focus is on structural correlates of college rank, the correlation between college and class capital seems to be increasing as contemporary education in South Korea offers consumers with economic means many new arenas for investment, foremost the option of study abroad prior to college. A $550 million venture in the first quarter of 2004, doubling the figures from 2002, the so-called early study abroad (*chogi yuhak*) is an escalating market (*Hankook Ilbo* 2004). Parents struggle as to how to best educate their children for a transformed South Korea in a transforming world (Park 2006). A not uncommon discussion is the one that asks, "Which will be more valuable into the future, a degree from Harvard or from Seoul National [South Korea's premier university]?" These options present new, and sometimes risky, human capital development strategies. In the self-development narratives of the students featured in this chapter, we will see that they enthusiastically embrace these risks. However, such a struggle—even just with second- or third-tier schools in both countries—is not separable from the student's class resources.

4. While we observe the interaction between patriarchal family forms and neoliberal subjectivity—particularly the ways in which gender and patriarchal norms mediate family investment in children and human development ideals—this chapter does not further larger discussions of the articulation of gender and neoliberal subjectivity, a still theoretically and empirically underdeveloped topic in the literature (see Walkerdine 2003; Anagnost 2000). Further, while we highlight persistent gender norms, it is important to note that South Korean families are among the smallest in the world, that son-preference has declined significantly, and that South Korean families make enormous economic and emotional investments in the next generation, investments that are arguably ever greater in the face of today's considerable class reproduction anxiety.

5. This chapter is based on conversations with students in the summers of 2003, 2004, and 2005. We usually met students in groups on or near college campuses, and in some cases we followed up with solo interviews. In most cases the groups were comprised of departmental or college club cohorts that followed the snowball networks of our recruitment. In total we spoke with about twenty students.

6. As neoliberal logics have spread worldwide, they take on specific trajectories in different places. See Anagnost 2004; Apple 2001; Borovoy 2004; Comaroff and Comaroff 2000; Du Gay 1996: 182; Ferguson and Gupta 2002; Fong 2004; Gee

1999; Kingfisher 2002; Rose 1990; Song 2003; Walkerdine 2003; Wallulis 1998; Yan 2003.

7. Comaroff and Comaroff (2000: 305) similarly describe the term: "Neoliberalism aspires, in its ideology and practice, to intensify the abstractions inherent in capitalism itself: to separate labor power from its human context, to replace society with the market, to build a universe out of aggregated transactions."

8. See Borovoy (2004) for a study of the ambivalence of Japanese young people as they struggle to meet the requirements of Japan's "new competitiveness." In parallel with the South Korean case in this chapter, these Japanese young people are asked to become a new generation of individualized and creative workers. Borovoy analyses both how class works, such that some youth are not afforded the opportunity to develop these new subjectivities, and how for elite youth these new requirements challenge deeply held values as well as ambivalences about American-style capitalism.

9. The complex political colors of the current education policy climate are easily observed through a recent *JoongAng Ilbo* editorial that denounced South Korean education as an "outdated steam engine" that hampers the "nation's competitiveness." The editorial continued, "Korea is still mired in the age of democratization, in which remnants of previous authoritarian regimes continue to linger. As such, the influence of ideology remains evident" (D. Lee 2004: 39–40).

10. Mok, Yoon, and Welch 2003: 61) summarizes South Korea's education transformation in terms of several key shifts: from standardization to autonomy, diversification, and specialization; from provider to consumer; and from classroom education to open and lifelong learning.

11. As Mok, Yoon, and Welch (2003: 62–63) characterize, "The Korean government openly acknowledges that the existing system has failed to equip the society with autonomous capacity" to solve the problems presented by the new knowledge economy. Former President Kim Dae Jung was committed to education reform that nurtured "autonomous" and "creative" human capital (Mok, Yoon, and Welch 2003; Song 2003).

12. English has long been a class marker in South Korea; that is, knowledge of, and comfort with, English has been a sign of educational opportunity, especially study abroad, and of social success, including successful jobs and career promotion in South Korea (see Park and Abelmann 2004). Several universities now have English course and examination requirements for graduation.

13. This refers to the list produced by *The Times* of London, a list that is well known in South Korea.

14. Here Heejin referred to South Korean state's long-standing ideological commitment to egalitarian education—especially the "high-school equalization policy." Her assertion echoed some neoliberal arguments that South Korea's recent educational turn is not a thoroughly neoliberal one because it has sustained equalization policies (D. Lee 2004: 39–40).

15. In informal on-line rankings of South Korean colleges and universities, Myŏngji University appears most often in the upper quadrant of schools; "second-tier" then would be more accurate.

16. See Borovoy (2004) for a fascinating discussion of college clubs as a mark of university status in Japan. More broadly, she takes college clubs as a key element of elite "college socialization" that prepares students for elite corporate work and social life. She both considers what it means that students at a provincial "low-level" college participate in clubs at significantly lower rates (30 percent) because many of them are commuter students as well discussing differences in the "easy come, easy go" way in which they participate in the clubs.

17. We are grateful to an anonymous reviewer for pointing out that it is not the story of forsaken or unattainable true love that is distinctive here but rather that Min's was a global tale.

18. Since July 2005, public servants work only five days, from Mondays to Fridays.

19. We are grateful to an anonymous reviewer who pushed us to think about the implication of our findings and argument for collective alliance.

Chapter Five

Smile Chaoyang

Education and Culture in Neoliberal Taiwan

NICKOLA PAZDERIC

Perhaps there are few better indicators of the scope of Margaret Thatcher's maxim "there is no alternative" to neoliberal globalization than the appropriation of Stuart Hall's critique of neoliberal economics to illustrate the imperative for educational reform in Taiwan. Hall's characterization of the new workplace and social environment as a "Brave New World" was adopted in a PowerPoint review of Taiwan's education goals presented by education professor Wang Hui-lan to an international conference on Globalization and Education Reform at Seoul National University in 2005.

Wang juxtaposes the quoted phrase with a Government Information Office (GIO) image of gleeful children supporting a globe—an image originally used to portray Taiwan favorably to the world in the aftermath of the 2003 SARS scare. Its use in this instance is unobjectionable insofar as it accords entirely with the impression that the government of Taiwan seeks to convey to the world. Hall's description of neoliberal economic life, which is drawn from the short-lived but influential anti-Thatcher journal, *Marxism Today*, follows as part of Professor Wang's presentation:

A shift of the new information technologies; more flexible, decentralised forms of labour processes and work organisation; decline of the old manufacturing base and the growth of the "sunrise" computer-based industries; the hiving-off or contracting-out of functions and services; a greater emphasis on choice and

product differentiation, on marketing, packaging and design, on the "targeting" of consumers by lifestyle, taste and culture rather than by the Registrar
General's categories of social class. (Hall 1988: 24, cited in H. Wang 2005)

Cultural critics should yet recognize Wang's substitution of *ought* for *is*. But,
ironies aside, Taiwanese know the score. Situated in an export-driven, high-
tech economy and aware that the neoliberal program outlined and criticized
by Hall is fast becoming a universal expectation, people act as if there is no
choice. The use of the image indicates, moreover, that Taiwan's so-called
e-generation is slated to become the smiling standard bearers of the brave
new world.

The transformation to a neoliberal economy began in Taiwan in the mid-
1980s as a result of policy decisions at the highest levels of government. Under pressure from the United States to reduce its trade surplus and from
local elites who were keen to profit by the privatization of state firms, Taiwan
changed its postwar economic course (Tsai 2001). The postwar transformation of Taiwan into one of the world's leading economies had depended on
manufacturing and restricted consumption, enforced by import restrictions
(Gold 1986: 67–73), which subverted the pretenses of conventional postwar trade practices (Chomsky 1998: 360). However, by the mid-1990s, the
Chinese Nationalist party (KMT), which ruled the island after 1945, began to sell shares of state-controlled industries. As a consequence, imports,
mandated by American trade agreements and World Trade Organization
(WTO) conventions, flooded the island. The Democratic Progressive Party
(DPP), which formed in the late 1980s as an outlawed political organization
with a populist social agenda, took control of the government via presidential elections in 2000 and moved even further in this direction to serve the
interests of its own financial and industrial elites.

The transformation has reached into every sphere of the economy, including education. The proposals that had been made for educational reforms
during and after the democratic transition of the late 1980s, which ranged
from humanistic education to ecological based programs (for example, Humanistic Education Foundation, 2007) have now been superseded by educational policies to promote the increased quality, autonomy, self-discipline, and
technological sophistication of the island-economy's work force (Kao 2003;
Mok and Lee 2001; Mok 2000, 2003). These buzzwords signal the disciplining of the labor force for the challenges of a global economy. However, the

urgency of the transformation stems from Taiwan's precarious geopolitical position. For the People's Republic of China, Taiwan is a renegade province, and its recovery is deemed a national destiny. For the United States, Taiwan remains a client-state base from which to project U.S. power in East Asia. Despite their bitter political struggle over Taiwan's national culture identity, both Chinese (KMT) and Taiwanese (DPP) nationalists tacitly agree that, in this unenviable position, the society appears to have but one hope to secure continued de facto independent political survival: ensure that its work force is a first-rate, high-quality knowledge machine, capable of seizing every niche, probing every market, and undercutting every competitor.

The pressurizing effects of this orientation have fundamentally shaped my former place of employment, Chaoyang University of Technology (CYUT) in central Taiwan. Since I began teaching there in 2001, I observed how the power of neoliberalism's dictates is felt in every sector of university life. CYUT provides a telling case study because its emergence and development are inseparable from the neoliberal educational reforms themselves. With over 13,000 students and 350 full-time faculty in 2006, CYUT first opened its doors in 1994, which was the same year that the Ministry of Education (MOE) adopted the principles of the neoliberal program. As I will show in greater detail, CYUT has thrived under these conditions to become by prevailing conventional measures a successful example of the private sector's capacity to establish and sustain a higher education institution.

I present a two-part thesis. First, although the values of neoliberalism are fundamental (indeed, the bottom line) to the development of the school, they operate within as they transform two conflicting and preexisting value systems. The emic designations of these preexisting systems are "traditional" (*chuantong*) and "Western" (*xifang*), whereas neoliberal values are referred to as "globalization" (*quanqiuhua*). I call these systems, for reasons I give in the following discussion, State Neo-Confucianism, Enlightenment, and Neoliberal Globalization, respectively. Each of these value systems incites, reinforces, and collides with the behaviors and attitudes of the other two in ways that are not very well understood by those who labor within their messy coexistence. The schema I present will, therefore, illustrate the local instantiation of neoliberalism's transformations.

The State Neo-Confucian value system is central to the formation of an East Asian identity structure, often glossed as "Asian values." It is cosmological insofar as it places the individual within an assured set of relationships and behavioral structures that in no way place the individual in a predicament of autonomy. While considered traditional, it functions as a *modern* adaptation of regional and local value systems. First in China and later in Taiwan, the Chinese Nationalist government has used mass-education techniques of standardized and printed curricula to educate the population to value the state above local factions and family (Wilson 1970). The modern nation-state became the embodiment of the cosmological hierarchy. That the State Neo-Confucian value system persists in the neoliberal environment is testament to its institutionalization in various school practices (Chun 2007), its inculcation in the minds of every Taiwanese schooled after Japanese colonial rule (1895–1945), its successful cooptation of preexisting local cultural patterns, and its utilitarian adaptation to the new bottom line.[1] CYUT also promotes a general Enlightenment system. This system finds its rationale in the utopian hope that universities will serve to liberate humans from drudgery and suffering through the application of reason to the problems of humanity (Aronowitz 2004; Borgmann 1984: 89; Readings 1996). Its stronghold is in the faculty trained at recognized universities in the United States, Europe, Japan, or Taiwan, and its strongest support comes from the Ministry of Education (MOE). The Enlightenment ideal assumes a prominent place in campus life, yet its position lies in tension with neoliberal and neo-Confucianist projects.[2]

Much of this chapter will be concerned with how these value systems influence daily life. But there remains a second part to my thesis, and it accounts for the title of this chapter. At CYUT, the appearance of happiness has become an induced discipline and produced commodity. Students and faculty alike are enjoined by administrative message to smile and say hello with posters, fliers, and quasi-scientific questionnaires. The most vivid of these are full-color posters placed at key entrances around campus, depicting faculty and administrators in the act of smiling and saying hello as an incitement to those so enjoined to reciprocate in kind.

This orientation has its advantages for an admittedly third-rate school (*sanliu xuexiao*), which is where Chaoyang fits in the local hierarchy of educational institutions. In Taiwan, public universities are the oldest and most highly funded, and they are the schools of choice for the children of Taiwan's professional classes. CYUT is a private tertiary-level institution in the technical track system. For the most part, students have found themselves in this track through their failure to gain high marks in the highly competitive Taiwanese examination system. Via informal interviews with students and administrators, I have come to understand that this emphasis on happiness is what sells CYUT to parents; it markets CYUT graduates to employers as a happy and compliant bunch, and it takes the pressure off students who have generally not shown high levels of academic performance.

The importance of positive energy, in the form of happiness-assuring "universal love," to subjective experience in Taiwan has taken on religious dimensions in some circles, as in the cultivation of *heqi* practices, a cultlike technology of the self that I have explored elsewhere (Pazderic 2004). In the United States, as well, one need only look to the most popular class at a supposedly first-rate school for an example of how happiness functions. Harvard University's Psych 1504, "Positive Psychology," is a course that explores happiness, self-esteem, empathy, friendship, love, achievement, creativity, music, spirituality, and humor; it leaves students after "the 90-minute-long class cheering and smiling" (Goldberg 2006). Although the yearning for happiness is no doubt genuine and, in fact, may be considered a realization of the Enlightenment hope, the campaign for smiles at CYUT suggests that the happiness most valued by Hall's brave new world is a form of embodied value in a world order that demands docile and cooperative (but not critical) knowledge workers to fill the lower ranks of corporations and businesses in need of the new competencies that define "human capital" in the global economy.[3] The preexisting state Neo-Confucianism and Enlightenment value systems have now become subordinated in service to these ends. This is the gist of the second part of my argument.

State Neo-Confucianism

In 1970, Richard W. Wilson published *Learning to be Chinese: The Political Socialization of Children in Taiwan*. During the Cold War, when mainland China was in the throes of a convulsive cultural revolution, many Western scholars received funding to seek out and analyze patterns of cultural life, including ancestor worship, family cohabitation structures, and market networks, in the hinterlands of Taiwan. The political purpose of this research is clear insofar as it served to support the Chinese Nationalist claim to be the legitimate, though temporarily exiled, government of China—a claim that fit nicely into the American Cold War anticommunist program. Wilson pursued the more politically troubling question of what children were learning during their mandatory elementary school educations. How were Chinese consciousness and behaviors incited, reinforced, and, for all intents and purposes, produced in a population that had only recently been taught to become Japanese?[4] Writing about the production of "large group unity," Wilson took note:

> There is a multiple-choice question in a review section on citizenship training where the children are asked: "The responsibility of young people is to (1) read books conscientiously, (2) exercise the body, (3) build society, (4) establish the family." . . . As the principal of the city school informed me, only (3) can be the right answer. (1970: 47)

During my tenure at CYUT, I have regularly taught two courses in which I discuss elements of this book with students. I ask them the same question. Undergraduates and graduate students have never failed to provide the correct answer, often in unison. Students find my wonder astounding. Why are we so disconnected? Every answer to this question is either a value associated with traditional Chinese cultural life or one promoted by the state. As such, the question appears entirely Kafkaesque to me. The difference lies with the fact that I have not climbed the same educational ladder.

One might think that the Democratic Progress Party would have dismantled this imperative after its defeat of the KMT in the 2000 presidential election, when Chen Shui-bian took office.[5] Although the DPP has transformed consciousness of Taiwan's cultural and political identity, the imperative "to build society" (*jianli shehui*) remains the universally recognized correct answer to this question of values. The pressures on Taiwan continue to give urgency to the answer to this question. The imperative to build society in a state not recognized by the United Nations as a sovereign nation apparently does not hinder the imperative to build a sense of national consciousness; rather Taiwan's uncertain status intensifies such a project. The keenly felt imperative remains in keeping with the dictates of neoliberalism, insofar as neoliberalism operates with scant regard to nation-states—but it does prefer disciplined populations.

States compete for investments to the point of weakening their own power. This has happened in Taiwan, and the new *Taiwanese* nationalism provides only a limited ground of resistance. Although the DPP government found political support through appeals to a Taiwanese consciousness, the long-term economic benefits of this position in the face of massive global pressure appear insufficient to turn it from following the KMT in this regard. As a result, state industries, from telecommunications to banking, have been systematically opened to international investment, and once-secure lifelong middle-class jobs in these sectors, which had served to support state structures during the postwar era, are being jettisoned. With little hope of turning their educations into state employment, young Taiwanese speak of themselves as part of an M-society (imagine the "M" representing the bipolar income distribution chart of a neoliberal economy).[6] Still, the values of State Neo-Confucianism persist in many social institutions. They persist, moreover and more importantly, not only in allegiance to an ambiguous state but in a variety of group behavioral patterns that can be viewed only from the standpoint of neoliberalism as useful though quaintly anachronistic.

I call these values State Neo-Confucianism due to a mechanism of transmission and discipline associated with the Civil Examination of Imperial China. Beginning with the Ming Dynasty (1368–1644), Neo-Confucian interpretations of Confucian teachings, which sought to incorporate popular Taoist and Buddhist ideas, determined much of the ruling class via the civil exam until 1905. After the Republican (Nationalist) revolution in 1911 and the consolidation of national power by the KMT in 1927, education became increasingly oriented toward producing modern subjects, specifically through the sciences and national indoctrination. The model of the universal exam, however, did not disappear with the revolution. It became a sign and device linking an imagined Chinese past to an equally anticipated future (Strauss 1994). An entire branch of the government was established at the time, devoted to testing for government jobs, school entrances, and licenses. The values expressed and reinforced by this system find popular expression in the benign, fatherly figure of Confucius, who can be seen, for example, in statues presiding at the gates of public libraries or school courtyards throughout Taiwan.

As this value system evolved into its contemporary form, heavy emphasis has been given to group consciousness. Stereotypes of East Asians as group oriented are as common as those that claim Westerners are individualistic; but this dichotomy can easily mislead. Conformity as a condition of the American corporate matrix is well known.[7] As currently practiced at CYUT, group orientation is a product of state programs to discipline people into becoming citizens who act in collectivities distinct from their families, clans, and villages. With a lock on forms of solidarity, all collectivities considered threatening to the Nationalist regime, such as labor unions, were severely repressed from 1945 until the 1990s (Chu 2001: 21–86).

One state-sponsored organization that prospered under state support is called the China Youth National Salvation Corps (known as The China Youth Anti-Communist National Salvation Corps since its founding on Taiwan in 1952 until the 1990s). This group is important to the culture of CYUT because the chairman of the Board of Directors was a one-time president of the corps, and many of the initial and current top administrators, including the founding and current presidents, were linked to the chairman and school via this organization. Its original aims were to prepare boys for mandatory military service, but later it became a Boy Scout–like service organization that seeks to harness youthful exuberance in service to the state.

According to one senior business department professor, the China Youth Corps provided an early business model for the school. In all my meetings with the first president of CYUT, he emphasized that he was most proud of the fact that CYUT was clean and free of major infighting. While the latter statement is misleading, the school was and remains one of the tidiest universities in Taiwan (no small selling point in 1994 when the average state school toilet reeked of urine and dust, thanks to the neglect of career state employees). At CYUT, however, this problem has been solved Boy Scout style: First-year students are required to clean the school as part of a labor education program. Monday through Friday at 7 a.m., they are out with brooms, mops, and cleaning fluids. This activity is part of a larger campus culture that moves from loathed service activities to hand-clapping fun in all school competitions, which are run regularly. Students singing in unison or posing together for photographs are images that sell well to parents who were brought up in a State Neo-Confucian educational environment. Moreover, schooled in such a system, many faculty members remain busy attending and supporting student functions. They receive no substantial official credit toward promotion and merit evaluations by participating in such activities, but they do get some service credit, opportunities to extend their campus networks, some recognition for themselves should their students win a prize, and personal enjoyment, expressed in terms of a shared feeling that comes with working with excited youngsters.

Similarly, group activities have been made subservient to the state. Teachers employed soon after the school's founding have told me of regular all-school national flag-raising ceremonies, during which the former president would exhort students to protect their sexual chastity, for example. As times and governments have changed and, perhaps more important, as the size of the student body has grown, the requirements have eased, and the flag ceremonies have been trimmed to one per semester per department. Teachers need not attend, but students dutifully and dangerously race on their motorcycles to school at the very last moment—the terrible early hour of 7 a.m. for senior students—to listen with feigned interest to speeches by departmental leaders. I have quizzed students afterward, and it seems that the thing they remember most clearly is the breakfast they bought in a rush on the way. Yet, despite the disinterest held by students toward the rituals of State Neo-Confucianism, these rituals persist, and students continue in their quiescent acceptance of their importance. As Slavoj Žižek (for example, 1994: 14) often remarks, completion of ritual is more important than belief itself—a theoretical point supported by the unquestioning, if indifferent, traditionalism qua nationalism of most students.

The highest values of this system are conformity to group norms, harmony of social relations, and respect for the face of superiors. Traditionalists and technocrats alike believe that these values are on the wane (Sun 1994: 106). While they may be fading from public allegiance, they persist as a default sensibility in everyday practice. To conform is to act harmoniously in the group and to recognize the power, measured as face (*mianzi*), of the leader. Leaders, in turn, are expected to act benevolently toward their underlings and do everything possible to insure the conditions of harmonious social relations. For the proponents of this system of values, traditional Chinese life is a highly dignified routine of mutual recognition and support (Tu 1985, 1995). At its best, the system gives rise to institutional structures in which hierarchy is keenly felt despite the fact that differences in wages or salaries may not be all that large.[8]

However, the utopia of service, harmony, and respect shows its unseemly side in cynicism, factions, and corruption.[9] Because dissent is not encouraged, power blocks quickly form; because discussion of issues might lead to a leader's loss of face, rumor mongering and backstabbing become necessary parts of any sophisticated person's political toolkit. Because leaders depend on the dispensation of favors to maintain their groups, corruption and cronyism remain common.[10]

Enlightenment Values or the Democratic-Consumerist Nation

A rival but symbiotic system of values has been in place since the earliest moments of modern national consciousness and nation-state formation in turn-of-the-twentieth-century China. In the wake of China's monumental May 4th Movement in 1919, in which students took to the streets to protest colonialism and promote reform in China, Chen Duxiu of the New Culture Movement gave democracy and science the nicknames Mr. Democracy and Mr. Science. Expressing the yearning of the times, he asserted, "Only these two gentlemen can save China from the political, moral, academic, and intellectual darkness in which it finds itself" (E. Gu 2001: 589). As a matter of national cultural survival, science and democracy became stated aims of Nationalist education and policy. Science was given first place; whereas democracy, understood in terms of national father Sun Yat-Sen's "Three Principles of the People," was set to emerge after a period of tutelage.

After the so-called retreat of the KMT government to Taiwan, following its defeat in the civil war in 1949, research in the social sciences and humanities were quietly but effectively policed. This was possible because most local intellectuals were killed or imprisoned following the February 28 incident in 1947 (Kerr 1965) and because the default sensibility of State Neo-Confucianism was considered sufficient for the establishment of a public morality necessary for economic growth (Wilson 1970). Simultaneous with revolts against nationalist literatures and cultures in the West (as expressed in the emerging field of cultural studies), Taiwanese intellectuals began to question the national cultural ideology. In 1973, members of the philosophy department of National Taiwan University were fired for dissent, and later in the 1970s authors who published realistic works of fiction and literary criticism that reflected the transformations of Taiwanese society, a literary movement referred to as "nativist literature" (*xiangtu wenxue*), were severely criticized although not entirely repressed. However, with the death in 1988 of President Chiang Ching-kuo, the son of Generalissimo Chiang Kai-shek who had served as the head of Taiwan's secret police in the 1950s, a new independence swept through the humanities and social sciences. State policy dictated that the promised posttutelage democracy had arrived, and change followed. In the 1960s, owning a copy of Marx would have likely landed one in jail; in the early 1990s, the leading national university in Taichung at which I taught had no shortage of Marxist books on its library shelves. The university was released from the national, anticommunist, and Cold War project of the KMT, just as the KMT began to divest from institutions that maintained its power.

What is more, during the 1990s researchers returned to Taiwan with advanced degrees from universities in the United States and elsewhere. The returnees in many cases disturbed the practices of faculty at the national universities where they found jobs. National schools were not as highly traditionalized as CYUT, but the model of affective student–teacher ties held sway. Moreover, many teachers at the state schools considered themselves entitled to live a relaxed life of scholarly repose; thus, most faculty were not interested in (and often were not trained to handle) the demands of research. The conflict that emerged was clearly between those who valued research as defined by leading research institutions and those who valued teaching as defined by locally accepted practice.

While working at one of the national schools during the mid-1990s, I witnessed three women become objects of some resentment from traditional faculty. They had returned from top programs in the United States, and they took an aggressive approach to research—winning grants, attending international conferences, and publishing. The tensions were exacerbated by the fact that the women were conducting cultural and feminist research, which tacitly put traditional models of state–citizen and teacher–student relations into further question. The tensions persist to this day, especially in humanities departments. It finds islandwide political expression in resistance to MOE regulations from humanities- and social science–oriented national schools that have seen their rankings tumble as a result of the new standards (104 Education Information Web, 2007).

Many faculty members at CYUT continue to act out the idealized teacher role; others seek promotion through research. While the politics can be intense, graduate students find themselves in a state of confusion. Should they stay close to the friendly teachers with whom they are familiar or risk the pains of intellectual discovery with demanding research-oriented faculty, who promise nothing less than the reconstruction of their finely inculcated worldviews?

The question is made more difficult because the MOE has decreed that every master's degree student write a thesis (unlike American universities, for example, where many MBA or education degree students finish without a major research project). The goal is to raise the research profile of Taiwan in the hopes of establishing a research center in an emerging global knowledge economy. Unfortunately, the test-heavy educational system does not afford training in independent inquiry—especially in fields as ideologically essential to state control and reproduction as the humanities and social sciences. Thus, not trained to conduct independent research, familiar with the State Neo-Confucian model of friendly teacher–student ties, and hoping for ease, many students choose the less demanding route.

From the standpoint of short-term gain, the problem is easily solved. Students are themselves consumers of education, which they are promised will add value to their human capital. Accordingly, students can gain leverage over the divided faculty via complaints that course content and curriculum design are insufficiently practical for future success. Success is usually undefined but understood to mean occupational pathways that lead to increasing consumer power (see Ren, Chapter One in this volume, for a comparable argument regarding the Chinese mainland). Because it is devoid of concrete content but overdetermined by the mandate for the state's construction qua economic growth, raising the problem of student success during meetings has the power to frighten administrators to alter curricula. It is simply and unquestionably logical that students must succeed; and, to be successful, they must be practical; and to be practical is to possess marketable skills. Naturally, teachers must supply these skills pleasantly.

Thus, students consume education and in turn produce themselves as consumable. It is here that the promise of Enlightenment slides into a subjectivity that I term *democratic consumerist*—following a description of the general culture of contemporary Taiwan made by the former vice president and current president of the university during a meeting with teachers in 2002. Acutely aware of this feedback loop, he referred to the demands on CYUT for efficiency of operations (experienced by the administration in terms of parental and student complaints) as something that is natural in a "democratic nation" (*minzu guojia*). His resigned reference to democracy struck me as strange but very pronounced insofar as it conflates the demands of consumers with the sovereignty of the people in a social environment in which democracy has only tentatively replaced authoritarianism as the accepted form of political life during the past twenty years.

Ironically, this new subjectivity is possible only because the liberatory promise of the Enlightenment has been realized for many in Taiwan. The days when people labored for poor wages in factories or bent over in rice fields have been all but forgotten. Taiwan now imports manual labor to build buildings, take care of its old people, and work on computer chip assembly lines. The crisis of personal autonomy is apparently resolved for students via two messages: Study for a future of success and consume (see Hsu, Chapter Two in this volume)—though to study at a school like CYUT might simply mean to consume education with no sure guarantees that the skills they acquire will have a purchase on the future. What if the promised future of a new global order fails to deliver? People can defer this possibly by appeal to the cargo-cults of Pan-Chinese, Pan-Asian, or Pan-Taiwanese identity. In the public sphere, democratic choice has been reduced to a seeming life-or-death struggle over ethnic/state identity that leaves the substantial and difficult questions about Taiwan's future largely unanswered *democratically*; rather they have *already* been answered in terms of the supposedly necessary choice of neoliberal reforms. As relatively impoverished elements of society, students practice so-called choice on the morning ride to school as they spend their petty cash to purchase the taste that they want or by making demands on the system to ensure their proper value-added transformations. The full extent of this consumer orientation is felt by the school itself, which is competing with other schools for student dollars, not unlike streetside breakfast venders.

Neoliberal Reforms and the Dominion of the Bottom Line

Although people connected to the highest reaches of the KMT government founded CYUT, the neoliberal reforms, which contributed to the downfall of the KMT state, ironically proved to be perfectly timed for the prosperity of the emergent institution. One year after CYUT started taking students, there were only seven institutes of technology and no universities of technology. In haste commensurate with the inflating aims of the state, CYUT was promoted to university status, along with four other schools in 1997. By 2003, seventeen institutions were accredited as universities of technology. The administration of CYUT took advantage of its head start and aggressively opened and expanded programs, hoping to establish a reputation and an alumni base on which to compete in the future for students from the vocational high schools of Taiwan. The extent of the competition is made even more clear by noting that there were only two dozen institutions of higher learning in Taiwan in 1975, whereas by 2005 there were over 150 schools, all competing for a shrinking number of students (Chang, Chen, and Huang 2005).[11]

This growth in higher education occurred simultaneously with the flight of Taiwanese industry and capital to Southeast Asia and China in the search of cheaper labor, land, and other production costs. It is no coincidence, therefore, that the new emphasis on life-long learning, practicality, and student quality became guiding principles (Kao 2003; Peters 2003). Taiwan had depended on economic success for national survival since the KMT found itself stranded on an island within easy attacking range of its civil war enemy. It had prospered to become one of the top manufacturing economies in the world, and the government had invested in education to promote this success (Green et al. 1999). During the 1990s, the precariousness and pressures of Taiwan's position were becoming increasingly evident. No longer saddled with the censures that immediately followed the Tiananmen Square massacre and prospering in part due to the transfer of Taiwanese industry and know-how, China could and does muscle Taiwan politically, militarily, and economically. Other parts of the world, including Taiwan's great benefactor the United States, are now in direct competition with the island. And in the case of the United States, intellectual copyright and other measures designed to secure American preeminence offer little protection to innovative Taiwanese companies that see their patents, for example, violated by powerful multinational corporations that simply have the power to do so. Taiwan's prosperity seems to most intelligent people to lack sufficient footing to insure the prosperity necessary for political survival.

Poor in easily extractable natural resources, Taiwan must now rely on a service economy that cannot generate the surplus necessary to keep intact the status quo of rising expectations and economic growth. What is more, local trades are subject to global market penetration. The former president of the university reminded the faculty in more than one schoolwide meeting that, with Taiwan's entry into the WTO, even education would become a tradable commodity, and the local market might be opened to mainland institutions that could undoubtedly undercut prices. Teachers are accordingly put under pressure to assure student satisfaction with their courses, lest certain departments or the university eventually be forced to close. Likewise, the state is under pressure to make Taiwan an educational producer to draw foreign capital to the island in the form of tuition payments. For this reason, the government seeks to raise the profile of Taiwan's research institutions. It has adopted measures of academic success from the United States, in particular faculty productivity in publications, to do so. The MOE has decided that to create in Taiwan a university ranked in the top 100 in the world and to secure the competitive quality of research necessary to establish a new culture of high-level achievement, schools are ranked by their publications in international science indexes (ISI), including the Science Index (SI), the Social Science Index (SSCI), the Arts and Humanities Citation Index (A&HCI), and the Engineering Index (Ei) (see Cheng 2001; National Science Council Information Center 2005). The pressures on teachers are multiple. They must satisfy the consumer-like demands of students, expand their course schedules (which keeps salary costs low), and compete with scholars from the world's top-tier research institutions.

This is easier said than done. But the demands are completely consistent with the capitalist logic, expressed obliquely in the discourse of Taiwan's supposed miraculous achievement. Just as capitalism seems to create wealth from nothing in abstract markets, and just as modern Taiwan had once been proclaimed to have emerged miraculously from its prior status as a former colony of Japan, many now exhort the population to "create a second Taiwanese miracle" from a society not really prepared to act according to the new economy's (perhaps impossible) dictates. In the case of universities, the bidirectional pull of assuring student satisfaction and publishing in ISI and Ei journals is new to all schools in Taiwan, including big-name national schools. The pressure to succeed at everything falls heaviest on the upstarts such as CYUT. Yet even the national schools, with their monopoly on the recruitment of the best students from college-prep high schools, now find their budgets only approximately 80 percent funded by the state. They must aggressively seek out new forms of revenue to keep their budgets balanced or, at least, modestly in the red. For this reason, attractively titled programs, such as Executive Masters of Business Administration (EMBA) and International Masters of Business Administration (IMBA), have been established at nearly all major institutions to bring in the tuition money of adult lifelong learners who hope to advance their careers, cap their positions with titles, or bide their time waiting for better jobs to open. In turn, some departments at leading schools have made it a requirement of PhD students to publish in an ISI or Ei journal to graduate (with their advisor as first or second author)—a move that departments hope will bolster the rankings of their universities without regard to the inflationary expectation that students will suddenly become experts. The state has also funded the tuition of foreign students who enroll in these programs to establish a basis in the global network of knowledge workers for Taiwan's full-scale entry into the global education market as a manufacturer of value-added (if in name only—for example, *Executive* MBA) diplomas and to raise Taiwan's precarious status via its graduates.

The push to have it all (devoted teachers, efficient administration, and top publications) seems to be paying off for CYUT on two fronts. On the first front, CYUT was recognized by the MOE as the finest school in its class in 2006. This judgment was based on the number of programs rated as top quality in teaching, research, and service. Aware of the bounty this rating brings in the forms of tuition income and MOE support and fearful of losing ground to aggressive upstarts, the university is pushing for further reforms. Departments are constantly under pressure to improve service to students, promote new teaching programs, and develop new plans to expand the university's outreach to businesses in central Taiwan. Understaffed to maintain profitability and, hence, stretched in every direction to meet the demands, my department is not unique in facing this condition. For example, the China Medical University Hospital in Taichung has announced its intention to be a first-rate hospital for customer service and *the leader in all of Asia* in research in the area of Chinese and Western medicine. This leaves the staff exhausted; but it must seem absolutely necessary to top administrators, who are anxious about increasing international competition.

Regardless and perhaps because of these tensions, times remain good at CYUT on a second front: profitability. In 2004, its revenues from tuition reached approximately US$36,000,000. After all expenses, it recorded a profit of approximately US$10,000,000 (Chaoyang University of Technology Accounting Department, n.d.). That these figures are available shows the extent of MOE regulation of nonprofit universities (Laws and Regulation Database of the Republic of China, 2002). According to these rules, most of these profits are turned over to the university's foundation, which is itself regulated on how it uses this money. Half of the profits must be returned to the university for reinvestment in the school; the other half may go to outside investments, which are further regulated to prevent, for example, university profits being used to prop up the stock prices for the founder's conglomerate. Despite all the safeguards, it is well known in Taiwan that universities and other schools can generate substantial income for investors. One well-known form of graft involves the relation of construction companies to the institutions. Schools take enormous loans for construction and funnel them to chosen companies with close links to the school. Tax deductions are taken, corners are cut, and insiders line their pockets, while schools pay back loans with tuition and other income in the years to come.

The founding conglomerate of CYUT saw its fortunes decline dramatically after the assumption of power by the DPP. In my discussions with rank-and-file employees, the university is often called a *dian* (company)—implying it is, from the unofficial standpoint of the conglomerate, an income-producing unit. Nonetheless, there is good evidence that CYUT has avoided the worst kind of corruption. For, although the founding conglomerate includes a construction company that gets awarded university contracts for construction, the university has been superbly built. The crucial test in this regard was the September 21, 1999 earthquake, which destroyed numerous public schools built in the vicinity, exposing the corruption that continues to plague public building projects. Although it was built adjacent to the fault line, CYUT suffered only relatively minimal damages, which were quickly repaired. Nonetheless, although CYUT has a reputation for competent administration, there is an underlying assumption among faculty that graft, if not certain, is surely possible. In fact, the underlying message in conversation is that it would be naïve to assume otherwise.

Smile Chaoyang

What is not naïve? Everyone must find his or her way through competing value systems. For a functioning faculty member, in particular, to keep things smooth, to not expose cracks, and to bridge the fissures are as important as *lux et veritas*. This much is clearly not naïve. However, ironic implications arise for this writer. For although this chapter is critical of the institutional context of its production, the substance of this critique matters little to the university, so long as it is published in an international forum of some repute. In part, this is because this publication will appear in English and have little import to the local customer base; but, more important, the school profits from *research numbers* via MOE inflows of capital and judgments.

Bill Readings has cannily compared the contemporary university to a financial market that extracts surplus value "as a result of speculation on differentials in information" (1996: 40). Publications in number reduce risk exposure. As the published production of information in local and international journals adds to the school's spreadsheet, the university becomes further entrenched as a node in the global information exchange system. Critical intellectual projects dissipate into universal exchange systems. From the standpoint of the contemporary university, all intents transform into activity (student assistants, grant processing, interlibrary loans, database management) that serves, according to Readings, to advance "the optimal input/output ratio in matters of information" (1996: 39). As Readings further notes, the activity does little more than guarantee "technology's self-reflection" (1996: 39). This chapter certainly exemplifies the latter point, though its intended target publication misses the former, as ideally defined by the MOE.

The MOE—or what I will call here Taiwan's "Central Bank" of Education—has determined that the coin of the realm is marked by ISI and Ei indexes, though all currencies are useful because convertible. International research publication numbers (or foreign currencies) are only a small part of the university's holdings, however. Students (or rather their images) become the local banknote by which the institution turns its productive capacities into a profit stream for all involved. This includes myself, as I work away in an air-conditioned office that overlooks the foothills of Taiwan's central mountain range, and it also includes students, who trade on CYUT's good name for future considerations that include economic advantages.[12] New Taiwan dollars generated by this exchange can be traded for greenbacks, which are backed by nothing, save investments in U.S. debt instruments. The arrangement is secured by the U.S. military, which serves policy objectives that sustain the dollar's place as *the* global coin of the realm (Frank 2004). We might naïvely say the system is quite corrupt, unreasonable, and unsustainable; but, at least in the short term (depending, of course, on your point of view), it does seem smoothly efficient (the temporary disruption of the global financial crisis of 2008 notwithstanding). Via universal exchange, the global financial system turns anything local into its component.

The despair of traditionalists can be inserted here. Traditional notions and practices of harmony and reciprocity become as convertible as utilitarian science. The school is aware of this and trades openly in its capacity to manufacture well-behaved and technically skilled youngsters. On the front page of the October 2006 edition of the university newspaper, this predilection is given clear exposition in an article entitled, "The President Says Hello: The University Promotes a Successful Courtesy Campaign":

The sun has risen. President Chung, Dean of Student Affairs Peng, administrators, and teachers stand in front of the gate to greet fervently students and teachers who have just arrived. It makes everyone feel warm, as if this is a home-like school full of politeness.

To make a happy school and to carry out the plan of full-blown life education, our school has continuously promoted the "courtesy demands reciprocity" school politeness campaign. A year has gone by . . .

President Chung with sincere words and earnest wishes said, "While IQ affects the learning of professional abilities, EQ affects the development of interpersonal relationships. But what really can promote the competitive attainment of employment is something called BQ, which includes the appearance of bearing, manner, accomplishment, and attitude." . . . After graduation from Chaoyang, everyone can be trusted by employers and show the characteristics and tolerance of people at Chaoyang. . . . In the research of "the most trustworthy freshman in business in 2006," our school was chosen as the most trustworthy technology university among all of the universities in central Taiwan by the 1111 Manpower Bank website. At the same time, personality education has already become one of Chaoyang's accents that can make us proud. (*Chaoyang Times* 2006)

The Manpower Bank, an online service that links employers with workers, passes judgment,[13] and the school receives recognition (perhaps equivalent to a bond rating if we are to continue with this metaphor) for its production of BQ, which can then be traded in turn for more students, jobs, and profits.

But what exactly is BQ? Following Goleman's (1996) quasi-intellectual book, *Emotional Quotient,* and Howard Gardner's humanistic manifesto, *Frames of Mind: The Theory of Multiple Intelligences* (1983), many different Qs have emerged—often disseminated by business consultants intent on finding a competitive advantage for their clients (for example, Freedman, n.d.). While many top administrators and faculty at CYUT find the humanistic approach elucidated by Gardner to represent a high point of Western thought and have urged subordinate faculty to take this approach to teaching, the choice of Qs (or intelligences) appears determined by the bank as *Beauty Quotient*—that is, brains, beauty, and behavior. The market accomplishes what teachers can only hope to do: define standards that discipline students (for example, *Administration Magazine,* 2007).

The two twentieth-century value systems at work at CYUT fit nicely with brains and behavior; beauty (in the form of a smiling CYUT) puts an appropriate face on it. Everyone is to be warm as if a part of the family—precisely the rule of the state in the twentieth century; everyone should have technical skills to enhance the march of progress; and all are to be happy, not because they are young and healthy—a fact elided, assumed, or ignored; rather students should be happy to insure that everyone who graduates from CYUT can be trusted by the job bank and its investors/customers, called employers.

While students often treat this injunction with the same indifference that they bring to the flag-raising ceremonies, the bottom line remains: They act out the smiles, and they expect others to put on a face for the school, too. The injunction is reinforced via seemingly insignificant and perhaps unconsciously crafted devices. For example, the title for this chapter was found on a university-wide questionnaire handed to all students early in the spring semester of 2006. Under a large-font English heading in bold, "Smile Chaoyang," students were asked in Chinese about their general satisfaction with all university units. For example, "Are you extremely satisfied, satisfied, a little satisfied, a little dissatisfied, not satisfied or extremely dissatisfied with the library?" At the bottom of the page, students were given room to write comments, which they generally ignored. Meant to provide feedback that spurs administrative staff to higher levels of customer service, no effort was made to create a statistically reliable survey. Students were only asked to rate their satisfaction; nothing was learned of the dedication and intentions of those surveyed. In its presumed anonymity, equality, and terms of inquiry, it resembled a cross between a consumer survey and a democratic ballot. It served, moreover, as a circuit through which the imperative for satisfaction moves from producer to consumer and back. It is no coincidence, therefore, that the command to "Smile Chaoyang," which hovers above the survey, is written in English—the sign of globalization par excellence. Even when filling out a bureaucratic evaluation, students sense they are standing before a higher power for which they must practice their BQ. The smiles say it all.

Numbers determine rankings as they emulate sales figures, which further determine rankings and so forth in yet another feedback loop. Each response is itself numbered, and one can be certain the feedback received by the administration is numerical. The focus on numbers is similar to teaching evaluation forms, handed to students a full month before instruction ends. Scores in the humanities and social sciences tend to be highly inflated, with average scores ranging around 4.3 on a scale of 1 to 5. CYUT is indeed a school where all teachers are above average; for to receive scores between 4 (agree or good) and 3 (no opinion) is to put one's teaching methods and classroom charisma in doubt. In fact, an administrator will exhort occasionally all teachers to teach *above average*. Impossible. Yet in the context in which marketing rules, it makes sense. This sensible irrationality is demonstrated insofar as this very measurement device is unscientific.[14] Consider the types of questions asked and their numerical responses. The first question: Is the teacher on time? There are only two logical answers, yes or no. Yet on the survey, there are no fewer than five possible replies, which ask only the degree of the student's *agreement*. Moreover, the fact that agreement, like satisfaction, is expected of both producers and consumers is given expression in the mantralike repetition of the first phrase *feichang tongyi* (uncommonly agree). As has happened elsewhere in the global educational marketplace, teachers are told that the evaluations are used only for reference; yet they have become the primary means by which promotion recommendations are made in the area of teaching precisely because they are expressed as a numeric measure in a system demanding some kind of metric. Thus, teaching is not evaluated in terms of empirical facts but in term of student *perceptions of facts*—the preferred perception of which is uncommon agreement or satisfaction. Teachers naturally become perception managers or, simply, marketers. It should come as no surprise that demanding lessons are as unpopular with teachers as they are with students, as consuming subjects invested with the power of evaluating the measure of their own satisfaction.

Baudrillard writes, "The globalization of exchanges puts an end to the universalization of values. This marks the triumph of a uniform thought over a universal one" (2003). The message is simple: The hope of universal Enlightenment has become one with marketing (see Yan, Chapter Six in this volume). Graduate students in my department demonstrate this fact. They copy the questionnaire methods of the school as they research the perceptions of students, parents, or teachers toward certain teaching methods or parenting styles. Such studies become tools for their professional advancement on graduation insofar as they give a quasi-scientific aura to a new and improved teaching method that they claim to possess. Up front with their bias toward perceptions, students are not concerned with the empirically testable reality of student achievements or failures; they have simply adopted the methods of CYUT, which has adopted these common and poorly constructed research designs from business and education journals. Students, therefore, know that these methods are valued. Moreover, they learn that perceptions can be traded for hard currency, which buys houses, cars, trips abroad, stable families, more education, and all the trappings and signs of middle-class success (for comparison with PRC constructions of middle-class status, see Ren, Chapter One in this volume).

Where does this leave us? Confucians believe, as they have since the turn of the previous century, that the world is on the wane. Bill Readings tells us we now dwell in the ruins of the Enlightenment University. On the wane and in ruins, State Neo-Confucianism and Enlightenment values nonetheless structure much of the activity that occurs at CYUT insofar as these values serve to facilitate the new terms of universal exchange.

Looking out my window, everything appears perfect. The air-conditioner hums; Radiohead plays through the computer's speakers; students cheer occasionally; the electronic bulletin board, posted permanently in the central commons, flashes neon messages amid subtropical trees and smiling students.

Notes

1. Asian values were reenvisioned as a form of Confucian capitalism during the rise of the Asian Tigers in the 1970s and 1980s. Following the Asian economic crisis of 1997, however, their cachet as the cultural infrastructure for economic success has begun to unravel. See, for example, Arai, Chapter Seven in this volume.

2. Readings (1996) argues that the modern university found its rationale in its support of national-cultural projects; for example, English departments at British universities. National culture and Enlightenment ideals have been practically intertwined. The nation was certainly a great hope for common people as a ground of resistance to monarchy. Similarly, early-twentieth-century Chinese intellectuals thought that Chinese national culture would provide resistance to colonialism. In this way, reactionary nationalism was tied to progressive Enlightenment. In Chinese history, State Neo-Confucianism seemed antithetical to modernity; yet State Neo-Confucianism depended on modern technology for its propagation and its importance as a ground for Chinese identity.

3. I have considered the problem of posing before the world in greater detail in a chapter on Taiwanese photography; see Pazderic 2009.

4. Taiwan had been a colony of Japan from 1895 to 1945, ending with Japan's defeat in World War II.

5. After eight years in office marred by scandal, Chen Shui-bian was defeated by the KMT candidate in 2008 and then imprisoned on petty charges

6. This parallels the bipolarization of the work force in Japan as discussed by Arai (Chapter Seven in this volume) and is arguably causally connected to the phenomenon of Chinese society as "pyramidal" in structure (see Ren, Chapter One in this volume) as Japanese and Taiwanese corporations seek sources of cheap labor on the Chinese mainland.

7. The difference between individualism and conformity in the United States can be chalked up to differences between collective endeavors and individual ones—in particular consumption; it is in consuming practices where people generally have the broadest scope of choices (Borgmann 1984: 140). In Taiwan, there is a similar division.

8. For example, in the state telecommunications industry that I studied in the 1990s, the difference in pay between an average engineer and a local general manager was only US$2,000 to US$3,000 per month (Pazderic 1999: 83–120).

9. For a discussion of how this value system in its contemporary institutionalization affects the production of academic knowledge at Taiwan's leading national research institute, see Chun 2000.

10. As recently as May 2006, the deputy minister of the National Science Council was indicted on corruption charges, to provide but one example (Ex-Science Council Deputy Minister Indicted for Graft 2006).

11. The history of population control in Taiwan can explain the shrinking student base for these new educational institutions. Although space constraints do not allow a full treatment, it should be noted that the population policies in Taiwan have been as influenced by Cold War politics as economics. Once acclaimed for its success in the 1960s and 1970s for implementing fertility limitation as a strategy of development, Taiwan is now facing a population implosion. Presently, the Taiwanese government seeks to increase the population of the island for its political purposes. The irony, of course, is that Taiwan's population would rise very quickly if the labor imported to produce success were allowed to remain and reproduce. Instead, Taiwan pursues neoliberal globalization through the production of human capital for its postindustrial economic future alongside off-shoring industrial labor elsewhere and importing a temporary workforce for low-skilled jobs at home.

12. See Song (Chapter Ten in this volume) for a discussion of the relative privileged labor status of PhD students in government responses to the IMF crisis in South Korea.

13. See 1111 Manpower Bank 2006, 2007.

14. Other problems of proper scientific investigation implicit in the student evaluation process include lack of reliability checking, lack of multiple scales to measure latent variables, validity (are questions understood as they are meant to be understood?), and descriptive statistics (including the problem of normal distribution).

Chapter Six

"What If Your Client/Employer Treats Her Dog Better Than She Treats You?"

Market Militarism and Market Humanism
in Postsocialist Beijing

YAN HAIRONG

In May 2002, the Beijing Fuping Professional Training School opened in a suburb of Beijing. As a private boarding school for training rural young women as domestics for urban households, Fuping appeared to fill an unmet need. State-funded professional training schools are part of the system of formal education. They parallel junior or senior high school education, with programs lasting several years. Workers in state-owned enterprises or other formal sectors have formal apprenticeships. Migrant workers, however, often learn their skills on the job. New migrant domestic workers are sometimes given a brief "training" by recruitment agencies, which may take from thirty minutes to a couple of hours of lectures on labor discipline. Fuping offers a dozen or so courses in its month-long training program and has pioneered a new style of training with private initiatives.

It was not long before both domestic and international media picked up the story.[1] Less than twenty years before, the establishment of the first government-affiliated company to recruit rural women as domestics for Beijing households had still faced some uncertainty about the ideological correctness of this business for a country with a socialist heritage. Since then, many private recruitment agencies have mushroomed. In 2002, the newsworthiness of the Fuping story was in its being a private training school and the brainchild of two eminent economists, Mao Yushi and Tang Min. In 1999 Mao had stepped down as director of Unirule Economic Research Institute (Tianze jingji yanjiusuo), a nongovernmental think tank, a post he had assumed after retiring from the Chinese Academy of Social Sciences. With connections to the Cato Institute in Washington, D.C., he is a self-proclaimed supporter of the neoliberal economics of Friedrich Hayek. Unirule has produced economists influential in Beijing policy circles. Tang Min, Mao's former student, was the chief economist of the Asian Development Bank.

Fuping is a play on words for the Chinese phrase meaning "poverty alleviation." Accordingly, on entering the school's main office building, one would see the publicity board:

> Renowned economist Professor Mao Yushi, Dr. Tang Min, the Chinese chief economist in Asia Development Bank, and other well-known figures, taking upon themselves the task of social development, established the nonprofit Beijing Fuping Professional Training School and Beijing Fuping Domestic Service Center in 2002. By providing professional training and creating job opportunities, they hope to contribute their own meager strength to help the urban and rural *ruoshi qunti* [literally, "weak-powered groups"] to gain employment and set themselves on the path of development. At the same time, the [provision of] professional and standard domestic service and community service will enable urban residents, who have the means and the need, to attain a higher quality of life.
>
> Tuition: 700 Yuan [just under US$90]
>
> Qualifications for Recruitment:
>
> (1) Age 17–40. Female, with a height above 1.55 meters. In good health and able to speak and understand Mandarin.
>
> (2) Have full documentation (ID card, health exam card, marriage-fertility card, migrant work permit, and academic diploma).

The Fuping School is nonprofit in the sense that the proceeds do not accrue to shareholders but are reinvested in the operation and expansion of the school. The required academic qualifications for enrollment were not specified, but most of the trainees have a junior or senior high school education. Located on the grounds of a former driving school, it has a spacious campus with classrooms, dorm rooms, a cafeteria, and even a sports field. Classes begin with the sound of an electric bell. Trainees, mostly in their teens or early twenties, wear pink uniforms and address the staff as "teacher" (*laoshi*).

At the beginning, Fuping operated strictly as a private institution following market principles. The school initially tried to recruit trainees from among urban laid-off workers, graduates from junior high vocational schools, and rural women. This private model of recruitment proved unsuccessful, bringing in fewer than 200 recruits in seven months. Mao revealed to me that potential trainees tended to distrust institutions that lacked government support. With too few recruits and some not being able to afford the tuition, the school found it difficult to survive. Fuping revised its strategy by entering into a partnership with the Anhui Provincial Government's Poverty-Alleviation Department. This affiliation ensures a supply of 2,000 trainees a year and an allocation from the local government's poverty-alleviation fund to cover half of the tuition for each trainee. The other half is deducted through installments from trainees' wages once they are employed. With the assistance of the Central Government Poverty-Alleviation Department, the partnership has quickly expanded to other provinces. Graduates of the school are channeled into the domestic service labor market in Beijing. This practice of "a private establishment with public/government assistance" (*min ban gong/guan zhu*) is now stylized as the Fuping model. Since its establishment, mainstream media and researchers have expressed only praise and support for Fuping and Mao Yushi. In the story of the school's development, however, we can see very clearly how Mao's utopian vision of the private sector providing training and jobs had to be adjusted to the complexly sedimented history of postsocialist China. The partnership is telling in several ways: It speaks volumes about popular distrust of the market in an environment where there is little regulation or protection from state oversight; it also suggests the historical paradox on which this neoliberal project rests, in which the state is both the legitimating power but also the constraint against which neoliberalism constructs its project.

Nonetheless, the idea behind this partnership is the commodification of labor power. China's Mao-era (1949–1976) state ideology valued workers and peasants as the political foundation, with manual labor as an important basis for class identity. By way of contrast, an institution such as Fuping trains migrant women to embody a new ideal of what it means to be a proper worker in postsocialist China. Neoliberalism, promoted as a global hegemonic ideology since the Thatcher-Reagan era, has become embedded in labor relations reform in China, creating a discourse of self-enterprising individuals as millions of urban workers are laid off and millions of rural migrants are brought into urban areas as the informal workforce.[2] The case of Fuping demonstrates the deployment of neoliberalism as a pedagogical process that teaches trainees how to understand their labor in a rapidly marketizing and stratifying society. This should be seen as a project of social engineering producing new kinds of worker-subjects. In this regard, the production of domestic labor is a process parallel to the self-making practices of the middle class explored by Hai Ren in Chapter One of this volume. The restructuring of the postsocialist economy requires an integral "restructuring" of the worker's subjectivity.

This chapter is based on several trips I made to the school in 2005 and my interviews with Mao Yushi and some of the school teachers. However, my analysis is also grounded on my research on domestic service first begun in 1998. My interactions with trainees were limited to conversations with them during the breaks, but some of the comments made by Mao and the teachers I interviewed reveal how some trainees have reacted to the training. Liberal intellectuals, such as Fuping's founders, view migrant workers as a "weak-powered group" (*ruoshi qunti*). Intellectuals, media, and nongovernmental organizations latch on this term to voice their concerns about justice, social cohesion, and development in the context of growing inequality and instability. But what role of mediation and representation do these actors take on themselves in using this term? What might be the limits embedded in the invocation and mobilization of this term? Is not empowerment a governance technology? How is it that the problem is seen as one of reforming the consciousness or the capacity of the worker rather than one of the economic system itself?

The Logic of Equivalence: Potatoes, Pork, and Trainees

Let's visit the school to observe how trainees are taught about their relationship with their employers. It is instructive to note here that one of the first lessons is a shift in language. Students must discard their customary use of the term "employer" (*guzhu*) for the school's term "client" (*kehu*). This apparently insignificant substitution is nonetheless loaded with significance. This language form becomes the sign of the worker's "professionalization" and also of her "empowerment" as a sovereign subject who is a service provider. It registers her service as a commodity form severed from any association with a master–servant relationship. Just as the concept of human capital is invested with the notion of the worker as his or her "own capitalist," so the domestic worker becomes an entrepreneur. The class relation is thus made invisible in language.

At the time of my visit, there were about fifty trainees in the school. Sometimes a class has as many as 100. Courses include cleaning, cooking, ironing, caregiving, and babysitting. The program ends with an intensive preparation for job seeking and a practice job interview. During training, trainees rise at 6 a.m. to receive one hour of military-style physical training prior to attending eight to ten hours of class a day (including weekends). In the evenings, they watch television until lights go off at 10 p.m. But even their evening leisure relates to their training, as we will see in the following discussion. The military training, supervised by two ex-soldiers, consists of disciplined line formation, running, and group exercise. When I expressed surprise at this, Teacher Lu explained, "Because clients have various demands, the school's training strategy is to extend our battle line (*lachang zhanxian*) and enhance trainees' adaptability for all situations."

The class that prepares trainees for upcoming job interviews was taught by an experienced Teacher Yin. The class I visited had more than forty students from Shaanxi Province. In this session, Yin was to go through the list of "do's and don'ts" each student had learned as part of their curriculum. In noting the possibility of two different job options for them—domestic work plus either childcare or eldercare, she instructed, "You cannot be picky. You cannot say 'I just want to take care of babies' or 'I just want to look after the elderly.' If you are picky, then you will have fewer employment opportunities." According to the guideline, trainees must sign a one-year contract with their clients. "You are obliged to honor the contract and cannot leave at will. Otherwise, you will have to bear all the consequences. Do you have any objections?" Yin did not specify what these consequences might be; however, the threat of reduced employability enunciated just a moment before still lingered, and the trainees seemed to understand. They answered in a chorus, "No."

In Yin's lecture, trainees were taught to view their labor as a commodity and their training as added value that comes from "professionalization." First, Yin compared selling the trainee's labor power to selling potatoes. "If you do well, then it will be easier for us to recommend you to other clients.

It is like selling potatoes. Usually people say, 'Come and look at my potatoes, big and good.' I can't say, 'Come and look at my potatoes, black and small.'" She later stressed that trainees must be prepared to do a superior job, because in 2005 their beginning wage at 450 yuan per month (about US$55) was significantly higher than the average of 350 to 400 yuan for domestic work in Beijing. To illustrate the concept of added value, she made use of a pork analogy: "The higher your wage, the higher expectation your clients will have for you, right?" Some trainees replied, "Right." "Why?" asked Yin. No reply. Yin continued, "You raise your pig. Others also raise their pigs. Others sell their pork at 2 yuan per *jin* [500 grams], but you sell yours at four yuan. Why can you do that? Do your pigs have more legs? What do you have that is different? Well, you have had training. Anyone can sweep the floor and dust the desk. What do you have that is different? You've got a qualification [for being better paid]." Another wall slogan echoes her words, "A trained domestic worker is different from others [*yu zhong bu tong*]! Your training should show!" This exhortation teaches them the value added from the professional training in which they have invested through their tuition payments. The school becomes a brand that acts as a guarantee for nervous prospective employers about the reliability and quality of their maids. While the luster of Mao Yushi generates much of this brand value, it can be sustained and reproduced only by these workers delivering labor to the satisfaction of their clients.

In Yin's teaching, the analogy between pork and the trainees' labor power is a clue to the commodity logic of the training school. Disparate things—potatoes, pork, domestic labor—are linked together in this teaching as they all speak the language of commodities. The subsumption of labor to the market is articulated through this prosaic commodity objectification. Labor power is made to appear "like" pork and potatoes despite its potential to produce more value than it costs. What the trainees were taught was not the Marxist critique of the commodity form but a neoclassical economic logic of commodities in its most naked and objectified form without any sentimental veiling. Marx's analysis of the commodity reveals that commodification and objectification of labor power, rather than being natural and universal in human history, is a particular problem of capitalist relations of production. Marx's analysis of labor under conditions of capitalism is thus a historical and specific critique of capitalism and points to the historical instances and future possibilities of decommodification. In contrast, neoclassical economics not only takes commodifiction to be natural and ideal but is also used as the basis for policy advocacy and employment training.

Neoliberalism challenges the state's function in managing and distributing public goods and in providing regulations to protect domestic industry and the domestic market against transnational competition. It codes privatization, or the conversion of public goods into commodities, as "liberty" and "freedom" and calls for governmental encouragement of labor migration. Educating laborers to embrace their own positioning as commodities in the market is both a crucial condition and effect of neoliberal marketization. In the case of Fuping, provincial governments have subsidized the tuition for these rural young women to learn to think less about their expectation of the state and more about themselves as autonomous and self-willed agents in the market as service providers.

Yin has just done that: She unsentimentally teaches about the object-ness and value added of their labor power so that the young women would come to act consciously as a commodity of some distinction. The fact that Yin is not an ideologue but an ordinary teacher reflects how widely neoliberal ideology has become disseminated as a social common sense, which needs only to be reinforced through formal instruction for rural young women who lack an awareness of their own commodity status.

In Yin's instruction, however, there are multiple codings for the domestic worker. A subtle shift is implicit in moving from the question "Do your pigs have more legs?" to "What do you have that is distinctive? Well, you have had the training." The first "you" is the owner of the pigs to be sold and the third "you" is the worker as seller of her labor power. In Yin's language here, however, the second "you" is at once both the first "you" (owner and seller) and the third "you" (worker and seller). The three iterations of the second-person pronoun are placed in a chain of equivalence, and thus each "you" is mobile and can therefore become transmuted into the other. The trainees were thus told that not only does the same logic of value operate in these different instances for the owner/seller and worker/seller alike but that as workers/sellers they can also become owners/sellers. It is implied to the trainees that this transformation from workers/sellers to owners/sellers follows the same logic of value. Hence we could recall the shift in calling one's employer a client, as already noted.

The trainee's television viewing in the evenings reinforces this lesson. For example, the melodrama *Oshin*, produced by NHK (Japan Broadcasting

Corporation) in 1983, tells the story of how a young girl from a poor tenant farmer family in Japan who had worked as a domestic servant became founder and owner of a supermarket chain.[3] Although the metamorphosis of Oshin allegorizes the transformation of Japan from a rural society to a high-growth economy, in noting the circulation of this series throughout developing countries and regions in Asia, Leo Ching argues, "Through the drama's regional distribution, this national allegory is then narrated into a regional story that dramatizes the parallel but belated economic development of Asian countries such as Taiwan, Singapore, Indonesia, and more lately, China and Vietnam" (2000: 250). *Oshin* was shown on Chinese television in 1984 and became a huge hit among urban Chinese who had just begun to have access to television sets. The story inspired the imagination of its primarily urban audience for the opportunities that the economic reform would open up to them in the 1980s. This replay of *Oshin* twenty years later is for a new generation of young women coming from rural areas not yet exposed to this TV series and presumably not yet transformed by this new consciousness. Oshin's specific humble beginnings as a domestic worker from the countryside and her eventual business success must speak with particular force to these rural trainees about both personal and national teleologies of economic development in a way that is undisrupted by the uncertainties of the global market economy. The Chinese broadcasting of *Oshin* has the theme song titled "Always Believe" (*yongyuan xiangxin*).

As if to echo "Always Believe," Yin concluded this lecture by reciting a hortatory passage, which she asked one of the trainees to write on the blackboard so that the rest will always remember it: "You are not allowed to detest [*yanwu*] your work in any situation. Detesting one's work is the worst thing. Even if you are forced by circumstances to do some tedious work, you should find some joy [*lequ*] in it. You must understand that you should find joy in all that should be done and must be done." She paused here and asked the class, "Should you or shouldn't you make money?" The class answered in unison, "We should." She continued, "This is the right attitude we should have toward work. If you have this attitude, no matter what work you do, you will achieve a good effect [*hao de chengxiao*]."

Yin instructed trainees that, when they encounter difficulties in their work, they should read this paragraph. If the foregoing analogy of potatoes-pork-trainees has revealed a thorough objectification of labor as a commodity on the market, then the would-be domestic worker is also required to develop an affective relationship with labor and to invest her own subjectivity in it. The subsumption of labor to capital, as Marx wrote, does not end in objectification (her labor power and labor time purchased and thus owned by another), but it also requires a reanimation. The trainee must find joy in her work. Objectification and alienation in the process of work is anticipated in Yin's lecture but is preempted through a militarized command of discipline, "You are not allowed to detest your work in any situation. Detesting one's work is the worst thing." This command is aided by an appeal to the moral imperative to make money.

No Excuse: The Military as a Concept-Metaphor

On the classroom wall hung a banner that greets trainees silently every day: "Do not be a deserter once you enter the battlefield. You will never earn sympathy or respect if you are afraid of difficulties, choose desertion, or look for excuses for laziness." Another banner hails them: "I cheer you on in your courage to walk out of isolated mountainous villages; I applaud your every effort to overcome difficulties." The classroom environment thus transmits the message that the market is a battlefield and that trainees are soldiers who need to prove themselves through determination and discipline. Mao Yushi, the school founder, had once remarked, "The market finely and fairly sorts out each and everyone." This is not a minority view of a single economist but is part of the dominant discourse in reform-era China.[4] For example, the *Beijing Review* echoed this view with an article titled, "Let the Market Sort Talent Out" (2004: 5). In these slogans, the market is a battleground that sorts out winners and losers.[5] In Fuping's education, the war metaphor gathers into itself both a moral imperative against quitting. "Deserters" are considered worse than losers because they constitute a threat to the game of competition. If it is bad enough to be poor and needy, desertion would amount to complete unworthiness: "You will never earn sympathy or respect." Here we see spelled out the consequences of not measuring up to the standard of Fuping's brand hinted at earlier by Yin.[6] It is perhaps not a coincidence that Teacher Lu had used the words *battle line* to talk about the training that the school provides. However, this battle line is not one that is formed collectively by the trainees. It is built in each trainee so that each and every one of them is prepared to assume responsibility for all possibilities and risks. The market as the battleground compels an internalization of the battle line within individual subjectivity.

Why is the battlefield a privileged metaphor in this context? "A business field is like a battlefield" (*shangchang ru zhanchang*) is a common enough saying, but those involved in battling are presumably entrepreneurs and their chief executives. In Fuping this metaphor is extended to each and every worker. Or is it more than a metaphor? Is this market-cum-battlefield a unique discourse of Fuping, or is it an idea that circulates more widely? How are we to understand this new kind of "militarism"?

Perhaps we can address this last question by way of a detour into popular books that advocate the military as the source of management and leadership skills necessary for business success today. However, Chinese military training is not the model promoted. Chinese military involvement in business in the reform era has been a public secret. Its association with corruption and abuses of power has generated so much public resentment that in 1998 President Jiang Zemin ordered the military to cease its commercial activities. Rather, U.S. military training comes ready to hand in an English-language literature promoting its value for business success.

It is no accident that the U.S. military has become a source of managerial inspiration. As the largest military establishment, with the most overseas operations, it has nurtured a militarism that has become a national ideal.[7] Chalmers Johnson quotes Andrew Bacevich, a West Point graduate and a Vietnam War veteran, "Americans in our own time have fallen prey to militarism, manifesting itself in a romanticized view of soldiers, a tendency to see military power as the truest measure of national greatness. . . . To a degree without precedent in U.S. history, Americans have come to define the nation's strength and well-being in terms of military preparedness, military action, and the fostering of (or nostalgia for) military ideals" (Johnson 2006: 20).

Yet militarism is not just promoted in its association with nationhood. It is touted as a template for social and individual management. For example, the book *The West Point Way of Leadership* speaks to a civilian readership: "The differences that exist between military and civilian leadership are differences in degree, not in kind." (Donnithorne 1993: 9). This is substantiated in the book's list of West Point graduates who have succeeded as CEOs of major corporations, presidents of many colleges and universities, and officials in all levels of government. This book was translated into Chinese and published in Taiwan in 1994 and then in mainland China in 1998. This view also resonates in business circles, as an article in the U.S. magazine *Business Week* tells of how military skills honed in the war against Iraq are becoming a human resource asset to corporate America: "It turns out that the U.S. involvement in Iraq . . . has become an unlikely but effective business boot camp" (Plameri 2004: 80). Brace Barber's *No Excuse Leadership*, translated in 2004 and very popular in China, also makes a similar link:

> *No Excuse Leadership* illustrates for leaders in all fields how to lead and succeed in difficult circumstances by using the leadership principles that the U.S. Army Ranger School experience helps people develop and that anyone can strive to master. . . . There is no opting out. . . . You either develop yourself and your leaders through purposeful, planned effort or you choose the alternative—suboptimum performance and profit. In today's elbow-throwing world, you need every advantage. . . . You live your professional life in competition. . . . It is a tiring life and one that can wear you down if you are using trial and error to search for methods that create success. Leave chance to someone else as you adopt a No Excuse philosophy.
>
> Truly, winning *is* the name of the game. . . . To win you must change the way you approach day-to-day situations. . . . (2004: 1–2; italics in the original)

Militarism is a new model of self-discipline and self-management and a new way to engage the world as society comes to be seen as an unending and intensified process of competition.

Chinese publishers and business circles are quick to borrow this inspiration when management in postsocialist China faces the problem of disgruntled labor and social unrest. The Chinese Social Sciences Press has created a book series called "Learn management from the military" (*xiang jundui xuexie guanli shu xi*) that so far has published nine books, eight of which are translated from English and include those discussed in this section. On Amazon.com, a blurb from *Fortune* magazine promotes *The Marine Corps Way* (Santamaria 2005) as follows: "The book makes a convincing case that battlefield techniques really do work in the business world." *Publishers Weekly* says of *Team Secrets of the Navy Seals* (Anon. 2003): "The armed forces are a wellspring of managerial concepts." Indeed, an explicit adoption of the military as a way of thinking about the business field is the premises shared by all these books and their promoters.

Mainstream media in China have embraced uncritically leadership ideals associated with a variety of U.S. military units as part of a larger literature on "studies for success" (*chenggongxue*).⁸ The Military Academy of West Point is said to be even better than Harvard's MBA program for training entrepreneurs. It not only incubates militarists and entrepreneurs but also reveals the shortcomings of higher education in China (Fan 2003: 82).

With the neoliberal notion that the social sphere be brought into the economic domain (Lemke 2001: 197), the military and market have become interpenetrating spheres. In thinking about their relationship, we have to go beyond viewing the military as merely a metaphor and into thinking of it as a discourse that has the power to perform a certain reality into being in the production of new kinds of subjects.⁹ Martha Banta writes of the narrative productions in the age of Frederick Taylor and Henry Ford, both pioneers in scientific management in the early twentieth century, "Everyone caught up in the times had tales to tell that 'spoke' the times into being" (1993: 5). The question for us is what times are now being spoken into being by narratives that make a corporate military-market world not just imaginable but as an imperative for survival. In our neoliberal time, we have highly rated reality shows such as "The Apprentice" and "Survivor" that beam out a message espoused by Barber: "Winning is the name of the game." Society is a battleground, whether it is in the boardroom, on the street, or on an island. These shows are being broadcast in Asia. To broaden its transnational appeal, "Survivor" has its "Survivor: China" series. The neoliberal reform is telling a new story of the time. With tens of millions of urban workers losing their jobs and their livelihoods devastated with the reform of state-owned enterprises, with tens of millions of migrant workers toiling in substandard conditions for a substandard living while a few magically accrue astronomical wealth, "hard work" is no longer an economic and social guarantee of a livelihood (c.f. Ehrenreich 2001). "Winners" and "losers" are propagated as the basic binary characters in the tale of our new time that renders society as a battlefield.

From Literary Humanism to Market Humanism

If Yin's class taught trainees to objectify their labor as a commodity, then the psychology class was to teach them how to reanimate themselves through an affective attachment to their work. In his midthirties, Chen had himself grown up in the countryside. He opened the class as follows: "A year has four seasons, and our life has high points and low points. . . . Today we talk about how to deal with human relations [*yu ren da jiao dao*]. If you are good at dealing with human relations, then you will be happy; if you are not good at dealing with human relations, then you will feel relatively painful." Then he asked the class what kinds of skills one should have in dealing with others. Some trainees were eager to reply, "smile," "be polite," "be careful with one's words and behaviors" (*zhuyi yanying juzhi*). Chen nodded approvingly but wrote his first point on the blackboard: "Respect" (*zunzhong*). "Do you like yourself? Can you accept yourself?" he asked. Trainees, "Yes!" "Good! Only if you accept yourself can you accept others." He wrote this adage on the blackboard. His second point, "Self-presentation" (*da ban ziji*), was divided into natural appearance, appropriate dress, and proper deportment. He especially emphasized "words and behaviors" (*yanxing*) because "the moment you move your hand or foot (*jushou touzu*), you pass information about yourself to others." In elaborating this point, Chen provided a comparison between rural and urban people:

> The image that impressed me most was a peasant in Northern Shaanxi: old, wearing a white towel on the head, perhaps with a sheep prod in hand, his eyes without any expression. The eye is the place where urbanites are different from rural folks. And you also need to pay attention to walking. Rural folks walk differently from urbanites. [To mimic the rural style of walking, he hunched his back a little bit and walked slowly. The trainees all laughed.] In short, you should be energetic. You should like yourself and learn to look at yourself in the mirror everyday. You should look for shortcomings and for places where you can improve yourself.

The image of an elderly man as a symbol of rurality is perhaps not accidental. It strongly evokes the famous oil painting named "Father" by artist Luo Zhongli. This painting was awarded the first-class prize in the 1980 China Youth Art Exhibition and is now in the collection of the National Art Museum of China in Beijing. The Chinese Central Television's special program on this painting offers a familiar interpretation: "[This painting] gives a tragic shock [*beiju xing de zhenhan*] in its representation of an old peasant in poverty. The realistic details of his parched lips, wrinkle-furrowed face, and his crude bowl diminish the distance between the viewer and the image. Through this painting, the artist offers a reflection on the traditional culture and the nation."[10] The artist had intended to create an image of national allegory and a portrayal of humanity.[11] However, for many urban Chinese, this painting has become a stereotypical image of the peasantry, an aged figure stupefied by the impoverished conditions of his existence and static tradition. Chen was not unique in his view of rural culture. In a recent documentary that follows the artist Luo Zhongli to the mountainous area where the prototype of "Father" had lived, a film critic again described the look in the eyes of rural people:

> Their eyes all have a kind, meek, and indifferent look, like that of a camel in a desert. Sailing on the sea, one can reach the shore; hiking on the mountain, one can reach the summit. Only in a desert can one feel the indifference of the endless yellow sand to human effort. It hurts us to see the desertlike indifference in the eyes of the children. It shows us the history.[12]

Contrary to the intention of the artist, viewers are not brought closer to the figure of the peasant by the realistic details. Rather, this close-up view of a peasant face was produced precisely at a moment of historical reversal to the relationship between intellectuals and peasants in the Maoist revolutionary legacy. The revolutionary process had compelled a recognition of self-inadequacy of the radical intellectuals as the sole subject of revolution and had nurtured a "combined" (*xiang jiehe*) agency between the intellectuals and the peasantry in the making of a social revolution. The negation of the radical content of Maoism, followed by the cultural turn in post-Mao China historiography, helped to reconstitute the intellectuals as the self-adequate subject of modernity.[13] The close-up ironically forebodes an unbridgeable chasm that opens up in the reform period between the cosmopolitan urban subject and the "backward" peasants now seen as a drag on China's modernity project.

Paradoxically, this took place in the emerging liberal discourse of universal humanism in the early 1980s. The liberal discourse of humanism is a negation of the leftist view that there was no universal humanity in a class-divided society and that "universal humanity" as such is a bourgeois ideological imagination.[14] The official negation of the Cultural Revolution in 1976 signaled an end to China's short twentieth century of revolution (1919–1976) (Wang 2006). Following the official ending of revolution and class politics came a tidal wave of humanism that first emerged in the field of philosophy of aesthetics around the issue of whether there is universal aesthetics and hence universal humanity (*pubian renxing*). In the same time period, the question of literary subjectivity (*wenxue zhuti xing*) was also raised and widely discussed in the field of literary criticism. "Literary subjectivity" emphasized the self-realization and agency of authors, literary characters, and literary critics as self-affirming sovereign subjects. Although this view of subjectivity encountered critiques from the perspectives of Marxist historical materialism, it won out in the debates and became the dominant and popular concept of self-hood after 1985. With the hindsight of the present it should be clear that this theory of subjectivity reflected the rapid rise of the intellectuals in the early to mid-1980s to resume their status as elites and that they thereby "expressed their expectations of their own agency and position as the subject (*zhuti*) above the object (*keti*), which included social environment (*shehui huanjing*), state, and the masses" (Zhu 1998: 120).

The rapid expansion of the market in the 1990s enriched some intellectuals who were associated with business. Those in fields of management, economics, and technology have seen an ascendance in their prestige and wealth. Humanistic intellectuals, on the contrary, experienced a social marginalization and bemoaned a loss of humanism that once flourished as an intellectual ideal a decade before. As a response, both Zhu Dongli and Wang Hui critically reflect that an imaginary of universal humanism has lost its social relevance to address the new reality of commodification, social disparity, and fragmentation created by the expanding market economy (Zhu 1998: 169–172; Wang H. 2003: 167).

Following this critique, I argue that although, by the late 1980s, aesthetic-literary humanism as intellectual discourses had declined, it had prepared the way for the rise of a market humanism that imagined global capitalism as the space of utopia. This is not to say that aesthetic-literary humanism directly gave birth to market humanism by any sort of logical continuity but that the market appropriated the social fermentation brought out through these intellectual debates and created its own version of humanism. Or one could say that the issue of humanism migrated from the spheres of aesthetics and literary practices to the increasingly dynamic and dominant sphere of the marketplace and in the process was remade into market humanism.[15] Indeed, many intellectuals followed this migration themselves into the sea of commerce (*xia hai*) and transformed themselves from self-styled liberal humanists to self-styled entrepreneurs. Some of those remaining in academic institutions practice part-time *xia hai*, capitalizing on their credentials in numerous ways. What was felt to have been lost as aesthetic and literary humanism is indeed thriving as market humanism.

The question of what market humanism is will be clearer as we move further into Chen's lecture. For now we should note a repetition with a difference in Chen's invocation of the image of the old peasant. He appropriates the legacy of 1980s humanism that speaks on behalf of the nation via an objectification of the peasantry. Of course he does so because this objectification is enmeshed in a historicist view that has become common sense since the 1980s. When the commentator on Luo's painting found a history in the eyes of "desertlike indifference," this history has been reconstructed by the post-Mao intellectual discourse, culminating in the 1988 six-part TV series "Heshang" (River Elegy). In that series, the liberal national intellectual surveys a series of objects: the nation, history, (agrarian) civilization, and peasant mentality—from the position of the self-appointed reflective, autonomous, and enlightened subject. Hence Chen's performative invocation of the peasantry is a citation of this familiar discourse. However, the difference is that this citation here is no longer made in the context of culture but in the labor market for an audience of prospective workers who are in fact from the countryside. In other words, humanism has been brought into quite a different context in its becoming transformed into market humanism. Let us follow Chen's lecture to explore this relationship.

The highlight of the lecture was to stress that everyone freely owns and expresses his or her own feelings (*qingxu*), attitude, and ultimately the power of a smile. Chen told two stories. The first was about Conrad Hilton, the founder of the Hilton hotel chain, and the second was about the Japanese salesman Hara Ippei (1904–1984), both of whom are noted for their emphasis on the importance of the smile for success. According to Chen, Hara Ippei's smile was worth millions of dollars, but he acquired it only after intensive practice. One has the ownership of one's smiles, but the ownership now entails an acquired discipline whose logic is lodged in the commodification of the self. With that note, Chen introduces a testing situation:

> Nobody is perfect, and you should not expect others to be perfect, including your future boyfriends and your clients. If you look for a boyfriend who must be 1.8 meters tall and with this and that, you may never find such a boyfriend. Similarly, you cannot expect your clients to be perfect either. There was a

trainee who quit her job and came back to the school. She said that her clients treat their dog better than they treat her. If your clients treat their dog better than they treat you, can you accept that?

Some trainees replied hesitatingly, "Yes." Chen nodded his head and continued:

Think more about what you want out of migration. You come to the city to make money for your family. Think about this. Gradually you will surely take the place of the dog. Everyone is her own boss. You, a boss, in order to make money, need to serve your clients well, but you do not need to think too highly of them. For each of us, if we want to change ourselves, we can.

Finally, like Yin, Chen also wrote the following inscription on the blackboard as a parting gift, which he asked the trainees to copy into their notebooks. It appears to be a translation and adaptation of a nineteenth-century poem in English:

A Smile
How easy it is to smile,
Yet the value it creates is limitless.
Those who receive it become instantly rich;
Those who give lose nothing.
None is too rich to accept it;
None is too poor to give it.
It brings joy to the home
And is a wonderful expression of friendship.
It is a miraculous antidote for stress,
And gives courage to those in despair.
If someday you meet a person
Who does not smile to you,
Then generously give yours to him,
For nobody needs it more
Than those who have no more to give.

Chen recommended, "When you feel gloomy, you can read this poem and remember Hara Ippei's million-dollar smiles." Chen then suggested that the trainees conclude the class by singing together the song "Zhenxin yingxiong" (The True-Hearted Hero), a song sung by Taiwan and Hong Kong singers such as Zhou Huajian and Jacky Chan, which is also popular on the mainland: "In my heart there used to be a dream. My singing will let you forget all the hurt. . . ." Although the class sang heartily, Chen kept shouting, "Louder! Louder!" The volume of the chorus rose still higher with each wave of his hand, celebrating a sentimentalized and romanticized militarism via an image of a hero who struggles in the battlefield of life:

> Let our song bring out your hearty smile.
> Let (us) wish that your life from now on will be different.
> Grasp every minute of life.
> Go all out for the dream in our heart.
> Without enduring wind and rain, how could we see rainbow.
> Nobody can succeed without effort.

The Power of a Smile

The lectures by Yin and Chen may seem contradictory, with one comparing trainees to pork and potatoes and emphasizing the thinglike aspect of human labor, and the other celebrating the ability and agency of the individual. One emphasized the role of the domestic worker as a seller of her labor power, while the other stressed her being a self-possessing sovereign subject (the boss of herself). Yet the two aspects are in fact two sides of the same coin of market humanism. In fact, I propose here that market humanism involves at least three separate instances of a contradiction packaged neatly within an apparently continuous logic. First, one is equally the thinglike "you" (a commodity) and the bosslike "you." We might note that the discursive origin that Chen drew on was humanism, and then he talked about domestic workers taking the place of dogs. If we were to find this surprising, Yin would remind us about the logic of continuity and equivalence between the thinglike you and the bosslike you. The thinglike you is objectified as something less than human, but, instead of rebelling against this treatment, the bosslike you must take charge of the situation and discipline the self to endure hardship to attain ultimate transcendence as a successful person. As dictated by market humanism, your self-worth will be sorted out in the market!

Second, in Chen's lecture, he stressed the importance of accepting yourself and that only if you accept yourself can you accept others. On the other hand, he performed an image of a peasant in front of the class that all were told to reject and denigrate. His own rural origin, which he had shared with the trainees, combined with his cosmopolitan status, which he was able to exhibit in front of them, added authority to the advice he gave as a living testimony of his teaching, "You must like yourself. You must learn to look at yourself in the mirror everyday and look for shortcomings."

This contradiction is also found in the biography of Hara Ippei. He invented his own self-critique sessions, inspired by a motto from Johann Wolfgang von Goethe, "Never by reflection, but only by doing is self-knowledge possible." His narrative emphasized the pains and shame in the process of struggling against the self and how difficult it was to reform oneself. One conclusion Hara drew from his six years of struggle is that "you are your own worst enemy" (1993: 23). Yet Hara's book also teaches that "a person who can love himself is then capable of loving others." Hara emphasized this love of the self again through a quote from Oscar Wilde, "To love oneself is the beginning of a life-long romance" (1993: 30–31).

Third, related to this project of reforming the self is an emphasis on attitude: "Attitude is everything." Chen advised the class, "If you want to change yourself, you can. . . . [But] the extent of your career is determined by your imagination." This philosophy assumes that the originary productive force is the mind that produces not only an individual's self-identity but also his or her relationships with the surrounding world. It also assumes that the production of the self motivates and propels all other social productions. If a now widely ridiculed Great Leap Forward slogan, "The size of harvest matches the degree of audacity" [*ren you duo da dan, di you duo da chan*], articulated a collective ambition in the Mao-era, the market version asserts an individual voluntarism in the sphere of self-production that will spur production in all social spheres.[16] Yet this form of voluntarism, much more extreme in its assumption, goes unremarked. In the poem Chen offered, a smile is such a matter of voluntarism. Not only is it a free material for social lubrication and mobility, but it itself creates value endlessly and enriches all—if we just have the will. It is all a question of attitude.

What is described as a voluntary act in the poem all too quickly will be encountered as a market coercion in reality. Here we see how market voluntarism also has its contradiction: Chen told the class that there are classes in Japan and Korea that provide training on smiling and warned, "If you don't know how to smile, Hilton will not hire you."[17] Voluntarism, however sentimental and romantic it may appear, reveals itself as a hard discipline integral with the ruthless bedrock of market dictatorship.

Human Engineering and Its Limits

How do domestic workers respond to the training that they are given at Fuping? I did not ask for permission to poll the opinions of the trainees in my field research, doubting that the trainees would feel free to speak their minds. However, indirect evidence is quite revealing. A teacher who taught at Fuping revealed that a trainee wrote in one of the textbooks, "Fuping is a prison." It is unknown who wrote it or how many trainees may have seen this note, as textbooks are recycled to new trainees, and they pass through many hands. Mao Yushi himself also offered evidence on the difficulty in transforming the minds of rural women. At a seminar in 2003, he expressed his worries about two ideas still held by trainees in his school:

> It doesn't matter whether they are peasants or ordinary urbanites. They have been under the influence of thousands of years of imperial power and have a deep-rooted mindset of subjection on the one hand; on the other hand, they have also experienced "thought reform" [*sixiang gaizao*] in more recent times, especially since 1949, and thus they tend to seek solutions via violence. At present, two dangerous concepts exist among wider circles of people. The first is the idea of "exploitation," that is, they think that to *dagong* [work for a boss] is to "be exploited." For example, trainees in the school I established in Beijing all have quite a low level of education, but nonetheless they have a strong anti-exploitation sentiment. They think to work is to be exploited, . . . The second is the idea that "to rebel is right" [*zaofan youli*]. That is, if there is exploitation and oppression, then there should be revolution and rebellion, and "equality and justice" should be pursued by expropriating the "exploiters." For these ideas to be changed requires a thorough repudiation of the ideology on which the Communist Party claims legitimacy, which is very difficult. (quoted in Lao Tian 2004)

Mao Yushi fears that, despite their youth, the trainees at his school might still be influenced by the Maoist idea "to rebel is right" and that the training, however forceful, has not succeeded in totally transforming their minds. For Mao Yushi, the problem is not the structural relations of inequality and exploitation embedded in these market relations but that trainees should harbor such an understanding. In faulting ideas of "exploitation" and "oppression" for distracting the minds of his trainees, he complains that the legacy of the Communist Party is not completely repudiated. Here we see a good example of how neoliberalism is a utopian vision that touches down in places with deeply sedimented histories that condition how these ideas will work out in practice.

However, it is not only these migrant workers who refuse their objectification as commodity but also the cohort of China's knowledge workers. White-collar professionals are ordered by their employers to read *No Excuse Leadership* (*Meiyou renhe jiekou*) on their own.[18] Heated discussions may emerge from this practice.

When a blogger posted his reflection on the book, it attracted 175 comments. Among them, thirty-three were positive about the book, fifty-seven negative, thirty ambiguous, and eight with mixed views. Thirty-one reported that their employers distributed the book and demanded that they turn in a written reflection. Those who were positive found it useful to push themselves harder. The first blogger, for example, "discovered that making excuses is a poison" and that it incapacitates oneself. Some agreed. One even offered a scathing self-reflection. Still another summarized the lesson, "[It] explains . . . why losers are losers!" Yet more are critical about the book, demonstrating an awareness of the unequal power relations between labor and management operating in real life contexts. Response number 19 snaps:

> It is easier to demand of oneself to work hard without excuses, but it is very difficult to put such a demand on one's superiors in China. To give up one's personality and self, to talk only about submission and teamwork, and then finally reach one's self-development—this is another intoxicating trap that works like a multilevel sales system [*chuan xiao*].

Response number 22 is still more direct about power politics, "Your boss hopes that you have no excuse! *No Excuse Leadership* gives bureaucrats an excuse to bully and oppress you!" Response number 25 exclaims, "This dog fart tries to brainwash [us]. When you read it, it seems reasonable and good, but it completely goes nowhere when you put it in specific reality." Response number 39 elaborates his analysis by comparing the book with the magic headband in the Chinese classic *Journey to the West* that gives the Buddhist monk Xuanzang control over the fearless and powerful Monkey King to make him his servant:

> The modern-day boss is fucking (*zhen tama de*) "clever" and has learned the trick by turning *No Excuse Leadership* into a modern-day headband. . . . If any idiot wishes to have a taste of the experience of the Monkey King, then go read *No Excuse Leadership*. But I will mourn for him [the reader], a walking corpse.

Response number 42 agrees, *"No Excuse* is a mental shackle put on slaves by the slave masters." Response number 151 asks, "Don't you find that it is bosses or leaders who ask you to read this book? Doesn't this vindicate Grandpa Marx that it's about extracting more surplus value from you?"

Although we cannot draw the simplistic conclusion that all who are critical of the book are critical of market economy, Mao Yushi would find enough evidence here to confirm his worries. He and his fellow neoliberal warriors will continue to battle against common people's perception of "exploitation" while supporting the continued hegemony of the market economy. The military as the concept-metaphor of society disciplines Chinese workers with a new life philosophy, but, at the same time, it arouses significant disgust and resistance among them and wakens them to the reality of the employment relationship, as demonstrated in these web discussions.

Fuping's mission statement represents migrant workers as "weaker-powered groups," a new social label that has become popular since the late 1990s and refers to popular masses (peasants, urban laid-off workers, rural-to-urban migrant workers). Invocations of this term, by NGOs and other civil and political elites, are often in the sympathetic context that these people are in need of empowerment. But we have seen how the benevolent Mao Yushi is so upset and worried when poor and relatively uneducated trainees are opposed to exploitation and dare to think of expropriating the rich. This kind of self-empowerment is something that Mr. Mao and Fuping's board members are quick to condemn. Thus it is revealed that the discourse of helping weaker-powered groups is a governing strategy: Rather than empowering the workers, it enhances the power and agency of the elites to govern, discipline, and shape the workers' agency by remolding their subjectivity. Perhaps this discourse, too, is a modern-day magical headband?

Notes

1. For example, the story appeared in *The Straight Times* (Singapore) and *Reuters*. An Internet search produces three pages of reports on the school.

2. See Yan (2003) for an analysis of the operation of neoliberalism in the process of migrant labor recruitment. A prominent character of neoliberalism in China is a strong state involvement in marketization and privatization. Those who are troubled by the seeming incongruence between the strong party-state and neoliberal reform in China might find a useful comparison in Graham Harrison's analysis of the neoliberal project in Africa, which demonstrates that "those states that have (relatively) succeeded in implementing neo-liberal foundations have relied on distinctly non-liberal forms of politics to do so" (Harrison 2007: 98). David Harvey (2005, 2006) shows that the illiberal politics of neoliberal reforms are not so exceptional after all.

3. According to www.nhkint.or.jp/us/history_e.html (accessed on May 15, 2007), the drama series was shown in more than fifty countries and regions. In April 2007, the drama was rebroadcast by the Hunan Satellite TV with a high reception rate.

4. Hayek's ideas about the power of the market as a rational ordering force were considered eccentric until Margaret Thatcher and Ronald Reagan brought them into mainstream respectability.

5. Not coincidentally, battleground and survival games have become a common trope in Japan that figures ominously in Japan's anxiety about its future global competitiveness (Arai 2003).

6. Note here the echoes of how the South Korean state marks out categories of the deserving and undeserving poor, as discussed by Jesook Song in Chapter Ten of this volume.

7. See Perry and Welkos 2007 on audience reception of the Hollywood film *300*, which celebrates an ideal militarism embodied by ancient Spartans.

8. A search using "West Point" as the keyword in the China Academic Journals Full-Text Database turns out 419 articles from 1979 to 2006. Of those articles, 398, or 95 percent, were published between 1994 and 2006 (retrieved on June 25, 2007 from the China Academic Journals Full-Text Database).

9. Derrida's critique on reason and rhetoric through the hyphenated concept-metaphor might be very useful here. In "White Mythology" (1974), Derrida critiqued the classical opposition between concept and metaphor, in which the concept seeks an essential or truthful relationship between the Mind and the World, while metaphor is a linguistic relationship within language that sets up an analogy between two entities. The concept is at the center of metaphysics while the metaphor is at the margin and is "admissible in philosophy, but only to the extent that it promises a return, with augmented resources, to the literality of the concept"

(Harrison 1999: 513). Derrida's project is to show that "metaphysical discourse is derivative from *(reléve de)* metaphor, not what is left over when—impossibly—language has been purged of all trace of metaphor, periphrasis, and ellipsis" (Harrison 1999: 516). In the context of our discussion, Derrida's critique is ironically paralleled by military-corporate executives who endeavor to show that the two are not metaphors for each other but are spheres that increasingly interpenetrate each other.

10. CCTV, "The Story behind Luo Zhongli's 'Father'" (*Luo Zhongli 'Fuqin' beihou de gushi*), October 16–17, 2007; retrieved on November 20, 2010, from http://longquanzs.org/articledetail.php?id=12998. The painting is now in the collection of the National Art Museum of China and can be viewed at www.namoc.org/en/Collection/200902/t20090205_66388.html (retrieved on June 13, 2012).

11. CCTV International, "Luo Zhongli—Days in the Daba Mountains" (*Luo Zhongli: dabashan de rizi*), September 27, 2003; retrieved on November 20, 2010, from www.cctv.com/west/20030927/100316.shtml.

12. See Su Ning, "Retell the Story of Father" (*Chongsu fuqin de gushi*), October 31, 2002; retrieved on July 4, 2007, from www.filmsea.com.cn/newsreel/commentator/200210310034.htm.

13. For the constitution of the intellectual identity, see Barlow 1991; for intellectuals in the 1980s Enlightenment, see Wang 1996; for the relationship between intellectuals and workers, see Rofel 1994.

14. See Zhu 1998 and Gu 2001. Zhu (1998, especially chapter 2) details the discursive formation of humanism and the defensive position of Marxist class theory in the 1980s.

15. See Barlow's critique of market feminism (2004: 253–301).

16. "Volunteerism" in the Mao era refers to collective willpower that can overcome daunting material constraints. This thesis came to the ultimate test during the Great Leap Forward, in which millions of peasants were mobilized for massive projects to build the rural infrastructure. This mass mobilization was caught up short by three years of famine (1959–1962), exacerbated in part by the redirection of rural labor from grain production to dam building. A significant number of people died of hunger. This history is important for understanding the irony that I note here. If Maoism is dismissed as voluntarist, market humanism is no less so, but in ways that have become "decollectivized"!

17. Pazderic, in Chapter 5 of this volume, shows how the smile figures in the creation of embodied capital in Taiwan as well.

18. See http://blog.wespoke.com/archives/000655.php (last retrieved on June 27, 2007; the URL is no longer active).

Chapter Seven

Notes to the Heart
New Lessons in National Sentiment and Sacrifice from Recessionary Japan

ANDREA G. ARAI

In 1882 the French theologian Ernest Renan wrote "What Is a Nation?" in which he set out "to analyze an idea which, though seemingly clear, lends itself to the most dangerous misunderstandings" (Renan 1996: 42). In this seminal essay, Renan argues that, in the association of the nation and nationality with the natural and inevitable outgrowth of former dynastic realms, the historical novelty and the affective power of national identifications had been mostly overlooked. His poignant intervention was to redirect attention to the nation as a new relationship of sentiment—or what he called a "soul, a spiritual principle" (1996: 52). Born of the obligatory processes of "forgetting" and "remembering," the nation is the result of the singular stitching together of a rich legacy of memories, or rather, remembering only the things that bond and the present-day consent that is born of forgetting to remember the differences and inequalities that are inevitable in the formation of nations. As the culmination of sentiment and sacrifice, the "large-scale solidarity" we know as the nation is regenerated through a "daily plebiscite," or habit of "remembering to forget and forgetting to remember" the endeavors, sacrifices, and acts of devotion made in the past and those that one is prepared to make in the future (Renan 1996: 53).

Nearly a century later, Benedict Anderson returned to Renan's discussion of the deep attachments and colossal sacrifices generated by the nation in an effort to locate the birth of this new sentiment and sacrifice within the larger context of capitalist modernity. Through his notion of "imagined communities," Anderson uncovered the particular technologies of remembering to forget and forgetting to remember—technologies such as print capitalism and other forms of mechanical reproduction that made it possible to imagine commonality and camaraderie with fellow citizens that one is not likely to ever meet (Anderson 2006). For Anderson, these contradictory and necessarily repetitive habits of the nation that result in sentiment and sacrifice in common are historically contingent and modular; that is, within changing historical conditions, across national contexts, and as a result of the pressures that these differing national contexts place on each other, the means of regenerating this affective tie for a national citizenry may shift.

This has never been more evident than in a statement written by Takahashi Tetsuya, a well-known scholar of war memory, in reference to Japan in one of his lesser-known works, *Hearts and War* (*Kokoro to Senso*): "These days, even if you wanted to reproduce the spirit of the prewar period, it would not be possible. And, by the way, this is not what is needed today" (2003: 12). What is at stake is precisely this shifting basis for an affective relationship between citizen and nation.

The context in which Takahashi is writing is a nation in crisis—Japan in the early twenty-first century—and it is this sense of crisis that would seem to compel a shift in the forms and requisites of the rituals of forgetting and remembering. Following a decade of severe economic downturns, beginning with the bursting of the first of the real estate and stock market bubbles of the early 1990s, the Japanese economy contracted to almost half its former size, resulting in what Carl Cassegard (2008: 10) has called the "collapse of the self-complacent space of Japan." Along with major reforms and restructurings of the economy that radically changed the structure of labor and education, the new recessionary context brought with it a profound anxiety about the naturalness of the imagined community of the Japanese nation and the ability of its youngest members to participate in the habits of forgetting and remembering that had naturalized national sacrifice and devotion and that had defined the will of their parents' generation to labor almost without limits.

The impossible return of prewar spirit referenced in the preceding paragraphs is concerned with a particular moment of this recessionary context at the conclusion of 2006. In December of that year the Abe government succeeded in revising the Fundamental Law of Education (*kyouiku kihonhou*), which was often referred to as "the educational constitution" for its close association with the postwar peace constitution of 1947. Therefore, this "prewar" spirit is a reference to an even earlier law, the nineteenth-century Imperial Rescript on Education (*kyouiku chokugo*), which had been revoked during the American Occupation of Japan because of its emphases on patriotism, the family-state, and the figure of the Japanese emperor as symbols of the antiquity and sacredness of the national community. With the revocation of the Imperial Rescript, education, which had been one of the chief arenas of the inculcation of national spirit and devotion in the period leading to Japan's role in the Pacific War, was stripped of its imperial symbolism. The 1947 postwar education law replaced a discourse of duty with a discourse of rights. It became the focus of both progressive leadership as well as continued contestation on the part of conservatives from the middle to the late twentieth century, as the Japanese nation continued to wrestle with the conflicts and contradictions of its modern nationhood.

As justification for overturning the 1947 Fundamental Law of Education in 2006, the Japanese government targeted the putative deterioration of the sentiment of sacrifice for the nation among the youth. Similar concerns about the youth of Japan had been made repeatedly over the course of Japan's modern history. However, following a decade of recession and economic crisis, as Japan saw itself losing its hard-won position as a model modernizer, these claims took on a new and powerful valence. Worldwide representations of Japan during the previous half century had portrayed it as a "modernizing miracle"—miraculous because the Japanese had become modern while "keeping their culture." In other words, it was said by foreigners and Japanese alike that Japan had been able to modernize while remaining different, and this difference was endowed with the charisma of economic success. This is precisely what lay in ruins as the recessionary economy of the 1990s stubbornly refused to end.

Takahashi entered the education debates when it became clear that the Japanese public and its elected officials could be, for the first time in over half a century, persuaded into undoing a historical legacy by failing to remember what they were about to lose and by being unaware of what forms of control might be instituted in its place. In *Hearts and War*, he focuses on the difference between the prewar period and the present in terms of the form and atmosphere of ideological control and its relation to the larger international context of each period. He points out how forms of pedagogy can be and have been used to restrict, police, and produce a military mind-set.

While the question of national spirit has again moved to the center of national debate, Takahashi argues that the claims of both Japanese conservatives and progressives are misguided with regard to the articulation of this spirit in the revised education law. The 2006 revisions to the Fundamental Law of Education are neither a simple return to the prewar education law (*kyouiku chokugo*), as progressives bemoan, nor are they a simple reinstating of the spirit of sacrifice and the values that underwrote the postwar social and political order, as conservatives hope for. In writing that "this (spirit) is not what is needed today," Takahashi draws our attention to how these revisions and the focus on the heart constitute a new affective relationship to the nation that is in the making. This focus brings him to the conclusion that prewar forms of governance are no longer viable in a Japan that can no longer offer its citizens the guarantees, public protections, and the kinds of direct national management that undergirded the postwar economic order.

In this chapter, I argue that these discourses of "love" and "heart" that have (re)emerged so strongly in the recessionary context of Japan are vehicles for subjectification "by other means."[1] It is this *other means* that concerns me here as I historicize and extend critically the way that individualizing techniques of power meet up with anxieties of national fashioning in the Japanese context past and present. The foregrounding of "love" (for the nation) and "heart" represent long-standing and unresolved issues of the relationship between national reproduction and the pressures of global competition. Together, they have produced a new focus on where new frontiers of value production can be found, where transformation must happen, and where the new responsibility for these changes will lie.

Couched in language that is both old and new, the new requirements to love your country and develop your heart (*kokoro*) strongly resonate with what Barbara Cruikshank has called "a new science of the self that places the hope of liberation in the psychological state of the people" (Cruikshank 1996: 233).[2] In the case of the self-esteem movement that Cruikshank examines, the target population was poor urban people of color in the United States. The goal of the program launched first in California was for this group to learn to "align their personal goals with the goals of the reformers" (1996: 232). In the contemporary Japanese context, the objects of this science of the self—this learning to be self-sufficient and to align your personal goals with the goals of the reformers and their new forms of governance emerging in the recessionary era—are the subjects of education, whether these be parents in the homes, children and youth in the schools, or teachers and the public at large. Therefore, it is important to note that these shifts are not limited to discourses about the youth but reflect a shift in the relationship between citizen and nation for all Japanese.

Since the beginning of the Japanese modernity project in the mid-nineteenth century, the changing requirements of sentiment and sacrifice have been a key arena for ongoing negotiations over the forms and expressions of nationhood and nationality, especially within the realm of educational policy. These changes and negotiations intensified as a result of the recessionary period. Of particular note in this sense in the 2006 revisions to the Fundamental Law of Education are the new sections on "patriotic education" (*aikokushin kyouiku*) that target the project of "creating youth who will love their country." These sections address a concern for a loss of the will to sacrifice on the part of the youth even as the form this sacrifice must take has changed: Once it would have meant giving your life to the nation in wartime, and in the era of high growth this might have taken the form of sacrificing one's health through laboring without limit in Japan's economic miracle (for example, the "death by overwork" afflicting male salaried workers). In the wake of the recession, this sacrifice now takes the form of relinquishing all those social guarantees such as job security, health care, and old-age pensions that had existed in the compact between Japan and its citizens in the era of high growth. No wonder there is a concern for whether the youth and children of the nation as the next inheritors of this national burden would willingly take up the call to "be what you were and be what you are" (Renan 1996: 52). Not only is this concern for the nation not about a return to the prewar spirit, but it also marks a shift in the production of national sentiment within these seemingly classic forms of return. In other words, not only is the "love" conjured by the patriotic call not the same, but the "heart" (*kokoro*) or the soul that loves is also not the same. The youth are now called on "to create independent hearts" (*jiritsutekina kokoro*) and to "raise themselves" (*jibun de sodatsu*), while also being asked to love and sacrifice for their country. This suggests an entirely new affective relationship to the imagined community of the nation.

However, this is not a phenomenon that can be explained in terms completely internal to Japan; it encompasses regional and global processes that situate Japan in the world. The crises of individual and national uncertainty that occurred in the late 1990s brought to the fore the ways in which the period of miracle growth (roughly 1955 through 1973) had obscured the tensions of this system that lay under the surface reality of an amazing period of economic prosperity and international recognition of Japan as a successful model of modernization.[3] When I first wrote about how these unresolved problems were materializing in social and political reality around the sites of social and national reproduction, home, school, and child, there seemed little to compare it to in the United States or Western context (Arai 2004). This has, as we know, all changed within the last few years. In the aftermath of the financial crisis of 2008, the Japanese example or "the Japanese disease," referring to the Japanese recession of the 1990s, can no longer be viewed as something particularly Japanese.

In Japan, the new technologies of self-reliance and self-development have been written into the system of education through the 2006 revisions to the Fundamental Law of Education and actualized through the creation of specific pedagogies that take the form of *Notes to the Heart* (*kokoro no no-to*), a set of educational materials distributed in the schools that focus on a "revolution within." Although this emphasis on heart would seem to speak about the interiority of the subject, "There is nothing personal about self-esteem" (Cruikshank 1996: 231). This pedagogy of self-reliance and development has larger goals of social reform.

In the Japanese context, the development of the individual heart is a pedagogy that engages both directly and indirectly with anxieties about national fashioning. These anxieties first took the form of a concern about the "incompleteness," in sense of an immaturity or temporal inferiority, of Japanese modernity during the prewar and immediate postwar periods.[4] These concerns returned in the recessionary period of the 1990s in the claims of neonationalists that the nation had been weakened by the American Occupation of the late 1940s. According to these critics, the stripping of war powers from the Japanese state and the continued reliance on laws such as the 1947 Fundamental Law of Education, which regulated the teaching of nationalism in the schools, has produced weakened and "strange" youth, whose impaired development has robbed the nation of its ability to complete itself. The focus on individual development now has been made to speak to these concerns as well; however, the current impetus for national completion has become very much removed from how it was once struggled over and envisioned.

The 2006 revisions to the education law must therefore be understood in relation to a history of struggle in Japan over a form of social and national re-production that was first conceived during the modernity project of the late nineteenth century and recast in the climate of postwar theories of growth and modernization.[5] However, today, the conditions of possibility for this set of national and cultural expectations are no longer available. These deeply ingrained views of what the Japanese nation should be, how this nation is to be reproduced, what is necessary for this reproduction, and its mismatch with the current government policies of less support and fewer guarantees for its citizens are all questions that I pursue in the following pages through an ethnographic investigation of the discourses, debates, products, and ef-fects of the pedagogies of "the heart."[6]

National concern about the formation of the individual child's heart both occludes and highlights the paradoxes of intertwined histories of modernity and neoliberal globalization.[7] The dissolution of the social contract in Japan during the recessionary period has led to the highly specific focus on the heart as a means to restore the affective relationship to the nation, while at the same time preparing the youth for a national context in which they can and should expect less from the nation-state but, nonetheless, be willing to be and do more. This is a context that I think of as neoliberal (Arai 2005). What concern me here are the specific cultural effects and products of neo-liberalization. As Ann Anagnost outlines in the Introduction to this volume, this includes the emergence of discourses of "freedom" and "responsibility." As she makes clear, citing Anna Tsing and others, while seeming to gesture to a new individualization, a relaxing of former expectations and disciplinary pedagogies of the state, in fact, these new discourses have a very different lineage from traditional liberalisms of the mid-twentieth century. The relax-ing of controls and regulations and the reductions of curricula in the sphere of education are accompanied more generally by a shifting of the burdens for citizenship and success to the individual, but these shifts are transacted through a means that is sociohistorically specific.

My discussion of this new relationship resonates with Inoue (Chapter 8 in this volume), who raises similar questions about the absence of a discourse of loyalty among the female workers in the Japanese corporation she studied.

Inoue reveals here a means for the company to ask for new forms of sacrifice from its female employees. The contradiction she finds here is similar to the one represented in the production of an independent or individualized patriotism. The new structures of sentiment and sacrifice are intentionally less equal and less communal but nonetheless figured through the idiom of the "heart" as *nationally Japanese*. The securing of the national future, it appears, no longer guarantees that all will participate in the ongoing prosperity of the national community.

Creating a National Citizenry and Crises of Capitalist Modernity

The 1947 Fundamental Law of Education has been referred to by many as the Heisei Rescript (recalling its adoption into law under the reign of the son of the wartime emperor Showa while also recalling references to the Imperial Rescript of the prewar period). It has been both praised and faulted for its continuities with Japan's prewar education past—a past that was from the beginning central to the unification, standardization, and consolidation of the heterogeneous peoples who inhabited the discontinuous geographic space of the Japanese archipelago. As Takashi Fujitani (1993) describes in his dramatic study of the early Meiji pageants and ritual performances around the figure of the young emperor in the latter half of the nineteenth century, the inhabitants of Japan had to be instructed to acquire a self-consciousness of the nation, even as they came to know themselves through what we might call "structures of comparison," or ways that Western modernizing discourses put pressure on non-Western peoples to "civilize and enlighten" themselves during the early nation building and colonial modernity moment of the mid-nineteenth century. Toward the end of the nineteenth century, the Meiji government shifted away from its initial focus on "civilization and enlightenment" (*bunmei kaika*) to a singular focus on economic growth and military might, encapsulated in the phrase "rich country and strong military" (*fukoku kyōhei*). Among the various laws and decrees of this late-nineteenth-century moment, promulgated to ward off threats to national sovereignty, was the Imperial Rescript on Education. Teruhisa Horio explains the significance of the Rescript as follows: "To today's eye the Rescript appears as a series of piously vague statements about the duties of loyal Imperial subjects; in the context in which it was written, however, it was a masterful formulation of the moral base created to mandate the switch in the people's loyalties from the family and clan to the Emperor and nation" (1988: 68).[8]

Subsequent to Japan's defeat in the Pacific War in 1945, a major reform of education was enacted along with the establishment of a new national constitution. Welcomed in the name of a different modernity, the 1947 Fundamental Law of Education and the so-called peace constitution seemed a refreshing release from wartime history. These two pieces of legislation created the foundations of the postwar order by renouncing war, turning education into an individual right rather than a duty to the state, and shifting the control of education back into the hands of the people and educators (Fujita 2000). With changes in the international balance of power following the end of the war, however, the American Occupation forces, which had been actively involved in the drafting of these laws, began to shift directions. The spirit of democratic reform that had energized postdefeat Japan was overridden by the American urging of Japan back into the militarized fold, a concern over a rising tide of domestic protest, and the sensing on the part of education officials and others that "democratization had gone too far" (Horio 1988: 147). In the late 1950s, as industry was gearing up for rapid economic growth, the government realized it would need to create a new kind of citizen to produce this miracle. Its answer at the time was a series of policy documents known as "The Image of the Desired Japanese" (*kitai sareru ningen zo*).

Seen through the eyes of the government bureaucrats who drafted "The Image of the Desired Japanese," the 1947 Fundamental Law of Education was an impediment to economic growth because of its focus on the rights of the individual and the prohibition placed on the central government to manage education from above. Faced with powerful popular opposition to any revision of the law, government policies focused on eroding its protections (Horio 1988: 160). However, it would be incorrect to represent the Image of the Desired Japanese as simple "restorationism"—its structure and function were very different from the model of citizenship associated with the imperial system. In its emphasis on "creating people" (*hitozukuri*), the Image of the Desired Japanese aimed to adapt education to the needs of high growth. These reforms included an emphasis on "academic competency" (*noryokushugi*), the addition of a national achievement test, and a sharp acceleration in the difficulty and amount of curriculum. Horio calls this legislation "ideological camouflage" (1988: 159) because of the way in which they "provided an ideologically charged series of representations which legitimized the values of the welfare state in the stage of monopolistic capitalism by appealing to the idea of "being uniquely Japanese" (1988: 159). By the early 1960s, the "peace and prosperity" slogan of the reforms was in the process of being transformed into a one-track focus on economic growth, within which education played the role of creating a highly skilled and totally absorbed workforce willing to sacrifice their private lives to the needs of industry and nation.[9]

This focus on creating the people to produce a high-growth economy coincided with the development of modernization theory in the United States as a Cold War technology for heading off the socialist threat posed by China and on the Korean peninsula. Japan was set up as a model for capitalist development—Japan, Inc.—the incorporated nation, seemingly immune to the vicissitudes that had characterized industrial capitalism elsewhere and based on the economic stages of growth of modernization theory. What it also meant, however, was that a nation just emerging from a war of aggression against its neighbors was encouraged to turn away from its past and toward the new modernizing future that awaited it. As Leo Ching (2001) reminds us, this trajectory had dramatic consequences not only for the postcolonial citizens of Taiwan and elsewhere but also for the postwar creation of Japanese national identity.

Following the oil shock and the shift in Japan from high to moderate growth in the late 1970s and 1980s, attempts were made once again to redefine and reorganize education to meet the economic challenges of postindustrialism and the demands of corporations for more flexible workers skilled in informational technologies. In 1984, Prime Minister Nakasone responded to this shift with slogans of building "social awareness" and putting a stronger emphasis on individual responsibility. The Nakasone agenda resonated closely with the changes being made in the United States under Reagan and in the UK under Thatcher as the first stage of "roll back" neoliberalism. This phase of neoliberalism is sometimes called "destructive" because of its stripping away of social protections and programs, as opposed to "roll-out" or so-called creative neoliberalism, which Peck and Tickell famously identified as a different or later stage, in which programs and protections are not so much restored as new forms of control and management, such as the practices and discourses mentioned earlier of self-esteem or the technologies of the heart in Japan, are created (Peck and Tickell 2002). In Japan, the "rollback" phase took the form of calls during the Nakasone era for privatizing education to lighten the financial burden on government and to adjust to a more flexible and less homogeneous—less standardized and increasingly less equal—workforce for the period of sustained lower growth of the late 1970s and 1980s. Postwar high economic growth had been built on the strict standardization of education in an effort to create a highly efficient, but also highly homogenous, workforce. This model had proved highly efficient for the post-Fordist structures of work known as Toyotism. However, Nakasone's program, including a proposed revision to the education law, lacked sufficient popular support at the time.[10]

However, there were signs that not all was well in the sphere of education. Increasing numbers of students were having trouble leaving their homes in the morning to go to school, others were subjected to unrelenting forms of bullying, still others were taking their frustrations out on school property and teachers directly (*konai boryoku*), and cram schools were rapidly proliferating. Nonetheless, social critique aimed at the economics of growth was drowned out by representations of stability, success, and homogeneity (Field 1993). The apparent prosperity of Japanese society served to obscure questions about the sustainability of economic growth (Hein 1993). Thus, Japan was imagined by foreigners and Japanese alike not only to be a leader in the race to build a new knowledge-economy but also as a place for the rest of the world to "learn from."[11]

The 1980s was a moment when the Japanese seemed poised to supersede the West, leading the next revolution in production with their notion of the "information society" and its knowledge economy. Tessa Morris-Suzuki demonstrates how the concept of the information society was developed to address the challenges faced by Japanese industry as the conditions that had made high-growth possible changed. Policy documents of the time promoting the idea of the information society were instrumental in shaping the future they predicted (Morris-Suzuki 1988). Including utopian projections about the end of manual labor, the information society was imagined as the next step in human evolution from an industrial society centered in the production and consumption of goods to a society founded on a new principle of "time-value." This notion of time-value, proposed by government bureaucrats and popular information gurus, was to inaugurate a transformation in the time required of workers in the production of value. As Morris-Suzuki makes clear, however, the utopian projections and policies of the information society leading up to the bursting of the economic bubble in 1989 should be seen as responses to a series of economic crises following the high-growth era.

The long economic recession of the 1990s has been narrated predominantly as the sudden and surprising collapse (*houkai*) of a wonder economy. The unanticipated quality of the recession has attracted a broad range of explanations that blame overly traditionalist politics and policies, the apparent reluctance of Japanese bureaucrats to react more quickly and dramatically to the collapse of the financial sector in the early 1990s, and even a supposed breakdown in the realms of social and cultural reproduction. There is of course no denying the very real repercussions of the plummeting property values and stock prices that occurred in the early 1990s following the bursting of a highly inflated real estate market and an artificially low discount or borrowing rate.[12] The period of the economic downturn is filled with stories of dramatically changed individual futures, personal mortgages that now exceed property values, and four-hour daily commutes without an end in sight for the many families whose hopes of moving closer to the city have been dashed. There was and is much more at stake than financial futures in the failing economy. As Marilyn Ivy argues, "Since then, the deep recession has pulled out the primary support for Japanese national subjectivity in the postwar period: the economy itself had functioned as the forcefully empowered and proper stand-in for the 'improper' and split nation-state itself" (Ivy 2006: 143). In other words, Japanese economic success and the purportedly unique systems of production and reproduction that had seemed so effortlessly to support it had made the very particular relationships of sentiment and sacrifice of the postwar nation seem natural. The collapse of the financial system and all it stood for and all that it shielded from sight ruptured the conditions of possibility for this prior affective relationship of the nation, opening up, as Ivy suggests, unresolved issues about national identity.[13]

At the level of the everyday, these representations produced a powerful sense of the normative, in which the specificity of class, region, gender, and historical change were absent. At a moment of uncertainty and change such as this, one might have expected tremendous social unrest, protest, and a potential questioning of the production of the normative (from within Japan and without). This was foreclosed in part through the dismissal of Japan (uninteresting now that it was no longer the unflappable, incomparable incorporated nation), on the one hand, and, on the other, a burgeoning literature of collapse published within Japan that began to establish a link between the problem with the nation and something amiss or strange about the reproduction of this nation and its future citizen-subjects.

In the mid-1990s, the national focus began to a shift strongly to this arena of reproduction. An all-male teachers' association (*prokyoshi no kai*) met once a month for several decades to debate the changing climate of education and nation and published their discussions on the deteriorating relationship between teacher, parent, and student and the changed position of the school, once considered "holy ground" for its production of a homogeneous and dedicated workforce, whose future, along with the nation it served, had seemed so secure. Under other circumstances, this collection of informal essays entitled *The Child Is Turning Strange* (*Kodomo ga Hen da*) might have been ignored completely (Kawakami 1995). They describe how the Japanese child (much like the nation) had become unknowable and unrecognizable. The strangeness of which they spoke was articulated to me in an interview I had with one of the spokesmen for the group, Kawakami Ryoichi, a junior high history teacher and later the author of the best-selling book *School Collapse* (*Gakkou Houkai*) published in 1999:

> In the 1950s and 1960s, human relations were simple. The child of this new era [1990s] doesn't understand what his teachers are all about. In the 1970s, the radicals had the necessary form [*shisei*]; we need a return to radicalness. The student movement and the inner-school violence [*kōnai bōryoku*] of the 1980s were preferable to the 1990s strange [*hen da*] child. We can't get through to these children; they're incomprehensible [*tsujinai; wakaranai*], and we don't have a clue what they're thinking. (Kawakami Ryoichi, personal communication)

The focus on the strangeness of the child intensified and changed in 1997, following the "Youth A" incident in Kobe. Over a period of approximately ten months, Youth A, a fourteen-year old junior high school student from a middle-class neighborhood, headed down a path of personal and social destructiveness, including vengeful messages about having been robbed of his existence and terrifying descriptions of deriving pleasure from killing. The wounding and killing of several children younger than himself finally ended in the beheading of a sixth-grade acquaintance of his family, placing the decapitated head at the school gate, and sending a jeering note to the police.

Education officials in the city of Kobe were faced with having to explain how this kind of monstrous incident could have been carried out by an "ordinary," which is to say middle-class, child and of course how they had missed warning signs all along. Their search for an explanation resulted ultimately in the emergence of two explanations that significantly changed the nature of the discourse on education and the nation. The first of these took shape within the local community of education officials in Kobe charged with finding a new language with which to explain the Kobe youth's violent deeds and his indictment of a system that he believed had rendered him "invisible" and against which he had sworn revenge. The choice of terms is notable because of the way in which they direct the focus of the problem within the child and children in Japan more generally. Borrowing from the writings of Kawaii Hayao, a Jungian clinical psychologist, who had recently been appointed as the director of the center for the study of Japanese culture (*Nichibunken*) in the neighboring city of Kyoto, education officials began to speak of the need to address the "interior" (*naimen*) of the child and of a problem with the child's heart (*kokoro*). One of the key effects that the use of these terms had on the understanding of the event was to remove it from the larger economic, political, and historical context within which it had taken place, and that Youth A himself had referenced in his own writings. The new language also transferred responsibility for the event from the educational system to the family, repudiating the culture of homogeneity and dependency within which this individual (or strange child) was produced. The second explanation emerged out of the first. In the huge media outpouring on this event, linkages began to be made between the strange internal make-up of the young (*kodomo ga hen da*) and the strangeness of the nation arising from the accumulation of the past and converging with a recession that threatened the national future. Individual development that was supposed to have been an effect of the success of national development was now turned on its head. It began to seem that it was the young who were making it impossible for the nation to continue to succeed.

"Raise Yourself!" New Lessons in National Loving and Laboring

A full-scale reform of education, which promised to correct the excesses of postwar education, was launched at the end of the 1990s under the slogans of "the strength to live" (*ikiru chikara*), "education of the heart" (*kokoro no kyouiku*), and "the frontier within" (*Nihon no furonteia wa Nihon no naka de aru*). Couched in a language of improvement, these slogans and the commentary behind them evoked all that was wrong with the nation and the youth. Examples and remedies proliferated. Young people were criticized for their lack of endurance, will, toughness, and social skills, including their lack of consideration for others, all which seemed to add up to a lack of devotion and ability to sacrifice for others, especially their nation. The most significant remedy was the conservative government's proposal to finally alter the Fundamental Law of Education to include a stronger emphasis on the relation between the individual and the nation—a relation that was now increasingly being defined in terms of the formation of the individual heart of the child.

Education reform committees had been established as early as 1998, producing in the interim a language specifying the need to make the Fundamental Law of Education more suitable (*fusawashii*). This suitability was explained in two different senses, which were related by implication more than explanation: the first, the changed environment (*kankyou*) between the nation from the immediate postwar period and the present moment of "globalization"; and second, the decreasing morals and a loss of devotion to study of the young and the weakened strength of the home and community in the project of education. Conspicuously lacking from these anxiety-ridden accusations and high-level discussions were the vastly changing conditions of individual and national security in the context of recessionary life, including mounting household debt, corporate restructuring, bankruptcy, and a frozen job market for the youth throughout the 1990s. As Yuji Genda writes in his insightful discussion of the labor economics of the period, the youth were being blamed for changed attitudes regarding their individual futures and national allegiance. Genda's argument is that this is not an original cause but rather the effect of the recessionary context of their lives (Genda 2005).

On December 15, 2006, the Japanese Diet passed the revisions. The new version of the Fundamental Law of Education is much longer than the original, including four new sections and a series of goals, one focused on correcting the home (discussed in the following paragraphs) and another intended to most directly repair the affective relationship to the nation among the youth. In the name of making education more "suitable," this goal, which became known as the patriotic education clause, states that one of the central purposes of education will heretofore be to learn to "cultivate a respect for the tradition and culture [of Japan] and love the country and homeland." As already mentioned, this suitability was defined in terms of what seemed to be lacking or missing in the citizenry, suggesting an original point in time in which morals, will, and devotion to the nation had occurred naturally, rather than having been produced historically through intentional cultural programs in the nation-building period (Fujitani 1993).

According to Miyake, the revisions did not cause significant public concern because of the way in which they left sections of the original language intact, while making calculated additions of new sections and omissions of older language to "completely alter the meaning and intention of the original" (Miyake 2006: 12). The changes in tone and context of the revisions are evident from the new preamble, which omits mention of respecting the individual in favor of the future of the nation, and the first two sections on educational principles and aims, which begin by talking about academic freedom but then temper this freedom with a new set of five targets (*mokuhyo*). These targets place a new emphasis on the feelings, desires, and attitudes of the individual as items for appraisal. Miyake argues that the vague wording of the patriotic clause was also an intentional compromise of the ruling conservative party to appease its less conservative government partners, but it was nevertheless sufficient to provide the context for the inclusion in school curriculum, and in some cases it appeared on report cards as a new category of assessment entitled "developing a heart that loves Japan."[14]

Moreover, in the new section on "education of the home," the revised law conveys the message that successful children are made by parents, not by the schools, and those students who fail to produce the required forms of devotion to the nation have only themselves and their parents to blame. Parents are newly identified here as the key providers of "the inculcation of independence in everyday habits to the production of the heart." And while there is mention of parenting classes (*hogosha gakushu*) and pamphlets for proper child rearing offered to teach parents their new responsibilities in this realm, as my interviewees suggested to me, this new responsibility delegated to parents feels "frightening" (*osoroshii*). In the popular realm, this new focus on parental responsibility has been encapsulated in book and magazine titles like *How Not to Raise a Part-Time Worker* [*furiita*], referring to the now legions of permanently underemployed youth entering the workforce after the miracle had ended. Uncertain about how to take on this new responsibility, parents are nonetheless motivated by the specter of failure, which has created a new mass market for privatized solutions through the growth of the cram school industry. A new psychologically informed literature on "raising a global child" is all too often a euphemism for new ways to help your child become more competitive in a much more constricted and uncertain job market and national future. With the exception of the leftist teacher's union *Nikkyoso* and academics like Takahashi, most of the public seemed unaware of the seriousness of these revisions, in some cases admitting to not knowing much about the Fundamental Law of Education and expecting the schools to inform them of the changes if they were serious.[15]

Exemplary of the conflicting messages of devotion to the nation, while being responsible for oneself, is a series of supplementary textbooks called *Notes to the Heart* (*Kokoro no No-to*), first produced and distributed to all elementary and junior high school students in 2002. The impetus behind the production of these colorfully designed and grade-specific booklets was precisely the (re-)creation of the daily plebiscite of the nation for Japanese students, a means of reminding them of the necessity of forgetting and remembering their affective relationship, albeit with the now important difference: The formerly ritualized *imagined community* of the Japanese nation is *not* that which is remembered and forgotten in the *Notes*. In the materials prepared for grades 1 through 3, the environment is bucolic and the focus is on students' independent performance of their daily routines at home and in school. The covers are adorned by a scene of two blissful youngsters, hugging their *Notes* to their hearts and floating above an area somewhere outside of the cityscape. By grades 5 and 6, the scenery has changed and the message has become more involved: Two adolescents stand in a forest with doves flying overhead; the scene is again in an uninterrupted countryside, and the messages on the cover proceed from "knowing yourself" to "raising yourself." Students are asked to reflect on the meaning of "freedom" (*jiyu*), their relations with their peers, and also their relation to their homeland (*furusato*). They are asked to think about how they can best contribute to their society with a "rich heart." What is additionally remarkable about these "heart notes" is their poignant absence of context and relationship to national history. Reading through them is an experience of being transported to another time and place, outside of the realm of ongoing recession and future uncertainty, to a space, it would appear, of the heart, in which the contradictions of the new affective relationship of less security and more individualization can be linked with former kinds of devotion and sacrifice.

To bypass the onerous textbook approval system in Japan, the *Notes* were given to the students as presents from the government, with instructions to open anytime during the school day. Their use was to have been extended beyond the regular class session into what is intended to become a routin-ized practice (Takahashi 2003: 18–21). As they proceed through the *Notes*, students are instructed to view their attachment to their nation with the will to succeed academically. Moreover, although the *Notes* are given as gifts, it is the student's responsibility to use them for his or her own self-enhancement and success. Above all else, the *Notes* help the students to see themselves as solely responsible for their own success or failure.

This new responsibility is also articulated in the very form of distribution—the gift—individualized and totalized in its form and content. Routinization of use is not promised here, nor is the kind of standardization of message and purpose common to other government-approved curricular materials. In fact, because of the informal manner of distribution and use, there is no way of tracking how the *Notes* have been used by schoolchildren on a nationwide scale. So, then, why go to the trouble of giving this massive gift, particu-larly in recessionary times? The answer lies, I believe, in the very informality and ubiquity of this gift to all the schoolchildren of Japan. While free to be opened when and as the students wish, the *Notes* impart a series of highly specific images to the child as student, images of a new form of individual and national development, a development that is predicated on new condi-tions of national belonging and new requirements of the national subjects-in-the-making. Indeed the extracurricular character of these materials suggests that the students must assume for themselves the responsibility of using them as a resource.

If *Notes to the Heart* conveys to the youth the new terrain of self-responsibility in a highly sentimentalized form, a key moment in the now cult film classic *Battle Royale* offers a harsher look at the conditions of reces-sionary restructuring in hyper-violent terms. Playing the role of an embat-tled middle school teacher in one of the "collapsing classrooms" of the 1990s, Beat-o Takeshi, famous for his violent portrayals of tragic figures in Japanese society, awakens his students, who have been drugged and abducted to a re-mote island where they will be forced to play a game of warfare of all against all, in which only one of them can survive as the victor. Reading the horrific rules of the government-mandated survival game, Takeshi's final message to his students as they are cast out to battle to the end: "Life is a game. Get tough. Battle and survive to become adults of worth."

The phrase *adults of worth* reveals the new affective conditions of the indi-vidual's relationship to the nation. The filmic world of *Battle Royale* shows us teachers that do not instruct, advise, and socialize students but instead condemn them to death; parents who are absent and do not know where their children are or what has become of them; and a state that no longer takes responsibility. What is evoked, only to be revoked, in this final instruction to "battle to become adults of worth" is no less than the tightly enmeshed relationships of the modern nation-state in which individuals were hailed as subjects and whose sacrifice to the nation, through work or military service, was rewarded with guarantees for life. In *Battle Royale* and the teacher's injunction to kill or eliminate those who are the same, so that the nation might survive, there is a critical inversion of the affective relationship to the nation. This battle-to-the-end intentionally turns on its head the linkages between shared sacrifice and shared sentiment. In this world, only the individual with the strength to live will win. The film forecasts the changed conditions of the affective relationship that the "adult of worth" can (and has no choice but to) enter into.

The scene described in the preceding paragraphs pushes the heart idiom of our earlier discussion yet a step further. Refigured here are not only the children, who are required to learn a new means of fashioning their own subjectivity for the various battles of the futures that they must learn to wage on their own with little guarantee of a secure future, but also the adult, who is also reconfigured as the completion of a set of values and a social compact discursively produced as distinctly Japanese.

The national context surrounding these "adults of worth" is no longer the nation-state as great equalizer, homogenizer, and socializer of the population. The prerecessionary, "learn-from-Japan" past is exactly what is revoked in the idea of the survival game and its officially mandated conclusion of sole survivor. The new "adult of value" is one whose time is not the developmental era of the postwar national past, in which the micro- and macrotechniques of standardization and homogeneity suited the needs and requirements of capitalist modernity in the latter half of the twentieth century. In the language of government policy documents, those overwritten, prescribed, and inculcated habits and virtues of the Japanese miracle are no longer suitable (*fuzawashiikunai*) to the situation in which Japan now finds itself.

The survivors of capitalist globalization are those for whom the former conditions are no longer available, and thus the former limits of work and life do not obtain. These limits have been redefined within the conditions of labor restructuring—the new contract and part-time labor force and educational reforms that attempt to obscure the new realities of sacrifice by making the devotion to country a matter of the individual heart. As one entrepreneur in the recession battered area around Osaka described for me recently: "Those who will succeed are those who have small feelers or antennae out in every direction to try and detect where the places and new sources of value will be created." He talked about how this new value is connected intricately to the values that are emerging among the young, "This is a labor reality," he said, "in which limits had become unknown [*genkai wa doko ni aru no ka*], so very different from before." He described with a sort of nostalgia the category of *zangyo* (overtime hours); even though this resulted in men who spent more time at work than with their families, some of whom in severe instances died from the effects overwork, at least even this was seen as a kind of limit.

The 2001 report "The Structure of Japan in the 21st Century" defines the new national values of this era of the heart, who will produce them, and how these adaptations will occur (Kawai 2000). Written by the Jungian psychologist Kawai Hayao, this new set of values in terms of the nation were located newly within Japan and the Japanese subject. Japan's new frontiers of growth, potential, strength, and survival are to found within. The sites of social reproduction would need to change to create this new value, producing subjects to be potentially endless sites for value creation. If within, where is this limit? According to a long-time acquaintance who is a member of the teachers' union, this new frontier within means that the new Japanese subject is on his or her own; having been stripped of whatever protections (job security, health care, pensions) remaining in the compact between capital and labor from the high-growth era, he or she is left "bare naked" (*maru hadaka*).

The combination of a sense of growing national crisis, a resurgence of patriotism, anxieties about the youth, and calls for devotion to the nation, as individuals struggle to maintain their own jobs, is not unknown in the United States or in other parts of the world. It is a shared experience of capitalist globalization as jobs are outsourced and whole industries are relocated offshore. But the effects of these changes take their specific forms in different places, reflecting prior histories and national formations. Under the name of the new patriotic education and heart notes, young Japanese citizens are being asked to adapt to the end of a system of social protections and relative income equalities. Patriotic education does not mean more direct control by the state but rather more responsibility placed on the individual for securing his or her own future at a time when the social safety net for which Japan became famous has been removed, the path from education to work is shifting, income gaps are widening dramatically, and the securing of personal futures is more uncertain. Patriotic education in Japan is as much about strategies of self-strengthening, maintaining position, and navigating the much-changed present, not only of national futures but also personal ones. Individuals must take responsibility for themselves, yet they are no less called on to sacrifice themselves for the nation.

Notes

ACKNOWLEDGMENTS

In the preparation of this chapter, I have benefited from the helpful comments of colleagues at the University of Washington, Stanford University, University of California at San Diego, and Whitman College. In particular, I would like to thank Miyako Inoue for help in thinking through the problem of patriotism in a neoliberal age and to Ann Anagnost for ongoing discussions, feedback, and careful attention to all stages of the writing of this chapter.

1. "By other means" is a notion borrowed from Gordon Lafer's discussion of the "war on terror" as a "strategy for advancing a neoliberal agenda" (2007).
2. Jennifer Robertson, in writing about a pre–nation-state form of education for women, called *Shingaku* (heart learning), describes the idea of *kokoro* (heart) in Japanese as "one of the most compelling and ubiquitous terms in the Japanese language" (1991: 88). Including both the heart and mind, it can refer to a locus of feelings, consciousness, and authority.
3. The Japanese economy expanded at a historically unprecedented rate with double-digit growth from 1955 through 1973 as a result of a national campaign led by the Ikeda government. For more about the income-doubling campaign of the Ikeda government and the sustained growth period of 1974–1990, see Hein 1993.
4. Igarashi (2002) uncovers how neonationalist sentiment is linked to a set of concerns about national incompleteness that have been one of the troubling mainstays of the modernity project in Japan. He uncovers the resonances between Maruyama Masao's use of the notion of "incomplete modernity" in partial explanation for the totalitarian programs and ideologies of the 1920s through the 1940s and present-day cultural critic Kato Norihiro's argument about the necessity of

war as a means to complete the modernity project in Japan. According to Kato, only with the (re)addition of the right to war will Japan emerge as a whole or "normal" nation that can mourn those who were once the victims of Japanese imperial aggression.

5. Modernization theory, as Takashi Fujitani (1993) discussed, was along with many other things an effort to posit, but then also to translate, the violence of the 1930 and 1940s into a postwar campaign of economic growth.

6. As Ann Anagnost explains in the Introduction to this volume, the power of ethnographic investigations is in their ability to engage with transformations at the everyday level, while attending to historicity and complex crossings among national contexts. In the case of the present chapter, the ethnographic work takes the form of tracking the Japanese context and its effects.

7. In the aftermath of the revisions to the Fundamental Law of Education at the end of 2006, a number of interesting discussions of their content have been published; see, for instance, Leibowitz and McNeil 2007. I am indebted to their discussions. The revisions have also been carefully documented on the website of the Japanese Ministry of Education and Technology in Japan (MEXT); see www.mext.go.jp.

8. For the English-language versions of the Imperial Rescript on Education and the 1947 Fundamental Law of Education, see Horio 1988: 399 and 400–401, respectively.

9. See Horio 1988: 153–158 for a discussion of an important document on "The Image of the Desired Japanese" (*Kitai Sareru Ningenzo*).

10. For a thorough discussion of the Nakasone period education reform agenda, see Hood 2001.

11. "Learn from Japan" references a period in the late 1970s and 1980s when the Japanese government under prime ministers Masayoshi Ohira and Yasuhiro Nakasone began to refer to their nation as having achieved their long-term goal of catching up with the West (in particular the United States, following the Occupation of Japan). The notion of catch-up had been a complicated one in that it referred variously to a combination of economic and cultural might and the ability to influence world events as a result. As the Japanese began to talk about their new plan to go beyond Western paradigms of modernity with plans for an information and knowledge society, Western writers began to describe the differences of Japan in terms of what they were doing better than Western nations, or how we could learn from the particular forms of discipline, social organization, and strong educational system that resulted in an envious combination of high math and science scores, historically high GDP, and low crime and divorce rates. The claim was often made that Japan now had things to teach the West.

12. For more on the financial collapse in Japan of the early 1990s, see Katz 1998 and Saxonhouse and Stern 2004.

13. In this quotation, Ivy is also referring to a series of neonationalist debates of the recessionary period over the postwar peace constitution with its antiwar clause. In the aftermath of the financial collapse, falling international credit status, and other signs of the loss of international status and power, questions about the "abnormality" or impropriety of a nation that cannot wage war were raised with a new fervor.

14. The emphasis on emotion was first included in 2002 in the national course of study and has been unofficially included as a category for evaluation on many elementary and junior high report cards.

15. One of my first direct experiences with the lack of public awareness of the contemporary issues surrounding the Fundamental Law of Education took place in April 2002. My husband, two daughters, and I had returned to the area outside Tokyo in which we had lived during my fieldwork (1999–2001) so that my older daughter could participate in her Japanese elementary school graduation. At the conclusion of the graduation ceremony, the principal, who was retiring the following year, and with whom I had had many conversations, handed a small laminated card to each of the graduating sixth graders. On the card was the text of the 1947 Education Law. None of the parents or students I talked to seemed to understand why they were being given this text. Born in the immediate postwar period, Principal Majima was keenly aware of the changes this law had made in postwar education, and he wanted these students and their parents to know what they were in danger of losing.

Chapter Eight

Neoliberal Speech Acts
The Equal Opportunity Law and Projects of the Self in a Japanese Corporate Office

MIYAKO INOUE

Long before there were *freeters*, NEETs, and *purekariāto* (*precariato*), there were "women."[1] They were perhaps the first category of workers whose labor was to be made flexible and to become fragmented and whose subjectivity was to be reshaped by a new governmental universe of economic and political programs for "liberating" people from regulations and enterprising their lives and selves. Even before the dawn of what turned out to be a decades-long recession in the early 1990s marked by rapid disappearance of regular employment and a living wage, some feminist scholars had seen it coming. As feminist economist Adachi Mariko (2007: 141) somberly notes, "The fact of the disintegration of the wage labor category and the liquidation of employment was something that had already been 'perfectly foreseeable' in feminist/gender analysis by the late 1980s."

Economic euphoria in the late 1980s contributed to one of those fleeting historical moments in Japan when the alignment of the stars made it possible to think the idea of gender equity. The unprecedented economic boom seemed to open a widely celebrated door, but, with the burst of the "bubble," the door of historical possibility slammed shut for Japanese women.[2] During the economic expansion, labor shortages led to the mobilization of women into the workforce, mostly as contingent workers. The ever-expanding world of consumer goods and services further empowered them as discerning and informed consumers, all of which *rendered women publicly visible* as the sign of the times. Proclaiming it a national goal "to promote equal opportunity and treatment between men and women in employment in accordance with the principle contained in the Constitution of Japan ensuring equality under the law,"[3] Japan's original Equal Employment Opportunity Law (EEOL), which went into effect in 1986, symbolized a moment of the seemingly harmonious reconciliation between political liberalism and that of economic empowerment "for all."

However "toothless" it might have been, the original EEOL prescribed a Fordist dream, which was, after all, about to be eclipsed as the Japanese political economy embarked on a post-Fordist, neoliberal regime of restructuring in the 1990s. The original EEOL was based on a model of collective welfare (finally) extended to women as a politico-legal remedy for Fordism's own obdurate institutional mandate of the gendered division of labor and "family wage." By the time it arrived in the late 1980s, however, "gender equity" as was understood and envisioned within the Fordist paradigm had fundamentally been displaced, and the EEOL had been co-opted as yet another limb of neoliberal projects, producing female workers as the subjects of self-government whose aspirations and hopes would be well adjusted to free market governance.

What was also at stake in this historical moment was that the original EEOL was implemented during Yasuhiro Nakasone's term as prime minister (1982–1987) along with a series of comprehensive neoliberal reforms based on market fundamentalism, by which "government itself becomes a form of enterprise whose task is to universalize competition and invent market-shaped systems of action for individuals, groups and institutions" (Lemke 2001, 197). Major publicly owned industries, including Nippon Telephone and Telegraph (NTT), Japan National Railways (JNR), and Japan Tobacco (JT), were privatized between 1985 and 1987. The merger of public employee unions with labor unions in the private sectors (*Rengō*) in 1989 meant the corporatization of organized labor in compliance with the broader neoliberal transformation. Revitalization of the economy was sought through market-friendly deregulation of land use, construction codes, finance, taxation, and foreign trade. These reforms in the 1980s were of a piece with those of other industrial superpowers seeking globalization as a solution to the worldwide crisis of Fordist regimes in the form of flexible accumulation. New pools of cheap labor and new consumer markets were the name of the game.

Characterizing the postwar universal (and egalitarian) education system as depriving children of individuality (*kosei*), and thus as not only undemocratic but also guilty of leaving citizens ill equipped for the coming age of global competition, Nakasone advocated decentralization and privatization of the national public education system and attempted to introduce competition and a market in education, according to which both schools and students (and their parents) would be granted the "freedom of choice" in selecting schools and curricula (Cave 2001; Hood 2001; Okada 2002; see also Arai 2000, 2003; Ivy 2000). It was understood, of course, that there would be winners and losers in this market, but this would be both good management and socially ethical. Revisions of the Health Insurance Law (*kenkō hokenhō*) in 1984—Japan has had universal social insurance since 1905—for the first time charged individuals a 10 percent copayment for covered medical expenses.

These reforms were accompanied by neonationalist cultural work to obscure the social fragmentation of cultural citizenship brought on by the widening gap between the haves and the have-nots. Nakasone was the first postwar prime minister to make an official visit to the Yasukuni Shrine, where not only the war dead but also Class A war criminals (as convicted by the Allied tribunals in Asia) were enshrined. Combined with the steady increase in Japan's military budget, the prime minister's visits to the shrine were a reminder for many Asian countries that Japanese imperialism was not only unrepented but could be resurrected at any time.

The EEOL thus paradoxically coexisted with a series of reforms that would further abandon all minoritized social categories, including gender as well as race, class, and ethnicity. How can one make sense of this? What was the shared condition that enabled a conjunctural—if not conspiratorial—articulation between the rise of neoliberal political economic reforms and the arguably democratic policy in the form of the EEOL? How did it shape the ways in which men and women, as well as management and labor, imagined what gender equality would look like and ought to be?

It probably comes as no surprise then that, as many scholars have rightly noted, the EEOL turned out to be toothless (see Creighton 1996; Edwards 1994; Gelb 2000; Lam 1992; Molony 1995; Parkinson 1989).[4] The impetus for the EEOL was a somewhat reluctant response to the 1979 U.N. Convention on the Elimination of All Forms of Discrimination against Women (CEDAW), which required signatory nations to enact laws to implement the terms of the convention. After six years of debate following Japan's signing of the convention in 1980, which involved effective organized opposition from the business community, the end product appears to be a total concession to the standpoint of management. Although gender discrimination in training, benefits, dismissal, and retirement is prohibited and subject to civil court penalties (albeit with complaints against employers to be mediated by the government), equality in recruitment, hiring, and promotion is not enforceable but subject only to an employer's good faith effort.[5] Thus, the law did not assign judicial surveillance to key practices. Men get better and higher-paying jobs than women because of bias in recruitment and hiring, and training and benefits are always linked—formally in a gender-neutral way—to the rank and compensation of the job title. Therefore the law's ability to prohibit gender discrimination has been severely limited from the start because men and women are offered different jobs at the point of hiring. Accordingly, any violation in the areas of dismissal and retirement would be equally missed because it would be hard to claim that a woman was fired or forced into retirement because of her gender when her job is effectively available only to women. The EEOL marked the triumph of management (Gelb 2000): The law itself shifted the terms in which gender equity was to be achieved from the employer's *legal* responsibility to its *social* and *moral* responsibility as "duties to endeavor" at equity.[6]

To develop my argument, I draw on my ethnographic research in the early 1990s in a corporate office of "May Japan, Limited" (a pseudonym). MJL management had just begun to implement various programs in compliance with the EEOL at a time when a historic corporate restructuring (*risutora*) was looming in response to increasing global competition. Giving an ethnographic account of how gender equity was imagined by managers, working women, and their supervisors at that conjuncture, this chapter presents an analysis of how the original EEOL was translated into concrete programs and practices of gender and labor politics. The Fordist remedy for gender equity as was envisioned in the original EEOL was transformed into a powerful apparatus that prepared women to liberate—and govern—themselves as subjects in a post-Fordist neoliberal political economy.

My ethnographic analysis is guided by Foucault's concept of "governmentality." The term *governmentality* refers to a particular political rationality of governing whose power-effects lie in "guiding the possibility of conduct and putting in order the possible outcome" (Foucault, 1991: 221; see also Dean 1999; Miller and Rose 1990). What is at issue here is a form of power that structures the field of possibilities for an actor, making it easier to come to think of oneself in terms of certain interests and not others and difficult if not impossible to think in practical terms of rational alternatives to defining the self and one's interests. Foucault's contribution was to see this political structuring not as the imposition of false consciousness by the powerful on the powerless but as the mundane working out of everyday practical arrangements by which individuals make themselves into subjects of a determinate form and, thus, govern themselves, even if not just as they please. Ultimately, the everyday practical arrangements that interest students of governmentality may have an autonomy and effectivity that counts more than any intention or strategy on the part of the powerful (the state, the ruling class, men). Foucault's notion of governmentality offers an effective key to understanding neoliberalism in general and to the way the EEOL in fact simply *restructured* gender inequality by showing how the modern dichotomies of freedom and domination, the state and the (market) economy, the personal and the political, and the private and the public are in fact the functions of the way neoliberal governmentality exerts its power (Lemke 2002). Foucault reminds us that freedom and domination are not mutually exclusive and that freedom is the necessary condition for domination, for "power is exercised only over free subjects, and only insofar as they are free" (1983: 221).

Women's happiness, sense of fulfillment, and aspirations came to be the concern of government agencies, employers, women's advocates, media commentators, public intellectuals, and informed individual women themselves—all of which constituted a complex public sphere around the issue of women, women's welfare, gender equity, and the EEOL. Within corporations, management gathered and analyzed information about their women employees. But women workers also constructed knowledge about women workers, even if not as systematized or recognized as the management's growing archive. In this chapter, I examine the concrete techniques and technologies of improving women's lives through empowerment programs (Cruikshank 1999) and discuss how women were guided to freely choose a particular relationship to their selves, one that was avowedly based on their welfare.

A framing in terms of governmentality draws our attention to the specific practices and actions directed at women by management at MJL: company surveys, workshops, and task forces that produced a specific (cultural) truth about the MJL female workers. Through these communicative events and modes of knowledge production, the management asks, "What do women want?" This, of course, is an incitement to discourse, as Foucault might have said, and a way of encouraging women workers to engage in new forms of participation in the workplace. As much as it is a democratic speech act of inclusion and enfranchisement, the interrogative address sets up female workers as "other" insofar as it is equivalent to management's saying, "We don't know what you want because you are not us." Rather than simply extending inclusion or entitlement to women, management claims that they first must know what women want. The surveys, workshops, and task forces constitute "speech acts" (Austin 1962; Butler 1997), or, more specifically, what I would call "neoliberal speech acts," prompted by the question of "What do women want?" and thereby hailing women who respond to it by interpellating themselves into the subject position of neoliberalism. Under the framing of neoliberalism, of course, gender equity cannot be a structural issue but is rather an issue of the ethics and aesthetics of how one conducts one's relationship to oneself and one's relationship with others. These communicative events imaginatively take place in an ideal public sphere (Habermas 1989), putatively realizing what Habermas (1979) calls the "ideal speech situation" of modern participatory democracy, where citizens freely, rationally, and truthfully express their opinions and where they fully and equally participate in discussion.

The "felicity condition" of neoliberal speech acts is that those who are hailed by them must be autonomous and free subjects who know and communicate what they want. This in turn gives birth to neoliberal subjects who are capable of taking responsibility for sovereign management of their own best interests. These communicative events *feminized* gender inequality and its correction under the EEOL, transforming the responsible subject from the employer to female workers themselves.

Not unlike Avery Gordon's (1995: 17) notion of "liberal racism," which entails the paradox of an "antiracist attitude that coexists with support for racist outcomes," sexism in the era of neoliberalism would easily escape the liberal-democratic notion of domination and oppression. The original EEOL was not so much ineffective as it became the means of a new mode of subjection of women—to the family, to the corporate employer, and to the nation-state. Sexism no longer needed to resort to the outright exclusion of women but could operate—perhaps even more effectively—by *liberating* women from the older and familiar mode of sexism-by-exclusion. It subjects women by treating them as autonomous individuals and fully integrated corporate citizens who affirmatively respond to, and imitate the pleas of, aspiring female employees: "We want to be treated not as women, but as individuals (*kojin to shite mite hoshii*)."

Women and Men at May Japan, Limited

May Japan, Limited, first established in 1966, was a midsized subsidiary of a European pharmaceutical and chemical multinational corporation dealing in the production, import and export, sale, and research and development of pharmaceutical and other chemicals with a total of 2,670 employees in Japan as of 1993. This is where I conducted ethnographic research from April 1991 through August 1993. This company de facto no longer exists. By the time I had left the company in fall 1993, it had began to undergo a drastic downsizing with some departments closed down or merged into another company and many full-time male employees forced out of work.

Before the downsizing, MJL had followed its standardized personnel management procedures. Men and women were segregated both vertically and horizontally, an arrangement reinforced by hiring practices and occupational tracking according to gender. Recruitment and hiring were the decisive points where men and women were differentiated and where the EEOL was least effective in facilitating reform. As with most Japanese white-collar organizations in the early 1990s, MJL preferred to hire predominantly men who were new university graduates for the core of the workforce. The EEOL did not prohibit this practice, which was outwardly discriminatory both in intent and in effect. Male recruits were largely baccalaureate graduates, except for those in research and development facilities with master's or doctoral degrees or those in manufacturing facilities or in some offices and facilities with only high-school diplomas, vocational school certificates, or junior college degrees. Male workers were organized into a larger, rigorously graded age (or seniority) hierarchy in the primary sector in cohorts that were internally relatively egalitarian (education being equal). All male workers were full-time employees except for a handful of contract workers (*shokutaku*) hired to fill specific job assignments, such as warehouse security. Women were recruited mainly as flexible and contingent labor and were consistently found in lower-ranked positions and career grades in the company hierarchy. This meant that they were systematically confined to support, as opposed to line (profit-making), functions within the company. All part-time workers were female, making up 22 percent of the female workforce at MJL. The major path of entry into MJL for full-time female workers was through mid-career employment (*chūtosaiyō*), an irregular form of recruitment in contrast to the strict age-based system in which male primary-sector recruits entered the company as a cohort immediately on graduation.

"The Year of the Employee"

After EEOL was first promulgated in 1986, MJL adjusted its pay system to equalize men and women's base salaries among cohorts with the same education level. This equal-pay system, however, applied only in the first five years of service. After that, the pay system incorporated discrimination based on gender as well as rank, age, occupation, education, and ability. Those in sales positions received sales-based increments, which made up the bulk of their total pay. Because sales jobs were available only for male workers, the salary gender gap inevitably grew, and the new pay system did very little to equalize pay.

In 1990 MJL management rolled out a mission statement, for the first time in its company history, titled "The Guiding Principle." In addition to articulation of its business goals, its pledge to customers, and its assurance of good citizenship in the community, it showcased the company's dedication to the welfare of employees in their "MJL life":

> Based on the principle that the employees are the most important asset for the company, MJL will value the individuality of each employee and will endeavor to bring out the best in him or her through well-planned programs. Job assignment and delegation of authority and responsibility will be made in accordance with individual ability and aptitude. MJL will endeavor to provide the employee with a rich and fulfilling MJL life by guaranteeing the fair evaluation of the individual's job responsibility and performance.

"The Guiding Principle" was followed by the designation of the year 1990 as "The Year of the Employee" (*shain no toshi*). Between 1990 and 1992, a dozen task forces were organized to revisit the existing personnel and benefit programs, all of which were meant to provide employees with better working conditions to make their work and private lives more rewarding. The company also implemented new management programs that harnessed white-collar worker initiative and active participation and were meant to implant the employee's active engagement with the company's business goals and the big picture.

"The Guiding Principle" and "The Year of the Employee" marked the increasing responsibility given to *all* employees, not just women or those on the production line. For example, in April 1991, the company set up an ad hoc interdivisional office that promoted "total quality improvement" (TQM) and implemented "quality improvement teams" in the workplace. While MJL's manufacturing plant had adopted TQM several years previously, the new initiative introduced for the first time the ideas of "quality" (*kuoritī*) and "quality improvement" to employees in corporate administration, sales, and research and development. All full-time employees were required to work in small teams, proposing and executing concrete projects to improve office productivity. Twice a year, the Quality Steering Committee selected the best project and widely publicized it within the company. The CEO made a speech to MJL employees in 1991: "We think it important to achieve higher quality in all aspects of company life by each of the employees actively participating in the company objectives and goals and identifying them as their own objectives and goals." TQM thus facilitated a particular mode of self-governance by making company goals and personal goals mesh—by linking work responsibility to the individual's project of the self through making a responsible and ethical self that would be accountable to the work process.

The ethical construction of the self was also linked to productivity and efficiency. In June 1991, the company appointed a new task force focusing on employees' business manners that produced and distributed a brochure to teach the aesthetics and ethics of everyday conduct and sociality, including how to use honorifics and how to bow appropriately according to the relative rank of the person one greets. In February 1992, the company hired a business consulting firm to conduct the first "climate survey" (*kigyō fūdo chōsa*), which purported to identify the company's culture or the composite of its organizational and psychological characteristics. A lengthy questionnaire specifically tailored for MJL was administered to all the full-time employees, soliciting detailed demographic, personal, and attitudinal information.

The results and analysis of the survey were reported back to the employees in a video presentation.

From the management's point of view, as I was told, the quality improvement teams, task forces, and the survey were, together, meant to create a sense of unity as a business organization and thus boost the morale of the workers. It was part of management's broader effort to comply with EEOL and achieve gender equity. But it is important to ask why such managerial initiatives came to be thought of as necessary in the early 1990s for the first time in the company's history. These programs—perhaps far beyond their intention of community building and corporate identity making, not to mention increasing worker productivity—occasioned a self-making project in which the employee's awareness was brought directly to him- or herself and to his or her relationship with others. These self-making techniques were designed to turn the individual worker into an agent who recognizes the self as a project in which he or she must invest, and they encourage the employee to understand his or her labor as a concrete object that he or she can control.

TQM/TQC programs, worker responsibility, and the engineering of employee-subjects in the 1990s might not sound new. But what was different about the new government or self-government of workers under discussion here was the incitement of and mobilization of "the individual." It was the individual *in her or his particularity* who was marked out as a new kind of corporate employee—especially among *women* employees—and this marked the birth of neoliberal corporate governance in Japan.

In the same year, management also announced the upcoming implementation of a new personnel evaluation system that more actively involved and implicated the employee's self-evaluation (*jiko shinkoku seido*). Unlike the traditional personnel system, in which the supervisor unilaterally evaluated the worker's job performance, the new system was more of a joint task between the supervisor and the employee, which took into consideration the worker's self-evaluation and her preferences for job type, promotion, or transfer. Objectives for the next term of performance review were also to be set jointly by the supervisor and the employee, so that the employee came to be personally and reflexively accountable in a way she had not been when assignments were made without consulting employees. One's *career goals* were thus materialized and subjected to joint management by the supervisor and the employee. Coercion and consent, as Foucault might tell us, here became more difficult to distinguish.

This self-evaluation system was part a new "ability-based grade system" (*shokunō shikaku seido*), called the Job-Execution-Competence Grade System (JEC Grade System). While the existing personnel management system (job evaluation, salary, and promotion) was based on length of service and seniority—criteria that the company, perhaps grudgingly, recognized could be discriminatory against women—the JEC Grade System was to be based only on ability. Under the new system, jobs were clearly identified and de-limited; they were carefully described in terms of concrete tasks and responsibilities; and they were categorized into specific grades. Pay raises and promotions would be based on measurable or otherwise objective performance standards in executing the job as formally described. The JEC Grade System was thus meant to replace the existing age-based system (*nenkōjoretsu*). In conjunction with the self-evaluation system, identifying and describing the job, its skill level, and other details would be done in a "consultative" exchange between the supervisor and the employee.

The management claimed the new participatory job description and employee evaluation systems as its affirmative response to the EEOL. The new personnel systems were intended by management to be the ultimate remedy for any gender inequality that might reside in the workplace. One of the company task forces on gender equality explained:

> Due to the increasing shortage of labor and increasing business competition, a high-quality female labor force has been more in demand than ever before. The next ten years will see more women interested in working in corporate offices. There has, however, not yet been established any system in the business world that can provide women with equal opportunities. It is our view that the implementation of the Job-Execution-Competence Grade System, which is to be introduced in the next few years, will enable "equal opportunity" to be guaranteed *automatically* [as an integral part of routine personnel processes] and that the unwritten rule that prescribes gender-based job assignment will eventually become a thing of the past. . . . It is our hope that talented and motivated female employees at MJL will benefit from the JEC-Grade System and will no longer be discouraged by persistent social inequality. [emphasis added]

The presentation of the JEC-Grade System as a remedy for gender inequality clearly illustrates the company's approach to the goal of equity. Gender and gender discrimination were understood as individual attributes with no structural linkage to systemic patriarchy or structural sexism. The JEC system was thus based on the "atom" of an individual worker abstracted from her historical and social context—that is, from concrete social relations of domination and subjection. The company thus managed to avoid introducing a personnel policy that could have as its target what are called "effects" in the affirmative action debate in the United States on the basis of which it could be evaluated.

Such programs inevitably discipline (or "empower") workers to produce knowledge about themselves and their relation to their work. The climate survey provided them with an "empirical" and "scientific" narrative of who they are and how they are doing. The quality circles and the "business manner" campaign, described in the preceding paragraphs, disciplined them to learn how to monitor themselves as well as their co-workers in terms of job performance. Labor is converted into a concrete object that the individual worker can own and therefore manage by improving, economizing, standardizing, and streamlining. It masks the worker's profound alienation from her own labor under capitalism by inaugurating her as an entrepreneur who invests in her own skills. The individual worker is, in this mode of governmentality, the owner and agent of her labor. The self thus becomes interchangeable with the objectification of the worker under capitalism: The worker is labor power and vice versa. Work is then one's self-identity (Miller and Rose 1995).

What Do Women Want? The Equal Opportunity Task Force and Workshops

One of the task forces created in 1990 as part of "The Year of the Employee" campaigns was The Equal Opportunity Task Force (EOTF) (*Kikai kintō tasuku fōsu*), to which five section chiefs (*kachō*) (four men and one woman) from different divisions of the company were appointed. Defining equal opportunity as "job assignment on the basis of ability, potential, and qualification, regardless of gender," an EOTF official memo states its mission as "realizing the coexistence of male and female employees based on the principle of 'the right-person-in-the-right-place.'" The EOTF's activities and reports in 1990 laid the foundation for the subsequent EEOL-related programs and policy initiatives.

The EOTF survey was administered to female employees and male managers, and the following results were reported: (1) Little discussion takes place between male superiors and female workers regarding women's career development. (2) Equality in pay is present only in the first three years of employment. (3) Women have little access to training programs for acquisition of new skills and knowledge. (4) Women have little participation in important meetings and conferences, which results in their receiving limited information in comparison to men. (5) Women are dissatisfied with male managers who view office chores (*zatsuyō*), such as serving tea, answering the phone, and copying, as "women's work."

In its report, the EOTF noted a significant gap in response between male managers and female employees to the last item on the survey, "Male managers know how to treat female employees." While as many as 85 percent of male managers responded in the affirmative, 68 percent of the female employees answered in the negative. This consciousness gap (*ishiki kakusa*) between male managers and female subordinates came to be viewed, in the wake of the survey results and by both male and female employees, as the major source of gender inequality within the company and an urgent problem to be solved to achieve equal opportunity. On this, women and men, workers and managers, could agree.

The EOTF called for a self-enlightenment plan (*jiko keihatsu puran*), in which nonmanagerial employees, both men and women, were to evaluate their own job performance, plan personal career development, and discuss all this with their supervisors for feedback at least once a year. Tellingly, the EOTF's final recommendation was that male supervisors should learn how to treat female subordinates. With the intent to expand women's job opportunities, the EOTF concluded:

> In the process of repeatedly giving female employees opportunities to expand their job territory, men (superiors) and women (subordinates) should mutually learn how to cooperate to work together. As a result, male superiors must rethink how to utilize the female work force. The accumulation of such experience will eliminate the rift between male superiors and female subordinates.

The six-year incremental plan for equal opportunity drafted by EOTF, which was never realized at MJL, exemplified the extent to which "equal opportunity" was contained by the discourse of individual psychology and consciousness:

Phase A (1990): Self-awareness (*jikaku, ishiki*);

Phase B (1991): Changing mentality (*ishiki kaikaku, arainaoshi*);

Phase C (1991–1993): Anticipating chaos and confusion (*konran*);

Phase D (1994–1995): The new consciousness sinks in (*ishiki e no shintō*);

Phase E (1996): Implementation of equal opportunity (*kikaikintō no jitsugen*).

Although some of the EOTF recommendations related to women's access to training and job assignment, the terms in which all the recommendations were ultimately couched and implemented displaced attention from structural and organizational imperatives to individual—and gendered—psychology. One might say that any suggestion of structural change, or seeking equality of results, was "deradicalized" (see Klare 1978) by translation into the project of changing how individuals think. Locating the truth in the individual's psychology is, as Rose (1996) argues, a central characteristic of advanced liberalism as a mode of governance in democratic societies.

In 1991, the MJL management appointed a group of five female workers (aged twenty-six to thirty-four) to organize the Working Group for Women (WGW). The management assigned the WGW to work on two major issues: the expansion of women's job categories and nondiscriminatory hiring. Assuming responsibility for complying with the Equal Opportunity Task Force initiatives, WGW members were to speak both *for* and *to* the MJL female workers and to mediate between the management and female workers as the latter's interpreters. As one member of the task force put it, the WGW's role is "to pump up the voices of women from the company's bottom and to let them be heard by the management." As did the EOTF, the WGW first administered a survey, but this time to all full-time female employees at MJL. The WGW's role was then to make a narrative from the numerical data generated by the survey.

The narrative carefully constructed by the WGW with selected survey results gradually emerged to take this story line: Contrary to the stereotype that women plan to quit MJL on marriage, most women take their careers seriously and do not think of their current jobs as temporary, although childbirth and child rearing might complicate their career plans. The real problem is that they are not equipped to plan careers systematically, and for this reason many women have never discussed their professional goals with their superiors. Many women are also not satisfied with their current jobs and workplace, and they feel that they cannot grow there (*shigoto wo tōshite seichō suru*).

Based on their identification of the barriers to equal opportunity, the WGW proposed a theme for its task force activities: "Power-Up for MJL Women" (*mezase pawā appu*). It entailed two concrete objectives for its second one-year project:

1. "Consciousness reform" (*ishiki kaikaku*) of female workers by female workers: To think about what we as women should be and what we should do to realize equal opportunity.
2. Proposing ideas to improve the existing benefits program in a way that enables women to balance work and home.

The WGW thus translated equal opportunity from a legal right and entitlement into a rhetoric of individual responsibilities, merit-based privileges, and accountability on the part of female employees in terms of work ethics, self-discipline, and professionalism. The policy issues of expanding job categories for women and nondiscriminatory hiring practices were reframed as personal issues of women's relations to their work. Taking on themselves the kind of obligations that the state (and the employer) might owe citizens and workers under a welfare-state regime (of the kind the American occupation envisioned in the aftermath of World War II), the WGW ended up presenting equal opportunity as a reward for women taking responsibility on themselves to become ideal gendered citizen-workers in an increasingly commonsensical neoliberal universe. It is not employers or government, but female workers themselves, who are to be held accountable for the realization of equal opportunity. All of this, of course, required a fundamentally new kind of gendered subjectivity.

"Improvement" on the matter of equal opportunity is to be sought at the individual level, in the individual psychological capacity to feel joy, fulfillment, and achievement through one's job (Donzelot 1991). At the annual managers meeting, the WGW emphasized critical self-examination, urging each woman to trust her own sovereign self: "In order to implement equal opportunity, the most important thing is for all of us, the MJL women, to examine ourselves closely, to assess our own individuality and goals in work, and to have our own vision of career and opinions to express." Regardless of the content and condition of her job, the worker with the appropriately "reformed consciousness" is capable of optimizing her potential and of growing to be a fully responsible adult—equal to men—through performing her job. Before anything else, be it a matter of entitlement or what the law prohibits or prescribes regarding the employer, equal opportunity is a reward for the fully-formed, gendered subject's ethical and even aesthetic relationship to herself on the one hand and to her work on the other.

In a 1991 in-house newsletter article entitled "The Future Roles of Female Employees in the Changing MJL," executive management declared it official policy to promote the idea of equal opportunity. Stressing the unique quality of women in having a closer and more natural relationship with "life" (understood to include both the natural and human-made worlds, including modern technology, products, and services), the article celebrates women's potential to play a critical role in bringing insight to management regarding the company's latest products. But to achieve this potential, the article continues:

> Women must participate in all aspects of business activities. In other words, it is essential that women not only manage people and advance the careers of others but also that they must be prepared and determined to manage themselves individually, and they must have the desire to be involved and to participate in doing so. *It is all up to how motivated, committed, and determined you* [women] *are to accept responsibilities and take on challenging jobs.* [emphasis added]

Just as the WGW called on female workers to reflect critically on their readiness and willingness to take their jobs seriously and improve themselves through their work, the management also demanded that women prepare themselves to compete and accept the challenges in the new world of (ostensibly gender-blind) equal, merit-based opportunity. What unites capital and labor here is the figure of the neoliberal subject, an independent, self-determined and self-determining, responsible individual, whose conduct simulates the logic of the market. The article continues:

> We at MJL are not simply considering equal opportunity but seriously thinking about the full involvement and participation of all female workers in all aspects of our business. *Now it is all up to whether or not you* [women] *take the initiative fully to contribute to the growth of MJL as well as to the benefit of the society.*

You have roles to play. So don't hesitate. In the next ten years, we want more of you to take positions with various responsibilities, and some of you even to take senior managerial positions. It is realizable, and our organization is already prepared for it. *So it now all depends on whether or not you accept challenging roles.* [emphasis added]

Both management and the WGW collapse the distinction between the social and the economic on the one hand and ethics and money on the other. Individual actors are to strategize on new terrain appearing with the neoliberal erosion of the social. But management and the WGE *invoked this framing for different reasons.* The WGW invested the neoliberal subject with the image of a professional woman—an economically independent and socially worthy individual, who knows what she wants and wants what she chooses, who optimizes her potential in the merit system, and who thus realizes her ideal self through work. On the other hand, as is seen in the preceding paragraphs, when the management endorses the idea of equal opportunity, saying that "our system is ready [read: nondiscriminatory], and it is all up to women," it envisions a risk-taking, self-motivated, citizen-worker in the merit system who will, in the case of suboptimal performance or disruption on account of family obligations, be mercilessly cut off from any company safety net, traditionally understood (for men) to reside in the system of seniority and lifetime employment.

By "equal opportunity," the management means "the full participation of all female workers in all business activities"—a remarkable displacement of the possibility of democratic inclusion into simply more of the same labor-control system, one historically designed for the male family-waged breadwinner-citizen-worker. Equal opportunity for women, if management could have its way, would not compromise the existing labor system's rules and forms of gender-based exploitation and exclusion. The difference is that this new sexism seamlessly fits into the neoliberal total mobilization of the population into its own responsibilization and self-governing. Business is happy indeed to be truly gender blind, as long as what it needs from employees at the bottom line is not tinkered with.

This all recalls the discourse of neoliberal welfare reform in the United States. In U.S. welfare-to-work programs, in which welfare recipients—predominantly minority women with children—are required to get job training, and eventually, a job, in exchange for welfare benefits, women on welfare

are presumed to be underresponsibilized as individuals. Being unemployed is considered to be an ethical and moral failure on the part of welfare recipients—as is clear in the prevailing welfare stereotypes of laziness, "welfare queens," and intergenerational dependence. What gets elided, of course, is the inevitable existence of capitalism's reserve army of labor, as well as other structural political-economic arrangements that guarantee the presence of the unemployed and the poor. The brilliance of neoliberal welfare reform discourse is to convert outwardly racist and sexist stereotypes—these have not disappeared but rather have become rearticulated into cases for practical self-improvement and individual empowerment. In the same manner, the MJL management repeats the point that it all depends on how women are (morally) self-prepared to accept challenging jobs; it is not a question of whether they deserve to receive equal treatment. In a statement that, with only minor alteration, could have been disseminated by anti–welfare-rights ideologues in the United States, the MJL management wrote:

> The reason that we stress this point to such a great degree is that we have an impression that only a handful of women are prepared to accept challenging jobs, while others seem to welcome as an excuse the view that male employees and colleagues, and most of the male management, are opposed to equal opportunity. This is, of course, true with particular cases, but it is not our policy, and therefore, it can no longer be used as an excuse [for women not to accept challenging jobs].

Now that the company supports the idea of equal opportunity and invites women to the full range of company business activities, they no longer have any excuse not to respond to its "total mobilization"—through the magic of the universal, gender-blind, free market—to fully and responsibly engage in their work. It would only be because of women's moral failure—by their being lazy and irresponsible, lacking in motivation and a sense of professionalism, escaping from freedom—that they might not get hired or promoted or be satisfied with their jobs. Don't blame the company or your supervisor for being sexist. And if you quit, this is your completely free "choice."

"POWER UP FOR WOMEN" WORKSHOPS

The workshop was another technology to produce the "truth" of female workers and their interests. While the survey assumed the rational subject to be expressing her subjective view with regards to the questions, the workshop relies on the technology of confession and the confessing subject (Foucault 1978), one who is willing to speak her secret, authentic experience and feelings as a female worker at MJL. It was the WGW's mission in these workshops to bring women's private voice—repressed and ignored—into public expression and to have it be heard by management. It is important to recognize the extent to which the workshop is a medium of communication endemic to liberal democracy, both enabled and constrained by a specific political rationality. As Foucault (1978: 62) shows in his discussion of how the truth of sexuality is brought into being, confession is a ritual that "produces intrinsic modifications in the person who articulates it: it exonerates, redeems, and purifies him [sic]; it unburdens him of his wrongs, liberates him, and promises him salvation." The woman-in-the-workshop is thus freed by confessing and sharing her secrets with her peers, and by doing so she is constituted as the subject of the discourse of gender equity (and inequality) she speaks.

At the same time, the workshop format sets the boundary of legibility in terms of what makes sense to speak and what does not. The confessed content must derive from the confessor's singularity as an autonomous, sovereign individual. The condition of the confession's veracity is "the bond, the basic intimacy in discourse, between the one who speaks and what he is speaking about" (Foucault 1978: 62). This sets up the fictitious boundary between the *personal* and the *political*. Truth lies in the woman's inner emotive self. What this pragmatic rule does is to preclude talk about anything but oneself as an individual, excluding any reference to structural, organizational, or legal issues as *political* and thus external to the workshop theme. One is not forbidden to speak about such issues, but they are understood as exogenous factors, akin to a death in the family or the weather.

In November 1991, the WGW organized workshops in Osaka and Tokyo, where MJL's largest branch offices and headquarters (Tokyo) were located. Recruited on a voluntary basis, forty-four women participated altogether. After opening remarks by a member of the WGW, each participant was asked to write down on three different cards respectively: (1) problems she was aware of in daily work; (2) anything she was not happy with at work; and (3) anything she wanted to share with other participants. In a neoliberal global assemblage, the participants then broke into small groups, categorized the responses of individuals in the group into themes, and chose which of these they would discuss as a small group. The discussion leader of each group was asked to write down on an overhead transparency three points: (1) the problem-topics the group discussed, (2) the characteristics of the workplace that caused the problem(s), and (3) possible solutions and strategies for improvement.

The workshop participants almost universally pointed out the persistence of gender stereotypes and their use by men and management as an explanation of the (unfair) gendered division of labor in the workplace. The majority of the groups thus chose as a discussion topic the issue of differential job allocation in the workplace, in which even motivated and aspiring women were systematically assigned to a clerical support role, what they referred to as an assistant-like role (*ashisutanto-teki*).

One common discussion topic concentrated on *zatsuyō*, which literally means "miscellaneous affairs." It refers to routine odd jobs in the workplace, such as serving tea, copying, filing, handling mail, ordering office supplies, and other repetitive, noncumulative, support work for core or line employees. These were exclusively assigned to women at MJL, where, I observed, gender consistently overrode age and years of service in assigning such menial tasks. Even the youngest and newest male member of the office was exempt from *zatsuyō*. A new young male employee would hesitantly but politely ask a female worker senior to him with much longer tenure at the company to order the office supplies he needed. Or, at around 11:50 a.m., when the bento lunch boxes for the workers had arrived, all the female workers would stop their work and start preparing tea for lunch. All women, whether full-time or part-time employees, temporary or permanent, shared the load of *zatsuyō* duties.

The most symbolically (and politically) charged of these *zatsuyō* duties is serving tea (*ochakumi*). A daily duty reserved for company women is to serve tea (or coffee) not only to visitors, but, more generally, to colleagues and superiors, throughout the day. At MJL, it was not uncommon for female workers to serve tea three times a day. In some offices, women might serve tea to as many as sixty people. All of this was an everyday material reminder of the differential treatment of women in the office and the deferential position they were expected to take.

The workshop discussions also invoked the familiar figure of the male supervisor who nipped his female subordinate's aspirations in the bud. It was agreed that the company-wide promotion of the idea of equal opportunity would not change a bit of his traditional view of women. He would continue to treat women as disposable temporary labor, as support staff with no chance of promotion, and to show no sense of duty for or even interest in mentoring female subordinates.

It is undoubtedly the case that women share more or less similar job dissatisfaction in their shared position in the stratified labor process. But serving tea was problematized as a workplace issue for women not only because it was universally experienced but, more important, because it was "legible" and "speakable" within the discourse of gender equity, something that made sense to talk about. In contrast, for example, none of the participants brought up the issue of salary, much less promotion. The workshop organizers also confirmed this observation and offered a couple of explanations. One was that salary and promotion were matters not precisely "about gender." One organizer surmised that women wanted to talk about things over which they felt that they had some control. One participant also said to me that it was not about money, but, as she put it, "I think all they [women] want is to feel their job more worth doing (*yarigai ga aru*) and to have others recognize (*mitomeru*) how hard and seriously they are working."

The WGW pointed out the importance of creating an environment that supports women's career development and their effort to balance work and family. But this "privilege" of women-friendly programs can be enjoyed *only if* women themselves understood the achievement of equal opportunity in a two-way model. First, a woman employee must have a genuine commitment to her career; second, (male) managers must be willing to nurture and train female subordinates. For the WGW, then, the key was smooth communication (*enkatsu na kominikēshon*) between female subordinates and male superiors. At the end of its term, the WGW concluded its presentation at the annual business managers' meeting as follows: "We need to strive toward the implementation of the MJL 'Guiding Principle' by recognizing each other's role in smooth communication between superiors and subordinates and person-to-person."

The surveys, workshops, and task forces objectified the firsthand accounts of attitudes, values, experience, feelings, and other "truths" about female workers, truths that were then used to guide the conduct the female workers—much of it, of course, as *self*-guidance. Following up on the WGW report at the annual business managers' meeting, in July 1992, the Personnel Department organized a three-day retreat, "The First Strategic On-the-Job-Training Workshop," targeting midlevel managers, or section chiefs (*kachō*). They were the direct supervisors of the female clerical workers, with whom they had everyday, face-to-face contact, and they held the interlocutor equally responsible—along with their female staff members—for "smooth communication." With the goal of improving their managerial skills and sensitivity to training, mentoring, communicating, and working with female workers, the main activity of the workshop was group discussion and an analysis of the data produced in the previous workshops, surveys, and task forces on equal opportunity.

Prior to this workshop, the participants' superiors received a questionnaire soliciting their evaluation of the participants as managers. The female subordinates of the participants were also surveyed on their views of the participants as managers. The participants received the survey results of their female staff at the workshop, and they were asked to reflect on the kinds of skill, attitude, and behavior expected both by their supervisors and by their supervisees.

The workshop was intended to demonstrate to managers how little they understood their female subordinates. They were to be enlightened about what women want and were treated to a wide range of comments about themselves as seen by their subordinates: "Don't try to fondle me when you get drunk!"; "Don't pick your nose hair at work"; "Don't come closer to me than necessary"; "I want my supervisor to treat all of his supervisees equally"; "I want my supervisor to give more precise feedback and instructions. He lacks in logical thinking"; "My supervisor does not take me seriously because he thinks women have no loyalty to the company"; "My supervisor has more frequent contact with his male supervisees and gives them detailed job instructions, but he does not seem to do so with his female supervisees. For the sake of efficiency, I want him to give us clear instructions." The participants also saw comments about themselves by their supervisors, for example, "He is too lenient with his female supervisees"; "I think he is always passionate about the effective mentoring of his supervisees, regardless of gender. But he seems to have difficulty communicating with female supervisees because of gender difference"; "Men and women have different sensitivities and habits, and their ways of expressing emotion differ. It requires more sensitive care when it comes to communicating with women"; "He seems to have little frank conversation with his female supervisees, which includes conversations about work."

Unlike the WGW workshop, where the participants were expected to confess their personal feelings and experience, the male managers' workshop required the participants to be analytical and objective about how to supervise their female supervisees and how to be effective (male) managers. While saturated with business language such as "identifying and diagnosing problems" and "seeking solutions," the workshop discussion zeroed in on interpersonal communication: how to give instructions and feedback to female workers; how to scold, reprimand, compliment, and encourage them; and how to be a good listener when they speak. At the end of the retreat, Mr. Kawai, an external consultant and authority on organizational behavior, management, and personnel training, who attended the retreat as an observer, formally closed the workshop by introducing the idea of *kyōsei*, the closest English translation of which would be "coexistence" or "symbiosis." During my research in the early 1990s, the term *kyōsei* was widely circulated and used in the media as well as in various documents promoting the EEOL. "Gender equity" deradicalized and desocialized (individualized) as *kyōsei* entails congenial interpersonal relationships between fundamentally different *others*, in the pursuit of pragmatic working relations conducive both of productivity and of personal fulfillment; gender difference—and implicitly gender inequality in the "results" of fair competition between men and women—is inescapably naturalized here and presumed to be inevitable. I heard the male managers using the term *kyōsei* to put on an appropriately "progressive" display of their support for gender equity. As Mr. Kawai explained the reasoning (of both men and women) of the company: "It is necessary frankly [for male managers and female staff] to *recognize and respect each others' distinct value system* . . . and to strive to move toward *kyōsei*" (emphasis added). The idea of the symbiotic relationship between the male supervisor and the female supervisee effectively depoliticized structural antagonism multiply organized by rank, age, and gender in the corporate organizational hierarchy.

Conclusion

The prevalence of the idea of *kyōsei* signaled a profound displacement of the vision of "gender equity" from the protection of women as a class to the feminization and individualization of gender inequality. It was reflected beyond the corporation in 1999, when the Basic Law for a Gender-Equal Society (*Danjo kyōdō sankaku kihonhō*) was implemented,[7] providing legal guidelines to promote equal participation (and responsibilities) in the society between men and women, including positive action to provide opportunities *to either women or men*. In the same year, amendments to the EEOL took effect. Major revisions included the *prohibition* of discrimination in the domains of recruitment, hiring, assignment, and promotion, which previously required only a good-faith effort on the part of the employer. Labor dispute mediation can now be sought without the employer's consent, whereas under the previous law both parties had to agree to seek mediation by a government agency. The employers who violate the law are now sanctioned by means of publicizing their names.

The most significant amendment, in terms of the present analysis, was the prohibition of specifying gender in recruitment literature and job advertisements. But it is not illegal for the company to hire only men or only women for a specific job category. Thus, in the end, systematic patterns of gender discrimination in the workplace count for nothing in the policies promoting equal opportunity. In a neoliberal Japanese public culture, it is not the deeply historical and social structures of gender that are responsible for an individual's fate but the individual woman's *self* as defined by the sovereign individual. And women's plea to be treated as an individual worker, not a female worker as defined by sexist stereotypes, came to be transformed into gender-blindness in the laws of gender equity—a passionate neoliberal commitment to be incognizant of the stubborn reproduction of gender difference.

The original EEOL's impact on company management and labor practices and the experience of female workers are best understood in historical context: the ongoing shift away from the welfare state and its associated modes of subject formation and governing-beyond-the-state, to post-Fordism and the increasing erosion of the social by the market logic as a mode of producing free subjects given the responsibility to govern themselves. Beyond its strictly legal horizon, and perhaps beyond its intended consequences, the EEOL, in its historically contingent articulation with neoliberalism, regulated both the working life of the women at MJL and the way gender equity was to be imagined by various parties in the workplace. Before, women were simply contingent workers (in both the narrower and larger sense of *contingent*) in whom the company made no investment. They would come and go, as disposable and replaceable labor. The discourse of liberal inclusiveness, however, embodied by the EEOL, invited women to become part of the (ostensibly gender-equal) majority with the promise of "equal" access and opportunity. Women were endowed and empowered with the ideas of individual autonomy and personal sovereignty and were promised reward for their efforts to remake themselves into self-optimizing, self-responsible, and self-disciplined subjects. I have discussed how the corporate rendition of public spheres such as workshops, surveys, and task forces mediated the EEOL not as rights-protection but as neoliberal self-actualization. These activities and events served as sites and tactics of neoliberal governmentality by producing the truth and subjectivity of the female worker and by reducing the fundamental contradiction between capital and labor to interpersonal communication skills and personal (gendered) psychology, all of which, far from protecting workers' rights, served to normalize the ever-intensifying flexibilization of labor and liquidation of (full) employment in the "global futures" we are all now encouraged to imagine and embrace.

Notes

1. *Freeter*, *NEET*, and *purekariāto* are all terms referring to the phenomenon of precarious labor increasing since the Japanese recession began in 1991. NEET is an acronym for those workers, primarily youth, "Not in Education, Employment, or Training."

2. For excellent cultural critiques on gender and its relations to Japan's broader geopolitics in the 1980s and 1990s, see Iida (2000) and Yoda (2000). Miyazaki (2003) and Riles (2004) also offer compelling theoretical discussions on Japanese culture and society in general in an age of neoliberalism.

3. For English translation for the EEOL, see Milhaupt, Ramseyer, and Young 2001.

4. See also Mikanagi (1998) and Osawa (1993) for analysis on how the division of labor was further reinforced in the 1980s.

5. Article 7 states, "with regard to the recruitment and hiring of workers, employers shall endeavor to provide women equal opportunity with men," and Article 8 states, "with regard to the assignment and promotion of workers, employers shall endeavor to treat women equally with men workers."

6. For a comprehensive study of gender and work in the postwar Japan, see Brinton 1993. For comparative purposes, see Ogasawara (1998) for her thoughtful sociological study of gender politics in a banking office during in the early 1990s.

7. A full examination of the revised EEOL is beyond the scope of this article. See Araki (1998), R. L. Miller (2003), and Weathers (2005) for the history and the impact of the revised EEOL.

Chapter Nine

Workplace Dramas and Labor Fantasies in 1990s Japan

GABRIELLA LUKACS

In the first episode of the series *Shomuni* (General Affairs),[1] Tsukahara Sawako is transferred to the section of general affairs—the "graveyard" for office ladies (*OL no hakaba*)[2]—as retribution for her love affair with a married employee in the sales department. Located in a dim basement of a trading company known as Manpan Shōji, the section of general affairs (*shomuni*) is home to unsold and useless merchandise with employees to match: a male section chief who cannot complete a sentence without getting garbled in his mannerisms, his plus-sized cat, and four other "loser office ladies" (*ochiko-bore OL*) who were similarly disposed of for being too old, too outspoken, or otherwise ill suited to the more high-profile departments of the corporation. Tsukahara's vicissitudes are far from over once she is assigned to her new post. As the seating order is determined by the number of sexual partners one has had (the more the higher the rank), she is ensconced in the lowest rank that the space entails. At the climax of the episode, when she teeters on the verge of emotional meltdown, Tsuboi Chinatsu, the spiritual leader of the section and the protagonist of the series, reveals her philosophy to her: "You don't exist to serve your company or your male colleagues; it is they who exist to serve you. What matters is that you get some fun out of your work; the rest is irrelevant."

Chinatsu and her unorthodox attitude toward her company made the show wildly popular, earning it a megahit status with ratings over 28 percent,[3] con-

tracts for three additional seasons, and two feature specials. *Shomuni* epitomized a new prime-time genre, the workplace drama (*shokugyō/shigoto dorama*),
developed by the commercial networks[4] in the late 1990s in response to the
sliding ratings of love-oriented trendy dramas (*torendii dorama*).[5] In the late
1990s, television producers began lamenting that producing trendy dramas
preoccupied with consumer trends and packaged in trite, scripted dialogues
about love was pure escapism in the midst of a nagging economic recession.
They surmised that "socially responsible" entertainment (*shakaisei wo obita
entāteinmento*) would appeal to broader cross-segments of the audiences as a
growing number of young people were marginalized from career-track employment and often lacked the expandable income to enjoy the lifestyles that
the trendy dramas propagated. These producers critiqued an overwhelming
preoccupation in love dramas with the happiness of the individual and emphasized the importance of revitalizing an interest in the "social." The effects of
these dramas, however, were far less noble than the agenda producers articulated in public forums. Work dramas further promoted individualism by valorizing the autonomy of workers in ordinary workplace settings. By insisting
on the importance of individualism in the realm of wage labor, these dramas
played a key role in mobilizing their viewers to satisfy a volatile economy's
demand for workers who were willing to invest in their work not only their
labor power but also their subjectivity: their beliefs, communicative skills,
and affective commitments. Workplace dramas such as *Shomuni* marked an
important milestone in the processes of neoliberal labor mobilization. These
dramas acclimated workers to a recessionary economy in which employers
demanded more commitment for less pay and even less job security.

An ideal subject of neoliberal philosophy, Chinatsu, as the heroine of *Shomuni*, understood that she *alone* was responsible for making her life (including her work) meaningful. Her popularity was largely due to her uncom-
promising insistence that no job was worth pursuing if there was nothing
enjoyable about it. In the wake of shrinking opportunities for career-track
employment and a growing demand for flexibly disposable labor, Chinatsu's
character is a fantasy of agency shaped by the logic of consumer capitalism.
By the end of the 1990s, Japan's economic crisis was increasingly severe. As
the national economy did not seem to be recovering from the recession that
had begun almost a decade before, large-scale corporate restructuring was
unavoidable.[6] A key strategy for corporations to stay afloat in a volatile economy was to dismantle the system of lifetime employment. While stringent

employment protection laws made it difficult for corporations to lay off older generations of their employees, they began excluding new employees from the system of lifetime employment. By reintroducing values such as fun and individualism into the realm of wage labor, workplace dramas such as *Sho-muni* offered labor fantasies that made the massive incorporation of youth into a precarious workforce more digestible. After discussing how the genre of workplace drama evolved in the late 1990s, I trace how the new dramas mediated and capitalized on the socioeconomic changes while producing new labor subjectivities in the process.

Workplace Dramas: Love Fatigue and Social Realism

The workplace itself is not an entirely new setting in Japanese television dramas. In detective serials (*keiji dorama*), the police department was a typical workplace setting that provided a rich ground for developing new story lines and articulating values vital to the reproduction of the dominant socioeconomic order (for example, *Taiyō ni Hoero!* [Howl at the Sun!], NTV, 1975–1982). The school drama (*gakuen dorama*)—preoccupied with the perennial conflict between individual and society—was another type of workplace drama (such as *Sannen B Gumi Kimpachi Sensei* [Third Year B Group Head Teacher Kimpachi], TBS, 1979–1980, 1982–1990, 1995, 1998–1999, 2001). The popularity of these dramas, however, declined in the 1990s when commercial television networks responded to market fragmentation by reuniting viewers into affective communities through offering them lifestyle-oriented trendy dramas (Lukacs 2010). Although commercial television had always served marketers by providing a programming environment amenable to advertising their products, the launching of trendy dramas in the late 1980s marked a new phase in the commercialization of the medium as it effectively destabilized the boundary between entertainment and advertising. In the second half of the 1990s, television professionals profusely commented on this trend with bitterness, pointing out that primetime drama serials had lost touch with reality and hence had lost their capacity to engage issues of social relevance.

In this section, I examine how producers talked about the need for reintroducing social awareness into drama production and what strategies they employed to achieve this goal. It was a particular type of realism television producers referenced in their criticism of love dramas. We might call this realism social realism. In relation to British soap operas, Ruth Mandel defines social realism as a strong assumption that television can raise consciousness and shape the beliefs of the viewers through didactic means. A long-running social-realist soap opera on BBC Radio 4 in the United Kingdom has been *The Archers* (1951–present), which was launched with the goal of teaching modern techniques of agriculture and animal husbandry to the audiences. Other British social-realist programs have raised such important issues as domestic violence; these aimed not only to educate the audiences but also to help victims by providing numbers of hotlines in the end of the programs (Mandel 2002). Similar to their British colleagues, many Japanese television professionals in the late 1990s increasingly resented that television had lost its role of serving the public sphere as a forum for the discussion of socially relevant issues. They reasoned that making programs of social importance would reverse the process of steady degradation in the quality of television entertainment and restore its role in reinforcing the social order by reproducing the socioeconomic structures and dominant subjectivities that underwrote it.

The social-realist mode of representation insists on the natural and the realistic; in other words, on creating believable characters and showing their everyday activities and surroundings. In love dramas, the heroines are dressed and coifed far beyond the means of the particular characters they play; however, this is not characteristic of workplace dramas. Their characters commonly don office attire, police uniforms, or scrubs. Yamaguchi Masatoshi, the producer of *Kirakira Hikaru* (Shining Brightly, Fuji 1998, 1999 Special, and 2000 Special) commented:

> Fuji TV is strong in the trendy drama genre. Trendy dramas portray characters as if they spent ten hours out of a day's twenty-four hours thinking about love. Apparently, these dramas are very popular, and I admit that it is difficult to make high-quality love dramas. It's just that in my environment there is no one who would spend that much time on managing his or her love life. Isn't it rather the case that most of us don't spend more than daily fifteen minutes on our love-related problems and personal conflicts? Grownups spend most of their time making money and worrying about their work. (cited in Komatsu 2000: 111)[7]

In opposition to love dramas, Yamaguchi emphasizes the importance of dramas that address socially relevant issues. Given the fact that prime-time dramas are the television programs most people watch, producers like Yamaguchi highlighted that these programs offer a great opportunity for commercial television networks to tackle problems that threaten the integrity and vitality of society. In most cases this effort has remained an unrealized ideal; nonetheless, the discourse on social responsibility has been efficient in serving other interests and producing other effects. I argue that television producers have come to use the notion of social responsibility as a discursive trope to negotiate their agency as their artistic aspirations have become constrained by the increasing commodification of the medium. At the same time, the strategy of making prime-time serials that impart a sense of realism also serves to draw, package, and deliver new audience segments (most notably, young men) to advertisers.

This is, however, not to say that these workplace dramas failed completely to realize the objectives of social realism. Scriptwriter Nakazono Miho's *Dear Woman* (TBS, 1996), for example, pioneered the trend of educating female employees about gender-based discrimination in the workplace. The serial followed the story of a young woman, Tsuno Reiko, who was trying unsuccessfully to find employment in Tokyo as a single mother. Finally she decided not to tell her employer that she had a child, earning her a non–career-track job as an office lady. In her new workplace, she was assigned to a project that aimed to monitor gender-based abuses within the company and to address complaints. In the mid-1990s, although sexual harassment was pervasive in Japanese companies, there was no public discourse to address the issue. The serial thus filled a crucial gap by discussing issues such as recruiters hiring female employees solely for their looks, male employees bullying their "aging" female colleagues (women in their late twenties!) so that they would quit and be replaced with younger employees, and bosses forcing female employees to participate in a swimsuit contest on the mandatory company trip. Scriptwriter Nakazono Miho recounted to me in an interview that many of the letters she and the network received claimed that viewers used *Dear Woman* as a reference point to fight sexism in the workplace.[8]

Dear Woman, however, was an exception. An early forerunner of workplace dramas, it targeted primarily female viewers by blending a love story with plotlines revolving around the vicissitudes of office ladies in the masculinist corporate world. However, in most workplace dramas, social realism was not so much a means of raising social awareness as a "promotional marquee" to draw new audience segments to television by making these serials clearly distinguishable from love dramas. A brief description of the strategies producers employed to reintroduce a concern with socially relevant issues into their dramas supports this claim. Commonly, producers mention three strategies. They claim that (1) these dramas do not capitalize on the *tarento* (celebrity) system, (2) their selling point is the well-crafted stories, and (3) they discuss character development not in a social vacuum but in the context of work. Note that these are precisely the features used to distinguish workplace dramas from love dramas.

First, producers of workplace dramas believed that, by not capitalizing on the *tarento* system, their dramas could relax the link between television and consumerism. The *tarento* system is specific to the Japanese media industries. The word *tarento* derives from the English word *talent*, but this is exactly what distinguishes the *tarento* from American celebrities: The *tarento* are often not talented. Rather, their popularity is a result of their extensive cross-genre and transmedia exposure to the viewers as Japanese celebrities simultaneously pursue careers in the television, music, and advertising industries. By capitalizing on the *tarento*, love dramas were embracing more and more the self-referential world of the *tarento*-system, and in parallel they were increasingly estranged from external social realities. Yamaguchi Masatoshi, producer of *Kirakira Hikaru*, lamented that the *tarento* and their capacity to mobilize references to consumer culture posed difficulties in making dramas of social relevance.

Second, Yamaguchi has noted that, unlike love dramas that exploit celebrity power, the strength of workplace dramas lies in the carefully crafted stories. In the production of workplace dramas, tremendous research is invested in the scripts to ensure the accuracy of details and the integrity of the narrative because the success of these shows depends on how compelling and convincing the stories are (Komatsu 2000). A focus on the story in serial drama production tends to correspond to a narrative style that considers the individual episodes both as independent units and as parts of a serialized program. This means that the episodes are enjoyable as discrete units, without requiring the viewers to commit themselves to watching the entire series. The producers of love dramas had counted on a continuing commitment to the series on the viewers' part. To keep viewers hooked, producers relied on cliff-hangers and what Modleski (1982) calls the "ever-expanding middle," a narrative strategy that postpones conclusions until the very end of the season finale. However, this deterred casual viewers who were not interested in making the commitment to watch serialized dramas that ran for twelve weeks. These viewers appreciated work dramas, as they could enjoy single episodes independently without having to watch the entire series.

Lastly, love dramas discuss the question of happiness for individuals in a social vacuum. Their characters are not members of particular social communities; we do not know what family background they come from and do not always get a clear sense of what they do for living. In contrast, workplace dramas contextualize characters as social beings who spend the majority of their time in their places of employment.[9] In late 1990s dramas, the workplace is not simply a background to the unfolding story line but the primary site for character development. The work environment is described in detail, and the characters' attitude toward work is scrutinized. Moreover, workplace dramas were in dialogue with media and government discourses on the need for institutional restructuring in the wake of the recession (*Shiroi Kyotō*, Fuji 2003, 2004), their primary target of criticism being the rigidly hierarchical corporate structure (for example, the seniority system), which they identified as a major source of inefficiency. Accordingly, one of the main conflicts of workplace dramas was the clash between junior and senior employees because it was in the course of struggles with their superiors that characters matured.

Work and Subjectivity in Trendy Dramas and in Recessionary Japan

Workplace dramas were particularly popular among young male viewers, who claimed that they enjoyed the refreshing portrayal of the characters and their relationship to work.[10] To understand why young male viewers found these aspects appealing requires an elaboration of the differences between love dramas and workplace dramas in representations of the drama protagonists (most of whom were women) and their relationship to work. Work was not a privileged theme in trendy dramas, mainly because producers believed that office ladies—the target demographic of the genre—were not interested in watching stories about work after a hard day of unrewarding labor. In love dramas, women's relationship to work was represented in two ways. First were those office ladies, who considered their employment as an interim period between school and marriage and quit their job after having a child. This is the typical heroine of love dramas. The second type of working women, which in reality is far less common, is the die-hard thirty- to forty-something career woman who is single and devotes herself to her work at the price of having a family (Suzuki 1999). The series *Single Lives* (TBS 1999) and *Brand* (Fuji 2000) were examples for this type of female protagonist.

Producers of workplace dramas have commented that this binarism in the representations of women in trendy dramas less and less reflected the realities of working women's lives toward the end of the 1990s. The scriptwriter Inoue Yumiko has observed that both portrayals were exaggerations:

> *Kirakira Hikaru* [Shining Brightly][11] was made before *Shomuni*, and there were not many dramas in which women were doing something together in a team. I personally badly wanted to see a drama in which four individualistic women (*koseitekina kyarakutā*) vigorously work, eat, and drink together. . . . When watching dramas I often had the feeling that they were made from a male perspective. Basically, you could see two types of women: the non–career-track office lady, who mostly wanted to get married (*kekkon ganbō no tsuyoi koshikake OL*) and the career woman type, who spent most of her time fighting her male colleagues. Real working women don't conform to these stereotypes. Career women have more pride than to fight men all the time; likewise, it's false to assume that noncareer office ladies spend most of their time thinking about love. My impression is that it is flawed to make that hard divide and put out a message that women do either work or love. Instead I wanted to show that women indeed work just as hard and responsibly as men do. I wanted to portray women who took pride in their professional identities. (quoted in Satake 2000: 41)

Similarly, the scriptwriter of *Shomuni*, Takahashi Rumi, has commented on the unrealistic portrayal of women in television dramas:

> The office lady of television dramas, who has a lot of money and a rich lover and spends most of her life having fun (*asobimakutteiru*), originates in women's magazines like *SPA!* The everyday lives of ordinary office ladies are far less joyful. They work hard for the 3 to 4 million yen [US$35,000–47,000] they make a year, and when they get home from work late in the night, often their only pleasure is to watch television in their tiny studios while eating some instant food that they picked up on the way home. (quoted in Satake 2000: 141–142)

This dominant opposition between women as future homemakers who are not invested in pursuing a job outside the home, or as career women who devote themselves to their professions and are not interested in having their own families, became increasingly discrepant with social realities by the second half of the 1990s. The Cinderella path to marry a Prince Charming who will provide for his sweetheart for the rest of her life—the dominant scenario love dramas echoed—was an option for a decreasing number of women in the late 1990s. Many women would have liked to quit their jobs and to become full-time homemakers once they had married, but in the recession married women faced growing pressure to contribute to the household income. In postwar Japan, corporations relied on the system of lifetime employment and seniority-based pay that entailed constant employment training and transfers between remote branch offices. This system applied only to a stable core of male workers, who, in return, were expected to commit themselves to their companies (Rohlen 1979). Female employees were not part of this core workforce. Most typically, female employees in the corporate world were office ladies whose average tenure in their companies spanned three to eight years.[12] They performed mainly clerical work such as filing, the operation of office equipment, accounting-related work, reception, or document and data processing. These women could neither maintain a continuous labor history, nor could they reenter the labor force as career-track employees, because the systems of lifetime employment and seniority-based pay foreclosed their reintegration into the corporate hierarchy. These women were the target audiences as well as protagonists of love dramas.

During the postwar period, the turnover of these female employees was high, which saved money for companies because these workers received a minimum wage that did not increase at the same rate as the salaries of male employees. In addition, companies did not pay social welfare benefits or bonuses to their nonstandard employees (Broadbent 2002; Joohee Lee 2004). Thus, the flexibility that women's underpaid labor provided offset the high costs of the lifetime employment system. Whereas the nonstandard workforce was overwhelmingly feminized throughout the postwar period, the 1990s witnessed a marked shift in the composition of this workforce. During this period, young men joined the nonstandard workforce in massive numbers.[13] Under the banner of the *freeter* phenomenon, popular as well as social-scientific discourses have explored the changing place of youth in the labor market. *Freeter* (a hybrid of the English word *free* and the German word *Arbeiter*, or worker) refers to the twenty- and thirty-something young people who drift from one short-term job to another. The average *freeter* is reported to stay in a job for about nine months, during which period he or she earns about US$1000 a month.[14] In 2003, 20 percent of the youth population identified as *freeters*, and their number has been increasing (Driscoll 2007). In 2009, approximately 35 percent of young workers between the ages of fifteen and thirty-four were employed in temporary positions.[15]

Many top-ranking trendy dramas such as *Long Vacation* (Fuji, 1996) or *Beach Boys* (Fuji, 1997) have glamorized the *freeters'* flexible lifestyle and iconoclastic, antisalaryman attitude. This celebration of *freeters* was part of a broader popular discourse on the changing attitude of youth toward labor. A journalist has written, "If the icon of the 1980s was the salaryman who sacrificed his private life for his company, today's icon is the *freeter*—the young Japanese who take odd jobs to make just enough money to enjoy their personal interest or choose their way of life" (Ōnishi 2004, A3). However, *freeters* are not always objects of celebration; they are also a source of moral panic. The sociologist Yamada Masahiro has played a key role in promoting a more unfavorable judgment. Yamada blames *freeters* for not paying their state pension contributions, thus putting further stress on a fund already burdened by a growing elderly population. He also accuses *freeters* of exacerbating Japan's falling birthrate, as they marry later and have fewer children, if any at all. He refutes the image that *freeters* devote themselves to pursuing their dreams. On the contrary, he argues that *freeters* are just using such dreams as excuses not to work because it is rarely the case that they give up full-time jobs to realize their ambitions. He concludes that *freeters* indeed have no dreams and characterizes them as weak willed, lacking in ambition, irresponsible, spoiled, and self-absorbed (Yamada 1999). I would stress that both of these approaches are problematic because they discuss the *freeter* phenomenon in a vacuum disconnected from the economic recession and the decline of the socioeconomic structure that underwrote the high-growth era. It is not so much that young people in Japan are decreasingly willing to sacrifice their lives to their companies, but they often no longer get the chance to do so.

The diminishing prospects of youths for secure employment have led to the loss of a familiar scenario for a predictable future. In searching for new directions, different social institutions imagined different possibilities for youths, not unaffected by their own political and economic investment in this segment of society. And although these visions were not necessarily consistent, even within distinct institutional discourses, drama producers seemed to be in agreement in that they did not want to upset their sponsors by playing up concerns about the insatiable appetite of the new economy for flexible labor or the ideas that *freeters* were "a new economic underclass in the making" (Yoda 2000: 656). Instead, they suggested that young people should get the best out of their new freedoms not only in the context of consumerism but also in the realm of work. Trendy dramas, however, conveniently avoided the question of where this new freedom came from. They timidly suggested that it resulted from the diversification of choices as the high-growth economy with its promise of life-long employment came to an end (*Beach Boys*, Fuji 1997). The idea that freedom was indeed the new obligation (and the new mandatory life-course) for many did not seem compatible with the expectations of commercial sponsors for television networks to create a consumption-friendly media environment. Valorizing the link between freedom and choice was preferred over emphasizing the connection between freedom and obligation.

This indifference to the origins of freedom tended to conceal the connection between freedom and neoliberal initiatives in the rhetoric of commitment to ideals of personal freedom. David Harvey has noted that neoliberal initiatives, to which ideals of individual freedom were essential, have always been

> . . . backed up by a practical strategy that emphasized the liberty of consumer choice, not only with respect to particular products but also with respect to particular lifestyles, modes of expression, and a wide range of cultural practices. Neoliberalization required both politically and economically the construction of a neoliberal market-based populist culture of differentiated consumerism and individual libertarianism. (Harvey 2005: 42)

In other words, while the encouragement of narcissistic consumerism in love dramas was merely supporting a neoliberal rhetoric, workplace dramas went a step further by mobilizing against hierarchical and highly bureaucratic institutional structures (that is, forms of regulation other than the free market) that, they stressed, stifled the realization of freedom and stood in the way of economic growth.

Trendy dramas celebrated the courage of young people to steer clear of secure employment, which would require them to sacrifice their individuality by becoming a part of a homogeneous and highly disciplined workforce.

(Note the resonance between this position and neoliberal theory that considers unemployment voluntary.) However, in the wake of diminishing pathways to regular employment and the growing dominance of irregular labor as the only available work option, the television industry's position does not seem socially responsible. *Shomuni* was appealing because it reconciled the contradictory expectations young viewers were experiencing in the late 1990s. On the one hand, as *producers* these viewers were expected to continue sharing in the postwar work ethic that required them to subordinate their desires for a fun-loving lifestyle to their companies' needs for a docile workforce that could revitalize the country's underperforming economy. On the other hand, as *consumers*, they were encouraged to pursue their aspirations by experimenting with an ever-expanding multitude of consumer choices. Viewers' responses suggest that workplace dramas—and *Shomuni* in particular—evoked their sympathy because the female protagonists transposed their "true" fun-seeking selves onto their jobs. By bridging the gap between these different expectations, the office ladies of *Shomuni* represented a new breed of workers whose willingness to connect fun and work resonated with neoliberal initiatives to push individuals to become autonomous and entrepreneurial. In the following section I continue interrogating how the struggles of Chinatsu (the heroine of *Shomuni*) to integrate fun and work articulated with the changing place of youth in the labor market.

The Shomuni *Series: The Office Lady as the New Cultural Icon of Lifestyle Employment*

The *Shomuni* series was based on a *manga* written by the young artist Yasuda Hiroyuki, who himself lived a *freeter* life. The series first appeared in the magazine *Shūkan Mōningu*, which targeted a male readership, and was published between November 1995 and June 1997. An article in *Tokyo Keizai Shinbun* in 1996 stressed that the story was popular because it featured a new type of office lady who was different from the protagonist of love dramas and did not sacrifice her interests to help the hero advance his. Instead, these women were portrayed as powerful, autonomous, and courageous enough to defy corporate hierarchy. The article concluded that male readers found it liberating to see these characters refusing to abandon their own personal values within the corporate setting (*jibun no kachi de ikiru*).[16]

Despite this suggestion that *Shomuni* might appeal to a young male audience, producers did not have high expectations, as young men did not constitute a demographic known to be committed to viewing prime-time television (7 to 11 p.m.). The program's exceptionally high ratings pleasantly surprised both the production team and the programming department. The serial did not feature any top *tarento*, without whom producers believed no drama could make it to the top of the popularity charts in the 1990s. Moreover, the serial was hastily put together when a new slot for dramas (Wednesday, 9:00 to 10:00 p.m.) was created shortly before the start of a new season. This slot had previously been reserved for variety shows, but the programming department decided to reassign it for dramas in response to the network's success in the genre.

The hit drama maker of the programming department Ōta Tōru was in charge of assigning staff and of casting *tarento* to this drama and did not want to grant a huge budget to a serial that did not have much of a chance of achieving high ratings. He assigned the lead role to Esumi Makiko, who was not well known in 1998. (Indeed, *Shomuni* earned her fame.) The supporting cast was similarly assembled from second- and third-tier *tarento*, who were recruited randomly depending on their availability. He assigned the new serial to the producer Funatsu Kōichi, who was known for his affinity for unconventional "art-house" programs that drew low to moderate ratings. He was also one of the producers in charge of the more successful, but far from mainstream, *Yo ni mo Kimyōna Monogatari* (Weird Stories in the World), which had been broadcast as special features since 1990. These programs allow the drama production staff to do something more in the realm of the absurd, the cynical, and the artistic.

Director Suzuki Masayuki was the most experienced member of the production staff. Like the producer, he too had a flair for nontraditional drama formats. As Suzuki was an accomplished director with high credentials, Ōta entrusted him with the freedom to do whatever he pleased (Uesugi and Takakura 2001). At the same time, Suzuki had already been engaged in another project scheduled for the following season (*Sekaide Ichiban Papa ga Suki*, Fuji 1998, [I Love Dad, He's the Best in the World]) that involved larger budgets and top-tier tarento. He concentrated on the preparation of *Sekaide Ichiban*, as the network expected it to draw higher ratings.[17] Not surprisingly, the two scriptwriters recruited for the project, Takahashi Rumi and later Hashimoto Yūji, were also neophytes in the field. Interviews with production staff suggest that a reason for the high ratings was that the drama was produced in a vacuum. The programming department had modest expectations, and thus it refrained from exerting pressure on the production staff.

Why did then the serial become such a smash hit? Viewers claimed that the series was easy to follow as each episode offered a whole story with a resolution at the end, thus making each episode independently enjoyable. As already suggested, this reflected a conscious strategy to draw viewers who were not willing to commit to watching entire serials. Male viewers also stressed that they found female characters wearing uniforms with improbably short skirts particularly appealing. Here a brief mention of the widespread appropriation of work uniforms in the Japanese sex industry as a form of erotic costume play should suffice. And the more popular the serial became among male viewers, the shorter the skirts of the heroines grew and the more often the main character was found atop a ladder changing lightbulbs as the camera filmed her from below. Most important, however, viewers reasoned that they enjoyed *Shomuni* because they found the portrayal of office ladies appealing. They claimed that they derived pleasure from seeing these office ladies talking back to their bosses.

Viewers loved the new bohemian working heroine, Tsuboi Chinatsu, who became a cultural icon.[18] The scriptwriter Takahashi Rumi, who drafted the drama series and wrote the first episode, played a crucial role in creating the character of Tsuboi Chinatsu. Takahashi recounted to me that she did not follow the original *manga* closely. First of all, she could not avoid readjusting the characters because of the cast. Although in the original version Tsukahara was the protagonist, the scriptwriter was more inspired by a supporting character, Tsuboi Chinatsu. Takahashi was convinced that this character was a better match for the lead *tarento*, Esumi Makiko. This is why she decided to place the character of Chinatsu in the center of the drama.[19]

The other plotline in the original *manga* that the scriptwriter kept for the television drama was the opposition between Chinatsu and an elite office lady, Misono. What turned these women against each other were their irreconcilable philosophies. Misono believed that the value of a woman was determined by the status and financial background of the man she dated, while for Chinatsu it was the *number* of men a woman has dated that defined her worth. This conflict was reminiscent of the antagonism between the heroine of love dramas and her rival in their competition for the attention of the hero. While the heroine was the epitome of the *shōjo* (the young girl whose life centers on fun and consumer culture), her rival was the traditional woman, who conformed to postwar gender ideals and became a stay-at-home mother. In the workplace dramas, the role of the traditional female character is very similar and provides a foil to emphasize the freshness of the new bohemian character. This conflict, however, did not become the central theme in the serial but degenerated into catfights, which some viewers found particularly sexy, as expressed in comments on fan sites.

The conflict between women is not completely abandoned in workplace dramas, but it is subordinated to a new conflict arising between a progressive young female and older male employees (*oyaji, ojisan*), "mainstream, reactionary, middle-aged men who cannot grow out of their old-fashioned identification with a work-centered life" (Yoda forthcoming). The *ojisan* is also the enemy of young men (among them *freeters*), who prefer a more consumerism-driven lifestyle. The protagonists of this conflict occupy starkly opposed positions: The older male employees believe that young women should follow the path of early retirement because women's place is in the home. The young women claim that stupid geezers should all retire (*Baka oyaji inkyo se yo*) because they are good for nothing. What is important to note here is the gendering of an antagonism that is not between men and women but between the values of the high-growth economic order and those underlying neoliberal restructuring.

The opposition between young progressive women and old retrograde men is the key conflict in the serial that survives not only from one episode to the other but also from one season to the next. This conflict translates into the basic narrative framework in which Terasaki, the manager of the human resources section, is determined to liquidate the section of general affairs. To prove that the section is an unnecessary expense to the company and that its members are incompetent, Terasaki and his assistant Nonomura keep cooking up new challenges such as health exams, crime prevention campaigns, and fire drills, which they assign to the office ladies in the section of general affairs. Terasaki deliberately schedules these drills for days reserved to host precious potential business partners when it is crucial that company executives impress their guests with a cleaned-up version of the company. As planned by Terasaki and Nonomura, the company is turned upside down, but the representatives of the human resources section do not succeed in getting the office ladies fired because these women always end up cleaning up the mess with admirable efficiency and they always impress the guests with their capability for organizing the company into a single, task-oriented body. In each episode, when they get their new assignment, the women start panicking and begin to talk retirement. Chinatsu, however, looks at the fun side of the new challenge. She stays levelheaded, folds her arms, and concludes: "It sounds like a good adventure. Let's get some fun out of it." According to the show's director: "These women turn upside down the traditional structure of the company, but they win the hearts of not only women but male viewers as well with their message to have a little more fun with life."[20]

What was so compelling about this character? What kind of new agency did she represent that so closely resonated with the imagination of a positive role model by male and female viewers alike? As scriptwriter Inoue Yumiko's quote has already illustrated, in workplace dramas the representation of the heroine has undergone significant changes. The producers wanted to make more realistic dramas by featuring characters that develop through their struggles with workplace problems such as conflicts with bosses. The typical heroine of workplace dramas no longer finds the meaning of her life in love and marriage. Some of these female protagonists devote themselves to their careers (as in the series *Kirakira Hikaru*); others work because of financial necessity (as in *Dear Woman*) or simply because they find their work entertaining (*Shomuni*). Marriage does not bring an end to the development of female characters as happens in love dramas.

Chinatsu is an extreme character in the original *manga*. Her life story only sporadically comes to the surface in the drama. From the original graphic novel we learn that her family disowned her after she embarked on a career in the adult video business. She entered the corporate world as a career-track employee, but she was soon transferred to the section of general affairs after having knocked out her male boss for smacking her butt. A scene from the first season illustrates her brashness. Tsuboi and Tsukahara are having dinner at a ramen stall, when a group of gangsters joins them. Tsuboi bets one of them that if she loses in arm wrestling, the gangster can spend the night with Tsukahara. Tsukahara runs off, while Tsuboi (not surprisingly) loses. The next day she tells Tsukahara that she owes her big time because she had to sleep not only with the gangster she lost to but also with his friends. Tsukahara responds that she cannot believe what nonsense Chinatsu is capable of saying without shame.

The only thing that Chinatsu values is freedom and occasionally solidarity with those of her colleagues who are also disadvantaged in the corporate system. She often confronts Tsukahara for letting her male colleagues order her about and for not having a strong sense of self. She is also at odds with Misono, who spends her time in the company searching for a potential husband. Chinatsu criticizes these women for not being independent and for relying on men to define who they are. But what unites these women is that they share an archenemy in Terasaki, the manager of human resources. When Terasaki picks on the twenty-nine-year-old Misono and starts pressuring her to get married and retire, Chinatsu stands by her.

This bohemian protagonist becomes a mature manifestation of the love drama heroine, which, I argue, is also a stand-in for the male *freeter*. What is new about Chinatsu is that she does not expect anyone else to make her happy but relies on herself to define who she is and how she imagines happiness for herself. This character fully internalizes a sense of self-orientation that marketing and social scientific discourses associate with *freeters* in the late 1990s. Moreover, while the selfishness of the love drama heroines invited criticism from male viewers, Chinatsu turns this personality trait into an attractive role model. She justifies it as a source of the freedom, autonomy, and entrepreneurial spirit that she advocates as necessary to survive in a recessionary economy. She represents a new type of labor subjectivity in that she rejects the highly hierarchical and group-oriented corporate structure, for it represses individualism[21] and forces employees to give up their freedom and autonomy.

In the late 1960s, the social anthropologist Nakane Chie (1970) argued that the frame (institution, place) was the principle for group formation in Japan, as opposed to a common attribute of individuals that constituted a group in Western societies. She stressed that this principle of group formation came from the household structure (*ie*) of the Tokugawa period (1603–1867), which still persisted in various group identities such as villages, educational institutions, and business corporations. This social structure was based on the principle of groupism (*shūdan shugi*) and the minimization of individual autonomy. She saw proof in the fact that Japanese employees identified themselves not by their occupation but by the institution (that is, the frame) itself. Her study legitimized the postwar ideology of corporate management, which required employees to commit themselves to their companies, by arguing that the frame-based pattern of group formation was founded on historical precedents in Japan since the beginning of the Tokugawa period.

This is exactly the ideology Chinatsu defies by constantly reminding her colleagues that this frame of groupism no longer offers employees a stable sense of belonging and a meaningful future. Chinatsu becomes the superego of the company in the era of corporate restructuring. Her responsibility is to replace lightbulbs, so she carries a ladder as a work tool in every episode. But this is not just a ladder; it serves as the "corporate ladder," the old socioeconomic order of Japan, Inc. (*kigyōka shakai*). She carries this symbol around as a reminder of its existence and its impact on employees. She herself denounces any effort to climb the corporate ladder because she equates such efforts with abandoning one's self.

For example, in one episode the *shomuni* staff vow to help a career office lady win a competition for the position of project manager against the star male employee Ukyo Tomohiro. To devote herself to her work, this office lady had abandoned her baby to the care of her divorced husband. The husband, unable to take care of the baby, leaves the child with a note addressed to the mother in the lobby of her company. The mother denies that the baby is hers because her being a single mother would severely reduce her chances to win the competition. In the end, Chinatsu tells the young career woman that their efforts to help her are a waste if it means that she has to become a man and compete like men who abandon their families for the sake of their work. If the *shomuni* women were to help her become a soulless corporate cyborg in the process of building her career, then their mission would be a failure.

When Chinatsu claims that no career is worth it if the person is lost in it in the end, one may wonder about this insistence on a right to freedom in a time of shrinking opportunities for career-track employment. Chinatsu's character should be understood in a context in which young women had come to symbolize social change. To identify with them was to approve the values commonly associated with them such as individualism and self-centered lifestyles. By the late 1990s, however, social discourses had lumped together young women with male *freeters*, who came to epitomize the same values in the popular imaginary. This is why *Shomuni* could so seamlessly blur the line between the identities of office ladies and male *freeters*. Chinatsu is garbed in the uniform of office ladies, but she has the spirit and attitude that sympathetic portrayals attribute to *freeters*. This is curious, as *freeters* and corporations occupy the opposite ends in popular discussions of Japan's future in the 1990s. *Freeters* represent the new Japan, while corporations stand for the postwar order, which ended with the recession in the early 1990s. By introducing a *freeter* attitude into the corporate world, Chinatsu becomes a reminder that a symbiotic dependence between corporations and employees is at odds with the demands of the new economy for entrepreneurial spirit, mobility, and flexibly reconfigurable work skills. By representing these values, Chinatsu epitomizes a new kind of worker subjectivity. Yet the answer she offers is nothing more than a labor fantasy; an uncritical celebration of freedom obliterates the fact that neoliberal economies thrive on a liberal rhetoric recognizing freedom as an unalienable property of individuals. In the context of economic deregulation, freedom is not only the freedom of the worker to flexibly employ or redefine her skills but also the freedom of the company to dispose of workers as market and labor demands fluctuate.

Scriptwriter Takahashi Rumi recounted to me that she thought of *Shomuni* as a recession drama in that the main preoccupation of the characters was to redefine themselves in conditions where they could no longer count on their companies to provide them with job security and welfare benefits. The message that "no work was worth doing if there was nothing enjoyable about it," however, reads not so much as a realistic strategy for youth but rather as a fantasy of agency and desire to be entitled to the freedom of choice in the wake of shrinking prospects for secure employment. Political scientist Steven Vogel has argued that in the 1990s both the Japanese government and corporations aimed to reform the employment system not by completely abandoning existing institutions but by cautiously modifying or even reinforcing them (2006). These choices, however, were more to protect an aging workforce (to comply with stringent employment protection laws) than to allow youth to enter the system of secure employment (Genda 2006). *Shomuni*'s suggestion to link work and enjoyment is thus discrepant with the demands of the new economy for flexible labor, which is, one may argue, often not all that enjoyable. Often, irregular work requires the same commitment from workers as career-track employment, but this commitment is not equally justified for employers and employees who will not equally benefit from the product of the worker's labor. Takahashi has commented:

In the men-oriented workplace dramas such as *Sarariman Kintarō* (Salaried Man Kintarō, TBS, 1999, 1999 Special, 2000, 2002, 2002 Special, 2004) or *Kachō Shima Kōsaku* (Section Chief, Shima Kōsaku, Fuji 1993, 1994, 1994,

1998), the main themes are how men are climbing the corporate ladder [*shusse suru*] or how they confront evil. Conflicts between junior and senior employees serve as the main sources of struggle. Ordinary office ladies in *Shomuni* have a lot of other problems than climbing the corporate ladder (which is way out of their league). . . . Of course, they are not in the position to fight evil. All they want is to make their jobs more fun for themselves. (Takahashi, cited in Satake, 2000: 142)

Given that affect management has always been a key job requirement for office ladies, this is a curious fantasy.[22] While the politics of drama production offer some insights to understand why this particular message was encoded in the script, this is just a partial explanation. I mentioned earlier that the serial was scripted by two writers, the other being Hashimoto Yūji. Although Takahashi played a more important role in writing the scripts for the first season, in parallel with the growing popularity of *Shomuni* among male viewers, the other (male) writer, Hashimoto, took over as lead author. As Takahashi was no longer allowed to pursue her agenda of crafting story lines that she believed office ladies (and female viewers in general) would find empowering, she withdrew in the middle of the second series of the *Shomuni* enterprise. She resented that the male staff members of the production team kept insisting on shortening the skirt length of the office ladies while increasing the number of catfights between Misono and Chinatsu (personal communication; see also Satake 2000: 146).

The message that "office ladies should get some fun out of their work" is by no means radical given that non–career-track female employees have long been involved in what anthropologist Ogasawara Yuko calls "offstage resistance" (1998). However, she argues that these acts of sabotaging work by arbitrarily deciding job priorities or by not taking initiatives end up promoting stereotypes that women get carried away with emotions and thus are irresponsible employees. Connecting the idea of pleasure and work, however, opens a space of redemption to male *freeters*.[23] Unlike office ladies, male *freeters* cannot aspire to secure a stable future for themselves by marrying men in career-track positions. In *Shomuni*, Misono represents this possibility for office ladies. Thus, by introducing pleasure into work, *Shomuni* offers a possibility for positive self-identification for *freeters* who reinterpret their unemployed status as the realization of the very freedom they are entitled to and as a step toward finding meaningful and enjoyable work.

In other words, Chinatsu's character explains the flexibilization of labor as a potential for *freeters* to enjoy their freedom, which is portrayed here as a matter of choice. There is a curious gender politics at work here. While different institutional discourses interpret the *freeter* phenomenon differently, they converge in viewing *freeters*—who are either female or male—as collectively effeminate. Although it is becoming more and more socially acceptable for Japanese men to be consumers, devoted involvement in consumerism is still coded as effeminate. Correspondingly, when discussing Japanese men's increasing participation in consumer culture, scholarly and popular discourses dominantly talk about the feminization of men—thus reinscribing the postwar divide between male producers and female consumers (see L. Miller 2003). In the 1980s, a consumption-led definition of self-hood defined by personal style became more characteristic. Yet this was discussed as a feminine trait in that it challenged the principle of unity and uniformity—the founding values of the masculine corporate structure of the postwar period. In this gendered binary, therefore, the resistance to an earlier ideal of masculinity epitomized by the salaryman, "especially of images of short, stocky, dark-suited *oyaji* [geezer] with pomade-plastered hair" (L. Miller 2003: 52), is inextricably tied up with femininity. And this is exactly why Chinatsu becomes popular with male viewers; in addition to refashioning the indecisiveness of youth as an insistence on one's right to freedom, she offers an alternative, more attractive ideal of masculinity.[24]

Conclusion: Workplace Dramas and Labor Fantasies

The prolonged recession has marked the end of Japan's rapid economic growth and all that it meant: steadily rising standard of living, low unemployment rates, mass middle-class stratum society, and the system of lifetime employment (or for women and the self-employed sector the possibility to aspire to it for their children). On the one hand, Japanese government officials and industry leaders agreed that introducing more flexible labor market laws was unavoidable; however, they remained ambivalent about abandoning the postwar labor contract (Vogel 2006) or, at least, its ideological support for formidable work discipline and workplace hierarchy.[25] On the other hand, the service industries pushed less hesitantly for neoliberal restructuring, flexibility, and new worker subjectivities. In these conditions, commercial television networks played an important role in reconfiguring the field of possibilities and mediating the tensions between young people's narrowing opportunities for meaningful employment and growing desires to use their labor power to realize themselves in conditions in which employers expect intense commitment from them.

The televisual discourse on social responsibility was both a marketing strategy to sell workplace dramas to new market segments (most notably young men) and a means for television producers to negotiate their agency under the massive commodification of the medium in the 1990s. However, this discourse was pertinent not only to producers but also to the viewers. Workplace dramas reminded them that their workplaces were no longer capable of securing predictable futures to them. Instead, they had become institutions of uncertain futures that constantly had to be saved from bankruptcy. By portraying this reality as the order of things under a stagnating economy, workplace dramas such as *Shomuni* tended to naturalize the withdrawal of corporations from guaranteeing lifetime employment. At the same time, the serial tended to encourage individuals to redefine themselves as enterprising and autonomous subjects, who were on their own to secure their own psychological or economic well-being.

In Japan, where over 95 percent of television content is domestically produced, television—and television dramas, in particular—plays a vital role in reinforcing particular social orders by reproducing the socioeconomic structures and dominant subjectivities that underwrite them. From the mid-1960s, family-oriented home dramas, for example, valorized selflessness, a key behavior to organize the national community into an entity united under the desire to ascend to the ranks of Western economic superpowers. Producers of workplace dramas claimed that they aimed to revitalize the tradition of home dramas by reintroducing a concern for the "social" into commercial broadcasting; however, work dramas were in fact not much different from love dramas. Both subgenres of trendy drama promoted self-centeredness as opposed to selflessness. Although work dramas were more concerned with society than love dramas, a preoccupation with the individual and his or her happiness remained in the center of both genres. Love dramas encouraged their viewers to be self-indulgent in the realm of consumption, while *Shomuni* extended this sensibility into a new frontier: the corporate world, which was the last bastion of the postwar socioeconomic order. While love dramas portray work as an unavoidable nuisance of life, in work dramas work becomes the very force field within which individuals can enact their freedom. In the late 1990s, workplace dramas mediated an ongoing recalibration of the social contract between individuals and postwar social institutions and produced new labor subjects in response to the demands of the new economy. The labor fantasies offered by these dramas served to make neoliberal initiatives for individual responsibilization more palatable.

I have argued that Chinatsu, the heroine of Shomuni, was a female stand-in for the male *freeter*. In the 1980s, young women's burgeoning power as consumers was part of a broader sea change in the popular imaginary. By the end of the 1990s they had come to embody new values such as a more robust enjoyment of life and a more relaxed relationship to work. While the service (mainly entertainment and leisure) industries have made enormous profits targeting these young women, other industries have also exploited them as a source of cheap and disposable labor. Mary Brinton has argued that, in postwar Japan, gender served as a readily available criterion by which a reservoir of unskilled labor could be maintained or shut down as business cycles fluctuated (1993). Although women have been steadily supplying flexible labor, in the wake of the recession the demand for disposable workers has dramatically increased, and masses of young men have been incorporated into a flexible labor force. In *Shomuni* these socioeconomic trends serve as the background to the story lines, but they are glazed over with a hypocritical message suggesting that there is no unrewarding work that cannot be transformed into fun. This breakdown of the boundary between pleasure and wage labor marked a milestone in mobilizing workers into a new labor regime and in socializing them to accept their employers' increasing demands for more commitment but for less pay.

Notes

ACKNOWLEDGMENTS

An earlier version of this chapter appeared as Gabriella Lukacs, "Labor Fantasies in Recessionary Japan: Employment as Lifestyle in Workplace Dramas of the 1990s" in *Scripted Affects, Branded Selves*, Gabriella Lukacs, pp. 147–176. Copyright, 2010, Duke University Press. All rights reserved. Reprinted by permission of the publisher. www.dukeupress.edu

1. *General Affairs II* (also translated as *Power Office Ladies*), Fuji, 1998, 1998 Special, 2000, 2000 Special, 2002 Final, and 2003 *Shomuni* Forever Special.

2. *OL* (for office ladies) is borrowed from the English language, and it refers to single women in their twenties who pursue non–career-track clerical and secretarial work that does not require expert knowledge or management responsibility.

3. In the second half of the 1990s, a rating of 15 percent (approximately 15 million viewers) was considered a hit program; a rating of over 20 percent equaled megahit status.

4. The Japanese television industry is self-sustaining, meaning that the local media market is controlled by the public channel NHK and five domestic commercial networks whose key stations in Tokyo are Fuji Television (Fuji TV), Tokyo Broadcasting System (TBS), Nippon Television (NTV), Asahi Network (TV Asahi), and TV Tokyo. Television dramas are a major form of prime-time entertainment in addition to such game shows as *Iron Chef.* There are four seasons in a broadcasting year, and Japanese prime-time dramas have ten to twelve episodes (aired weekly in the same program slot) in a season.

5. Indeed, the original idea for trendy dramas was to provide them with subtitles giving information to the viewers on the clothes, accessories, and other consumer items featured in the drama.

6. Free market principles into Japan's government-guided economy were introduced soon after the recession's onset. See Inoue, Chapter Eight in this volume.

7. All translations from the Japanese language are mine.

8. Interview with Nakazono Miho, July 1 and 9, 2003, Tokyo, Japan.

9. These dramas are not action dramas like the American *E.R.* or *Law and Order.* We have to remember that Japanese producers work with incomparably smaller budgets than their American colleagues, and they emphasize character development, rather than action scenes and special effects.

10. *Shomuni* had aired on Fuji Television before I began my fieldwork research on the Japanese television industry in the 2001. Although I was unable to interview viewers during the period when the series was shown, I was able to talk to my informants about the show later. Between 2001 and 2003, during my stay in Tokyo, Fuji aired reruns of the drama in afternoon program slots. I also include in my study discussions on the show that appeared on fan sites and comments that were posted on Internet chat boards. Lastly, I have reviewed articles accounting for the popularity of *Shomuni* published in print media.

11. Fuji, 1998; *Kirakira Hikaru Special* 1999, 2000. Producer: Yamaguchi Masatoshi. Scriptwriter: Inoue Yumiko.

12. This was the dominant life course in the postwar period. In this period, similar to Western societies, female participation in the labor force fell; and, by the 1980s, a particular pattern of gendered employment had evolved. Namely, women temporarily stopped working after giving birth and returned to the workforce,

mainly as part-timers or blue-collar workers in their late thirties or early forties (Brinton 1993; Roberts 1994).

13. In 1998 protective labor laws were further relaxed. Recruitment practices (including the employment agency business) were deregulated. Overtime work became exploitable without regulation, and the time limit of one year on part-time employment was abolished (Itoh 2005).

14. See "Japan Report Worried about Young Part-time Workers." *Jiji Press English News Service*. May 30, 2003.

15. *Kōseirōdōshō: Heisei 21-nen Jakunensha Koyo Jittai Chōsa Kekka no Gaikyo* (Ministry of Health, Labor, and Welfare: Summary of the Survey Results of the Employment Condition for Young People in 2009); retrieved on March 21, 2011, from www.mhlw.go.jp/toukei/itiran/roudou/koyou/young/h21/jigyo.html.

16. See "Danseishi, OL Manga Pawā Zenkai, Honpōsani Kassai" (Male Magazines, OL Manga Full Power, Applause to the Wildness), *Nihon Keizai Shinbun, Yūkan*, May 13, 1996, p. 13; see also "Kore ga Osusume 'Oshigoto Manga'—'Shomuni' no Sakusha ga Kataru" (Workplace Manga That We Recommend: Interview with the Author of "Shomuni," Yasuda Hiroyuki), in *Josei Jishin*, November 24, 1998, p. 151.

17. Interview with Takahashi Rumi, April 27, 2003, Tokyo, Japan.

18. See for example: "98nen Ninkisha Rankingu TOP 50 'GTO' Sorimachi & 'Shomuni' Esumi, Nidai Outlaw no Kyōtsūten?" [Top 50 Popularity Ranking in 1998: GTO's Sorimachi and Shomuni's Esumi: Commonalties Between the Two Outlaws], in *Nikkei Entāteinmento*, January 1999, pp. 48–49.

19. Yasuda, the author of the original *manga*, had no experience working in the corporate world; thus the original portrays the company as a space of ultimate absurdity where the characters are all unfit losers and only luck prevents the company from drifting to the brink of bankruptcy.

20. http://web-japan.org/trends98/honbun/ntj980911.html; accessed on January 15, 2011. Web Japan is sponsored by the Japanese Ministry of Foreign Affairs (MOFA). It aims to provide information on Japan in English.

21. *Individualism* and *difference* were keywords in 1980s marketing, marking a shift from mass consumption to a diversification of consumer demands. A decade later, when individualism was discussed in relation to work, it acquired a new meaning. In the new context, individualism was not simply the opposite of a group-oriented social structure but rather a recognition that individuals could no longer rely on institutional guarantees and social solidarity. For an analogous discussion, see David Harvey's (2005) description of how a discourse on individualism served Thatcherite economic reforms by dissolving all forms of social solidarity in 1980s Britain.

22. Arlie Hochschild (1983) argues that women's caring work in workplace contexts is a form of emotional labor defined as the management of feeling.

23. Judith Farquhar's (1999) analysis of the Chinese film *Zhao Le* (Looking for Fun) is instructive here. The film portrays a group of retired men who practice Beijing opera in search of fun. Marginalized from all forms of power in reform China, the retirees struggle to imagine a positive future for themselves in which their new role as guardians of Chinese heritage restores their sense of pride and usefulness.

24. One of my informants told me that in recent years Chinatsu has become a gay icon. This does not simply illuminate the fluidity of Chinatsu's gender identity, but it also reveals how struggles for recognition of one's vision of a meaningful future open redemptive possibilities. It, however, goes beyond the scope of this chapter to elaborate on this discussion.

25. However, I would like to note that this ideal often remains a political ideology in which opposition to neoliberalism becomes a discursive strategy to define Japanese identity in contrast to a ruthless West.

Chapter Ten

Governmental Entanglements

The Ambiguities of Progressive Politics in Neoliberal Reform in South Korea

JESOOK SONG

Neoliberalism is a logic that operates through diverse social actors to engineer certain forms of social governing. It is not just an economic system in which state governments and macromonetary institutions such as the World Bank and the International Monetary Fund (IMF) are the only actors in constructing a "regime of truth" about economic reason (Foucault 1976).[1] It also exists at the level of individuals pursuing a certain understanding of how to live their lives. The definition of *neoliberalism* that I am using in this chapter is therefore double sided. On the one hand I am referring to a liberal ethos of individual notions of freedom to pursue goals and enjoy autonomous lives without collective surveillance, intervention, or dependency on the state (Foucault 1991; Rose 1999). On the other hand, I am referring to state-led initiatives to restructure the South Korean economy, industry, and finance in the wake of the Asian Debt Crisis (1997–2001) and in response to transnational projects pushing for free-market policies and privatization of state services (Harvey 2005).

My particular focus in this chapter is the somewhat paradoxical position experienced by South Korean intellectuals as political actors implicated in this shift in the logic of government. Motivated by the core values of liberal democracies such as freedom, equality, independence, entrepreneurship, and rational decision making, these intellectuals nonetheless found themselves inadvertently participating in neoliberal logics that were shaping policies with which they were ideologically at odds. How could a political investment in liberal values and social justice lead to neoliberal policies scaling back government responsibility for vulnerable populations? The implementation of homeless policies during the Asian Debt Crisis reveals the paradoxical working out of neoliberal logics in South Korea.

Neoliberalism is a variant of advanced liberalism in response to existing liberalisms (Hindess 2004). The relationship between neoliberalism and prior liberal regimes is not necessarily oppositional but very likely resuscitating. Although it tends to be more centered on economic and market expansion, it nonetheless builds on the principles of democracy as much as earlier liberalisms. Socially conscious South Korean intellectuals may have helped to reproduce forms of neoliberal social governing by applying liberal ideas as strategies of intervention. Simultaneously occupying a position as state agents and state subjects, these intellectuals as critical thinkers and actors were caught between competing projects of how to govern society and the self after democratization. This fact alone requires me to locate the positions of activist intellectuals in the process of knowledge production. In their taking for granted their progressive and critical stance, they may fail to recognize their complicity as agents of the sort of neoliberal projects of which they might be otherwise critical. In agreeing to take an active role in civil society, they unwittingly enabled the state to download the responsibility for social governance to the civil society sphere and thereby facilitated the rollback of the state's responsibility for social provision. Producing knowledge without reflecting on one's own epistemological frameworks and daily practices reifies a dualistic divide between "us" and "them" in an unequal power relationship between oneself and those one studies—between those who see and write and those who are being seen and written about (Hall 1996).

A timeline of recent history demonstrates the complexly layered past that underlies this complex positioning of South Korean intellectuals. During the period from 1960 to 1987, South Korea was ruled by a developmental state under the leadership of a military dictatorship committed to maximizing economic development. This was followed in 1988 by a democratized state established in response to widespread social protest. Retaining a state-planned economy in line with the old military government, this new regime lasted only until 1997 with the establishment of a true liberal democracy in South Korea. The election in 1997 of President Kim Dae Jung, the former leader of the democratization movement (*minjuhwa undong*), was the most

significant political development since the beginning of the military dictatorship in 1960. South Korean activists who had opposed the military government prior to 1997 now found new forms of political agency, but this
time as actors within state government.[2]

However, Kim's presidency marked a new political beginning that was
contemporaneous with the Asian Debt Crisis, which hit in 1997 and became the worst economic downturn in South Korea since the Korean War
(1950–1953). Along with other Asian countries, such as Indonesia, Taiwan,
and Thailand, Korea encountered the crisis as a consequence of an abrupt
change in global financial markets. Foreign investors retreated from short-
term and unhedged loans, fearing a currency hike after the collapse of assets
and property-market bubbles. By signing the Standby Agreement with the
International Monetary Fund (IMF) on December 3, 1997, as a condition
for receiving IMF bailout funds, the South Korean government agreed to
restructure its economic, financial, and government management systems
along free-market lines. These measures contributed to the bankruptcy of
many large companies and banks and led to large-scale unemployment.[3] Although the debt to the IMF was eventually repaid and the crisis was officially
announced over in 2001, Kim's administration and following regimes—the
presidencies of Roh Moo Hyun (2003–2008) and Lee Myung Bak (2008–
present)—have been responsible for scaling back the costs of government by
privatizing public services and transferring financial responsibility from the
central government to municipalities but without granting them the fiscal
means to pay for them. For example, in 2008 the homeless policy granted
welfare benefits to homeless people; however, the fiscal responsibility for
providing these benefits was assigned to city-level governments, most of
which are not financially capable of providing support, with the exception of
the capital city Seoul, making this new entitlement impossible to implement.

The period since democratization in 1987 has therefore seen the formation of a vastly different political landscape in South Korea. South Korean
society has shifted from an oppositional mobilization against an oppressive
military regime to a society apparently in harmony with the ideals of liberal
government. Social movements organized through labor activism against the
policies of the national government and the corporations as well as middle-
class consumer activism against free-market tyranny no longer obtained
wholehearted support from the working poor, despite the negative conse-

quences that these policies pose for them. For intellectuals, once at the fore-
front of the political opposition, the liberalized political-cultural mood that
followed democratization could be characterized by inertia, lethargy, escapism, and cynicism (Lee 2007). The radical ideals of collective social change
have been displaced by the liberal pursuit of individual happiness.[4] Many less
advantaged members of the population lost their faith in collective resistance
as they saw resistance leaders acquiring the values and material goods symbolic of the capitalist practices these leaders had once claimed to abhor. One
example could be found in the bitter experience of laid-off part-time workers
of Korea Telecom, Inc., who were betrayed by the full-time workers' union
during the Asian Debt Crisis. Prior to the crisis, both groups of workers
were united in their solidarity against company owners and in their opposition to the bourgeois class. However, after successful unionization, resulting
in increased wages, many full-time workers were able to aspire to a middle-
class lifestyle. With the massive layoffs following the economic crisis, the
union ultimately betrayed the part-time workers by supporting only those
laid-off workers who had been full-time (Lee 2003).

The magnitude of this shift in political sensibility can perhaps be best
conveyed by the following literary passage excerpted from a short story entitled "Human Decency" by Chi-Yŏng Kong:

> "*Things around us, things inside us, things that seem trivial—those are the things
> we'll tackle first, all right?*" He said this with a smile on his face and a glow in
> his good-natured eyes. And then he fought those trivial things and went to
> jail, the sight of him dragged into court, gagged, in white traditional prison
> garb bringing us to tears . . . and he worked in a factory and married a factory
> girl with only a middle-school education. And here I was, five years later, go-
> ing to see this man, a man now quoted as saying, "*There was no use risking one's
> life for something trivial,*" a man who had inherited his father's bus company,
> who fathered two daughters and then separated from the factory girl with the
> middle-school education, after which she was committed to a mental hospital.
> (Kong 1997: 68–69, my emphasis)

These trivial things and their changing value signal a fundamental shift
in how one chooses to live one's life. Collective struggles have given way
to more individualized goals. Many one-time political activists had been

chased by riot police and tortured in detention.[5] They had fought for the rights of laborers and peasants, and some of them had married people less educated and poorer than themselves to demonstrate their political commitment and class solidarity. However, many of them later became office workers or business people pursuing economic security. Having lost their passion for engaging in social movements, some also turned to mainstream politics, keeping company with the older generation of politicians that they had once criticized. Many of those who had married working-class or rural partners during the heyday of their activism later divorced them, finding them no longer compatible. The social, mental, and physical wounds of these cast-off spouses illustrated in Kong's story are therefore emblematic of this shift away from social responsibility toward more private goals.

A Political Landscape of South Korea during the Asian Debt Crisis and the Kim Dae Jung Government

The historical shifts sketched out in the previous section are important for understanding the specific conditions under which neoliberal logics have been shaping policies in the wake of the Asian Debt Crisis. As a response to massive unemployment, the Kim Dae Jung government implemented "productive welfarism," resulting in a shift from welfare to workfare (Peck and Theodore 2001). This move intensified neoliberal social governing at the level of social policy and public discourse in terms of who would be eligible for government support. For the first time in its history, South Korea launched policies for dealing with the homeless as appropriate citizens of the welfare state; however, only those homeless men who were living on the streets temporarily as a direct consequence of the economic crisis were considered deserving of support. This was premised on the assumption that these men would resume their responsibilities as family breadwinners as soon as their employment situation was redressed (Song 2006; 2009). However, this assumed that the economic crisis was only a temporary aberration of South Korean economic growth. South Korea officially announced the end of the crisis in 2001 when it repaid the foreign debts to international financial institutes; however, as happened in post–economic recession Japan, the goal of lowering the unemployment rates to precrisis levels was nominally achieved only because of the increase of public works programs and irregular employment.[6]

Under the name of "productive welfarism," the first extensive welfare system to be established in South Korea prioritized "workfare" through reference to the apparent failure of welfare in advanced capitalist societies: This failure is construed as the draining of the public budget for social services that do not contribute to productivity and economic growth but result instead in forms of dependency on the state (Shin 2002). When Kim Dae Jung implemented the welfare state in 1998, he invited civic groups to respond to the Asian Debt Crisis as partners of government. Initially, the invitation was well received not only because of the urgency to address the crisis at hand but also because the idea of a welfare state for many of these groups was a symbolic entrance to social democracy and a commitment to economic justice. However, the program of productive welfarism as implemented by the government followed neoliberal models, the primary focus of which were to protect economic growth rather than to promote economic redistribution among disadvantaged populations. This represented a fundamental shift in the political commitment of the postdemocratization South Korean government in response to global logics of economic restructuring. Since the crisis officially ended in 2001, neoliberal ideas have become much more concrete in the daily lives of most South Korean people. They have become embodied in narratives of self-management of health and life style (Abelmann, Park, and Kim, Chapter Four in this volume; Song 2004) and in their perceptions of the value of refined living or "well-being" (Song 2004; Koo 2006). This conception of "well-being" is defined through consumption of certain commodities and practices of self-care (environmentally friendly electronics, organic food, and yoga and Zen exercise programs). The discursive and consumer practice of well-being is a continuum and culmination of a changed value of life from an emphasis on economic growth to one of quality of life after liberal democratization in late 1980s. While the period of rapid economic growth in South Korea (1960–1980) was appreciated for its contribution to quantity of living, such as the increase of GDP, middle-class social movements have become more focused on the quality of living—indicating the importance of pursuing individual happiness rather than sacrifice for collective survival—which Kim Dae Jung has picked up as a catchphrase for his welfare state.[7]

The need to improve the quality of life as an authentic concept of social well-being rapidly expanded during the crisis in conjunction with commercial products that individuals would purchase as a form of self-care (Song 2004; Wong 2005). This commitment to improving the quality of life along with the shift toward political democracy in 1997 raised expectations that Kim Dae Jung would promote significant social reform. Moreover, because the previous president, Kim Young Sam, was heavily criticized and ridiculed by the majority of South Koreans for his failure to prevent the Asian Debt Crisis, the moment was ripe for a political hero.

Kim Dae Jung's political achievement can also be attributed to his effective deployment of policies in welfare and education. During his exile in Britain prior to gaining the presidency, he began to develop his commitments to economic liberalization and governmental restructuring as an effective means to manage business–government relations and combat corrupt practices, especially bribe taking, which had been widespread in the South Korean government.[8] These developments, which were in line with the policies of the IMF and the World Bank, became more conspicuous during the time of the economic crisis. Even before he was inaugurated, Kim Dae Jung promptly executed a series of plans for reform and restructuring. He also expanded government funding for nongovernmental organizations (NGOs) and nonprofit organizations (NPOs) to elicit their participation in sharing the responsibility for helping the unemployed and homeless. In this fashion, Kim Dae Jung was able to secure the support of many long-standing members of progressive civic groups by mobilizing partnerships between government organizations (GOs) and NGOs in response to the crisis. For instance, civil groups took major roles in promoting a national campaign for gold collection to repay the debt in ways that were reminiscent of the Repay Debt Movement or the Korean Production Movement, which had taken place in 1920 during the Japanese colonial period.[9] In response to the economic crisis, gold came not only from middle-class citizens but also from lower-income people. The proceeds were handed over to respected delegates representing the three most popular religions (Buddhism, Catholicism, and Protestantism) to distribute to those in need as part of the National Movement for Overcoming Unemployment (*Sirŏpkŭkpok kungmin udong*).

The growth of civil groups during this time should be historically contextualized to understand the political atmosphere leading up to the crisis. The Great Democratization Movement in 1987 engendered mass protests demanding the end to a period of nearly three decades (1960–1987) of military dictatorship. In the aftermath of the 1987 protests, South Korea established an electoral democracy that led to the flowering of popular civil movements advocating for women's rights, gay liberation, environmental protection, and economic justice. These movements were distinct from pre-1987 political movements, which had featured collective opposition to the political oppression of the military dictatorship and the capitalist exploitation of low-income workers and farmers. By contrast, sociopolitical movements after 1987 emphasized individualistic values and included middle-class issues such as consumer campaigns as legitimate objectives for social activism. Middle-class citizens were the main supporters of these movements (Koo 2001).

Although there were allegations of marginalizing the working poor by South Korean progressive political activists, Kim Dae Jung's liberal platform remained steadfast, quashing any hopes of socialist democratic reforms. Kim Dae Jung's strategy of partnering NGOs with GOs optimized a regime of liberal social governing that grew in response to the national debt predicament (Haggard, Pinkston, and Seo 1999: 202–204). The increased participation of activist groups in different realms of social management enabled the Kim Dae Jung government to implement neoliberal policies to reduce the costs of government under the guise of social security and the welfare state. These were the social policies that came to be called "productive welfarism." At the beginning of Kim Dae Jung's administration, a general welfare plan was not articulated by the new government, even after the issue of unemployment burst on the scene as an issue of poverty. Rather, the government selectively implemented crisis-related relief policies for only certain categories of the unemployed and homeless. It was only after Kim Dae Jung's Celebration Speech during Independence Day (August 15) in 1999 that the blueprint for productive welfarism was introduced to the public and the Planning Committee to Improve the Quality of Life, equivalent to a U.S. White House executive office, was set up as the blueprint's brain trust.

The South Korean government presented this program as the first in South Korean history to guarantee a minimum standard of living for its population. A 1999 government white paper proclaimed that South Korean welfarism followed the "Third Way" by combining liberal and socialist systems (The Presidential Secretary Plan-Committee to Improve the Quality of Life 1999: 14–16). However, the "Third Way," as it was used originally by Tony Blair in Britain as well as by Kim Dae Jung in South Korea, can be better understood as a neoliberal model, rather than a combination of neoliberalism and social democracy. The emphasis on economic growth in neoliberal discourses and the blueprint for productive welfarism were strikingly similar insofar as the latter promoted unimpeded economic growth and restricted the use of state funds for addressing economic inequality. At first glance, the commitment for a guaranteed minimum standard of living appeared to contradict this. However, the goal was to establish the welfare state at minimum cost. The welfare cost was minimized through the requirement of employability and minimal public provision. "Welfare" was conceptualized as "workfare" or "postwelfare" in this first stage of South Korea's self-proclaimed welfare state. The criteria of employability and normative families were used to discriminate between "deserving" and "undeserving" welfare citizens. Laid-off workers reduced to living on the street temporarily due to the immediate effects of restructuring were labeled *nosukcha*—a new label created during the crisis, literally meaning "people who sleep in the street"—and deemed to be deserving of welfare benefits, whereas the chronically homeless (*purangin*)—a term with a longer history prior to the crisis that literally means "floating" or "rootless" people—were deemed to be undeserving. This distinction was produced through popular discourses of "family breakdown" in the wake of the financial crisis (Song 2006).[10] Hence, it is not a coincidence that "employable" and "familial" male breadwinners emerged as deserving welfare subjects under productive welfarism.

The new state welfare system also perceived newly unemployed members of the middle class (*chungsanch'ǔng*) as deserving welfare citizens along with those from the poor working class (*sǒmin*). It was the first time that members of the middle class had been recognized as deserving of state support. This seemed absurd to many lower-level state administrators accustomed to the idea that the government could afford welfare provision only to truly destitute people. This would have been compatible with the principles of a developmental state by minimizing the scope of beneficiaries of social policy to focus resources for economic development. Activists had expected Kim Dae Jung to pursue more leftist ideals (such as socialist democratic welfare), and they too were confused by the inclusion of middle-class citizens among deserving welfare recipients. However, this reformulation of welfare citizenship corresponded with the liberal account of deserving welfare citizenship; that is, employable and taxable citizens who do not depend on public provision but are self-sufficient and, preferably, responsible for other family members by virtue of being male breadwinners.

At the outset of the crisis, three tiers of laid-off or unemployed people were established by the state and city administration in Seoul. The first tier was made up of workers who had been laid off with employment pensions by *chaebŏl* (big conglomerates). They received unprecedented state benefits, including as much as 70 to 80 percent of their previous salaries for extended periods and free access to vocational education for reemployment. The second tier consisted of workers who were laid off without employment pensions but who were eligible to work in the Public Works Programs (*Konggong Kŭllo Saŏp*). The third tier consisted of unemployed people who were living on the street in despair. The "IMF homeless" (*ai-em-epŭ nosukcha*) were, therefore, the deserving recipients of government unemployment policies, although long-term homeless people were considered undeserving by definition and were further disadvantaged by the creation of this new category of "IMF homeless" (Song 2009). Although the government could have focused on the overarching issue of homelessness by setting up more inclusive public provisions or policies of entitlement in this new welfare system, homelessness was instead characterized as an extension of more temporary unemployment issues.[11]

Within this historical and sociopolitical context, I found myself an unlikely beneficiary. In the midst of my dissertation research on social minorities, I had proposed to do a study on homelessness for the Seoul City Committee for Unemployment Problems (SCCUP) and became temporarily employed through the Public Works Program under a new category, "unemployed person with higher education" (*kohaknŏk sirŏpcha*), a classification that had to be invented to cover this somewhat novel situation. The SCCUP consisted of a dozen high-ranking civilians (including faculty from various universities, researchers from government-sponsored research institutes, the chief editors of major newspapers, and leaders of NGOs) and upper-level city officials (two vice mayors and four major city bureau heads). My role was to lead short-term research projects on the relationship between unemployment and homelessness for youth, women, and disabled people. In the course of this research, I met many South Korean intellectuals who participated in GO–NGO partnerships around the issues of homelessness and who had become entangled in the engineering of neoliberal social policy.

Dr. Uh

I met Dr. Uh while doing a short-term research project assessing the needs of homeless women for the SCCUP.[12] We met at a time when state administrators had just declared that the government could afford to assist only those homeless men who had been living on the street for a short time. Long-term homeless men and all homeless women (whether short-term or not) were classified as undeserving citizens whom the government could not afford to help. In my work with the SCCUP, I had encountered great difficulty convincing state administrators to pay attention to the broader spectrum of homeless people, especially women. Dr. Uh's research on long-term homeless men and men who were at risk of homelessness (mainly day laborers) was influential in the creation of the first homeless policies in South Korean national history as a primary expert on homeless policy in Seoul and other cities during the crisis.

Dr. Uh and I often worked together to persuade state administrators to reconsider their narrow definition as to who was deserving of welfare benefits. However, even he expressed doubt about whether the plight of homeless women could be viewed with equal significance to that of homeless men. Dr. Uh's prioritization of class over gender reflected his background as a student activist in the 1980s, a period in which South Korean activism largely focused on labor exploitation and the political oppression of the military dictatorship at the expense of other social issues, including gender discrimination. To his credit, Dr. Uh did not dismiss women's needs, nor did he view homeless issues from the distanced perspective of a bureaucrat. Rather, he expressed sympathy toward marginalized people perhaps in part because he was himself a semi-independent researcher without secure employment.

However, Dr. Uh's perspective on homelessness gradually changed. When homeless people first emerged as targets of government workfare, the overall perspective was that homeless people should have the potential for rehabilitation and employment (Song 2009). At this stage, there were few experts in the field of homelessness. Although Dr. Uh was already employed as a regular researcher in a state-sponsored research institute, he soon joined the Presidential Secretary Planning Committee to Improve the Quality of Life. He then published a report on homeless women after I quit my work in the city office. His report concluded that due to the costs and complexities of welfare support for homeless women, it was not an appropriate domain for

state administration and therefore assigned responsibility for it to "civil society" groups. This astonishing shift in Dr. Uh's perspective is symptomatic
of how a leftist intellectual had become complicit with a neoliberal welfare
project.

Prior to joining the presidential office commission, Dr. Uh had told me
that he could not understand why the regime included middle-class citizens
as deserving subjects of the welfare state. He may have hoped that the welfare
regime would focus more on the working poor. However, in his policy recommendations, Dr. Uh ultimately relegated the responsibility for addressing
the needs of homeless women to civil society and urged the state to focus its
attention on the dire situation of male day laborers who were at risk of losing
their homes. Dr. Uh's willingness to accept middle-class men as proper targets for the state's new welfare system could be rationalized with his leftist
idealism as follows: The middle class bears the financial burden for the needs
of the working poor through taxes as well as through their voluntary labor
and resources for civic organizations to help the working poor. However, I
question whether this rationale truly meets the needs of complexly stratified
categories of deprivation.

Mr. Ku

While working on a report on the new homeless shelter system for the
SCCUP, I met Mr. Ku when I visited the House of Freedom Homeless Shelter. He had been assigned to coordinate the work of civil representatives of
the Seoul City Commission on Homeless Policies with city officials in related divisions. Mr. Ku was also head of the Homeless Rehabilitation Center
(*Nosukcha Tasisŏgi Chiwonsentŏ*),[13] a government-organized nongovernmental
organization (GONGO) that coordinated the work of 120 homeless shelters
with the government office that had been set up as an emergency response
to the Asian Debt Crisis to craft policies for the homeless. The shelters that
he worked with included the Houses of Hope, which I discuss later in this
section. Mr. Ku was a doctoral student in a department of social work at a
renowned university. As a former student activist from the 1980s, he made
it clear to me that the student movement of the 1980s had been much more
intense and difficult than what student activists of the 1990s such as myself
would have experienced.

It is notable that Mr. Ku did not immediately understand my status as a temporary researcher in the Seoul City Office, for I was neither a regular staff member nor a government-affiliated researcher. Rather, I had an ambiguous status, as both state agent (a government manager or government-affiliated researcher) and state subject (a citizen receiving workfare subsidy and a Public Works Program worker). However, Mr. Ku and I were in somewhat similar positions and, interestingly, we had become involved in city work in very much the same manner. We were both PhD students who had reluctantly but seriously undertaken government-related work that neither of us could have imagined ourselves doing because of our antiauthoritarian politics. Mr. Ku may have thought that his situation was unique and had not anticipated meeting another "reckless" intellectual willing to advance social causes through government programs and to risk being criticized by other activists as either an opportunist or a collaborator. Arguably, we were both attempting to carry out the militant leftist guerilla tactics of the 1980s by showing that strategic leadership and sacrifice can make a difference in the lives of working-class people. But, at the same time, I wonder if our strong, individuated sense of intellectual agency was, in fact, the sign of a liberal ethos. How was it possible that a liberal and leftist sensibility could coexist in the efforts of South Korean intellectuals such as Mr. Ku and myself in this period of postdemocratization?

Although it was intended as part of a critical intervention, Mr. Ku's role of managing homeless shelters that were run mostly by civilian organizations also helped to intensify practices of neoliberal social policy during the Asian Debt Crisis. Nonetheless, Mr. Ku also questioned the dichotomy between deserving and undeserving homeless people. As a front-line social worker meeting and living with homeless people, he contested this division as arbitrary. Along with many other social workers, he also questioned the image of the "IMF homeless" as middle class and therefore easy to rehabilitate.

Mr. Ku was a midlevel worker in an interstitial space between the NGO sector and city government. Seoul has two facilities for homeless shelters: the House of Freedom (*Chayu ŭi Chip*) and the Houses of Hope (*Hŭimang ŭi Chip*). The House of Freedom is a large building located in the Kuro industrial area of Seoul. The building is owned by the city of Seoul and was once the Pangnim Textile Factory. It had been one of the first and largest textile factories of the Korean economic developmental period during the Park Chung Hee regime. During the 1970s, it had been an early symbol of South Korean economic success, which had been based on the development of light industry. During the 1980s, as heavier industries such as automobile manufacturing began to represent South Korean prosperity throughout the world (E. M. Kim 1997; Cumings 1997), the Pangnim Factory was closed.[14] By the 1990s, the former factory building was housing thousands of homeless people.

The House of Freedom was named by the city government to suggest an environment that offered homeless people temporary shelter with fewer regulations and relative freedom, as compared to the Houses of Hope. The city government created the Houses of Hope to remove street people from public places. They are smaller shelters built specifically to accommodate the IMF homeless. Many homeless people dislike them because of their strict prohibitions against drinking, smoking, staying out after hours, and sexual relations. On the other hand, the advantage of staying in a House of Hope is that residents can be paid for work through a public works program and given free meals and a place to sleep. Although the House of Freedom does not offer work and wages, many among the homeless prefer it because it imposes fewer restrictions on their behavior.

A salient example of neoliberal state practices in South Korea through privatization of the public sphere is the outsourcing of administrative work to NGO or private consulting groups such as the Homeless Rehabilitation Center, a GONGO that is neither a grassroots organization nor part of the state machinery. The center works with the Homeless Commission in addition to various levels of the government, mediating conflicts between the commission's civilian members and its bureaucrats. It also runs the House of Freedom and determines which categories of homeless people can reside in the Houses of Hope. Very few operating shelters actually comply with the center's regulations because most of the Houses of Hope are run by small welfare agencies, which receive minimal state support and are funded by religious groups. For them, running a homeless shelter was an additional task without any government incentives or benefits. In view of the difficulties Mr. Ku faced in managing these small homeless shelters, he criticized the city government's policies as shortsighted and unrealistic. The problems of homelessness were long-standing and could not be solved by merely providing temporary shelter. He pointed out that the city's objective to remove all the homeless from public places to the Homeless Rehabilitation Center ran counter to its intention to provide services for IMF homeless only. Distinguishing the IMF homeless from long-term street people was not an easy task because the causes of homelessness ran much deeper than the recent economic troubles.

Mr. Ku's positions were therefore in conflict between his being both an agent of state policy and an advocate for the homeless. On the one hand, he was able to successfully use his mastery of social policy language in pursuit of social equity. He challenged the assumption of government officials on the causal association assumed between homelessness and the Asian Debt Crisis. During the annual ceremony for the Homeless Rehabilitation Center, he publicly announced that the premises of government homeless policies were false. Based on his own data, he argued that short-term homeless people who lived on the street were for the most part not homeless because of the Asian Debt Crisis. Further, he questioned whether such a category of homelessness could even be clearly distinguished and whether it was even possible for short-term street people to easily resume a normal social life.

However, Mr. Ku also actively participated in neoliberal social governing when he relied on conservative gender and family norms to endorse the idea of rebuilding middle-class stability and social morale.[15] At the same public event, for example, Mr. Ku noted that 55 percent of the homeless people at the Homeless Rehabilitation Center were classified as "single homeless people because of family breakdown," which is an example of how social anxiety about family stability had become magnified during the crisis. According to his report, the majority of homeless people had fragile family relationships. However, the boundaries that separated "normal" from "abnormal" families, in his view, are premised on heterosexual conjugal relationships, based on the cultural assumption that middle-aged men cannot live alone and require the unpaid labor of their female partners.

During the Asian Debt Crisis, when mass media represented the family and its breakdown as the cause of social problems such as divorce, homosexuality, teen prostitution, and homelessness, homeless welfare agencies responded to these representations by encouraging a variety of rehabilitation programs. The Homeless Rehabilitation Center held a contest in 1999 for the best rehabilitation program among the 120 Houses of Hope. The award-winning program included matchmaking services, wedding ceremonies, short-term reunion events with relatives, and transportation and gifts to families or visits to hometowns during the holidays.[16] These programs and events were designed to motivate homeless people to resume a "normal" way of life and to promote ideas of the nuclear family as the unit responsible for social needs.[17] Marriages between homeless men and women were represented as success stories by the hosting homeless shelter, the Rehabilitation Center, and the media. Many high-level government officials, as well as civil leaders, visited the winning shelter to express their approval of those willing to assume the status of "normal families."

In this way, Mr. Ku participated in the neoliberal governing of homelessness through disciplining gender and family relationships. As with Dr. Uh, Mr. Ku's perspectives as an intellectual appeared to shift from a leftist to a more liberal democratic position (or possibly, a complex amalgam of both), which has become symptomatic of neoliberal governance in South Korea. As a leftist, he created some space to address the problems of disadvantaged groups, in this case, homeless people; as a liberal, he acquired and employed a managerial position and competed with neoliberal social engineers to control and manage homeless issues. Ultimately, Mr. Ku's strategies for managing the homeless converged with the dominant neoliberal rhetoric, perhaps most significantly by supporting conservative norms about gender and family. Mr. Ku's reiteration of normative family ideology contributed to the discursive formation of "deserving" homelessness. Only employable male breadwinners, who could be rehabilitated to assume a normal family life, emerged as deserving welfare subjects. South Korean neoliberal logic aimed to preserve national prosperity by promoting norms of productive citizenship at the expense of excluding vulnerable homeless populations who were a drain on the public purse.

Reverend Kang

When I first met Reverend Kang through a personal connection, I immediately recognized that she could best help me understand the problems of homeless women.[18] As a religious leader, Reverend Kang occupied a vocation unusual for a woman. In the spring of 1998, she was also the first civil activist to address the needs of homeless women in Seoul City (Song 2009). In a City Commission on Homeless Policy, which consisted mostly of civil activists working in their local communities, Reverend Kang was the first to volunteer to run an emergency shelter for women. This decision reflected her ten-year experience as a minister serving in an industrial area of Seoul, during which she had observed at close hand the destitution of women living and working in that area.

Reverend Kang countered the demoralizing government portrayal of homeless women by organizing the Homeless Women Shelters Association (*Yŏsŏng Nosukcha Shimtŏ Yŏndae*). It consisted of eight shelters for women and families (six shelters sponsored by the city government's homeless policies and two funded by other agencies). From the time of the Debt Crisis, all eight women's shelters belonging to the association were run mostly by civil activists, religious organizations, or private welfare institutes. Reverend Kang gave some insight into the invisibility of homeless women. Many lower-class homeless women were victims of domestic abuse who became homeless after exhausting their stay with relatives or at inns, all-night church services (*ch'ŏryayebae*), and prayer houses (*kidowon*).

Homeless shelters were one of the outcomes of the partnership between civil society and government initiated by the Kim Dae Jung regime. The city government had originally planned to entrust the management of homeless shelters to established civil associations, especially religious groups such as Chogyechong (a popular Buddhist denomination in South Korea), as well as other Roman Catholic, Anglican, and other Protestant church groups. However, within a month, the city changed its strategy to pursue a bureaucratic top-down process due to the urgency imposed by the Asian Debt Crisis. This is an example of the intensified effects on homeless policies, combining neoliberal governance by the new presidential office (partnership between an NGO and a GO) with long-standing regulative governance (top-down bureaucracy).

The city partially subsidizes homeless shelters, which are run by about a hundred different welfare agencies connected to the city government. Although some civil groups volunteered to open shelters, the city did not fully address the difficulties that arose from the lack of experience of these groups with bureaucratic structures. For example, when Reverend Kang found a place for her shelter and needed to contract a yearly rent with the owner,[19] the city was not cooperative in providing the rental fee in the time that had been promised. Following the proper channels (*chŏlch'a*) of bureaucratic process would have resulted in six months of delay,[20] So Reverend Kang had to go to various levels of local governments to ask if they could assist with this problem. However, none of the officials in the city (*sich'ŏng*), district (*kuch'ŏng*), and ward (*tongsamuso*) offices was able to help. As Reverend Kang interpreted the situation:

> I do not think that all of these city, district, and ward office officials had de-
> cided not to help us. But, unfortunately, the ward office managers, who best
> understood the situation we were in, did not have enough authority to exert
> control over this issue [*unsin ŭi p'ogi chopta*]. And the city officials who had the
> power just did not understand the difficulty. (Interview with Reverend Kang,
> spring 1998)

Although the city had invited civil activists to help manage homeless issues in the name of a "partnership between a GO and an NGO," a liberal
technology of social engineering, they were not necessarily equivalent in the
power structure. Civil activists tended to experience more inconvenience
than did governmental officials in this unprecedented working relationship,
especially when civil activists became subjects of financing and auditing.
The state's administrative authority was not lessened despite its delegation of
responsibility to civil agencies and the downsizing of the number of governmental employees as compared to the previous interventionist state regime.
The various levels of government were, in a sense, contracting out homeless
service provision while retaining control over these operations in a "flexibilization" of government.

In addition to difficulties occasioned by unequal power dynamics, Reverend Kang faced more fundamental barriers in making government officials
understand the diverse needs of homeless women: For example, her concerns
for women as mothers came into direct conflict with the maternalist policies
of city officials. Homeless women who had to leave their children at home
suffered from "mother-aches" (*emi pyŏng*).[21] They became even more psychologically distressed when they stayed together with homeless women who
had their children with them. Reverend Kang asked city officials if she could
run separate shelters for women who were alone and for those who had their
children with them, either as two adjacent units in a building or through
spatial segregation by room. However, the city did not allow her to do this;
rather, it pathologized these women as members of the long-term homeless
(*purangin*) undeserving of welfare benefits. She saw these women as proper
mothers, but this conflicted with the views of city officials who viewed them
as women who had left their children.

Reverend Kang noted a further gendered impasse in the city officials' understanding of homeless women's needs. Their measure for determining how many homeless people should be assigned per shelter was inaccurate because they based this on the needs of healthy men who merely needed a place to sleep and eat when they returned to the shelter from a day at work.[22] Many homeless women also had a desire to work, but they needed to rest and recover their health first. They required a recovery and rehabilitation shelter (*chahwal/chaehwal shimpt'ŏ*) that could provide them with care appropriate to their needs.

Reverend Kang's rationale was based on an understanding that most homeless women living a street life needed psychological care. They had strong egos and had lost the ability of expressing emotional feeling. They also needed specialized care for women's reproductive health. Many had damaged reproductive systems from exposure to the cold while living on the street.[23] To motivate and prepare these women to work for a living, Reverend Kang recommended that the government provide coordinated services for psychological and physical recovery. In pursuit of this goal, she was able to draw on special funds available for homeless people by mobilizing governmental discourse of "rehabilitation" and "employability."

On the one hand, Reverend Kang contested the workfare regime's gendered valuation of employability and the negative effects of its maternalist biases. She advocated the provision of psychological services, recovery shelters, and education for children who were with their mothers in the shelters. On the other hand, her endorsement of "desire to work" resulted in excluding street life as an independent way of living. In pursuing governmental financial support for a recovery shelter, she inadvertently reproduced the ideology that homeless people can be supported only when they demonstrate their productive and reproductive value within the norm of the heterosexual family and a gendered division of labor.

Reverend Kang's location of "proper" motherhood within the imaginary of a normative family institution converged with the broader social concern for family breakdown that intensified during the Asian Debt Crisis. Her family experience with a brother who had become schizophrenic after police torture sheds a light on both her personal itinerary in understanding the family as the primary welfare institution for South Korean individuals and its link to the historical context of developmental regimes. She agreed with the Korean welfare system, in which the family functions as the primary institution of responsibility for social and individual well-being (particularly psychological well-being, for which public awareness is very low). But, at the same time, she urged social support for individuals who cannot or do not want to rely on their families.

Reverend Kang's reference to family is not necessarily contradictory to her aim of encouraging social accountability for individual well-being. Rather, it was symptomatic of liberal ideas among civil activists that burgeoned after the democraticization movement of 1987 and culminated in the social management of the Asian Debt Crisis. By relying so heavily on the ideal of a normative family institution as the foundation for social crisis management, she intensified the effects of neoliberal governmentality. She employed a discourse of crisis no less than did governmental officials as a device to orchestrate urgent social governing. These social agents, including civil activists as well as city officials who use crisis discourse for emergency social governing, are what I call crisis knowledge brokers.[24]

Locating Myself

As a researcher working for the city government while also making it the object of ethnographic inquiry as a feminist anthropologist, in what ways might I also have been complicit with practices of liberal social governing? I was not a distanced producer of knowledge but actively involved in the making of social policy. I was both a state subject and a state agent: I received a workfare subsidy as a worker in the Public Works Program, and at the same time I was a state-sponsored researcher.

I first became interested in this problem when I observed that many unmarried women in their twenties and thirties who had lost their jobs during the Asian Debt Crisis did not get financial support from the government. When I approached government officials with a proposal to do this study, although they agreed on the need for more research on homelessness, they were reluctant to hire a new research team in a time of downsizing. They were both doubtful and scornful about my suggestion that a research team might be a part of a Public Works Program. They could not imagine that qualified researchers with academic degrees would agree to take on minimum-wage jobs, given the stigma attached to workers in this program. Nonetheless, I volunteered to be the first, and this was how I came to be

registered in the state unemployment office under the new category: "unemployed person with higher education" (*kohaknŏk sirŏpcha*).

Throughout my research, I questioned (and continue to question) how to
employ a critical perspective without reproducing the hegemonic ideology
of the intellectual's representational power over a disadvantaged group. How
might intellectuals reinforce constructions of neoliberalism, even when it is
their intention to deconstruct it? In attempting to redress the invisibility of
homeless women in the eyes of social welfare workers, there is no guarantee
that this would lead to positive consequences. Many homeless women I met
in South Korea did not want to be exposed to public view, even though they
were in great need of resources. What risks would I be taking in crossing the
ethical boundaries between activist and academic modes of intellectual practice? Would I diminish my integrity as a critical thinker and actor, or was it
an inevitable element of my integrity? In the realization that I am not outside
a system of neoliberal social governing, at times I find that I am consciously
complicit with macrolevel institutions. At another level, my pursuit of social
justice must be held in balance with a need to keep my life manageable. I am
unavoidably supporting through my practice the institutional administration of neoliberal social governing to which I belong (for example, in classrooms, departments, and universities).

Anthropological knowledge is critical for people's ability to understand
how their own fragmented liberal reasoning interacts with shifting political
technologies related to governmental institutions. One final story about the
temporary research team that I was working for and their reflections on the
epistemological issues that arose in the application of ethnographic methods
in nonacademic contexts is a good illustration of this. A research methods
workshop was held in a corner of the Labor Policy Division office of Seoul
City. Because the corner could not be easily seen from the outside, it was a
hidden refuge and a safe space where we could talk freely.

One of the vivid memories that I have from that corner seminar was the
moment I introduced the issue of the "native anthropologist" to address the
problems of the dichotomy of objective and subjective positions for information gathering and the baggage of Enlightenment ideas of rationality. The
team members, however, were much more interested in the dilemmas of the
position of "native anthropologist" as it applied to their own lives in considering the limits of objective methodology. They were self-conscious that
many of their friends from college would be suspicious of what they were

doing in the state bureaucracy that had been historically the machinery of undemocratic state governance and oppressive actions against civil activism. The blurred position of "native anthropologist" reminded them of a critical question: whether their positions as semiofficial governmental researchers could positively affect the lives of the people they studied and the marginal groups among the unemployed, such as women, youth, the homeless, and those with disabilities. It was sometimes hard for them to separate themselves from the objects of their research because they themselves were unemployed working-class youth and/or women and, in some cases, living with disabilities.

Some of them made peace with their positions as state agents by focusing on the practical necessity of earning a living. Others attempted to assert their rights to be served by the state through being acknowledged as public works project workers. Nolja, who had long experience working in the Public Work Program, considered the team to be a rare politically strategic space to make some good changes in governmental policies on women's unemployment or at least an independent space to create a communication route between governmental personnel and nongovernmental and nonprofit organizations, and, in particular, local grassroots groups:

> In general, the meaning of the team for having created a new space for feminist policies seems to be waning; instead it seems that the primary meaning of the team is as a way of living for the individual. Because this team consists of "only young girls" [*ŏrin yŏjaaedŭl*], we are out of the authority loop for making policies. Nonetheless, we feel some rewards from doing this job. It is because we get more stubborn [*ogi*] for proving that we can do things despite the fact that we are young women [wearing a proud smile]. *We are still enduring—we have not been beaten* [that is, either by the city officials or by the experts of SCCUP].
>
> We are producing knowledge that will be used somewhere ultimately. Mr. To also cited our research content in his report to the subcommittee [SCYWU]. No matter how much he nags us, we know he uses our work often in his own. Although he does not treat us well, we have won this bureaucracy and office struggle as a result. In the future, I will be proud of recalling our work. *My strategy is subservience. . . . We shall see who ultimately wins. This strategy makes me feel like a tightrope walker, but still it is worthy because it creates a space for competition.* [Interview with Nolja, January 2000, my emphasis]

During the second round of research on "Underemployed and Partially Self-Employed Young People," our questioning of the boundary between researcher and "native" stirred the team members most. When they were in the field, they said, they were tempted to "go native" rather than maintaining a distance from their subjects as researchers.

Sometimes it was because their research subjects were the social group that they most identified with themselves (that is, underemployed or unemployed youth). Other times it was because their subjects were the subaltern working class poor (*minjung*) whom South Korean political activists have long considered to be the most exploited by the capitalist economy and suppressed by the military dictatorship. Team members tended to consider these people as most deserving of compensation and benefits from the society, and they felt guilty for not being able to help them more directly. However, when the team researched underemployed youth, middle-aged unemployed housewives, and runaway teen workers, they thought that paying more attention to these marginal groups among the unemployed addressed the need to diversify the category of "deserving" welfare citizenship.

A paradox of the team's reports and their understanding of their own positioning was, therefore, the conflicting but cohabiting logics of singling out those who most merited "deserving" welfare citizenship (that is, the working poor), while also attempting to diversify this category. This paradox is symptomatic of what happens when former leftist student activists turn into liberal intellectuals. Although they did not fully adopt the official rhetoric of bureaucrats, social policy experts, civil activists, and mass media ideologues, the team members were also agents whose competing discourses and practices produced new subjects as deserving welfare citizenship.

As the ethnographer of this research team, I also participated in the structures of neoliberal governing. No less than other team members, I have a conflicting sense of self-identity and fragmented subjectivity surrounding the knowledge I am producing. June was the member who had worked the longest among us in the Public Work Program. Her despair about the complexity of the team's situation still strikes me:

> I asked you before if there are many people who will read your dissertation after you have completed it. I was thinking then of the problem of limited distribution and consumption for both our reports and dissertation-based books. I thought, if writing reports are fundamentally limited in terms of distribution, we had better not write them. [Interview with June, February 2000]

June actively made meaning out of this experience in her personal career and feminist activism outside the city office, as did other team members such as Mimi, who joined a venture company in pursuit of going abroad to study NGO management.

We had attempted to apply anthropological knowledge to convey people's social realities to policy makers more vividly than mere statistics. We learned about the limitations of using this approach as an ad hoc on-the-spot application of theory. Only the long process of dissertation writing helped me to sort out the complexity of the social context we had been working in. Only then was I able to fulfill our expectations of making prolific meaning of the team's activities in tracing out the competing and fragmented liberal reasonings in this shift in South Korean governmentality. This could not have been accomplished by merely writing reports for immediate administrative impact.

Finally, the team's activities were not directed at assigning or judging who was "responsible for" or who were "victims of" the acceleration of neoliberal governing in the Asian Debt Crisis. This makes sense if we appreciate it as a cultural production embedded in people's historical experience, rather than as a set of economic policies realized by some conspiracy of ideologues.

During the 1990s, South Korean intellectuals shifted from a belief that tackling trivial things could be significant to a cynicism that it is "no use risking one's life for something trivial." Yet this shift is not clear-cut and remains highly contentious among the fragmented subjectivities of the Public Work Program workers described in this chapter. However, we find how liberal discourses, such as "freedom," "rights," "justice," and "improvement," are saturated in neoliberal welfare and labor subject formation in South Korea, Japan, and China. When recent South Korean history is remembered as deficient in freedom and in provision of well-being, projects to promote neoliberal market freedom and welfare reform preempt and co-opt liberal democracy. Just as Japanese *freeter* youth come to desire freedom from life-long employment, ironically job security for this generation is already no longer an option available to them (see Chapter Seven by Arai, Chapter Eight by Inoue, and Chapter Nine by Lukacs in this volume). As Chinese workers are liberated from the socialist structures of the Maoist era, the state still heavily engineers the promotion of self-improvement (see Chapter One by Ren and Chapter Six by Yan in this volume). The trivial things are actually still key to wrestle with neoliberal hegemonic practices in our daily lives in the name of freedom and rights. In this context, are liberal ideas readily separable from neoliberalism? Let us think about the sources of tension and our own complicities in neoliberalism made possible by our own liberal habits of thinking and living.

Notes

ACKNOWLEDGMENTS

Parts of this chapter appeared, in an earlier version, in "The Dilemma of Progressive Intellectuals" in Jesook Song, *South Koreans in the Debt Crisis: The Creation of a Neoliberal Welfare Society* (Duke University Press, 2009).

1. Of course, I am not arguing that macroinstitutions and state governments are exempt from such critical claims; rather, I wish to push us further by mobilizing analytically powerful paradigms in our daily politics.

2. See Chen 2010 for a similar history in Taiwan. Those who were political dissents under the KMT joined the new government when the opposition party assumed power in 2000.

3. The total population of South Korea is about 40 million, and the workforce population was about 10 million prior to the crisis. In one year, 1.5 million workers lost their jobs (U.N. Development Programme [UNDP] 1999: 40). The percentage change in real gross domestic product, or GDP, was 5 percent in 1997 and minus 5.8 percent in 1998. The percentage of population in poverty was 8.5 percent in 1996 and 1997 and 12 percent in 1998. The unemployment rate was 2.5 percent in 1997 and 7.3 percent in 1998, and the percentage of change in real wages between 1998 and 1999 was minus 10 percent (World Bank 2000; UNDP 1999).

4. This sensibility is not unlike the one that pervades the Japanese education reform described by Andrea Arai (Chapter 7 in this volume).

5. The intellectuals who participated in the student movement or in the worker/peasant movement were named in various ways. Hagen Koo labels them "students-turned-workers" (2001: 104–125). Seung Kyung Kim uses a term "disguised workers" (1997: 132). Another colloquial term is "3-8-6 *saedae*," referring to a generation of youth who were then in their thirties, had gone to college in the 1980s, and had been born in the 1960s.

6. See note 3 for the unemployment rate.

7. This shift in South Korea parallels a similar process of middle-class self-making in China (see the essay by Hai Ren, Chapter One in this volume). The concept of population quality (*renkou suzhi*) in China came increasingly to operate as a form of social distinction in the discursive production of a middle class (Anagnost 2004: 190). See also Liao 2006.

8. Hall 1984; Peck and Tickell 2002; and Peck and Theodore 2001 all show that Thatcher's introduction of workfare and its continuation in Blair's Third Way neoliberalism transferred to other nation-states.

9. The movement was created for countering Japanese colonial dominance over the Korean economy by building Korean national wealth.

10. Family breakdown (*kajŏnghaech'e* or *kajokhaech'e*) was a ubiquitous subject of discourse in the media, the academy, and government policy, indexing a widespread sense of moral deterioration of women as domestic caretakers. Song (2009) further makes a connection between this moralizing discourse and how the construction of deserving homelessness was gendered. Homeless women either became invisible to the public eye or were deemed as undeserving welfare recipients, while homeless men became recognized as deserving of benefits for rehabilitating their families through their normative male role as breadwinners.

11. See Song 2011 for the history of people in the street or people without place to live in a broader sense.

12. All names that appear in this chapter are pseudonyms.

13. The Homeless Rehabilitation Center was built as a response to homelessness in the Seoul Train Station and was part of the Commission on Homeless Policy that was created by the new mayor's attempt to establish a government–civil partnership for emergency social governing.

14. It is significant to note that, by this period, most textile workers in the lighting industry were young unmarried female laborers who had come to Seoul from the rural, mostly agricultural, areas looking for employment to support family subsistence and a male sibling's education (see Abelmann 2003; Kim 2000).

15. See Song 2006 for an analysis of the discourse of family breakdown. See also Kim and Finch 2002.

16. This is according to *The Homeless Rehabilitation Center Report* (1999). This is a different report from the one Mr. Ku used to criticize the city government.

17. The cover page of *Salimtŏ* [Place of Revitalization] *Newsletter* (Fall 1999) features a picture of a homeless shelter hosting group marriage ceremonies for homeless people. The issue also published follow-up stories of each couple's success.

18. I met Reverend Kang through a mutual introduction by her colleague from the Protestant civil activist group advocating for a social safety net rooted in local communities where poor urban working-class people reside. Although I knew the city of Seoul supported four shelters for women and two shelters for families out of all 125 of its shelters, it was hard to find someone who could provide information on the concrete conditions of homeless women without going through a personal connection.

19. Yearly leases (*chŏnse*) are the conventional term for rental contracts in South Korea. Monthly rent (*wŏlse*) is also possible, but it used to be very rare (Nelson 2000). In the crisis years, landlords who were also short of regular income began to rent their places with monthly contracts.

20. The practice of asserting "proper process" (*chŏlch'a*) is, like "responsibility holder" (*ch'aegim sojae*), a bureaucratic trope, indexing the defensiveness of middle and lower officials in the City bureaucracy under a heavy workload: It is used to excuse or mask evasion of one's responsibility and procrastination or rejection of orders from upper level, to accuse others, and to claim rights over a task.

21. *Emi* is vernacular version of mother, *pyŏng* refers to disease in Korean.

22. According to a senior staff member of a women's shelter, "Governmental policy is targeted to homeless men. When the city provides a handout for homeless people during the traditional holidays, it is all items suitable for men, and not a thing for women. And when we request some essential support from the Welfare Ministry, we often hear a dismissive reply: 'There are only a few homeless women, aren't there?'"

23. The reference to cold as destructive to women's reproduction is conventional folk wisdom in Korean traditional medicine (Kendall 1987).

24. Although it is likely that social activists, such as Reverend Kang, may the state rhetoric for maneuvering around it, nonetheless they both believed and reproduced the regime of truth around the notion of "family breakdown" and rehabilitation. As in liberalism, neoliberalism, in its various forms in sedimented historic contexts, is empowered only when it earns explanatory power from ordinary people as well as experts who believe in these truths of social improvement, especially for preserving heteronormative family morals and norms. I articulate this further in a paper on family independent women (Song, in press).

References Cited

References Cited

Abelmann, Nancy. 2003. *Melodrama of Mobility: Women, Talk, and Class in Contemporary South Korea*. Honolulu: University of Hawai'i Press.

Adachi, Mariko. 2007. "Gurōbaru shihonshugi to saiseisan ryōiki" (Global Capitalism and Spheres of Reproduction). *Gendai Shisō* 35(8): 138–147.

Adams, Vincanne, Kathleen Erwin, and Phuoc V. Le. 2009. "Public Health Works: Blood Donation in Urban China." *Social Science and Medicine* 68(3): 410–418.

Administration Magazine. 2007. "BQ, diyiyan jiouyao ying" (BQ, Win on First Sight). Retrieved on May 24, 2007, from www.books.com.tw/magazine/item/management/index0203.htm.

Ahern, Emily M. 1973. *The Cult of the Dead in a Chinese Village*. Stanford, CA: Stanford University Press.

Allison, Anne. 2006. "The Japan Fad in Global Youth Culture and Millennial Capitalism." *Mechademia* 1: 11–21.

———. 2009. "The Cool Brand, Affective Activism and Japanese Youth." *Theory, Culture & Society* 26(2–3): 89–111.

Anagnost, Ann. 1997. *National Past-Times: Narrative, Representation, and Power in Modern China*. Durham, NC: Duke University Press.

———. 2000. "Scenes of Misrecognition: Maternal Citizenship in the Age of Transnational Adoption." *positions: east asia cultures critique* 8(2): 390–421.

———. 2004. "The Corporeal Politics of Quality (*Suzhi*)." *Public Culture* 16(2): 189–208.

———. 2006. "Strange Circulations: The Blood Economy in Rural China." *Economy and Society* 35(4): 509–529.

———. 2008a . "From 'Class' to 'Social Strata': Grasping the Social Totality in Reform-Era China." Special Issue on "Developmental and Cultural Nationalisms." *Third World Quarterly* 29(3): 497–519.

———. 2008b. "Imagining Global Futures in China: The Child as a Sign of Value." In *Figuring the Future: Globalization and the Temporalities of Children and Youth*. Jennifer Cole and Deborah Durham, eds. Santa Fe, NM: School for Advanced Research Press.

———. n.d. *Embodiments of Value in China's Reform.* Unpublished book manuscript.

Anderson, Benedict. 1998. *The Spectre of Comparisons: Nationalism, Southeast Asia, and the World.* London and New York: Verso.

———. 2006. *Imagined Communities: Reflections on the Origin and Spread of Nationalism.* New York: Verso.

Anderson, Marston. 1990. *The Limits of Realism: Chinese Fiction in the Revolutionary Period.* Berkeley: University of California Press.

Andrews, Julia F. 1994. *Painters and Politics in the People's Republic of China, 1949–1979.* Berkeley: University of California Press.

Anonymous. 2003. *Team Secrets of the Navy Seals: The Elite Military Forces' Leadership Principles for Business.* Kansas City: Andrews McMeel Publishing.

Appadurai, Arjun. 1997. "Consumption, Duration, and History." In *Streams of Cultural Capital: Transnational Cultural Studies,* David Palumbo-Liu and Hans Ulrich Gumbrecht, eds., pp. 23–45. Stanford, CA: Stanford University Press.

Apple, Michael W. 2001. "Comparing Neo-liberal Projects and Inequality in Education." *Comparative Education* 37(4): 409–423.

Arai, Andrea G. 2000. "The 'Wild Child' of 1990s Japan." *South Atlantic Quarterly* 99(4): 841–863.

———. 2003. "Killing Kids: Recession and Survival in 21st Century Japan." *Postcolonial Studies* 6(3): 367–379.

———. 2004. *Recessionary Effects: The Crisis of the Child and the Culture of Reform in Contemporary Japan.* PhD Dissertation. Department of Anthropology. Columbia University.

———. 2005. "The Neoliberal Subject of Lack and Potential: Developing 'the Frontier within' and Creating a Reserve Army of Labor in 21st Century Japan." *Rhizomes: Cultural Studies in Emerging Knowledge* 10 (Spring).

Araki, Takashi. 1998. "Recent Legislative Developments in Equal Employment and Harmonization of Work and Family Life in Japan." *Japan Labor Bulletin.* 37(4): 5–10.

Aronowitz, Stanley. 2004. "Against Schooling: Education and Social Class." *Social Text* 79 [22(2)]: 13–35.

Austin, J. L. 1962. *How to Do Things with Words.* Cambridge, MA: Harvard University Press.

Badiou, Alain. 2003 [1997]. *Saint Paul: The Foundation of Universalism,* Ray Brassier, trans. Stanford, CA: Stanford University Press.

Banta, Martha. 1993. *Taylored Lives: Narrative Productions in the Age of Taylor, Veblen, and Ford.* Chicago: University of Chicago Press.

Barber, Brace E. 2004. *No Excuse Leadership: Lessons from the U.S. Army's Elite Rangers.* Hoboken, NJ: John Wiley & Sons.

Barboza, David. 2005. "The Great Malls of China." *The New York Times,* May 25. Retrieved on July 15, 2007, from www.nytimes.com/packages/khtml/2005/05/24/business/20050525_MALL_AUDIOSS.html.

Barlow, Tani E. 1991. *"Zhizhifenzi* [Chinese Intellectuals] and Power." *Dialectical Anthropology* 16(3–4): 209–232.

———. 2004. *The Question of Women in Chinese Feminism*. Durham, NC: Duke University Press.

Baudrillard, Jean. 2003. "The Violence of the Global." *ctheory.net*. Retrieved on June 15, 2007, from www.ctheory.net/printer.aspx?id=385.

Beck, Ulrich. 1992. *Risk Society: Towards a New Modernity*. London: Sage.

———. 1994. "The Reinvention of Politics: Towards a Theory of Reflexive Modernization." In *Reflexive Modernization: Politics, Tradition and Aesthetics in the Modern Social Order*, Ulrich Beck, Anthony Giddens, and Scott Lash, eds., pp. 1–55. Stanford, CA: Stanford University Press.

Beck, Ulrich, and Elisabeth Beck-Gernsheim. 2002. *Individualization: Institutionalized Individualism and its Social and Political Consequences*. London: Sage.

Becker, Gary S. 1992. "The Economic Way of Looking at Life." Retrieved on July 11, 2007, from www.nobel.se/economics/laureates/1992/becker-lecture.html.

Befu, Harumi, and Sylvie Guichard-Anguis, eds. 2001. *Globalizing Japan: Ethnography of the Japanese Presence in Asia, Europe, and America*. New York: Routledge.

Beijing Chenbao. 2006. "Luyou renshi cheng zhongguo youke nan cihou" (Tourist Industry Professionals Argue That Chinese Tourists Are Difficult). December 27. Retrieved on July 11, 2007, from www.qingdaonews.com/content/2006-12/27/content_7709208.htm.

Berlant, Lauren. 2007. "Slow Death (Sovereignty, Obesity, Lateral Agency)." *Critical Inquiry* 33 (4): 754–780.

Bernard, Mitchell. 1996. "States, Social Forces, and Regions in Historical Time: Toward a Critical Political Economy of Eastern Asia." *Third World Quarterly* 17(4): 649–665.

Blanchot, Maurice. 1987. "Everyday Speech." *Yale French Studies* 73: 12–20.

Boddy, Trevor. 1992. "Underground and Overhead: Building the Analogous City." In *Variations on a Theme Park: The New American City and the End of Public Space*, Michael Sorkin, ed., pp. 123–153. New York: Hill and Wang.

Boltanski, Luc and Eve Chiapello. 2006. *The New Spirit of Capitalism*. New York: Verso Books.

Borgmann, Albert. 1984. *Technology and the Character of Contemporary Life: A Philosophical Inquiry*. Chicago: The University of Chicago Press.

Borovoy, Amy. 2004. "What Color Is Your Parachute? New Middle-Class Subjectivities in the Post-Gakureki Society." A paper presented at the conference "Researching Social Class in Japan," Ann Arbor, Michigan.

Bourdieu, Pierre. 1984. *Distinction: A Social Critique of the Judgment of Taste*, Richard Nice, trans. Cambridge, MA: Harvard University Press.

Bramall, Chris. 2009. *Chinese Economic Development*. London: Routledge.

Bray, David. 2005. *Social Space and Governance in Urban China: The Danwei System from Origins to Reform*. Stanford, CA: Stanford University Press.

Brinton, Mary C. 1993. *Women and the Economic Miracle: Gender and Work in Post-war Japan.* Berkeley: University of California Press.

Broadbent, Kaye. 2002. *Women's Employment in Japan: The Experiences of Part-time Workers.* London: Curzon Press.

Brooks, Peter. 1976. *The Melodramatic Imagination: Balzac, Henry James, Melodrama, and the Mode of Excess.* New Haven, CT: Yale University Press.

———. 1994. "Melodrama, Body, Revolution." In *Melodrama: Stage, Picture, Screen,* Jacky Bratton, Jim Cook, and Christine Gledhill, eds., pp. 11–24. London: British Film Institute.

Bryman, Alan. 2004. *The Disneyization of Society.* London: Sage.

Burchell, Graham. 1996. "Liberal Government and Techniques of the Self." In *Foucault and Political Reason: Liberalism, Neo-Liberalism, and Rationalities of Government,* Andrew Barry, Thomas Osborne, and Nikolas Rose, eds., pp. 19–36. Chicago: University of Chicago Press.

Butler, Judith P. 1997. *Excitable Speech: A Politics of the Performative.* New York: Routledge.

Cassegard, Carl. 2008. "From Withdrawal to Resistance. The Rhetoric of Exit in Yoshimoto Takaaki and Karatani Kojin." *Japan Focus* (March), 4. Retrieved on April 10, 2010, from www.japanfocus.org/-Carl-Cassegard/2684.

Cave, Peter. 2001. "Educational reform in Japan in the 1990s: 'Individuality' and Other Uncertainties." *Comparative Education* 37(2): 173–191.

CCTV. 2007. "Chengdu shi sui baixuebing nühai zizuo "shengming juechang" [Chengdu 10-year-old Leukemia Girl Self-composes "Life Swan Song"]. Retrieved on December 26, 2007, from http://finance.cctv.com/special/C19961/20071127/107110.shtml.

Chang, Yu-Min, Ying-Chieh Chen, and Wen-Chung Huang. 2005. "Transformation and Development of Higher Technological Education in Taiwan." Paper presented at the conference, Exploring Innovation in Education and Research, Tainan, Taiwan, March 1–5.

Chaoyang Times. 2006. "Xiaozhang dui ni Say Hello: benxiao tuixing limao yundong chengguo feiran" (The President Says Hello: The University Promotes a Successful Courtesy Campaign). *Chaoyang Times,* October 23.

Chaoyang University of Technology Accounting Department. n.d. "Chaoyang keji daxue shouzhi yuchu biao" (Balance of Payment Surplus of Chaoyang University of Technology). Retrieved on May 24, 2007, from www.cyut.edu.tw/~account.

Cheah, Pheng. 1999. "Grounds of Comparison." *Diacritics* 29(4): 1–18.

Chen Chao. 2004. "China's Charities & Philanthropists." Retrieved on July 11, 2007, from www.china.org.cn/english/2004/Apr/94150.htm.

Chen, Kuan-Hsing. 2010. *Asia as Method: Toward Deimperialization.* Durham, NC: Duke University Press.

Cheng, Chao-chi. 2001. "2001 Nian guonei ge daxue lunwen fabiao SCI/SSCI/Ei ziliaoku paihangbang" (2001 Data Base Rank of SCI/SSCI/Ei Papers Published in Taiwanese Universities). *Chung Yuan University Journal* 126 (May).

Cheng, Hsiou-chuan. 2002. "Taiwanren de Dongjing Guanguang [Taiwanese Sightseeing in Tokyo]." *Cultural Studies Monthly*; retrieved in September 2005 from www.ncu.edu.tw/~eng/csa/journal/journal_14.htm.

"China's Gifted 'Superchildren' on a Fast Track to Success." September 27, 2006. *Asahi Shimbun* (English edition).

Chinese Academy of Social Sciences (CASS). 2002. *Dangdai zhongguo shehui jieceng yanjiu baogao* (The Report on Social Stratification Research in Contemporary China). Lu Xueyi, editor in chief. Beijing: Shehui Kexue Wenxian Chubanshe.

Ching, Leo T. S. 2000. "Globalizing the Regional, Regionalizing the Global: Mass Culture and Asianism in the Age of Late Capital." *Public Culture* 12(1): 233–257.

———. 2001. *Becoming Japanese: Colonial Taiwan and the Politics of Identity Formation*. Berkeley: University of California Press.

Chiou, Shwu-Wen, ed. 2003. *Japanese Popular Culture in Taiwan and Asia II*. Theme issue, *Envisage: A Journal Book of Chinese Media Studies* (2).

Cho, Younghan. 2008. "The National Crisis and De/Reconstructing Nationalism in South Korea during the IMF Intervention." *Inter-Asia Cultural Studies* 9(1): 82–96.

Chomsky, Noam. 1998. "Free Trade and Free Market: Pretense and Practice." In *The Cultures of Globalization*, Fredric Jameson and Masao Miyoshi, eds., pp. 356–370. Durham, NC: Duke University Press.

Chu, Jou-jou. 2001. *Taiwan at the End of the 20th Century: The Gains and Losses*. Taipei: Tonsan.

Chua, Beng Huat. 2004. "Conceptualizing an East Asian Popular Culture." *Inter-Asia Cultural Studies* 5(2): 200–221.

Chuang, Ya-Chung. 2005. "Place, Identity, and Social Movements: *Shequ* and Neighborhood Organizing in Taipei City." *positions: east asia cultures critique* 13 (2): 379–410.

Chun, Allen. 2000. "From Text to Context: How Anthropology Makes Its Subject." *Cultural Anthropology* 15(4): 570–595.

———. 2007. "Ethnography in the Anthropology of the Unreal." Conference paper presented at The Future of Ethnographic Practices, National Chinan University, June 2.

Chung, Shun-wen. 2004. *An In-Depth Guide to Twenty-Four Hours of Kaohsiung*. Kaohsiung: The Information Office.

Cohen, Lizabeth. 2006. "The Consumers' Republic: An American Model for the World?" In *The Ambivalent Consumer: Questioning Consumption in East Asia and the West*, Sheldon Garon and Patricia L. Maclachlan, eds., pp. 44–62. Ithaca, NY: Cornell University Press.

Comaroff, Jean, and John Comaroff. 2000. "Millennial Capitalism: First Thoughts on a Second Coming." *Public Culture* 12(2): 291–343.

Communiqué of the Sixth Plenum of the 16th CPC Central Committee. 2006. Retrieved on April 16, 2010, from www.chinese-embassy.org.uk/eng//zyxw/t279526.htm.

Corporate Synergy Development Center (CSDC). 1998. *Xinkujiang Shangdianjie Kaifa Tuidong Jihua* [The Development Plan for New Kujiang Shopping Streets]. Taipei: Department of Commerce.

———. 2000. *2000 Shangquan Anliji* [Examples of Business Cluster, 2000]. Taipei: Department of Commerce.

———. 2001. *2001 Shangquan Anliji* [Examples of Business Clusters, 2001]. Taipei: Department of Commerce.

Council for Economic Planning and Development (CEPD). n.d. *Changzao Chengxiang Xinfengmao Xingdong Fang'an* [Creating New Appearances for Urban and Rural Areas]; retrieved in September 2005 from www.cepd.gov.tw/land/town/creative/creative.htm.

Crawford, Margaret. 1992. "The World in a Shopping Mall." In *Variations on a Theme Park: The New American City and the End of Public Space*, M. Sorkin, ed., pp. 3–30. New York: Hill and Wang.

Creighton, Millie R. 1996. "Marriage, Motherhood, and Career Management in a Japanese Counter Culture." In *Re-Imaging Japanese Women*, Ann E. Imamura, ed., pp. 192–220. Berkeley: University of California Press.

Cruikshank, Barbara. 1996. "Revolutions Within: Self-Government and Self-Esteem." In *Foucault and Political Reason: Liberalism, Neo-liberalism and Rationalities of Government*, Andrew Barry, Thomas Osborne, and Nikolas Rose, eds., pp. 231–252. Chicago: Chicago University Press.

———. 1999. *The Will to Empower: Democratic Citizens and Other Subjects*. Ithaca, NY: Cornell University Press.

Crystal, David. 2003. *English as a Global Language*, second edition. Cambridge, UK: Cambridge University Press.

Cumings, Bruce. 1997. *Korea's Place in the Sun: A Modern History*. New York: W. W. Norton.

Davis, Deborah S., ed. 2000. *The Consumer Revolution in Urban China*. Berkeley: University of California Press.

———. 2005. "Urban Consumer Culture." *The China Quarterly* 183 (Sept.): 692–709.

Davis, Mike. 2011. "The Coming Economic Disaster." Retrieved on July 22, 2011, from www.tomdispatch.com/blog/175422/tomgram%3A_mike_davis,_the_coming_economic_disaster/.

Dean, Mitchell. 1999. *Governmentality: Power and Rule in Modern Society*. London: Sage Publications.

de Certeau, Michel. 1984 [1980]. *The Practice of Everyday Life*. Berkeley: University of California Press.

de Certeau, Michel, Luce Giard, and Pierre Mayol. 1998. *The Practice of Everyday Life: Vol. 2: Living and Cooking*. Minneapolis: University of Minnesota Press.

Debord, Guy. 1994. *The Society of the Spectacle*. New York: Zone Books.

Deng, Xiaoping. 1984. "Building a Socialism with a Specifically Chinese Character." Speech, June 30; retrieved on April 16, 2010, from http://english.peopledaily.com.cn/dengxp/vol3/text/c1220.html.

Derrida, Jacques. 1974. "White Mythology: Metaphor in the Text of Philosophy." *New Literary History* 6(1): 7–74.

Dohse, Knuth, Ulrich Jürgens, and Thomas Nialsch. 1985. "From 'Fordism' to 'Toyotism'? The Social Organization of the Labor Process in the Japanese Automobile Industry." *Politics & Society* 14(2): 115–146.

Donnithorne, Larry R. 1993. *The West Point Way of Leadership: From Learning Principled Leadership to Practicing It*. New York: Doubleday.

Donovan, Michael G. 2008. "Informal Cities and the Contestation of Public Space: The Case of Bogota's Street Vendors, 1988–2003." *Urban Studies* 45(1): 29–51.

Donzelot, Jacques. 1991. "Pleasure in Work." In *Foucault Effect: Studies in Governmentality*, Graham Burchell, Colin Gordon, and Peter Miller, eds., pp. 251–280. Chicago: University of Chicago Press.

Driscoll, Mark. 2007. "Debt and Denunciation in Post-Bubble Japan: The Two Freeters." *Cultural Critique* 65: 164–187.

Du Gay, Paul. 1996. *Consumption and Identity at Work*. London: Sage.

Dutton, Michael. 1998. *Streetlife China*. Cambridge, UK: Cambridge University Press.

Dyer-Witheford, Nick. 2002. "Global Body, Global Brain/Global Factory, Global War: Revolt of the Value Subjects." *The Commoner* 3: 1–30. Retrieved on July 29, 2011, from www.commoner.org.uk/index.php?p=6.

Edwards, Linda N. 1994. "The Status of Women in Japan: Has the Equal Employment Opportunity Law Made a Difference?" *Journal of Asian Economics* 5(2): 217–240.

Ehrenreich, Barbara. 2001. *Nickel and Dimed: On Not Getting by in America*. New York: Metropolitan Books.

Erwin, Kathleen. 2006. "The Circulatory System: Blood Procurement, AIDS, and the Social Body in China." *Medical Anthropology Quarterly* 20(2): 139–159.

Ewen, Stuart. 1988. *All Consuming Images: The Politics of Style in Contemporary Culture*. New York: Basic Books.

"Ex-Science Council Deputy Minister Indicted for Graft." 2006. *Taipei Times*, December 27, p. 1.

Fan Yutao. 2003. "Why MAWP Becomes the Base for Cultivating CEOs of Large Enterprises," *Beijing jixie gongye xueyuan xuebao* (The Journal of Beijing Institute of Machinery). 18(10): 76–82.

Farquhar, Judith. 1999. "Technologies of Everyday Life: The Economy of Impotence in Reform China." *Cultural Anthropology* 14(2): 155–179.

Farquhar, Judith, and Qicheng Zhang. 2005. "Biopolitical Beijing: Pleasure, Sovereignty, and Self-Cultivation in China's Capital." *Cultural Anthropology* 20(3): 303–327.

Feher, Michel. 2009. "Self-Appreciation; or, The Aspirations of Human Capital." *Public Culture* 21(1): 21–41.

Ferguson, James, and Akhil Gupta. 2002. "Spatializing States: Toward an Ethnography of Neoliberal Governmentality." *American Ethnologist* 29(4): 981–1002.

Feuchtwang, Stephan. 1974. "Domestic and Communal Worship in Taiwan." In *Religion and Ritual in Chinese Society*, Arthur Wolf, ed. Stanford, CA: Stanford University Press.

Field, Norma. 1993. *In the Realm of the Dying Emperor.* New York: Vintage Books.

Fong, Vanessa. 2004. "Filial Nationalism among Chinese Teenagers with Global Identities." *American Ethnologist* 31(4): 631–648.

Foucault, Michel. 1976. *Power/Knowledge: Selected Interviews and Other Writings,* Colin Gordon, ed. New York: Pantheon.

———. 1978. *The History of Sexuality.* New York: Random House.

———. 1983. "The Subject and Power." In *Michel Foucault: Beyond Structuralism and Hermeneutics*, Hubert L. Dreyfus and Paul Rabinow, eds., 208–226. Chicago: University of Chicago Press.

———. 1988. *Technologies of the Self: A Seminar with Michel Foucault,* Luther H. Martin, Huck Gutman, and Patrick H. Hutton, eds. Amherst: University of Massachusetts Press.

———. 1991. "Governmentality." In *Foucault Effect: Studies in Govermentality.* Graham Burchell, Colin Gordon, and Peter Miller, eds., pp. 87–104. Chicago: The University of Chicago Press.

———. 1995[1977]. *Discipline and Punish.* New York: Vintage Books.

———. 2008. *The Birth of Biopolitics: Lectures at the College de France, 1978–1979.* New York: Palgrave Macmillan.

Frank, André Gunder. 2004. "Paper Tiger—The United States and the World. Centre for Research on Globalisation." Retrieved on June 12, 2007, from www .globalresearch.ca/articles/FRA406A.html.

Freedman, Lucy. n.d. "Professional Coaches: What's Your BQ (Behavior Quotient)? Behavioral Skills for You and Your Clients." Retrieved on May 24, 2007, from www.coachuniverse.com/articles/behaviorskills.htm.

Friedman, Milton. 1998. "The Hong Kong Experiment." *Hoover Digest*, No. 3. Retrieved on October 10, 2006, from: www.hoover.org/publications/digest/ 3532186.html.

Fujita, Hidenori. 2000. "Education Reform and Education Politics in Japan," *The American Sociologist* 31(3): 42–57.

Fujitani, Takashi. 1993. "Inventing, Forgetting, Remembering: Toward a Historical Ethnography of the Nation-State." In *Cultural Nationalism in East Asia.* Harumi Befu, ed. Berkeley: University of California Press.

Gao Yaojie. 2005. *Zhongguo Aizibing Diaocha* [The Investigation of AIDS in China]. Guilin: Guangxi Normal University Press.

Gardner, Howard. 1983. *Frames of Mind: The Theory of Multiple Intelligences*. New York: Basic Books.

Gee, James Paul. 1999. "New People in New Worlds: Networks, the New Capitalism and Schools." In *Multiliteracies: Literacy Learning and the Design of Social Futures*, Bill Cope and Mary Kalantzis, eds., pp. 43–68. London: Routledge.

Gelb, Joyce. 2000. "The Equal Employment Opportunity Law: A Decade of Change for Japanese Women?" *Law and Policy* 22(3&4): 385–407.

Genda, Yūji. 2005. *A Nagging Sense of Job Insecurity: The New Reality Facing Japanese Youth*. Tokyo: International House of Japan.

Gladney, Dru. 1991. *Muslim Chinese: Ethnic Nationalism in the People's Republic*. Cambridge, MA: Council on East Asian Studies, Harvard University.

Gold, Thomas B. 1986. *State and Society in the Taiwan Miracle*. London: M. E. Sharpe.

Goldberg, Carey. 2006. "Harvard's Crowded Course to Happiness: 'Positive Psychology' Draws Students in Droves." *The Boston Globe*. Retrieved on May 31, 2007, from www.boston.com/news/local/articles/2006/03/10/harvards_crowded_course_to_happiness/.

Goleman, Daniel. 1996. *Emotional Intelligence: Why It Can Matter More than IQ*. London: Bloomsbury.

Gordon, Avery. 1995. "The Work of Corporate Culture." *Social Text* 13(3): 3–30.

———. 1997. *Ghostly Matters: Haunting and the Sociological Imagination*. Minneapolis: University of Minnesota Press.

Gordon, Colin. 1991. "Governmental Rationality: An Introduction." In *The Foucault Effect: Studies in Governmentality*, Graham Burchell, Colin Gordon, and Peter Miller, eds., 1–52. London: Harvester Wheatsheaf.

Green, Francis, Donna James, David Ashton, and Johnny Sung. 1999. "Post-school Education and Training Policy in Developmental States: The Cases of Taiwan and South Korea." *Journal of Education Policy* 14(3): 301–315.

Greenhalgh, Susan. 2005. "Globalization and Population Governance in China." In *Global Assemblages: Technology, Politics, and Ethics as Anthropological Problems*, Aihwa Ong and Stephen J. Collier, eds. Malden, MA: Blackwell.

Greenhalgh, Susan, and Edwin A. Winckler. 2005. *Governing China's Population: From Leninist to Neoliberal Biopolitics*. Stanford, CA: Stanford University Press.

Gu, Edward X. 2001. "Who was Mr. Democracy? The May Fourth Discourse of Populist Democracy and the Radicalization of Chinese Intellectuals (1915–1922)." *Modern Asian Studies* 35(3): 589–621.

Gu Haiyan. 2001. "The Discourse of Humanism and the Theory of Subjectivity (Renwen zhuyi huayu he zhutixing lilun)." In *Ershi shiji de zhongguo: xueshu yu shehui [wenxue juan]* (Twentieth-Century China: Scholarship and Society (Literature), Han Yuhai, ed., pp. 381–437. Jinan: Shangdong renmin chubanshe.

Habermas, Jürgen. 1979. "What Is Universal Pragmatics?" In *Communication and the Evolution of Society*, Thomas McCarthy, trans., pp. 1–68. Boston: Beacon Press.

———. 1989. *The Structural Transformation of the Public Sphere: An Inquiry into a Category of Bourgeois Society.* Cambridge, MA: MIT Press.

Haggard, Stephan, Daniel Pinkston, and Jungkun Seo. 1999. "Reforming Korea Inc.: The Politics of Structural Adjustment under Kim Dae Jung." *Asian Perspective* 23(3): 201–235.

Hall, Stuart. 1984. "The State in Question." In *The Idea of the Modern State*, Gregor McLennan, David Held, and Stuart Hall, eds., pp.1–28. Milton Keynes, UK: Open University Press.

———. 1988. "Brave New World." *Marxism Today.* (October): 24–29.

———. 1996. "The West and the Rest: Discourse and Power." In *Modernity: An Introduction to Modern Societies*, Stuart Hall, David Held, Hubert Don, and Kenneth Thompson, eds., pp. 184–224. Cambridge, UK: Blackwell.

The Hankook-Ilbo. 2004. "Significance of U.S. Educational Institutions' Entry into Korea." *Korea Focus* 12(3): 57–59. (Originally *The Hankook Ilbo*, May 1.)

Hara Ippei. 1992. *Tuixiao zhi shen Yuan Yi Ping* (The God of Salesmanship Hara Ippei), Hu Dongliang and Hu Yanhong, trans. Beijing: Zhongguo jingji chubanshe.

Hardt, Michael. 1999. "Affective Labor." *Boundary* 2 26(2): 89–100.

Hardt, Michael, and Antonio Negri. 2004. *Multitude: War and Democracy in the Age of Empire.* New York: Penguin.

Harootunian, Harry. 2004. *The Empire's New Clothes: Paradigm Lost, and Regained.* Chicago: Prickly Paradigm Press.

Harrell, Stevan. 1995. "Introduction: Civilizing Projects and the Reaction to Them." In *Cultural Encounters on China's Ethnic Frontiers*, Stevan Harrell, ed., pp. 3–36. Seattle: University of Washington Press.

Harrison, Bernard. 1999. "'White Mythology' Revisited: Derrida and His Critics on Reason and Rhetoric." *Critical Inquiry* 25(3): 505–534.

Harrison, Graham. 2006. "Neoliberalism and Persistence of Clientelism in Africa." In *The Neo-Liberal Revolution: Forging the Market State*, pp. 98–113. New York: Palgrave Macmillan.

Harvey, David. 1989. "From Managerialism to Entrepreneurialism: The Transformation in Urban Governance in Late Capitalism." *Geografiska Annaler. Series B, Human Geography* 71 (1): 3–17.

———. 1990. *The Condition of Postmodernity: An Enquiry into the Origins of Cultural Change.* Cambridge, MA, and Oxford, UK: Blackwell.

———. 2000. *Spaces of Hope.* Berkeley: University of California Press.

———. 2003. *The New Imperialism.* Oxford, UK: Oxford University Press.

———. 2005. *A Brief History of Neoliberalism.* Oxford, UK: Oxford University Press.

———. 2006. "Neo-Liberalism and the Restoration of Class Power." In *Spaces of Global Capitalism*, pp. 1–62. London: Verso.

Havel, Václav. 1992. "Stories and Totalitarianism." In *Open Letters: Selected Writings 1965–1990*, pp. 328–350. New York: Vintage Books.

He, Qinglian. 2003. "A Listing Social Structure." In *One China, Many Paths*, Chaohua Wang, ed., pp. 163–188. London: Verso.

Hein, Laura. 1993. "Growth Versus Success: Japan's Economic Policy in Historical Perspective." In *Postwar Japan as History*, Andrew Gordon, ed., pp. 99–122. Berkeley: University of California Press.

Hindess, Barry. 2004. "Liberalism: What's in a Name?" In *Global Governmentality: Governing International Spaces*, Wendy Larner and William Walters eds., pp. 23–39. London: Routledge.

Hochschild, Arlie. 1983. *The Managed Heart: Commercialization of Human Feeling.* Berkeley: University of California Press.

Hoffman, Lisa. 2006. "Autonomous Choices and Patriotic Professionalism: On Governmentality in Late-Socialist China." *Economy and Society* 35(4): 550–570.

Hoffman, Lisa, Monica DeHart, and Stephen J. Collier. 2006. "Notes on the Anthropology of Neoliberalism." *Anthropology News* (September): 9–10.

Homeless Rehabilitation Center. 1999. *The Homeless Rehabilitation Center Report.* Seoul: The Homeless Rehabilitation Center.

Hood, Christopher P. 2001. *Japanese Education Reform: Nakasone's Legacy.* New York: Routledge.

Horio, Teruhisa. 1988. *Educational Thought and Ideology in Modern Japan.* Tokyo: University of Tokyo Press.

Hsu, Ying-chie, and Yang Cheng-hsueh. 2001. "An Empirical Examination of Marketing and Service Quality of Business Community Building in Taiwan." National Science Council Project Report, NSC 89-2626-H-327-007. Taipei: National Science Council, Taiwan.

Hu, Angang. 2003. "Equity and Efficiency." In *One China, Many Paths*, Chaohua Wang, ed., pp. 219–233. London: Verso.

Huang, Wu-dar, Hideakira Ogawa, Tokutoshi Torii, and Akira Naito. 1992. "A Reconstructive Study on Urban Structure of Kaohsiung During the Japanese Rule Period," *Journal of Architecture, A.I.R.O.C.* 33: 21–35.

Humanistic Education Foundation. 2007. "Caituanfaren renben jiaoyu wenjiao jijinghui" (The Humanistic Education Foundation). Retrieved on June 15, 2007, from http://hef.yam.org.tw/index01.htm.

Igarashi, Yoshikuni. 2002. "The Unfinished Business of Mourning: Maruyama Masao and Postwar Japan's Struggles with the Wartime Past." *positions: east asia cultures critique* 10(1): 195–218.

Iida, Yumiko. 2000. "Between the Technique of Living an Endless Routine and the Madness of Absolute Degree Zero: Japanese Identity and the Crisis of Modernity in the 1990s." *positions: east asia cultures critique* 8(2): 423–464.

Ito, Ken K. 2008. *An Age of Melodrama: Family, Gender, and Social Hierarchy in the Turn-of-the-Century Japanese Novel.* Stanford, CA: Stanford University Press.

Itoh, Makoto. 2005. "Assessing Neoliberalism in Japan." In *Neoliberalism: A Critical Reader*, Alfredo Saad-Filho and Deborah Johnston, eds., pp. 244–250. Ann Arbor, MI: Pluto Press.

Ivy, Marilyn. 2000. "Revenge and Recapitation in Recessionary Japan." *South Atlantic Quarterly* 99(4): 819–840.

———. 2006. "Revenge and Recapitation in Recessionary Japan." In *Millennial Japan: Rethinking the Nation in an Age of Recession*, Tomiko Yoda and Harry Harootunian, eds., pp. 195–215. Durham, NC: Duke University Press.

Iwabuchi, Koichi. 2002. "Becoming Cultural Proximate: Japanese TV Dramas in Taiwan." In *Recentering Globalization: Popular Culture and Japanese Transnationalism*, Koichi Iwabuchi, ed., pp. 121–157. Durham, NC: Duke University Press.

———., ed. 2004. *Feeling Asian Modernities: Transnational Consumption of Japanese TV Dramas*. Hong Kong: Hong Kong University Press.

Janelli, Roger L. 1993. *Making Capitalism: The Social and Cultural Construction of a South Korean Conglomerate*. Stanford, CA: Stanford University.

Japanese Ministry of Education and Technology. 2006. "Kyouiku Kihonhou Hoan Nitsuite." (About the Fundamental Law of Education Bill). Tokyo: Japanese Ministry of Education and Technology Publicity.

"Jiang Zemin zai Guangdong kaocha gongzuo qiangdiao, jinmi jiehe xin de lishi tiaojian jiaqiang dang de jianshe, shizhong dailing quanguo renmin cujin shengchanli de fazhan" (During His Investigation in Guangdong, Jiang Zemin Emphasized a Close Integration of the New Historical Condition into the Strengthening of the Party's Construction to Lead the Chinese People to Promote the Development of the Productive Forces from Beginning to End). *Renmin Ribao*, February 26, 2000, p. 1. Retrieved on June 16, 2012, from www.people.com.cn/GB/channel7/35/20000428/52747.html.

Johnson, Chalmers. 2006. *Nemesis*. New York: Metropolitan Books.

Judd, Dennis, and Susan Fainstein, eds. 1999. *The Tourist City*. New Haven, CT: Yale University Press.

Kahn, Joseph. 2004. "China's Elite Learn to Flaunt It While the New Landless Weep." *The New York Times*, December 25. Retrieved in December 2004 from www.nytimes.com/2004/12/25/international/asia/25china.html.

Kao, T. C. 2003. "Promoting 'Holistic' Education in a Fast Changing World." Paper presented at the Twenty-Fifth PAPE (Pan-Pacific Association of Private School Education) Congress, Bangkok, Thailand, November 15.

Katz, Richard. 1998. *Japan, the System That Soured: The Rise and Fall of the Japanese Economic Miracle*. New York: M. E. Sharpe.

Kawai, Hayao. 2000. *Nihon no Furonteia wa, Nihon no Naka ni Aru* (Japan's Frontier Is Within Japan). Tokyo: Kodansha.

Kawakami, Ryouichi. 1995. *Kodomo ga Hen da!* (The Child Is Turning Strange!). Second edition. Tokyo: Bessatsu Takarajima.

———. 1999. *Gakkou Houkai* (School Collapse). Tokyo: Iwanami Press.

Kendall, Laurel. 1987. "Cold Wombs in Balmy Honolulu: Ethnogynecology among Korean Immigrants." *Social Science and Medicine* 25(4): 367–376.

Kerr, George H. 1965. *Formosa Betrayed*. Boston: Houghton Mifflin.

REFERENCES CITED *289*

Kim, Eun Mee. 1997. *Big Business, Strong State: Collusion and Conflict in South Korean Development, 1960–1990*. Albany: State University of New York Press.

Kim, Hyun Mee. 2000. "Modernity and Women's Labor Rights in South Korea" (Han'guk ŭi kŭndaesŏng kwa yŏsŏng ŭi nodongkwŏn). *Journal of Korean Women's Studies* 16(1): 37–64.

Kim, Seung Kyung. 1997. *Class Struggle or Family Struggle? The Lives of Women Factory Workers in South Korea*. Cambridge, UK: Cambridge University Press.

Kim, Seung Kyung, and John Finch. 2002. "Living with Rhetoric, Living against Rhetoric: Korean Families and the IMF Economic Crisis." *Korean Studies* 26(1): 120–139.

Kim, Yi Eunhee. 1998. "Home Is a Place to Rest: Constructing the Meaning of Work, Family and Gender in the Korean Middle Class." *Korean Journal* 38(2): 168–213.

Kim Young-Chol. 2003. *A Study of the System of Special Purposed High School (T'ŭksu Mokchŏk Kodŭnghakkyo Ch'eje Yŏnku)*. Seoul: Korean Educational Development Institute.

King, Samantha. 2006. *Pink Ribbons, Inc.: Breast Cancer and the Politics of Philanthropy*. Minneapolis: University of Minnesota Press.

Kingfisher, Catherine. 2002. "Neoliberalism I: Discourses of Personhood and Welfare Reform." In *Western Welfare in Decline: Globalization and Women's Poverty*, Catherine Kingfisher, ed., pp. 13–31. Philadelphia: University of Pennsylvania Press.

Klare, Karl E. 1978. "Judicial Deradicalization of the Wagner Act and the Origins of Modern Legal Consciousness, 1937–1941." *Minnesota Law Review* 62: 265–339.

Knapp, Ronald G. 2007. "The Shaping of Taiwan's Landscapes." In *Taiwan: A New History*. Murray A. Rubinstein, ed., pp. 3–26. Armonk, NY: M. E. Sharpe/East Gate.

Kohrman, Matthew. 2003. "Authorizing a Disability Agency in Post-Mao China: Deng Pufang's Story as Biomythography." *Cultural Anthropology* 18(1): 99–131.

Komatsu, Katsuhiko, et al. 2000. *Odoru! Oshigoto Dorama*. [Odoru! Workplace Dramas]. Tokyo: Dobun Shoin.

Kong, Chi-Yŏng. 1997. "Human Decency." In *Wayfarer: New Fiction by Korean Women*, Bruce Fulton and Ju-Chan Fulton, eds. and trans., pp. 42–78. Seattle: Women in Translation.

Koo, Hagen. 2001. *Korean Workers: The Culture and Politics of Class Formation*. Ithaca, NY: Cornell University Press.

———. 2006. "Globalization and Middle-Class Culture in Korea." Critical Korean Studies Workshop, Toronto, University of Toronto. November 10.

Koschmann, Victor. 2003. "Modernization and Democratic Values: The 'Japanese Model' in the 1960s." In *Staging Growth: Modernization, Development, and the Global Cold War*, David C. Engerman, Nils Gilman, Mark H. Haefele, and Michael E. Latham, eds., 225–250. Amherst: University of Massachusetts Press.

Lafer, Gordon. 2007. "Neoliberalism by Other Means: The 'War on Terror' at Home and Abroad." Worksite: Issues in Workplace Relations, available at www.econ.usyd.edu.au/wos/worksite/lafer.html.

Lam, Alice C. L. 1992. *Women and Japanese Management: Discrimination and Reform.* New York: Routledge.

Lamley, Harry J. 2007. "Taiwan under Japanese Rule, 1895–1945: The Vicissitudes of Colonialism." In *Taiwan: A New History.* Murray A. Rubinstein, ed., pp. 201–260. Armonk, NY: M. E. Sharpe/East Gate.

Lao Tian. 2004. *"Biao jiao 'xiao baomu' he 'daxuesheng' de renzhi"* (Compare cognition of university students and migrant domestic workers). Retrieved on June 26, 2007, from www.wyzxsx.com/xuezhe/laotian/printpage.asp?ArticleID=158.

Lash, Scott. 2003. "Reflexivity as Non-Linearity." *Theory, Culture & Society* 20(2): 49–57.

Laws and Regulation Database of The Republic of China. 2002. "Caituanfaren sili xuexiao xingxue jijinghui zuzhi ji yunzuo banfa" (Private School Foundation Organization and Operating Regulations). Retrieved on April 19, 2006, from http://law.moj.gov.tw/Scripts/PQuery4A.asp?FullDoc=all&Fcode=H0020049.

Lee, Chong-chae. 1998. "An Analysis of the Debate on the Relative Evaluation System of the High School Grades for Special Purposed High Schools" (T'ŭksu Mokchŏk Kodŭnghakkyo Pigyo Naeshinje ŭi Chaengchŏm Punsŏk). In *Review of Korean Education 1997 (Han'guk Kyoyuk P'yŏngron 1997)*, Korean Educational Development Institute, ed., pp. 201–219. Seoul: Kyoyuk-Kwahak-sa.

Lee, Deok-nyung. 2004. "Dreaming about a Revolution in Education." *Korea Focus* 12(1): 39–41. (Originally published in *The JoongAng Ilbo*, April 10, 2004)

Lee, Jiyoung, dir. 2003. *Friend or Foe.* Documentary film.

Lee, Joohee. 2004. "Taking Gender Seriously: Feminization of Nonstandard Work in Korea and Japan." *Asian Journal of Women's Studies* 10(1): 25–49.

Lee, Ju-Ho. 2004. "The School Equalization Policy of Korea: Past Failures and Proposed Measure for Reform." *Korea Journal* 44(1): 221–234.

Lee, Namhee. 2007. *The Making of Minjung: Democracy and the Politics of Representation in South Korea.* Ithaca, NY: Cornell University Press.

Lee, Tain-Dow, ed. 2002. *Japanese Popular Culture in Taiwan and Asia I.* Theme issue, *Envisage: A Journal Book of Chinese Media Studies* (1).

Leehey, Jennifer. 2010. "Open Secrets, Hidden Meanings: Censorship, Esoteric Power and Contested Authority in Urban Burma in the 1990s." PhD dissertation, Department of Anthropology, University of Washington.

Leibowitz, Adam, and David McNeil. 2007. "Hammering Down the Educational Nail: Abe Revises the Fundamental Law of Education." *Japan Focus*, July 9; available at www.japanfocus.org/-Adam-Lebowitz/2468.

Lemke, Thomas. 2001. "'The Birth of Bio-Politics': Michel Foucault's Lecture at the College de France on Neo-Liberal Governmentality." *Economy and Society* 30(2): 190–207.

———. 2002. "Foucault, Governmentality, and Critique." *Rethinking Marxism* 14 (3): 49–64.

"Let the Market Sort Talent Out." 2004. *Beijing Review* 47(13) [April 1]: 5.

Li, Changping. 2003. "The Crisis in the Countryside." In *One China, Many Paths*, Chaohua Wang, ed., pp. 198–218. London: Verso.

Li Dun. 2004. *HIV/AIDS in China: A Legal Assessment and a Factual Analysis*. Beijing: Social Sciences Documentation Publishing House.

Liao, Han-Teng. 2006. "Towards Creative Da-tong: An Alternative Notion of Creative Industries for China." *International Journal of Cultural Studies* 9(3): 395–406.

Liu, Lydia He. 1995. *Translingual Practice: Literature, National Culture, and Translated Modernity in China, 1900–1937*. Stanford, CA: Stanford University Press.

Liu, Sophia, and Yilin Ho. 2004. "Fall in Love with Kaohsiung." *Unity* November/December 2004: 38–39.

Low, Setha. 1996. "Spatializing Culture: The Social Production and Social Construction of Public Space in Costa Rica." *American Ethnologist* 23(4): 861–879.

Low, Setha, and Denise Lawrence-Zuniga. 2006. "Locating Culture." In *The Anthropology of Space and Place: Locating Culture*, S. Low and D. Lawrence-Zuniga, eds., pp. 1–47. Cambridge, MA: Blackwell.

Lu, Hsin-yi. 2002. *The Politics of Locality: Making a Nation of Communities in Taiwan*. New York: Routledge.

Lukacs, Gabriella. 2010. *Scripted Affects, Branded Selves: Television, Subjectivity, and Capitalism in 1990s Japan*. Durham, NC: Duke University Press.

Luo Gang. 1999. "Shui zhi gonggong xing?" (Whose public-ness?) In *Zai xin de yishixingtai de longzhao xia: 90 niandai de wenhua yu wenxue fenxi* (Under the Shadow of the New Ideology: Cultural and Literary Analysis in the 1990s), Xiaoming Wang, ed., pp. 64–70. Nanjing: Jiangshu renmin chubanshe.

Ma, Qiusha. 2002. "The Governance of NGOs in China since 1978: How Much Autonomy?" *Nonprofit and Voluntary Sector Quarterly* 31(3): 305–328.

Mandel, Ruth. 2002. "A Marshall Plan of the Mind: The Political Economy of a Kazakh Soap Opera." In *Media Worlds: Anthropology on New Terrain*, Faye D. Ginsburg, Lila Abu-Lughod, and Brian Larkin, eds., pp. 211–229. Berkeley: University of California Press.

Manthorpe, Jonathan. 2005. *Forbidden Nation: A History of Taiwan*. New York: Palgrave Macmillan.

Marx, Karl. 1976. *Capital*, vol. I. Harmondsworth, UK: Penguin Books, 1976. (Originally published in German in 1867.)

McMorrough, John. 2001. "City of Shopping." In *The Harvard Design School Guide to Shopping*, pp. 192–203. London: Taschen.

Mikanagi, Yumiko. 1998. "Japan's Gender-Biased Social Security Policy." *Japan Forum* 10 (2): 181–196.

Milhaupt, Curtis J., J. Mark Ramseyer, and Michael K. Young. 2001. *Japanese Law in Context: Readings in Society, the Economy, and Politics*. Cambridge, MA: Harvard University Press.

Miller, Laura. 2003. "Male Beauty Work in Japan." In *Men and Masculinities in Contemporary Japan: Dislocating the Salaryman Doxa*, James E. Roberson and Nobue Suzuki, eds., pp. 37–59. London: Routledge, Curzon.

Miller, Peter, and Nicholas Rose. 1990. "Governing Economic Life." *Economy and Society* 19(1): 1–31.

———. 1995. "Production, Identity and Democracy." *Theory and Society* 24(3): 427–467.

Miller, Robbi Louise. 2003. "The Quiet Revolution: Japanese Women Working around the Law." *Harvard Women's Law* 26: 163–215.

Miyake, Shoko. 2003. *Kokoro no No-to wo Kangaeru* (Thinking about Notes to the Heart). Booklet No. 595. Tokyo: Iwanami Press.

Miyazaki, Hirokazu. 2003. "The Temporalities of the Market." *American Anthropologist* 105(2): 255–265.

Modleski, Tania. 1982. *Loving with Vengeance: Mass-Produced Fantasies for Women*. New York: Routledge.

Moeller, Susan D. 1999. *Compassion Fatigue: How the Media Sell Disease, Famine, War, and Death*. New York: Routledge.

Mok, Joshua Ka-ho, and Michael Hiu-hong Lee. 2001. "Similar Trends, Diverse Agendas: Higher Education Reforms." In *Globalization and Changing Governance: Higher Education Reforms in Hong Kong, Taiwan and Mainland China*, pp. 1–21. Hong Kong: Department of Public and Social Administration, City University of Hong Kong.

Mok, Ka-ho. 2000. "Reflecting Globalization Effects on Local Policy: Higher Education Reform in Taiwan." *Journal of Education Policy* 15(6): 637–660.

———. 2003. "Similar Trends, Diverse Agendas: Higher Education Reforms in East Asia." *Globalisation, Societies and Education* 1(2): 201–221.

Mok, Ka-ho, and Anthony Welch. 2003. "Globalization, Structural Adjustment and Educational Reform." In *Globalization and Educational Restructuring in the Asia Pacific Region*, Ka-ho Mok and Anthony Welch, eds., pp. 1–31. New York: Palgrave Macmillan.

Mok, Ka-ho, Kiok Yoon, and Anthony Welch. 2003. "Globalization's Challenges to Higher Education Governance in South Korea." In *Globalization and Educational Restructuring in the Asia Pacific Region*, Ka-ho Mok and Anthony Welch, eds., pp. 57–78. New York: Palgrave Macmillan.

Molony, Barbara. 1995. "Japan's Equal Employment Opportunity Law and the Changing Discourse on Gender." *Signs* 20(2): 268–302.

Morris-Suzuki, Tessa. 1988. *Beyond Computopia: Information, Automation, and Democracy in Japan*. New York: Kegan Paul International.

Nakane, Chie. 1970. *Japanese Society*. Tokyo: Charles E. Tuttle.

Nakano, Yoshiko. 2002. "Who Initiates a Global Flow? Japanese Popular Culture in Asia." *Visual Communication* 1(2): 229–253.

National Science Council Information Center. 2005. "Biao 1-3-6 SCI geguo lun-wen fabiao pianshu ji mingci" (Table 1-3-6 Annual Papers and Rank by Nation-ality in SCI). Retrieved on May 5, 2006, from www.edu.tw/EDU_WEB/EDU_MGT/STATISTICS/EDU7220001/indicator/1-3-6.htm.

Nelson, Laura C. 2000. *Measured Excess: Status, Gender, and Consumer Nationalism in South Korea.* New York: Columbia University Press.

"New Healthcare Reform Plan." 2009. *People's Daily Online*; retrieved on April 25, 2010, from http://english.people.com.cn/90001/90782/90880/6634394.html.

NHK. 2005. *Friita—Genryuu—Monozukuri no Genba de* (From the Worksite: A Story of the *Freeter*). Documentary Film.

Oakes, Tim. 1998. *Tourism and Modernity in China.* New York: Routledge.

Okada, Akito. 2002. "Education of Whom, for Whom, by Whom? Revisiting the Fundamental Law of Education in Japan." *Japan Forum* 14(3): 425–441.

Ogasawara, Yuko. 1998. *Office Ladies and Salaried Men: Power, Gender, and Work in Japanese Companies.* Berkeley: University of California Press.

104 Education Information Web. 2007, "Taida: fenlingyu pingbi jiao jucanka-oxing, zhengda zhi lengmen shouxianzhi" (Taiwan University: To Compare and Estimate by Fields Is More Likely to Be Referenced; Chengchi Univer-sity Said It Is Not in Vogue and Limited). Retrieved on May 28, 2007, from www.104learn.com.tw/cfdocs/edu/iexam/show/iexam/cfm?autonumber=4863.

1111 Manpower Bank. 2006. "Chaoji xinxianren dianzibao" (Super Freshmen E-Paper). Retrieved on May 22, 2007, from www.1111.com.tw/ePaper/schoolfreshePaper/zoneschool/Fresh20061215.htm.

———. 2007. "2007 qiye zuiai xiaoxi xinwengao" (Report of Universities of which Industries Are Most Fond in 2007). Retrieved on May 31, 2007, from www.1111.com.tw/zone/pr/headline.asp?autono=1621.

Ong, Aihwa. 1999. *Flexible Citizenship: The Cultural Logics of Transnationality.* Dur-ham, NC: Duke University Press.

———. 2006. *Neoliberalism as Exception: Mutations in Citizenship and Sovereignty.* Durham, NC: Duke University Press.

———. 2008. "Self-fashioning Shanghainese: Dancing across Spheres of Value." In *Privatizing China: Socialism from Afar*, Li Zhang and Aihwa Ong, eds., pp. 182–196, 262–265. Ithaca, NY: Cornell University Press.

Ōnishi, Norimitsu. 2004. "This 21st-Century Japan, More Contented Than Driven." *The New York Times*, February 4: A4.

Organisation for Economic Co-Operation and Development (OECD). 2000. *Ko-rea and the Knowledge-Based Economy: Making the Transition.* Paris: OECD.

Osawa, Mari. 1993. *Kigyo chushin shakai o koete* (Beyond the Company-Centered Society). Tokyo: Jijitsūshinsha.

Park, So Jin. 2006. *The Retreat from Formal Schooling: "Educational Manager Moth-ers" in the Private After-School Market of South Korea.* PhD Dissertation. Univer-sity of Illinois, Urbana-Champaign.

Park, So Jin, and Nancy Abelmann. 2004. "Class and Cosmopolitan Striving: Mothers' Management of English Education in South Korea." *Anthropological Quarterly* 77(4): 645–672.

Parkinson, Loraine. 1989. "Japan's Equal Employment Opportunity Law: An Alternative Approach to Social Change." *Columbia Law Review* 89(3): 604–661.

Pazderic, Nickola. 1999. *Success and Failure in Post-Miracle Taiwan*. PhD dissertation, Department of Anthropology, University of Washington.

———. 2004. "Recovering True Selves in the Electro-Spiritual Field of Universal Love." *Cultural Anthropology* 19(2): 196–225.

———. 2009. "Mysterious Photographs." In *Photographies East: The Camera and Its Histories in East and Southeast Asia*, Rosalind Morris, ed. Durham, NC: Duke University Press.

Peck, Jamie, and Nik Theodore. 2001. "Exporting Workfare/Importing Welfare-to-Work: Exploring the Politics of Third Way Policy Transfer." *Political Geography* 20(4): 427–460.

Peck, Jamie, and Adam Tickell. 2002. "Neoliberalizing Space." *Antipode* 34(3): 380–404.

Perry, Tony, and Robert W. Welkos. 2007. "The Few, the Proud among Fans of '300.'" *Los Angeles Times*, March 14.

Peters, Michael A. 2003. "Classical Political Economy and the Role of Universities in the New Knowledge Economy." *Globalisation, Societies and Education* 1(2): 153–168.

Philo, Chris, and Gerry Kearns, eds. 1993. *Selling Places: The City as Cultural Capital, Past and Present*. Oxford, UK: Pergamon.

Plameri, Christopher, with Brian Grow and Stan Crock. 2004. "Served in Iraq? Come Work for Us." *Business Week* December 13: 78–80.

Presidential Secretary Plan-Committee to Improve the Quality of Life (Saech'ŏnnyŏn ŭl hyang han saengsanjŏk pokchi ŭi kil). 1999. Seoul: T'oesŏldang.

Pun Ngai. 2003. "Subsumption or Consumption? The Phantom of Consumer Revolution in 'Globalizing' China.'" *Cultural Anthropology* 18(4): 469–492.

———. 2005. *Made in China: Women Factory Workers in a Global Workplace*. Durham, NC: Duke University Press.

Qin Hui. 2003. "Dividing the Big Family Assets: On Liberty and Justice." In *One China, Many Paths*, Chaohua Wang, ed., pp. 128–159. London: Verso.

Read, Jason. 2009. "A Genealogy of Homo-Economicus: Neoliberalism and the Production of Subjectivity." *Foucault Studies* 6 (February): 25–36.

Readings, Bill. 1996. *The University in Ruins*. Cambridge, MA: Harvard University Press.

Redfield, Peter. 2005. "Doctors, Borders, and Life in Crisis." *Cultural Anthropology* 20(3): 328–361.

Ren, Hai. 2005. "Subculture as a Neo-Liberal Conduct of Life in Leisure and Consumption." *Rhizomes: Cultural Studies in Emerging Knowledge* 10 (Spring). Retrieved on July 11, 2007, from www.rhizomes.net/issue10/ren.htm.

———. 2007a. "From *Wenhua* to *Wenhua chanye*: A Review of Culture in the Contemporary PRC." *Modern Chinese Language and Culture*, June. Retrieved on July 11, 2007, from: http://mclc.osu.edu/rc/pubs/reviews/ren.htm.

———. 2007b. "The Landscape of Power: Imagineering Consumer Behavior at China's Theme Parks." In *The Themed Space: Locating Culture, Nation, and Self*, Scott A. Lukas, ed., pp. 97–112. Lanham, MD: Lexington Books.

———. 2010a. *Neoliberalism and Culture: The Countdown of Time*. London: Routledge.

———. 2010b. "The Neoliberal State and Risk Society: The Chinese State and the Middle Class." *Telos* 151 (Summer): 105–128.

———. 2012. *The Middle Class in Neoliberal China: Governing Risk, Life Building and Themed Spaces*. London: Routledge.

Renan, Ernst. 1996. "What Is a Nation?" In *Becoming National*, Geoff Eley and Ronald Suny, eds., pp. 42–55. New York: Oxford University Press. (Originally published in 1882.)

Riles, Annelise. 2004. "Unwinding Technocratic and Anthropological Knowledge." *American Ethnologist* 31(3): 392–405.

Roberts, Glenda. 1994. *Staying on the Line: Blue Collar Women in Contemporary Japan*. Honolulu: University of Hawaii Press.

Robertson, Jennifer. 1991. "The Shingaku Woman: Straight from the Heart." In *Recreating Japanese Women, 1600–1945*, Gail Bernstein, ed., pp. 88–107. Berkeley: University of California Press.

Rofel, Lisa. 1994. "Yearnings: Television Love and Melodramatic Politics in Contemporary China." *American Ethnologist* 21(4): 700–722.

Rohlen, Thomas. 1979. *For Harmony and Strength: Japanese White-Collar Organization in Anthropological Perspective*. Berkeley: University of California Press.

Rose, Nikolas S. 1990. *Governing the Soul: The Shaping of the Private Self*. London: Free Association Books.

———. 1996. *Inventing Our Selves: Psychology, Power, and Personhood*. New York: Cambridge University Press.

———. 1999. *Powers of Freedom: Reframing Political Thought*. Cambridge, UK: Cambridge University.

Ross, Andrew. 2006. *Fast Boat to China: Corporate Flight and the Consequences of Free Trade: Lessons from Shanghai*. New York: Pantheon Books.

Rutheiser, Charles. 1996. *Imagineering Atlanta: The Politics of Place in the City of Dreams*. London: Verso.

Salimtŏ [Place of Revitalization]. 1999. *Salimtŏ Newsletter* (Fall 1999).

Santamaria, Jason A., et al. 2005. *The Marine Corps Way: Using Maneuver Warfare to Lead a Winning Organization*. New York: McGraw-Hill.

Satake, Taishin. 2000. *Kanojotachi no Dorama: Shinarioraitā ni Natta Joseitachi* (Dramas for Women: Women Who Become Scenario Writers). Tokyo: Kinema Junpōsha, Kinejun Mukku.

Saxonhouse, Gary, and Robert Stern. 2004. *Japan's Lost Decade: Origins, Consequences and Prospects for Recovery.* Oxford, UK: Blackwell Publishing.

Schein, Louisa. 1998. "Importing Miao Brethren to Hmong America: A Not-So-Stateless Transnationalism." In *Cosmopolitics: Thinking and Feeling Beyond the Nation*, Pheng Cheah and Bruce Robbins, eds., pp. 163–191. Minneapolis: University of Minnesota Press.

———. 2000. *Minority Rules: The Miao and the Feminine in China's Cultural Politics.* Durham, NC: Duke University Press.

Schmid, Andre. 2002. *Korea between Empires.* New York: Columbia University Press.

Schmitt, Carl. 2005 [1922]. *Political Theology: Four Chapters on the Concept of Sovereignty*, George Schwab, trans. Chicago: The University of Chicago Press.

Scott, James. 1999. *Seeing Like the State: How Certain Schemes to Improve Human Condition Have Failed.* New Haven and London: Yale University Press.

Seo, Dong-Jin. 2008. "The Will to Self-Managing, the Will to Freedom: Self-Managing Ethic and the Spirit of Flexible Capitalism in Korea." A paper presented at the conference "Neoliberalism in South Korea," Feb. 1–2, 2008, Toronto, University of Toronto.

Seth, Michael. 2002. *Education Fever: Society, Politics, and the Pursuit of Schooling in South Korea.* Honolulu: University of Hawaii Press.

Shao, Jing. 2006. "Fluid Labor and Blood Money: The Economy of HIV/AIDS in Rural Central China." *Cultural Anthropology* 21(4): 535–569.

Shepherd, Robert. 2008. *When Culture Goes to Market: Space, Place, and Identity in an Urban Marketplace.* New York: Peter Lang.

Shin, Kwang-Yeong. 2000. "The Discourse of Crisis and the Crisis of Discourse." *Inter-Asia Cultural Studies* 1(3): 427–442.

———. 2002. "Economic Crisis and Social Welfare Reform in South Korea." Paper presented at the Korean Studies Colloquium, Cornell University, April 22, pp. 1–14. Retrieved on July 2, 2007, from www.people.cornell.edu/pages/tml5/korea.htm.

Shue, Vivienne. 1998. "State Power and the Philanthropic Impulse in China Today." In *Philanthropy in the World's Traditions*, Warren F. Ilchman, Stanley Katz, and Edward L. Queen II, eds., pp. 332–354. Bloomington: Indiana University Press.

Sigley, Gary. 2006. "Chinese Governmentalities: Government, Governance and the Socialist Market Economy." *Economy and Society* 35(4): 487–508.

Simmel, Georg. 1950. "The Metropolis and Mental Life." In *The Sociology of Georg Simmel*, Kurt H. Wolff, trans., ed., and introduction, pp. 11–19. Glencoe, IL: Free Press.

Simon, Scott. 2003. *Sweet and Sour: Life-Worlds of Taipei Women Entrepreneurs*. Lanham, MD: Rowman and Littlefield.

"Socialism with Chinese Characteristics." 2007. *People's Daily Online*; retrieved on April 16, 2010, from http://english.peopledaily.com.cn/90002/92169/92211/6275043.html.

Sohn-Rethel, Alfred. 1978. *Intellectual and Manual Labor: A Critique of Epistemology*. Atlantic Highlands, NJ: Humanities Press.

Song, Jesook. 2003. *Shifting Technologies: Neoliberalization of the Welfare State in South Korea, 1997–2001*. PhD Dissertation. University of Illinois, Urbana-Champaign.

———. 2004. "Neoliberal Governmentality of South Korean Welfare Society: Discourse Analysis of 'Productive Welfarism' and 'Well-Being Race' [Welbingjok]." Paper presented at the East Asian Welfare State Workshop, March 12, 2004, University of Toronto, Canada.

———. 2006. " 'Family Breakdown' and Invisible Homeless Women: Neoliberal Governance during the Asian Debt Crisis in South Korea 1997–2001." *positions: east asian culture critique* 14(1): 37–65.

———. 2009. *South Koreans in the Debt Crisis: The Creation of a Neoliberal Welfare Society*. Durham, NC: Duke University Press.

———. 2011. "Situating Homelessness in South Korea during and after the Asian Debt Crisis." *Urban Geography* 32(7): 972–988.

———. in press. *Living on Their Own: Single Women's Housing and Financial Security and Affective Baggage in South Korea*. Albany: State University of New York Press.

Spivak, Gayatri Chakarvorty. 1988. "Scattered Speculations on the Question of Value." In *In Other Worlds: Essays in Cultural Politics*, pp. 154–175. New York: Routledge.

Stewart, Kathleen. 2007. *Ordinary Affects*. Durham, NC: Duke University Press.

Strauss, Julia C. 1994. "Symbol and Reflection of the Reconstituting State: The Examination Yuan in the 1930s." *Modern China* 20(2): 211–238.

Su, Shuo-bin. 2010. *Invisible and Visible Taipei*. Taipei: Socio Publishing.

Sun, Chen. 1994. "Investment in Education and Human Resource Development in Postwar Taiwan." In *Cultural Change in Postwar Taiwan*, Stevan Harrell and Chun-chieh Huang, eds., pp. 91–110. Boulder, CO: Westview Press.

Suzuki, Kōichi. 1999. "Terebi Dorama "Shomuni" to "Dokushin Seikatsu" ni Miru OL Zō." ("Representations of Office Ladies in Shomuni and Single Lives"). *Hōsō Bunka*, (Broadcasting Culture), October: 29–37.

Ta, Trang X. 2011. "A State of Imbalance: Corporeal Politics and Moral Order in Contemporary China." PhD dissertation, Department of Anthropology, University of Washington.

Tai, Po-fan. 1994. "Who Are Vendors? The Historical Formation of Vendors in Taiwan." *Taiwan: A Radical Quarterly in Social Studies* 17: 121–148.

Takahashi, Tetsuya. 2003. *Kokoro to Senso* (Hearts and War). Tokyo: Shobunsha.

Thrift, Nigel. 1999. "Cities and Economic Change: Global Governance?" In *Unsettling Cities: Movement/Settlement*, John Allen, Doreen Massey, and Michael Pryke, eds., pp. 271–320. New York: Routledge.

Tomba, Luigi. 2004. "Creating an Urban Middle Class: Social Engineering in Beijing." *The China Journal* 51: 1–26.

———. n.d. *"Divide et impera*: Community, Space and Authority in Urban China." Unpublished manuscript.

Tsai, Ming-Chang. 2001. "Dependency, The State and Class in The Neoliberal Transition of Taiwan." *Third World Quarterly* 22(3): 359–379.

Tsing, Anna. 2000. "The Global Situation." *Cultural Anthropology* 15(3): 327–360.

Tu, Wei-ming. 1985. *Confucian Thought: Selfhood as Creative Transformation*. Albany: State University of New York Press.

———. 1995. "The Confucian Dimension in the East Asian Development Model." In *Confucianism and Economic Development*, Tzong-shian Yu and Joseph S. Lee, eds., pp. 47–67. Taipei: Chung-Hua Institution for Economic Research.

Uesugi, Junya, and Takakura Fumitoshi. 2001. *Terebi Dorama no Shigotonintachi* (The Makers of Television Drama). Tokyo: KK Besuto Serāzu.

United Nations Development Programme (UNDP). 1999. *Human Development Report*. New York: Oxford University Press.

Vogel, Steven. 2006. *Japan Remodeled: How Government and Industry Are Reforming Japanese Capitalism*. Ithaca, NY: Cornell University Press.

Walkerdine, Valerie. 2003. "Reclassifying Upward Mobility: Femininity and the Neo-Liberal Subject." *Gender and Education* 15(3): 237–248.

Wallulis, Jerald. 1998. *The New Insecurity: The End of the Standard Job and Family*. Albany: State University of New York Press.

Wang Hui. 2003. *China's New Order: Society, Politics, and Economy in Transition*. Cambridge, MA: Harvard University Press.

———. 2006. "Depoliticized Politics, Multiple Components of Hegemony, and the Eclipse of the Sixties." *Inter-Asia Cultural Studies* 7(4): 683–700.

Wang, Hui-lan. 2005. "Education Reform in Taiwan: Multiple Voices and Practices." Retrieved on June 15, 2007, from http://eri.snu.ac.kr/icer2005/down/Session4/education%20reform%20in%20Taiwan.ppt.

Wang, Jing. 1996. "Heshang and the Chinese Enlightenment." In *High Culture Fever: Politics, Aesthetics, and Ideology in Deng's China*, pp. 118–136. Berkeley: University of California Press.

———. 2001a. "Culture as Leisure and Culture as Capital." *positions: east asia cultures critique* 9(1): 69–104.

———. 2001b. "The State Question in Chinese Popular Cultural Studies." *Inter-Asia Cultural Studies* 2(1): 35–52.

———. 2005. "Bourgeois Bohemians in China? Neo-Tribes and the Urban Imaginary." *China Quarterly* 183 (Sept): 532–548.

Wang, Sung-hsing. 1974. "Taiwanese Architecture and the Supernatural." In *Religion and Ritual in Chinese Society*, Arthur P. Wolf, ed. pp. 183–192. Stanford, CA: Stanford University Press.

Wang Xiaoming. 1999. "Ban zhang lian de shenhua (The myth of the half face)." In *Zai xin de yishixingtai de longzhao xia: 90 niandai de wenhua yu wenxue fenxi* (Under the Shadow of the New Ideology: Cultural and Literary Analysis in the 1990s), Xiaoming Wang, ed., pp. 29–36. Nanjing: Jiangshu renmin chubanshe.

Wang Yi. 2003. "From Status to Contract?" In *One China, Many Paths*, Chaohua Wang, ed., pp. 189–197. London: Verso.

Weathers, Charles. 2005. "In Search of Strategic Partners: Japan's Campaign for Equal Opportunity." *Social Science Japan Journal* 8(1): 69–89.

Weller, Robert P. 1987. *Unities and Diversities in Chinese Religion*. Seattle: University of Washington Press.

Wilson, Richard W. 1970. *Learning to be Chinese*. Cambridge, MA: The M.I.T. Press.

Wong, Joseph. 2005. *Healthy Democracies: Welfare Politics in Taiwan and South Korea*. Ithaca, NY: Cornell University Press.

World Bank. 2000. "East Asia: Recovery Exhibits Greater Breadth and Depth, but Remains Uneven." Available at www.worldbank.org/eapsocial/index.html.

Wu, Shu-ling, and Chung-sheng Kuo. 2001. "Folk Culture and Consumption Society: An Investigation on Commodity of Taiwanese Folk Culture." *Journal of Ching Yun Institute of Technology* 21(1): 253–260.

Xiao, Xuehui. 2003. "Industrializing Education?" In *One China, Many Paths*, Chaohua Wang, ed., pp. 237–249. London: Verso.

Xie Lihong. 1995. "Beijing zhonghua minzu bowuyuan" (The museum of the Chinese nation in Beijing). In *Beijing bowuguan nianjian 1992–1994* (The Yearbook of the Museums in Beijing, 1992–1994), Beijing Bowuguan Xuehui, eds. Beijing: Yanshan Chubanshe.

Xue Yi. 1999. "Guanyu gerenzhuyi huayu" (Regarding the discourse of individualism). In *Zai xin de yishixingtai de longzhao xia: 90 niandai de wenhua yu wenxue fenxi* (Under the Shadow of the New Ideology: Cultural and Literary Analysis in the 1990s), Xiaoming Wang, ed., pp. 42–49. Nanjing: Jiangshu renmin chubanshe.

Yamada, Masahiro. 1999. *Parasaito Shinguru no Jidai*. (The Era of Parasite Singles). Tokyo: Chikuma Shobo.

Yan Hairong. 2003. "Neoliberal Governmentality and Neo-Humanism: Organizing Value Flow Through Labor Recruitment Agencies." *Cultural Anthropology* 18(4): 493–523.

———. 2008. *New Masters, New Servants: Migration, Development, and Women Workers in China*. Durham, NC: Duke University Press.

Ye, Su-ke. 1993. *Riluo Taibeicheng: Rizhi shidai Taibei dushi fazhan yu tairen richang shenghuo 1895–1945 [Sunset in Taipei City: Urban Development in Taipei and Taiwanese Daily Life in the Japanese Period 1895–1945]*. Taipei: Independent Nightly News.

Yoda, Tomiko. 2000. "A Roadmap to Millennial Japan." *The South Atlantic Quarterly* 99 (4): 629–668.

———. n.d. *"Kogyaru* and the Economy of Feminized Consumer Society."

Yu, Shuenn-Der. 1999. "Yieshi Yanjiou yu Taiwan Shehui [Night Market Research and Taiwanese Society]." In *Renluixue zai Taiwan de Fazhan: Jingyan Yanjiou Pian* [The Development of Anthropology in Taiwan: Experience and Research], pp. 89–126. Taipei: Institute of Ethnology, Academic Sinica.

———. 2004. "Hot and Noisy: Taiwan's Night Market Culture." In *The Minor Arts of Daily Life: Popular Culture in Taiwan*, David Jordan, Andrew Morris, and Marc Moskowitz, eds. Honolulu: University of Hawaii Press.

Yu Wenlie. 2004. "Jingji lujing de zhexue sikao" (A philosophical thinking on the direction of the economy). In *Kaifangxia de hongguan jingji yu qiye lilun yanjiu* (Macro Economy under Opening and Company Studies), Wu Yifeng, Ding Bing, and Li Zhong, eds. Beijing: Zhongguo Jingjin Chubanshe.

Zhang, Li. 2001. *Strangers in the City: Reconfigurations of Space, Power, and Social Networks within China's Floating Population.* Stanford, CA: Stanford University Press.

———. 2002. "Spatiality and Urban Citizenship in Late Socialist China." *Public Culture* 14(2): 311–334.

———. 2010. *In Search of Paradise: Middle-Class Living in a Chinese Metropolis.* Ithaca, NY: Cornell University Press.

Zhang, Li, and Aihwa Ong, eds. 2008. *Privatizing China: Socialism from Afar.* Ithaca, NY: Cornell University Press.

Zhang Tongze. 2001. "Aoyun jihuo waijingji" (The Olympics Fires up the Entertainment Economy). *Qingnian shixun*, August 10. Retrieved on April 23, 2006, from www.tyfo.com/news/financial/block/html/200108100297.html.

Zhongguo xinwen zhoukan. 2005. "Fengmian Gushi: Cuiruo de chengshi xuemai" [Cover Story: The Fragility of the City Blood Line]. *Zhongguo xinwen zhoukan* January 31: 18–27.

Zhu Dongli. 1998. *Jingshen zhi lü: xin shiqi yilai de meixue yu zhishi fenzi* (The Travel of the Spirit: Aesthetics and Intellectuals since the New Era). Beijing: Zhongguo guangbo dianshi chubanshe.

Žižek, Slavoj. 1994. "The Spectre of Ideology." In *Mapping Ideology*, Slavoj Žižek, ed., pp. 1–33. London: Verso.

Zukin, Sharon. 1995. *The Cultures of Cities.* Cambridge, MA: Blackwell.

Zukin, Sharon, and Jennifer S. Maguire. 2004. "Consumers and Consumption." *Annual Review of Sociology* 30: 173–197.

About the Contributors

Nancy Abelmann is Associate Vice Chancellor for Research (Humanities and Arts) and the Harry E. Preble Professor of Anthropology, Asian American Studies, and East Asian Languages and Cultures at the University of Illinois at Urbana-Champaign. She has published books on South Korean social movements, women and social mobility, film, Korean Americans, and, most recently, *The Intimate University: Korean American Students and the Problems of Segregation* (Duke University Press 2009). She is coeditor of *No Alternative? Experiments in South Korean Education* (University of California 2011) and *South Korea's Education Exodus* (in progress) and coauthor of *How Korean American Teens and Parents Navigate Immigrant America* (in progress).

Ann Anagnost is Professor of Anthropology and Chinese Studies at the University of Washington. She is author of *National Past-Times: Narrative, Representation, and Power in Modern China* (Duke University Press, 1997). Her forthcoming book is *Embodiments of Value in China's Reform* (Duke University Press). Her current research is on food sovereignty movements at both local and transnational scales of analysis. She was editor of *Cultural Anthropology* (2002–2006).

Andrea G. Arai teaches in the Japan Studies Program in the Jackson School of International Studies, University of Washington. Her publications include "The Wild Child of 1990s Japan," in *Japan After Japan: Social and Cultural Life from the Recessionary 1990s to the Present*, edited by Tomiko Yoda and Harry Harootunian (Duke University Press, 2006). Arai is completing a book entitled *Recessionary Times*, which traces troubled sites of national-cultural reproduction following the 1990s financial downturn. Arai's new ethnographic project, "Alternative Lifestyles and Livelihoods" engages with postbubble displacements and emerging notions of reclamation and recovery.

Ching-wen Hsu is Assistant Professor in the Institute of Anthropology at National Tsing Hua University, Taiwan. She earned her degree at the University of Washington and has published on tourism and place making in urban Taiwan. Her current project focuses on Taiwanese transnational families in the United States.

Miyako Inoue is Associate Professor of Anthropology at Stanford University. She is the author of *Vicarious Language: Gender and Linguistic Modernity in Japan* (University of California Press 2006). She is currently writing a book on a social history of Japanese stenography, which explores the idea of "fidelity" in the stenographic reproduction of speech and its cultural and political-economic implications in the context of Japanese modernization and modernity since the late nineteenth century.

Hyunhee Kim is a research fellow at the Institute of Cultural Studies, Seoul National University, Korea. Her research interests include Asian Migration and racializaion, (il)legality and citizenship, American and Korean legal cultures, Asians in popular culture. Her PhD dissertation, "Ethnic Intimacy, Race, Law and Citizenship in Korean America," discusses the New York Korean community and its struggles for American citizenship.

Gabriella Lukacs is Assistant Professor of Anthropology at the University of Pittsburgh. Her research explores televisual and new media, capitalism, labor, and subjectivity in contemporary Japan. Her publications include *Scripted Affects, Branded Selves: Television, Subjectivity, and Capitalism in 1990s Japan* (Duke University Press, 2010). Her current research examines questions of subjectivity and capitalism with a focus on new labor subjectivities such as the Internet idols who become famous by posting their photos and diaries on the Web, cell phone novelists whose novels have recently come to dominate literary bestseller lists, or entrepreneurial homemakers who accumulate wealth from day trading.

So Jin Park is a research fellow at the Institute for Social Development Studies, Yonsei University. Her research focuses on Korean family and gender issues, neoliberal subjectivities, study abroad of Korean college students, and Chinese students in Korean universities. Her published work includes "Educational Manager Mothers: South Korea's Neoliberal Transformation" (*Korea Journal* 2007) and "Reconsidering Korean Culture and Society and Seeking Self Identity in the World: Short-Term Study Abroad Motivation and Experiences" (*Comparative Korean Studies* 2010, in Korean).

Nickola Pazderic completed his doctorate at the University of Washington. He has taught at the University of Washington, Yale University, CYUT, National Taichung Institute of Commerce, National Chung Hsing University, and National Cheng Kung University. His article "Recovering True Selves in the Electro-Spiritual Field of Universal Love" appeared in *Cultural Anthropology* in 2004, and "Mysterious Photographs" was published in *Photographies East*, edited by Rosalind Morris (Duke University Press 2009).

Hai Ren is Associate Professor of East Asian Studies and Anthropology at the University of Arizona. He is the editor of *Neo-Liberal Governmentality: Technologies of the Self & Governmental Conduct*, which is a special issue of *Rhizomes: Cultural Studies in Emerging Knowledge* 10 (Spring 2005), and coeditor of *New Media Subversion*, a special issue of *Hyperrhiz: New Media Cultures* 7 (Spring 2010). He is also the author of two books: *Neoliberalism and Culture in China and Hong Kong: The Countdown of Time* (Routledge, 2010) and its sequel, *The Middle Class in Neoliberal China: Governing Risk, Life-Building, and Themed Spaces* (Routledge, 2012).

Jesook Song is Associate Professor of Anthropology at the University of Toronto. Her book *South Koreans in the Debt Crisis* (Duke University Press, 2009) deals with homelessness and youth unemployment during the Asian financial crisis in the late 1990s. A second book, *Living on Their Own* (SUNY Press, in press), is about single women's financial struggles in South Korea. Her edited volume *New Millennium South Korea* (Routledge, 2010) explores transnational movements and global capital. Her current research explores psychological health markets at the margins such as psychotherapists helping victims of state violence and LGBT advocacy organization counselors.

Trang X. Ta is Lecturer in Medical Anthropology within the School of Archaeology and Anthropology at Australian National University. She is a

Fulbright Visiting Scholar at the University of Hong Kong for 2012–2013, and her areas of research include medical anthropology, biotechnology, and global food studies. Her dissertation, "A State of Imbalance: Corporeal Politics and Moral Order in Contemporary China" (2011), traces the contours of the Chinese state, its projects of moral revitalization, and its use of neoliberal ruling technologies under conditions of economic liberalization that have transformed everyday life in late-socialist China.

Yan Hairong is an anthropologist at Hong Kong Polytechnic University. She is the author of *New Masters, New Servants: Migration, Development, and Women Workers in China* (Duke University Press, 2008), coauthor of *East Mountain Tiger, West Mountain Tiger: China, Africa, the West and "Colonialism"* (Maryland Monograph Series in Contemporary Asian Studies, no. 186), and coeditor of "What's Left of Asia?" (a special issue of *positions* 15(2), 2007). Her current research includes projects on China–Africa links and the rural cooperative movement in China. Her intellectual interests include labor, gender, rurality and rural–urban relations, and socialism and postsocialism.

Index

70, 129–30; international connections in, 66–72; Japan and, 55–56, 67–68, 73*n*5, 148*n*4; Neo-Confucianism in, 131–35; neoliberalism in, 128, 139–48; population policies in, 149*n*11; post-industrial development in, 16, 18–19, 59, 71; production of goods in, 70–71; street vending in, 58–66, 74*n*16, 75*n*17; United States and, 56–57, 73*n*6, 129, 131, 140

Takahashi Rumi, 229, 234, 235, 240–41
Takahashi Tetsuya, 175–77
Takeshi, Beat-o, 191–92
Tang Min, 150–51
Tarento (celebrity) system, 227, 234
Taylor, Frederick, 161
Television: Japanese industry, 245*n*4; love/trendy dramas on, 223–32, 243–44; social realism in, 225–28; workplace dramas on, 6, 22–23, 222–44
Thatcher, Margaret, 127, 183
Themed built environments, 36, 38–39
Third Way, 255–56
Tickell, Adam, 183
Tokyo Keizai Shinbun (newspaper), 233
Totalitarianism, 93–94
Toyotism, 184
Treaty ports, 55, 73*n*4
Trendy dramas. *See* Love/trendy dramas
Tsing, Anna, 7–8, 180

United Kingdom, 4
United Nations, 199
United States: and Japan, 183; military model of, 159–61; and modernization theory, 183; and Taiwan, 56–57, 73*n*6, 129, 131, 140; welfare in, 213–14
University education: in South Korea, 100–123; in Taiwan, 127–48

Value. *See* Human value
Vendors, street, 58–66, 74*n*16
Vogel, Steven, 240

Voluntarism, 168–69, 173*n*16
Volunteerism, 173*n*16

Walkerdine, Valerie, 122
Wang, Hui-lan, 127–28
Wang, Jing, 49*n*9, 88
Wang Hui, 164
Wang Tao, 47
Wang Xiaoming, 49*n*8
Weaker groups. *See* Disadvantaged groups
Welfare. *See* Social welfare
Wilde, Oscar, 168
Wilson, Richard W., 131–32
Women: education of, 19, 21–22; homeless, in South Korea, 258–59, 263–67; and labor, 19, 21–22, 197–221, 222, 226, 228–44; as responsible for gender equality, 211–14
Workers: and affective labor, 18, 18–19; in China, 33; as commodities, 152–56; in neoliberal contexts, 14–15, 152–54, 156, 161, 192–93, 223–24, 230–33, 240–44; and responsibility, 22–23, 205–6, 211–14; and self-development, 5–6, 18–23, 26*n*11; subjectivity of, 153, 205–8, 228–33, 240; women as, 19, 21–22, 197–221, 222, 226, 228–44. *See also* Domestic labor; Freeters
Workplace dramas, 6, 22–23, 222–44

Yamada Masahiro, 231
Yamaguchi Masatoshi, 225–26, 227
Yasuda Hiroyuki, 233
Youth: and labor, 1, 104; and popular culture, 58
Yu Wenlie, 33

Žižek, Slavoj, 135
Zhang Yuchen, 32
Zhao Le (film), 246*n*23
Zhou Huajian, 167
Zhu Dongli, 164

Japan's Dual Civil Society: Members Without Advocates
By Robert Pekkanen
2006

The Fourth Circle: A Political Ecology of Sumatra's Rainforest Frontier
By John F. McCarthy
2006

Protest and Possibilities: Civil Society and Coalitions for Political Change in Malaysia
By Meredith Leigh Weiss
2005

Opposing Suharto: Compromise, Resistance, and Regime Change in Indonesia
By Edward Aspinall
2005

Blowback: Linguistic Nationalism, Institutional Decay, and Ethnic Conflict in Sri Lanka
By Neil DeVotta
2004

Beyond Bilateralism: U.S.–Japan Relations in the New Asia Pacific
Edited by Ellis S. Krauss and T.J. Pempel
2004

Population Change and Economic Development in East Asia: Challenges Met, Opportunities Seized
Edited by Andrew Mason
2001

Capital, Coercion, and Crime: Bossism in the Philippines
By John T. Sidel
1999

Making Majorities: Constituting the Nation in Japan, Korea, China, Malaysia, Fiji, Turkey, and the United States
Edited by Dru C. Gladney
1998

Chiefs Today: Traditional Pacific Leadership and the Postcolonial State
Edited by Geoffrey M. White and Lamont Lindstrom
1997

Political Legitimacy in Southeast Asia: The Quest for Moral Authority
Edited by Muthiah Alagappa
1995